the Unofficial Guide™ to Buying a Home

Second Edition

Alan Perlis with Beth Bradley

WILEY

Wiley Publishing, Inc.

For general information on our other products and services or to obtain technical sup-port, please contact our Customer Care Department within the U.S. at 800-762-2974, outside the U.S. at 317-572-3993, or fax 317-572-4002.

Wiley also publishes its books in a variety of electronic formats. Some content that appears in print may not be available in electronic books.

Library of Congress Control Number: 2004101611

ISBN: 0-7645-4248-6

Printed in the United States of America

Manufactured in the United States of America

10 9 8 7 6 5 4 3 2 1

Second Edition

Book design by Lissa Auciello-Brogan

Cover design by Wendy Mount

Page creation by Wiley Publishing, Inc. Composition Services

To my five wonderful children, and to Beth Bradley, my wife and editor, who turned my tortured prose into something infinitely better.
—Alan Perlis

Acknowledgements

Throughout the writing of this book, Bob Sehlinger, Molly Burns, and Russell Helms offered their very concrete help and encouragement. For invaluable advice on the technical aspects of financing, inspecting, and closing, I relied on friends and colleagues Tony Robbins, Renee Webb, Steve Hines, Andrew Griffith, David Condon, and John Randolph. More than he will ever know, I have relied on the clear thinking of Bill Waldrip, whose guidance has made me a better real estate agent.

Contents

v

IV The Process Begins: Looking for and Getting the Home You Want..........................193

9 The Search Is On: Looking at Houses with Your Agent 195

About the Authors

Alan Perlis and **Beth Bradley** can tell you everything you need to know about buying a home. In 1990, Alan decided to pursue a full-time career in real estate, and he has been a multi-million dollar producer ever since. Currently a Broker Associate with Oxford Realty Company in Birmingham, Perlis is a frequent guest speaker on a wide variety of topics. Married to Beth Bradley and father of five, he is the author of numerous articles and the author of three previous books, all on literary topics. Beth Bradley graduated from Vanderbilt University in 1970 with a B.A. in English, and later earned her Master's degree from the University of Alabama at Birmingham. Her career highlights include five years teaching intellectually gifted high schoolers; 13 years marketing journals internationally for scholarly and scientific publishers; and, in a less lucrative vein, publishing original poetry in various small press magazines. She now spends most of her time raising her three kids with husband Alan Perlis, and painting.

For most of us, the thought of buying a home fires our imaginations with visions of comfort, an improved standard of living, and the opportunity to own that special, perfect home projecting our taste, lifestyle, and identity. We lie awake nights excited by the prospect of finally having sufficient space, a functional, well-designed kitchen, and enough closets to store the accumulations of a lifetime.

Deciding to buy a home is like falling in love. It's intoxicating, energizing, and scary as hell. There you are, one moment gleefully decorating your new living room in your mind, when the next moment you're seized by panic. This jangle of nerves is what we in the real estate business refer to as a *reality check*. Somewhere between hanging the floral print drapes and placing the 1950s retro recliner, it occurs to you that you actually have to go out and buy this house. Worse, rushing in come thoughts of Realtors, mortgage companies, lawyers, interest rates, credit applications, and days (if not months) of wandering through empty houses.

Buying a house is a big step. Also, for the record, it is complicated, expensive, and fraught with peril. But here's the good news . . . it's doable. Millions of people have purchased homes and survived the process, and you can, too. We pose this question:

"How do you eat an elephant?" The answer: "One piece at a time." Finding and buying a home, like eating an elephant, is a process that when contemplated in total is daunting. But taken one piece at a time, with a little guidance and a dash of patience, it's almost a snap. You provide the patience, we'll provide the guidance.

From cereals to cinema, we are often faced with too many choices. Fat-filled, reduced-fat, or fat-free? PG, PG-13, or R-rated? It's difficult enough to decide on a cup of coffee (plain, flavored, espresso, latte, cappuccino, caffeine-free, in small, medium, or large?), let alone a house! How do you decide—not only on the right house—but also on the right offer to make, the right mortgage to take out, and everything else surrounding such an important decision?

We're here to help you figure out what you're supposed to know and do. We've broken the whole house-buying process down into manageable portions, bite-sized chunks of the home-buying elephant that you can digest at your own pace. We also give you a reasonable time frame to follow.

We've pared it all down to the essentials, and, chapter-by-chapter, we serve it up logically, plainly, and honestly. Most importantly, we'll provide you with the inside scoop . . . genuinely useful terminology and unbiased information, complete with sample forms and documents, so that you'll feel confident being in charge.

Nerves That Jingle-Jangle-Jingle

As a culture, we're moving more frequently than ever before. Did you know that in the next year one of your five nearest neighbors will move? We remain in one dwelling for shorter and shorter periods of time.

As a nation, we're more prosperous than ever before. The 1990s saw nearly a 500-percent increase in the stock market. The result has been an unprecedented amount of individual wealth, and with it, the desire to protect some of that wealth by investing in a home.

But buying a home, as we have noted, is a frightening endeavor because, among other reasons, it costs a great deal of money. You buy Wheaties, you buy a toaster—but a whole house? To make matters worse, everyone from your parents on down has drilled into your head the ominous words, "It's the biggest purchase you'll ever make." What if you make the wrong purchase? What if the style of the home you choose gets on your nerves after a couple of months? What if your next-door neighbors assemble an arsenal and turn their home into a militia compound? The "What if?" list could go on and on . . .

Luckily, there's a bit of light to dispel those dark doubts. Buying a home today is in many ways an easier, and certainly more streamlined, process than ever before. Thanks to Equal Opportunity and Affirmative Action initiatives, as well as variety of real estate consumer and agency disclosure laws, everyone involved in the sale of a home must now provide full disclosure of their role in the process. The lender, the inspector, the appraiser, the real estate agent, and the home seller alike must lay bare to the prospective buyer all pertinent information about the home. Whereas previously, for example, your agent was not permitted even to advise you on the amount to offer, nowadays he can not only advise you, but can also share with you the amount of recent comparable home sales in the area. In fact, the relatively new phenomenon of buyer brokerage, which we explain in detail in Chapter 8, has vastly improved the both the degree and accuracy of disclosures involved in an real estate agent selling a home to you through an ethical set of steps.

The Home-Buying Process Revealed

The home-buying process, like the organization of this book, is linear and sequential. It starts with getting your act together and ends with moving into your new home.

In Part I, we cover the myriad loan options you have in making your purchase, along with an analysis (if you should need it) on how to clean up your credit to put you in the best position to obtain the type of loan that best suits your needs.

In Part II, we'll help you do your homework. Too many people rush into the home-buying process without preparing themselves mentally and physically. You and anyone else with whom you look for homes need to work through the decision-making process in advance, thinking creatively and establishing limits. Most books won't even mention this aspect of home buying, but it's the one that will give you the greatest leg up on a successful and enjoyable home-buying adventure.

We'll also give your search a major boost by providing you with up-to-the-minute information on using the Internet (no, you don't have to be a computer whiz to make the Internet work for you!) to find the perfect home or agent.

In Part III, we'll help you make preliminary decisions that will determine what kind of home you look for, saving you literally weeks of confusion down the road. We'll get right down to business and look at the purchase of a home as a personal investment: as a means to making home ownership a significant part of your wealth-building process. We'll also discuss issues involved in constructing your own home, and give you a scouting report on the major players in the home-buying game, telling you what they do and what their motivations are.

In Part IV, the process has begun! We'll give you tips for spotting special buying opportunities and working with your agent and other players to optimum advantage. By putting our suggestions to work for you, you'll have an advantage in the art of negotiation over people who walk into the process uninformed and unprepared.

In Part V, we will show you what to expect as the process wraps up. We'll explain what the inspection is (and as just importantly, what it isn't). After giving you the facts on title and homeowner's insurance, we'll take you to the big crescendo, the closing, and equip you with everything you'll need to make it painless (well, relatively painless!).

Most homebuyer guides abandon you at the moment you close the sale. In Part VI, we'll take you two extra steps further to ward off last-minute surprises. First, we'll give you tips for making a smooth transition to your new home. How do you make the move easier? How can you start things off right with your new neighbors? We'll give you lots of ideas, and, in a unique chapter, we'll also take you back through the entire home-buying process from the perspective of real estate law. You may think you have an intuitive grasp of what the law is, but unless you're a lawyer, you don't! We'll take you through all sorts of real-life situations you might face and what the law says about them.

Our advice throughout the book is detailed and serious, but you don't need to be a lawyer or accountant to understand the lessons involved. All you need is a sincere desire to arm yourself with excellent information. And we'll also provide you with samples of several documents you'll be seeing along the process, and checklists of things you should do. You'll find mortgage tables, worksheets for house hunting, moving, and various other tasks, mortgage notes, disclosure statements, and more.

Bad and Good Reasons for Buying a Home

Practically speaking, good reasons for buying a home are the ones you thought up. Bad reasons are reasons someone else originated.

Bad Reasons

Although there are several good reasons for buying a home and only a couple of bad ones, some of the bad ones can really come back to haunt you. Probably the worst reason of all to buy a home is to save a faltering relationship. The diversion of searching for and buying a home may foster some commonality of purpose, thus masking the underlying problems of your marriage or relationship for a while. But once you're settled into your new home and the cooperative spirit of house hunting is in the rearview mirror, all of your old troubles will resurface. At best, going through the process will buy your relationship some time. But in the long run, adding a good house to a bad relationship only provides an additional asset to fight over when the end inevitably comes.

Most other bad reasons for buying a home arise from a lack of introspection and self-knowledge, as well as misplaced priorities.

For some people, the purchase of a home seems to be wired to their biological clock. For example, just as surely as certain women feel drawn to have children by a particular age, many individuals feel internal pressure to own a home by a certain time in their lives. The bottom line is that using home ownership as a benchmark for success and self-esteem has the potential for diverting time and resources from other, possibly more important, aspects of your life. As surely as a house can be a status symbol and a tangible testament to substance and success, it can also be an anchor and a drag.

There is a trend in the United States toward a simplification of life that has been gaining momentum for some years. Many people who think they want one thing, discover after honest self-evaluation that they would be happier with something completely different. Concerning housing, our society has conditioned us to think within fairly narrow parameters. Instead of exploring various alternatives for housing, we gravitate more often than not to the traditional route of home ownership, usually a single-family dwelling. But what if you really don't have the time to maintain a home, or can't afford to have someone do it for you? Will living in a nice apartment take such a bite out of your ego that it's not worthy of consideration? Know yourself and your needs, and then be open to exploring the entire plurality of housing choices. Force yourself to rank your priorities. You may be surprised to discover that never having to mow a lawn or fix a leaking faucet (and the time that is thus freed for other pursuits) outweighs the benefits of home ownership.

Finally, not having a reason, or having a poorly defined reason, for buying a home, doesn't really cut it. You'd be amazed at the number of people who start out to buy a home without having a clue why they are doing it. First-time buyers, when pressed, might say, "Because it's time," or "I just want to own something." Others decide to buy out of peer pressure or a vaguely anticipated tax advantage.

Whether your own dynamic is based on desire, necessity, or a combination of the two, be sure you understand, before you buy, why you want to. A half-hearted or poorly thought-out reason for buying will certainly make it very difficult to find what you want. Even worse, a dud of a reason could stick you with a house you don't want.

Good Reasons

Most of the reasons that prompt the majority of people to become house-hunters have to do with issues such as space, privacy, and safety. They include matters of quality, in education, and in life in general. They can also stem from career choices. Not surprisingly, financial considerations likewise often play an influential role.

What constitutes a "good" reason for buying a home? How do you know when you have a good reason for purchasing a home, whether it's your first or fourth? You will know when you have a strong sense of how you need to live, or want to live—in other words, a powerful governing dynamic that motivates your impulse to move. You will know that you have a good reason when that reason is concrete, rather than abstract.

Here, in no particular order, are 10 good, well-considered reasons for buying a home:

1. You're tired of renting, including for financial reasons.

2. You want a better school system or a safer neighborhood.

3. You need something larger, particularly for a growing family.

4. The nest is empty; you may want a smaller or easier-to-maintain home.

5. You want more land.

6. You want a newer house with fewer chronic repair problems.

7. Mortgage interest rates are low.

8. You've been transferred.

9. You want a better, or more suitable, neighborhood—one closer to your workplace, family, friends, etc.

10. You've experienced a change in lifestyle or family dynamics, including remarriage, divorce, the death of a significant other, or the arrival of a new family member such as an elderly parent.

Buying as a Matter of Taste

Though there may be other benefits to be gained, you may wish to move primarily as a matter of preference or taste. You may find that one of the following common examples of this type of motivation strikes a familiar chord:

- You wish to move to a neighborhood that you prefer over your current one. (There's nothing terribly wrong with your current neighborhood; you're just irresistibly drawn to a different one.)

- You have decided that you would prefer a one-story to a one-and-one-half story or two-story home, or vice versa.

- You want a home with different features, such as large, modern bathrooms, a large kitchen, a fireplace, or garage.

- Your current home is old, tired, or dilapidated. You wish to move into a newer, fresher one.

- You want to make the move from one style of home (e.g., ranch, colonial, Victorian, contemporary) to another style, or to a different material, e.g., brick, clapboard, fieldstone, or stucco.

- You love to entertain, and you want to move to a home that is more suitable for frequent entertaining.

The list could go on and on. The main point is that there's certainly nothing wrong with moving because of such a preference, as long as three conditions apply:

1. You are in a good financial position to make such a move.

2. You have given sufficient thought to such a move.

3. You are confident that the advantages of such a move outweigh any drawbacks.

If these conditions apply to you, read on!

Slackers Need Not Apply

Each chapter in this guide is full of substantive "unofficial" money-saving, time-saving tips, ideas, and quotes from experts. The information is presented in a light, readable tone, in the exact order that corresponds with the home-buying process.

We can't choose your cereal, movies, or coffee. But we can help you choose the right home. Whether you're buying for the first or fifth time, whether you're buying it to live in or for an investment, we can help you feel confident rather than fearful about your purchase.

But be forewarned. If you're looking for a "how-to" book that treats you like anything less than an intelligent adult, this guide's not for you. We speak plainly, but we don't patronize. We support you, but in the final analysis, you're the soldier on the front line. If you prepare adequately with this guide as your companion and mentor, you'll be ready for anything the home-buying process dishes out. We wish you good luck, but remember (as an old soldier once said) that "good luck is where preparation meets opportunity."

Special Features

Every book in our series offers the following four special side-bars in the margins that were devised to help you get things done cheaply, efficiently, and smartly.

1. **Moneysaver:** Tips and shortcuts that save you money.

2. **Watch Out!:** More serious cautions and warnings.

3. **Bright Idea:** General tips and shortcuts to help you find an easier or smarter way to do something.

4. **Quote:** Statements from real people that are intended to be prescriptive and valuable to you.

We also recognize your need to have quick information at your fingertips, and have thus provided the following comprehensive sections at the back of the book:

1. **Drawings of the nine most popular home styles.**

2. **Important Statistics:** Facts and numbers presented at a glance for easy reference.

3. **Important Documents:** "Official" pieces of information you need to refer to, such as government forms.

4. **Glossary:** Definitions of complicated terminology and jargon.

5. **Bibliography:** Suggested titles that can help you get more in-depth information on related topics.

6. **Resource Guide:** Lists of relevant agencies, associations, institutions, Web sites, and so on.

7. **Index.**

Money Issues

PART I

GET THE SCOOP ON...
Taking out a contract ▪ Savvy leveraging ▪
"Gifts"and co-signers ▪ Types of mortgage loans
▪ Understanding amortization ▪ Truth-in-lending

Ready...Set...Finance!

This chapter contains a wealth of raw data and technical terminology. When you've finished reading it, you'll have at least a rudimentary knowledge of every kind of mortgage loan available for purchasing a home. Your head will probably be spinning with "mortgage vertigo." But, you'll have the know-how to zero in on the mortgage that suits you best.

In the following pages, we look at everything from types of contracts to categories of employment status. You'll learn how to determine the amount of your mortgage payment, depending on which loan option you choose. You'll be introduced to each of the five major loan options individually and—in between—explore how you can pay off your loan ahead of schedule.

After you're living in your new home, much of the whole financing experience may seem like an elaborate and even rather comical dream. You'll

3

> **❝** Every radish I ever pulled up seemed to have a mortgage attached to it. **❞**
>
> —Ed Wynn (1886–1966), explaining why he sold his farm

gradually forget the details, but you'll have a frame of reference for the next time you buy a home, when the whole process (we sincerely hope) will seem a good deal easier.

You're ready to look at houses—now what?

At this point, you're probably chomping at the bit to hit the road and look for houses. Many people have inflated expectations of what they can afford; others are unaware of skeletons in their closets that could haunt the whole loan process. Basically, if you have any intention to finance your home purchase, you will want to know in advance the amount and type of loan for which you qualify. Whether you wind up pleasantly surprised, doubtful, or even depressed, you will at least go into the home-buying process knowing your limits.

Many people, in fact, shop for houses with an official loan approval letter firmly in hand. Sellers and their agents are always impressed to see prospective purchasers whom they know will qualify for a loan. Having such a letter clears the air of uncertainty; it often helps you negotiate the best possible terms for your purchase. This is because most sellers would rather have an offer somewhat lower than list price that comes with a loan approval letter, than they would a full-price offer with a loan contingency that they're not certain can be removed or satisfied.

Even though you're not quite ready to go shopping, you should know about the purchase contract types you may one day be filling out. They are part of mortgage parlance. Moreover, their content comprises much of the financing details you're about to investigate. Basically, three types of contracts are available for purchasing a home, each specific to the financing options available to you:

- The "financed sale" contract—If, like the vast majority of homebuyers, you are taking out a new loan, you will execute this type of contract.

- The "equity sale" contract—If you are taking over an existing loan, also called *assuming* a loan, you will execute an equity sale contract. This means that you'll be making a down payment equivalent to the current owner's equity in his house. You'll most likely have fewer, and lower, closing costs than with a new loan.

- The "cash" contract—If you're one of the fortunate few who is paying cash, your only costs in addition to the contract price are a share of the settlement agent's fee and the fee to transfer title and record your deed.

What follows is an overview of the types of loans that correspond to the first two types of contracts, as well as the costs involved. For those executing a cash contract, we'll discuss other obligations of which you need to be aware.

The new loan: a basic anatomy lesson

Literally hundreds of mortgage loan products are available for those getting new financing. These products fall into a handful of basic categories that we will go over later in the chapter. They all have certain features in common. All new loans require that you pay closing costs (fees paid to your lender for processing a mortgage loan), although many loan programs enable you to share closing costs with the seller. You will also be responsible for what are known as *prepaids*, which include homeowner's insurance, prorated interest (from the day of closing until the end of the closing month), and a prorated share of the property taxes. If you are making a down payment of less than 20 percent, it may be necessary to include a private mortgage insurance (PMI) premium, although PMI is becoming something of a dinosaur. Your mortgage is actually a security interest to protect your *note*, which recites the terms of repayment.

Shopping for the best

Now that you're prepared to shop for a loan before you begin shopping for a home, how do you go about finding the right lender? Given the abundance of potential lenders, how do you shop around for the best one? Here are the kinds of questions commonly asked when selecting a mortgage institution:

- "Should I call each mortgage company and bank and then choose the one that offers the lowest interest rate?"
- "Should I choose the large bank or the small private mortgage company?"
- "Should I take the recommendation of friends?"
- "Should I accept the recommendation of my real estate agent?"
- "Should I respond to the most appealing ad in the Yellow Pages?"

These are all valid questions, but they are not necessarily the most relevant.

Let's get something out on the table right away. If you are creditworthy, you could call 10 different mortgage institutions, and all will quote you approximately the same interest rate, assuming you tell each one that you plan to borrow the same amount of money. This will be true whether you call a large bank or a small mortgage company, because both act as brokers whose job it is to secure a loan for you on the secondary market. However, there might be a very slight variation in the loan origination fee, which is usually about 1 percent and is quoted as

 Bright Idea

You may want to have a mortgage broker do your shopping. A mortgage broker represents multiple lenders and may know which bank has the most aggressive loan programs. Make sure, however, that you get a commitment from the broker that he is not charging you more than the bank would charge you for the same loan. The broker typically gets a *rebate* from the bank.

Watch Out!

The most common complaint about mortgage loan officers is repeated calls with a never-ending stream of questions and requests related to your credit and income. Don't let your loan officer hang up from the first call until you receive a confident "yes" when you ask whether he has elicited all the information and itemized all the documents needed to process your loan.

points of your mortgage amount and paid as a closing cost, and other administrative fees. The question is, "Should this slight variation sway your decision toward one mortgage company over another?"

No. When choosing a lender, one consideration is more important than saving these few dollars—saving your valuable time. Call several lenders. Your first question to each of them should be: "How many times do I have to visit or call you before you can complete processing a loan for me?" The answer should be "once." A good loan officer can tell you, within a few minutes, what documents you'll need to collect and turn over to him. Many good loan officers will come to you, toting a laptop computer, and be able to plug in the information from these documents, pull up a credit report, and have you approved for a loan (subject to a satisfactory appraisal on the home you buy) in an hour or less. Most of us lead busy lives, with precious little time to pay frequent visits to our loan officer prior to purchasing or closing on the purchase of a home. Just as efficient service should be a salient characteristic of every real estate agent, it should also be the hallmark of every mortgage lender. But (big surprise), often it is not.

The foolproof way to find the best lender is to ask these three questions:

- Do they have a comprehensive selection of loan packages?
- Can they give me the quickest, most efficient service?
- Will they come to me, if necessary?

Bright Idea

You should be able to do all your mortgage shopping over the telephone. After you've picked out two or three mortgage companies that provide one-visit processing, ask for their Web sites. A quick review from the comfort of your computer will probably narrow down your choice to the one mortgage company that has the particular loan you want.

If you find more than one potential lender that meets these criteria, then go with your instinct.

If you assume . . .

Even though it's a done deal at this point, let's review the questions you were supposed to ask yourself upon assuming a loan:

- Do I have enough cash to meet the seller's equity? (In areas where homes rapidly appreciate in value, the equity the seller expects is usually more than many people can afford. Or, the seller may have paid off so much principal that the equity is unaffordable.)

- Is the interest rate on the loan I'm assuming competitive with current interest rates? (If the interest rate on the assumable loan is significantly higher—a percentage point or more—than on a new loan, the monthly payment may be too high, even if the equity payment is low.)

- How many years will it take me to pay off the loan?

The ideal assumption is of a short-term loan (20 years or less of remaining payments) at a competitive interest rate and with low equity. This may seem to be a nearly impossible combination, but it happens from time to time. The explanation is the mobility factor: A seller is transferred, but there's not enough time to realize an increase in equity, nor enough time for interest rates on new loans to have risen much above the rate on the seller's existing loan.

If you do purchase your home through an equity contract that entails the assumption of the previous owner's loan, your

Bright Idea

You could be one of the fortunate few who finds a seller willing to provide his own financing in exchange for a certain amount of equity. In this type of arrangement, sometimes called a *promissory note* or *purchase money mortgage*, you promise to repay the debt on the seller's terms. You pay your homeowner's insurance and property taxes separately from the mortgage. Closing fees are minimal.

closing costs will be much lower than if you get a new loan. The seller will order a loan package from the original lender, and a settlement agent will transfer the package to you. Often, you'll be paying a transfer fee to assume the loan (the average is about $500). Conventional loans, which we'll discuss later in the chapter, are rarely assumable. But Federal Housing Authority (FHA) and Veterans Administration (VA) loans are almost always assumable, some without the extensive documentation required for a new loan application.

Cash now. But what about later?

Even if you purchase your new home with cash, you might someday be in a position where you'll want to consider mortgage loan options. A home is an investment. This means that you can borrow on the equity to finance other projects. By paying with cash, you achieve a 100-percent equity position. You could exchange all or part of your equity to buy a vacation home or a new car. You could pay off college tuition or offset the cost of some uninsured catastrophe. Read on, because you may want to consider a mortgage loan in the future.

How do you make your money?

Before we look at each basic loan option in detail, let's look at what type of buyer you are and how this may affect you. It's important for your mortgage loan officer to know what kind of employment situation you fit into. He will be less interested in the type of work you do—or if, in fact, you work at all—than in how you get paid. From a loan officer's point of view, there are three employment categories:

- The "1040 employee," who is paid regularly by an employer.
- The "1099 taxpayer," who is self-employed.
- The non-employed.

Of course, it's easy to figure out which type of employee you are. The important thing is to take note of how your employee status affects the type of loan you can get. So read on.

Like most people (the 1040 employee)?

You're a 1040 employee if you receive a regular paycheck from which Social Security (FICA) tax is deducted. If you're paid on a regular basis, your loan officer will determine how much you can afford to pay for a home by taking your gross monthly income and using the 28/36 percent formula (explained in Chapter 4) to determine a monthly payment ceiling. However, compensating factors may allow your loan officer to bend the ratios. If you receive regular payments from a trust account; if you've been receiving alimony and/or child support for more than two years; if you have a substantial savings account that could cover your mortgage payments if you were laid off or became ill and couldn't work; or if you're retired from one job that's providing supplemental income while you still work at another job, you may be able to afford a more expensive home than the basic ratios would allow.

Are you a self-starter (the 1099 taxpayer)?

You're a 1099 taxpayer, self-employed, if your income derives from commissions, fees, or bonuses and you pay your own Social Security tax. If you're self-employed, chances are that you're paid irregularly and are responsible for your own FICA tax. At the end of each year, you get one or more Form 1099s. You probably file a quarterly voucher estimating three months of income and include a check that coincides in amount with your federal tax bracket and three months of FICA tax. In all likelihood, your real estate agent himself is a 1099 taxpayer—often called an *independent contractor*—rather than a 1040 employee.

To qualify for a mortgage if you're a 1099 taxpayer, you'll have to demonstrate that your income has been consistent over a two-year period or longer. Why? Obviously, your lender will need assurances that you can generate enough income to meet all your expenses in the future. In other words, if you receive a Form 1099 that shows your gross income, you need it to demonstrate a consistent track record in your line of work.

Are you a mixed bag (the non-employed)?

Even though you may not be earning wages in the traditional sense of having a job, you may still have enough income to qualify for a loan. For example, from trusts, investments, or settlements (inheritance, alimony payments, accident-related compensation, disability insurance, and so forth). If your only regular income is from one or more of these sources, technically, you're non-employed. But, like the independent contractor, you're a taxpayer. And, you may be able to show consistent income over a long enough period of time to get whatever kind of financing best suits your needs.

> **❝** If you're non-employed, you're not a pariah in the eyes of a loan officer. Among the non-employed are a substantial number of people who receive income from any number of possible sources. The issue for your loan officer is income-earning consistency, not 'employment versus non-employment.' **❞**
>
> Tony Robbins, A.M. Robbins Mortgage Company

Even more importantly, you may be retired, have a substantial monthly or yearly pension fund, and use this fund instead of income in the traditional sense to finance a home. The Federal Government has strict sanctions for lenders who discriminate against purchasers on the basis of age. It has become more and more common, in this time of increased longevity, for people 80 years of age or even older to apply for and receive 30-year loans.

Show me the money—what are your choices?

Regardless of your employment classification, you may be eligible for four of the five types of loans available. (The fifth type is the Professional Association loan, which is usually available only if you are a doctor or attorney.) Now you're ready to consider the type of loan that best suits your finances.

Each of the loans we'll look at is designed to fit a particular set of needs. If you write a financed sale contract to purchase your new home, you'll specify on that contract one of the following categories of financing:

- Conventional

- FHA

- VA

- Community Home Buyer

- Professional Association

We'll look at each of these separately:

Presumably, you will seek advice from your real estate agent regarding loan types before you write your contract. At that time, you will also draw up an "Estimated Cash Required to Purchase" disclosure with your agent so that you will know your approximate closing costs in advance (see a sample in Appendix C).

On the odd chance that you've jumped the gun and secured a contract to purchase a home before visiting with or speaking to a loan officer (hopefully, you have, at least, calculated your ratios and checked your credit status), you will want to visit with your lender as soon as possible. After discussing your financial situation, the loan officer might recommend a different type of loan than the one indicated on the contract. That's okay, as long as the seller is informed and he nets the same amount of money at the closing as with the original loan. If the amount turns out to be lower because of mandatory seller-paid closing costs (as often happens with VA, FHA, and Community Home Buyer loans), you may have to renegotiate a higher sales price to make up for the difference.

When you have more cash than you need, should you leverage?

Each of the loan options we discuss in this chapter allows you to determine the amount of your down payment (within specified lower limits). However, if you have more cash available than you need for a minimum down payment, the question becomes, should you use it for a larger down payment or keep it for other purposes?

This is, of course, a very personal decision based on your lifestyle and the lifestyle of your family. If you enjoy traveling to distant ports, dining at gourmet restaurants, or participating in some other expensive extracurricular activity, then you may want to reserve the extra money for a ready cash supply. However, if you prefer investing to spending, you should consider a leveraging strategy. *Leveraging* means maximizing the amount of your mortgage loan while at the same time minimizing your out-of-pocket expenses—that is, your down payment and closing costs. The result is optimal use of your money.

For those of you who are investors, whether or not you should leverage depends on two factors: the current home mortgage interest rates and the condition of the financial marketplace. If the going mortgage interest rates are high—(in today's market, that would be 6 or higher)—it makes the best sense to

 Watch Out!

This is not a book about financial planning or accounting. Here, we are providing only some broad suggestions. Before following any of them, you should discuss them in detail with your favorite expert.

put as much money down on a house as you can, in order to reduce the interest payment portion of your mortgage. However, if the going mortgage interest rate is low—(6 percent or lower)—it may make more sense to leverage. The lower the interest rate, the lower your overall monthly mortgage payment, and conversely, the greater the amount you should finance.

The gift and the co-signer

Before we go through the five basic loan options, let's look at two ways you can boost your loan-getting power. The first is the gift. Exactly what constitutes a gift in the context of financing your home?

First, you should understand what a gift is not. A gift isn't something you can use on your loan application as a supplement to your income. For example, if you earn $30,000 per year but need to earn $35,000 per year to qualify for a particular loan, you can't use a gift commitment of $5,000 to make up the difference.

So what, then, is a gift? It is outside help with the down payment on your house. It can be for any amount. For example, even if you have enough of your own cash to put down 10 percent on a house, but you want to put down, say, 30 percent, you can receive a gift for the additional 20 percent. Therefore, even though a gift cannot be counted as regular income, it can substantially reduce your debt-to-income ratios and help you purchase a home that may otherwise be beyond your price range.

The gift must be offered to your lender in the form of a letter stating that the giver will provide the specified amount of money without your being expected to repay the debt. (Many gift recipients make private arrangements to repay the giver anyway.) The giver does not have to be a parent or even a relative. Why are lenders so receptive to different kinds of givers as well as the amount of their gifts? They're not. So, expect your giver to be subjected to an extensive credit check. Then, if your lender doesn't believe your benefactor can comfortably part with the specified amount, free and clear, the whole gift-as-down-payment plan may collapse.

Here is a sample of the type of gift letter that lenders require:

> "I, Jane Doe, the mother of John Doe, do freely give John and his wife Lucille $10,000 from the proceeds of CD [Certificate of Deposit] Number 1234567, drawn from The Bank of All Banks, which will mature on June 16, 2004. I do not expect or require repayment of this gift. If you need to examine my personal financial history, please contact my accountant, Harvey Flake, at (555) 555-5555."

Another type of benefactor besides the gift-giver is the co-signer, sometimes called the *guarantor*. A co-signer is someone whose name goes on a mortgage loan along with your own and who commits to helping you repay the debt. Your co-signer must agree to take over the debt in the event that you default. Like the gift-giver, the co-signer must undergo a thorough credit check and income evaluation. However, unlike the gift-giver, the co-signer's name appears along with yours on the trust (as opposed to ownership) deed and mortgage.

Some of you may balk at the idea of using a co-signer as a means of enabling you to buy a home. However, many co-signers regard the payment of part of their beneficiary's mortgage interest as a useful tax shelter. Or, you may simply have a parent, other relative, or friend who is generous and has the means to help you. Why deny them the satisfaction?

Your co-signer can always remove his name from your deed and mortgage at a later date. You can remove the co-signer's name simply by refinancing—that is, taking out a new loan—once you've saved enough money for the down payment.

A shopping list of loans

This brings us back to the subject of the various categories of loans available to homebuyers: the conventional, FHA, VA, Community Home Buyer, and Professional Association loans. We'll start our recap of these categories with the loan used by the majority of homebuyers and then move into some of the less conventional, but nonetheless viable, means of financing.

A loan most ordinary—the conventional loan

If you have at least 5 percent of your own money for a down payment and your ratios are in line with the 28/36 percent formula, you will probably want a conventional loan. Conventional loans adhere to Federal National Mortgage Association (FNMA, or Fannie Mae) guidelines. These and all other loans are set for a specific period of time until full payoff. The longer the loan period, the lower the principal and interest payment, but the higher the interest rate.

A crucial factor affecting your mortgage payments is the percentage (of the purchase price) of your down payment. If your down payment is under 20 percent, you may be required to get private mortgage insurance (PMI), which will be added to your monthly payments. But, as we said earlier, PMI is becoming a vestige of the past. Most lenders now offer blended loans—let's say an 80-percent first loan and a 15-percent second loan, which is usually financed at a slightly lower interest rate. As a result, your gross monthly payment for principal and interest is well below the payment on a 95-percent single loan with PMI.

You may have thought, with the information given, that you had a handle on the conventional mortgage. But, in fact your conventional mortgage options have increased considerably over the past few years. You don't have any money for a down payment? Okay. There's a 100-percent, no PMI program that could suit your need. The interest payment is usually slightly higher than that of a loan with 5 percent down, and the credit requirements are usually more strict. But, if you are truly eager to buy a home, if interest rates are low, and if you think it will

---

 Moneysaver

You usually are expected to pay all of your own closing costs, although surprisingly often, you'll find a seller willing to pay a share of them. In many states it's customary for you and the seller to divide equally the portion of closing costs that go to the settlement agent and title company.

take an unbearable amount of time to accumulate funds for a down payment, then a 100-percent plan may work for you.

Wait a minute! You don't have money for either a down payment or for closing costs? That's okay. If you have stellar credit (you *might* be able to slip by with one or two 30-days late payments over the last four or five years), some conventional loans will finance between 103 and 107 percent of your purchase to accommodate some or all of your closing costs—again at an only slightly higher interest rate than for a loan (one with 5 percent or more in a down payment).

Why, you may ask, would *anyone* consider putting money down on a home if these last two options are available? For two reasons: first, because credit requirements for these loans are rather strict; second, because it is wise, if you have cash to put down on a home, to have at least some equity in your purchase in case you should have to borrow on that equity or in case property values in the neighborhood should remain stable or decline over the next few years. You could find yourself unable to sell your home for more than you paid for it. I've seen people writing checks or, even worse, borrowing money to close on homes they purchased four, five, or six years earlier with 100-percent financing. The spectacle was not very pleasant. Finally, the total monthly payment on any of these loans is higher because of the higher interest rate and greater amount of money borrowed.

Another central issue pertaining to all forms of mortgage loans is that they have dollar limits. When you get an interest rate quote for a conventional loan, you need to know that the rate is only good for a maximum loan amount of $322,700 (based on the mid-year 2003 figure). The interest rates at or below the maximum is called the *conforming rate*. You may want to borrow far more than $322,700, and the only limits are how much you earn or have in savings and how your credit score comes out. You will need to apply for a conventional loan for this kind of money, but at a non-conforming, or jumbo interest

Moneysaver

PMI, if you have to have it, can add more than 10 percent to your monthly mortgage payment! But you can have your PMI removed after the principal balance of your loan is paid down to 80 percent of your purchase price. If you can demonstrate that your home has appreciated in value, you can reach the 80 percent point more quickly by submitting a new appraisal to your lender.

rate, which is usually between ⅜ and ½ a point higher than the rate for a conforming loan. No upper limit is placed on how much you can (hypothetically) borrow to buy a home, and no point exists at which you can be required to put money down. I know a few fortunate people who have financed 100 percent of home purchases well over one million dollars, though.

Let's look at an example of the most conventional of conventional mortgage loans to see how it works. Say you buy a home for $125,000. Your down payment is 5 percent of the purchase price, or $6,250. Your contract says you will pay your normal closing costs ($2,800) and prepaids, which vary greatly from state to state because of taxes. In addition, because you are putting down less than 20 percent, you will have to pay PMI, which you plan to fold into your loan. The PMI factor with 5 percent down is 1.05 percent of your loan amount, paid annually in 12 monthly installments, just like principal, interest, taxes, and insurance. Suppose that your loan is amortized over a period of 30 years at an interest rate of 7 percent. Table 1.1 can help you figure out your monthly mortgage payment.

Table 1.1. Figuring Your Monthly Mortgage Payment

1. Take your purchase price and subtract your down payment of 5 percent (including earnest money) to get the total amount of your mortgage:

Purchase price	$125,000.00
Down payment (including earnest money)	$6,250.00
Mortgage amount	$118,750.00

2. Now look at the P&I chart in Appendix B. The principal and interest for a 30-year fixed-rate loan at 7 percent is $6.65 for every $1,000 of loan amount.

   Therefore, $118,750 ÷ 1,000 × 6.65 = $789.68 P&I.

   If your annual property taxes are $1,200, then $1,200 ÷ 12 = $100.

   If your annual homeowner's insurance premium is $500, then $500 ÷ 12 = $41.66.

3. Finally, to calculate your PMI, take 1.05 percent of your loan amount and divide by 12:

   $118,750 × .0105 = $1,246.80 ÷ 12 = $103.90

4. Add all your figures together to arrive at a total monthly payment:

P&I	$789.68
Property taxes	$100.00
Homeowner's insurance	$41.66
PMI	$103.90
Total monthly payment	**$1,035.24**

To determine the total amount you will need at closing is a bit less daunting. Follow the steps given in Table 1.2.

Table 1.2. Determining the Amount Needed at Closing

Add your down payment, your closing costs, and 14 months of homeowner's insurance (14 × $41.66 = $583.24), which in most states is required for you to set up an insurance escrow account. Then deduct the amount you paid in earnest money—in this example, $1,000.

Down payment	$6,250.00
Closing costs	$2,800.00
14 months of homeowner's insurance	$583.24
Subtotal	$9,633.24
Earnest money	−($1,000.00)
Total amount needed at closing	**$8,633.24**

Moneysaver

The amount of PMI required decreases as your percentage of down payment increases. To calculate PMI with at least 10 percent down but less than 20 percent, multiply your loan amount by a factor of .0045 instead of .0105. Remember, if you put down 20 percent or more, you will not have to pay PMI.

We'll now move beyond conventional to three types of loans that allow you even more flexibility to bend the ratios used for conventional financing—the FHA loan, the VA loan, and the various loan programs usually lumped together under the Community Home Buyer's loan arrangement. We'll finish our discussion of loan choices with the Professional Association (PA) loan, usually available only to doctors and lawyers.

The cheapest—the FHA loan

Unless you are a doctor or lawyer, which we discuss later, the FHA loan may be your least expensive option. The primary reasons for getting an FHA loan are that you don't have to have cash for a down payment; you really need to bend the upper (higher) ratio to qualify for a loan; your credit rating is below the minimum set for getting conventional financing; or you're buying a home at a price that accords with the maximum amount that FHA allows you to borrow in your county. FHA allows all of your funds needed at closing to come from gift money. FHA also allows most of your closing costs to be paid by the seller—in fact, up to 6 percent of your loan amount. FHA programs include the one-year ARM, the buy-down (paying points, or prepaid interest, at closing to lower your interest rate), and the fixed-rate loan. Each metropolitan area fixes its own maximum loan amount allowable through FHA (plus MIP, which is FHA's version of PMI). The current average U.S. maximum, which varies from county to county, is about $150,000.

With an FHA loan, the down payment you are required to pay is lower than for most conventional loans: 3 percent down on a sales price less than \$50,000 and 2½ percent down less \$500 on a sales price greater than \$50,000.

FHA has two forms of mortgage insurance (MIP):

- An up-front lump sum of 2.25 percent of your loan amount, which is usually financed into the loan.

- A 0.5-percent annual premium included in your monthly payment escrows, which are funds in your loan to pay taxes, insurance, and PMI or MIP.

If you're tight on funds available to close, you can ask the sellers to pay part or all of your closing costs, even if this means bumping up the sales price to repay the sellers for their help. If this is not possible, some of your closing costs may be financed. In FHA financing, you're not allowed to pay certain closing costs, such as the underwriting fee, document preparation fee, courier fees, and assignment fees. FHA requires that the seller pay these fees. The Department of Housing and Urban Development (HUD) requires that your contract be very specific regarding who pays what.

It's commonly believed that with an FHA loan, the federal government provides financing. The fact of the matter is that while the FHA insures its loans, the government doesn't put up the money. FHA loans are brokered to the secondary market just as conventional loans are.

Several years ago, loan officers originating FHA loans had to apply directly to the state capital to order an appraisal. The time from contract to closing tended to be inordinately long and sometimes, downright unpredictable. Now loan officers can use

Watch Out!

Not all real estate agents can figure your payments or closing costs on FHA loans. Some may not even tell you about FHA—even in cases where it would be in your best interest to get FHA financing! If you're concerned about having enough cash to close, don't forget this option. You should go directly to your loan officer before writing a contract.

the FHA appraiser of their choice, which means that your loan can close in 30 days or less.

Finally, with an FHA loan, you can bend your ratios a bit. Instead of applying the 28/36 percent formula, FHA qualifying ratios are 29 percent and 41 percent, respectively. Some people have qualified for FHA loans with upper ratios greater than 50 percent! Moreover, some additional flexibility exists in the case of compensating factors, such as a 10 percent or larger down payment, a good savings pattern, conservative use of credit, cash reserves, your potential for increased income, or your purchase of an energy-efficient home.

No money down! The VA loan

A VA loan, sponsored but not insured by the federal government, is available to you if you are a veteran and you've applied for and obtained your full entitlement. The VA allows you to finance 100 percent of your purchase, up to a current national average of $237,000. At closing, you pay a one-time VA funding fee of between 1 and 3 percent of your loan amount, which is usually folded into your loan. (If you're a veteran on disability, you don't have to pay the funding fee.)

No "lower ratio" (percent of mortgage payment to gross monthly income) is taken into the consideration of your eligibility for VA funding. The total debt ratio may be 41 percent or higher, depending on compensating factors, such as the number of people in your family and how much you spend to support them. It is not uncommon to be approved with a debt ratio of greater than 55 percent. The government wants to support

 Moneysaver

As you negotiate your VA contract, you should be aware that the seller is allowed to pay all closing costs and prepaid items. It's entirely possible to obtain a VA loan with no down payment or closing costs. You may even get a full refund of your earnest money at closing!

you, the veteran, in your quest for financing, and therefore, allows your lender to be far more flexible in handling your ratios than with other types of financing.

The Community Home Buyer loan

The Federal National Mortgage Association (Fannie Mae) and the Federal Home Loan Mortgage Corporation (FHLMC, or Freddie Mac) have programs that allow you to pay less than the traditional 5-percent down payment. The Community Home Buyer program allows you two options: to put down 3 percent (all your own money) or to put down 5 percent, with 3 percent being your own money and the additional 2 percent coming from a gift or separate loan.

The program has some restrictions, the most significant one being an annual maximum family income (currently about $46,000) set by HUD. Fixed-rate loans are the only programs offered, and homebuyer education and credit counseling are usually required as part of your loan application. Typically, the interest rate for Community Home Buyer loans is slightly higher than for other types of financing.

The four advantages to the Community Home Buyer program are

- Only 3 percent of your money is required for a down payment.
- Only one ratio—income to total debt—is relevant, and it can run as high as 40 percent.
- You need have only one month's cash in reserve (most other loans require two).
- Some leniency on credit is usually given if you've had late payments.

For doctors or lawyers only

Most banks (but almost no private mortgage companies) have special loan programs called Professional Association (PA) loans, for doctors and lawyers. These are especially attractive if you're buying a home for the first time. Of course, you aren't required to get a PA loan if you're an attorney or physician, but this unique program is available to you if you need it.

A Professional Association is a bit like an exclusive club. It offers 100-percent financing if you need it and also allows you to fold almost all of your closing costs into your loan. Unlike conventional or FHA loans, which require you to pay PMI, MIP or, if not one of these, a slightly higher interest rate on a blended loan, if you put down less than 20 percent, the PA 100-percent loan is blended to enable you to forgo monthly insurance premiums and not necessarily pay a higher interest rate The first loan— usually in the 80- to 85-percent financing range—conforms to regular Fannie Mae guidelines; the second loan of 15 to 20 percent is amortized over a five-year period and is counted as a down payment in the sense that it relieves you of the insurance premium burden. Another attraction of the PA loan is that it enables you to reach an equity position of 20 percent in five years or less (assuming that your home doesn't depreciate in value).

That's not all. With the usual mortgage loan, mortgage companies and banks broker loans for lenders in the secondary market. These outside lenders buy hundreds or even thousands of loans at one time and service them by managing your escrow account (the account established at closing to pay your taxes, homeowner's insurance, and PMI). In contrast, the PA loan is monitored in-house. You make your payments to a local organization that usually provides you with a menu of additional services—free checking, in-house stock brokerage services, CDs that bear higher-than-usual interest, and the like.

To summarize the four loan options available beyond a conventional loan:

- **FHA:** You may want to consider the FHA loan program if you need a gift to make your down payment, or if your ratios are a bit higher than those allowed with conventional loans.

- **VA:** If you're a veteran and are eligible through state certification to receive a VA loan, you will want to look at the
  VA option. It enables you to obtain 100-percent financing,
  including your closing costs.

- **Community Home Buyer:** If your income falls below a certain level, you may want to explore this program, which
  enables you to buy a home through conventional financing for as little as 3 percent down.

- **Professional Association:** If you are a doctor or lawyer
  seeking to finance 100 percent of the purchase price of
  your home, this is an attractive loan option uniquely
  available to you.

Amortization and you

Amortization is a sadistic invention designed to make investors
a lot of money quickly! The mathematical principle is sound,
but its effect is jolting. To put *amortization* simply (which is an
oxymoron): in the initial years of your mortgage loan, the
amount you pay down in principal is usually less than 10 percent
of your total monthly payment, while the interest portion is
greater than 90 percent. The longer you make payments, the
lower the ratio of interest to principal until, near the end of
your loan period, your principal payment greatly exceeds your
interest payment.

A long time coming

The sadistic trick is that your principal payment does not equal
and then exceed your interest payment until about three-fourths
of the way through your total loan period. I've included two
sample amortization schedules in Appendix B: one on a 30-year
loan of $100,000 at 7 percent and the other on the same type of
loan, but at 10 percent. Note how much more total interest is
paid on the 10-percent loan. Regardless of interest rates, notice
how much interest will be paid in the first 10 or 12 years of the
loan period. Also notice that in both schedules, the principal

Moneysaver

To cut your loan payoff schedule in half, include your regular payment with the next month's principal payment. Simply follow your amortization schedule, adding the next month's principal into the check you write. Write "payment plus additional principal" on the lower left-hand line of your check.

payments don't exceed the interest payments until the year 23! The government has laws requiring that you be informed of all this at the closing . . . at least in a vague way. In Appendix C, I've included a sample note template that lays out the terms of a sample mortgage, and a sample mortgage template (the security instrument that demands repayment of the debt).

In Appendix C, you'll also find the Federal Truth-in-Lending Disclosure Statement. These are among the most important of the documents you'll be signing at closing. I've supplied them to help you understand how amortization works.

You can use the sample template in Appendix C to relieve some of amortization's sting. Look at item 4, "Borrower's Right to Repay." Your prepayment rights enable you to pay off your loan early to avoid a substantial amount of interest. Doing so will not lower your monthly payment, but it may significantly reduce the period of time it will take you to pay off your loan.

Mind-bending boxes

We suggest that you have your own mortgage repayment schedule worked out before you close, especially if you plan on living in your new home for longer than five years and have taken out a fixed-rate loan. If you look at the Federal Truth-in-Lending Disclosure Statement (see Appendix C), you'll see why. Called by many settlement agents the "federal confusion-in-lending statement," this disclosure form, meant to enlighten you, has four boxes near the top. These boxes require some explanation. The first is the "Annual Percentage Rate" (APR) box, which is not your note rate, but an interest rate derived from adding your closing costs to your loan amount to arrive at the "cost of your credit" expressed as a yearly interest rate. Don't be fooled; the first box does not tell you anything you need to know. Skip it and move right on to Box 2, "Finance Charge."

The finance charge is a euphemism for the amount of interest you'll pay over the life of your loan assuming that you pay at the note rate every month. Here's where you see how the going interest rate for mortgage loans really makes a difference. Look at the bottom of the two amortization schedules in Appendix B for $100,000 loans, one at 7 percent, the other at 10 percent. If you have a 7-percent loan, Box 2 will show a total interest payment of $139,502.20. If you have a 10-percent loan, your interest payment will be $215,909.34—a difference, in 30 years, of more than $75,000!

When you come to Box 3, "Amount Financed," you simply fill in the amount of your loan. Added together, the "amount financed" and the "finance charge" will give you the "Total of Payments" (Box 4) made over the life of your loan, assuming no prepayments or early payoff. The stark reality is that your total payments can wind up being three times or more than your initial loan amount.

The note, the Truth-in-Lending statement, and the amortization schedules should explain why adjustable-rate loans are so attractive if you're going to be a short-term homeowner and why the prepayment option is so helpful if you can budget to do it.

You won't actually see the documents we've been discussing until closing, except for the samples in Appendix C. But knowing

 Moneysaver

If you want to make additional principal payments, you don't have to do it every month. Some people make partial prepayments on an occasional basis as extra cash becomes available. Any prepayment anytime helps you save money. It's your loan servicing company's responsibility to keep up with your outstanding loan principal.

how they work as you plan the financing of your new home will help you anticipate the best way to pay off your loan as part of your overall financial plan. Your home purchase won't seem too daunting if you know what your real costs are!

Just the facts

- Shop for loans based on the type of contract you've signed: financed, equity, or cash.
- Understand what type of buyer you are.
- Choose the lender who can give you the best service with the least hassle.
- Select the loan that fits your financial/professional circumstances.
- Avoid huge interest payments by using an amortization schedule as a guide to making extra payments on your principal.

GET THE SCOOP ON...

How credit fosters home buying ▪ Credit for mortgages ▪ Reporting agencies ▪ Credit counseling rip-offs ▪ Restoring your good credit ▪ How lenders interpret credit

Cleaning Up Your Credit

Chapter 2

Credit. It's the American way. Even if we can afford to, it's rare for us to buy big-ticket items with cash. Increasingly, we write fewer checks. Instead, we consolidate our check writing into the relatively small number of checks we write monthly to make payments on our credit card bills.

Who among us has not received a regular dose of credit card offers by mail? Although we throw most of them away, some are just too tempting to resist. Your favorite department stores, all major gasoline companies, and many major grocery store chains provide credit cards, and those that don't provide them allow us to shop with the biggies: American Express, Visa, MasterCard, and Discover. Who among us does not carry at least one of these four?

With the proliferation of credit and the increasingly popular use of credit cards, we have accumulated far more debt than our parents' generation could ever imagine. This is the result of the minimum monthly payment, which can be as low as 2 or 3 percent of the total amount owed on any particular credit card. All of us have taken advantage of this at one time or another—in a crunch period, for example, when unforeseen expenses have forced us to pay the minimum and hope to pay off more later. On occasion, even that minimum monthly payment exceeds our available cash. Suddenly, we miss one month's payment entirely . . . or two, or three. And, all of our misses, indeed all of our late payments, are being reported to credit bureaus.

Now you have decided to buy a home. Alas, you may discover that your late payments, or even your consistently on-time payments of revolving (monthly) debt, have put home buying beyond your reach. In this chapter, we'll advise you on the following:

1. How to keep the amount of your credit card debt low enough that your ability to buy a home in a certain price range is not hampered.

2. How to clean up those negative aspects of credit—late payments or nonpayments—so that your ability to buy a home is not impaired.

The central point of this chapter is that applications for mortgages are entirely credit driven. Toward the end of the chapter, we'll examine how lenders take your credit reports from the three major credit bureaus and arrive at a composite score that determines the amount of money you can borrow, the interest at which you can borrow money, what types of mortgage programs you qualify for (literally hundreds of different programs are available), and whether you are qualified for financing at all.

More often than not, these determinations are made by computer and not by some mad actuary sitting in an office reading your credit reports. Most lenders use either a program called Loan Prospector (LP in mortgage broker parlance) or Digital Originator (DO) that can spit out loan approvals, cautions, or referrals within an hour or less. We strongly advise you, rather than waiting in agony for a computer to spit out an impersonal statement of what you qualify for or a rejection, to know as much about credit and how it affects your ability to buy a home in advance of undertaking either searching for a home or searching for the right loan. Even if you plan to buy your home with cash, most of you will have established a credit history. This chapter will, among other things, help you understand your own credit history and how it affects all your shopping habits. So, cash buyers, strap on your helmets and move forward through this chapter.

You mean they're watching me?

Have you ever wondered how all the gasoline companies, department stores, catalog ordering companies, major credit card companies, and others found your name and address to write to you and offer their amazing low-interest, high credit-ceiling cards? The answer is simple: Credit card companies publish a list of their debtors for the exclusive use of list brokers, who in turn sell your name to other credit card companies so they can solicit your business. The more credit cards you have, the more you're solicited. Why? Because the more credit cards you have, the more your name is sold to other credit card companies by list brokers.

> 66 Today, just having had one car loan or one student loan won't cut the mustard with mortgage lenders. You have to have an uninterrupted and fairly elaborate credit history to get a mortgage. As far as lenders are concerned, your credit history is your destiny. 99
>
> —Tony Robbins, A.M. Robbins Mortgage Company

This isn't necessarily bad. If you don't have credit, forget about applying for a mortgage. You'll be turned down. No mortgage company in America will approve you for a loan unless you've established a credit history. So, if you plan to buy a house and you don't have enough cash for its entire cost, you will need to have a history of credit payments to show that you've paid your bills in the past and are, therefore, an excellent candidate to make your mortgage payments in the future. In a way, then, these credit card companies are doing you a favor, helping you to establish sufficient credit to make you a viable candidate for a mortgage loan.

What credit card companies won't tell you is that three other ways of establishing credit are available to you besides using their particular rectangular piece of plastic: automobile loan payments, student loan payments, and payments on previous mortgage loans. If none of these conditions applies to you, these credit cards are indispensable.

I didn't only use them; I abused them

From the perspective of mortgage lenders, credit card use can turn into credit card abuse in the following two ways:

- When the minimum monthly payment on the amount of credit card debt you've accumulated, added together with your intended mortgage payment, greatly exceeds the 36-percent debt-to-income ratio threshold we discuss in Chapter 4.

- When you're late on or in default with your monthly credit payments.

The first way may not be so bad. Your mortgage loan officer could advise you to "pay down" your gross debt with available cash reserves so that you fall within the limits of the upper ratio. In fact, if your credit history is excellent, she may be able to submit your loan for approval even if your debt-to-income ratio is several percentage points higher than the 36-percent standard limit. In the past few years, in fact, the ratios have become less important to lenders than the amount and type of credit you have and how reliable you are in paying your bills. If you don't have the cash reserves to pay down your gross debt, or if your

 Bright Idea

If you find yourself in a position where you can't pay all your bills, at least make your mortgage payment. And make it on time, even if you have to beg or borrow. If there's only one bill you can pay, make it your mortgage payment.

upper ratio is significantly above the standard maximum, you may be approved for a smaller loan than the one you wanted, but one large enough to buy some kind of home. In other words, having a lot of debt is not necessarily an insurmountable problem as far as buying a home is concerned.

Having bad debt or bad credit, on the other hand, could be the kiss of death. Late payments or failing to pay (default) on car payments, student loans, or credit card bills are by far the most common reasons for the rejection of applications for mortgage loans. In addition, if you already own a home or have owned a home in the past, late payments on your mortgage loan will invariably clobber you when you make application for a new mortgage loan. Think of this from the lender's point of view. Even if your additional credit history is blemish-free, if you have been late on mortgage payments in the past, the lender is hardly likely to make you the very same kind of loan now. In her eyes, your past is your future.

They seem to know me better than I know myself

Let's face it: Your credit history is an open book. Given what's recorded about you in the files of the IRS, countless other government agencies, and credit bureaus, your life is not as private as you might think. What you bought on credit and how you've paid it back is a matter of record.

But we have the right to know what's been written about us, including our credit report. Although it may seem draconian that credit bureaus keep files of our credit history, it's comforting to know that they keep them for us as well as for possible review by lenders or other potential new creditors. Since we've arrived at the point where a mortgage lender is the next player in your home-buying quest, it's important for you to know exactly what these credit bureaus are, how they record your financial history, and, if anything derogatory appears in your credit report, how you can address and possibly eliminate this derogatory information before you visit a mortgage loan officer.

What a credit bureau does

Every time you make a payment on an outstanding debt, the total unpaid balance of that debt is noted in one or more credit bureau reports. Also noted is the date of your most recent payment and any time you have been more than 30 days behind in making that payment. Of course, any defaults are also noted, along with bankruptcies and judgments against you. The problem is that three major national credit reporting bureaus exist, and each records your credit differently. Before you can evaluate the status of your own credit and determine whether or not you need to clean it up and how to do so, you have to know how to read each of the three credit reports and understand how your lender will use it in determining your creditworthiness.

Reading consumer disclosures

The most important elements of any credit report are the statuses of your various accounts and your history of paying them. These elements are part of one, two, or three of the following credit bureaus' histories of your payments: Equifax Information Service, Trans Union, and TRW/Experian. Here's how each of these credit bureaus reports your credit history.

Equifax Information Service

>>>30 (2) 60 (3) 90 (0) 8/97-R3<<<

A notation like this will appear for all your monthly debt repayments. This particular notation indicates that payment on an account (the creditor will be indicated by the side or underneath the notation itself) has been 30 days late on two occasions,

---

 Watch Out!

If you should experience a foreclosure on any home you've owned, give up the idea of getting another mortgage; if you're late with your mortgage payment (especially more than 30 days) and don't have a stupendously good excuse, give up the idea of getting another mortgage in the near future.

60 days late on three occasions, and never 90 days late. The additional note, 8/97-R3, tells the date of the last 60-day late payment, with the R3 reiterating that this is the third time a payment has been made 60 days late. This is certainly derogatory credit information, but it's also sketchy information. For example, there's no way to tell when the two 30-day late payments occurred, and this makes disputes that you might have with your creditor or with Equifax itself exceedingly difficult. Moreover, Equifax only provides account history when some negative element exists in your credit. You may have only one account that's been delinquent in the past. The rest of your credit may be perfect.

From your Equifax report, you don't have any information to justify your otherwise perfect credit as a means of offsetting one or more delinquent accounts.

Trans Union

112112113111
111121111111
62 0 1 3

The 24 numbers in the top two lines represent the last 24 months of any credit payments you have made on a particular account. The first "1" is from 24 months ago; the last "1" refers to your most recent payment. The number "1" indicates that you made your payments on time; the number "2" indicates that you have been 30 days late; the number "3" indicates that you have been 60 days late. The account numbers on line three indicate that credit on this particular account has been paid for 62 months, that there are no 90-day late payments, one 60-day late payment, and three 30-day late payments. This information is far more complete than Equifax's for two reasons: you know exactly when an account was late, and you have information that goes two years back—the length of time lenders usually look back in their study of your credit history (exclusive of bankruptcies and defaults).

Bright Idea

Wait until you've received two or three credit reports and can get the full history of your credit before you begin to interpret it. Don't waste time and energy speculating on your payment history on the basis of incomplete information!

TRW/Experian

This credit-reporting bureau provides the most information about your credit history. It goes back seven years or more to gather information on credit you may have long since closed or maintained with a zero balance. On disclosures to you, the consumer, and to your lender, Experian explains facts such as whether or not you're the responsible payee on your own accounts, how much money you owe to each of your creditors, and whether you've been late. Unlike Trans Union, however, with Experian you're not told when you had late payments. Without knowing exactly when you've been tagged for making late payments, it's rather difficult to dispute them. In fact, you may have to use credit reports from all three credit bureaus and overlay them to get an exact picture of when you were late on payments and whether you have any chance to explain away these late payments or dispute them.

Here's a typical column of figures on an Experian report:

CUR-Was 30

nnnccc123ccc

nncc12nnnccc

"CUR-Was 30" indicates that a current account number was 30 days late at some period of time within the last seven years. The letter and number codes indicate a more recent payment history, with the first "n" signifying your account status 24 months ago and the last "c" representing the month the credit report was issued. The letter "n" means nothing was owed on the account; a "c" means that money was owed and was paid on time;

Watch Out!

Almost everyone reports being surprised by at least one piece of information on a credit report. It's important that all surprises be addressed before you apply for a loan.

a "1" means a payment was one month late; a "2," two months late; a "3," three months late. A "2" immediately following a "1," or a "3" immediately following a "2" means that there was a second or third month in a row in which payment was not made. Although it's very useful to know what months you failed to make payments within the past two years, Experian's manner of reporting is confusing because it's rather arbitrarily coupled with an account status of seven years or longer. Trying to reconcile the dusty old marks with newer ones can be a real brain twister.

How your lender handles the confusion

Your lender may be as confused as you are over the incompleteness or incomprehensibility of any single credit bureau's reporting of your credit history. As a result, lenders create their own full factual reports to evaluate mortgage loan applications. The full factual is a compilation of at least two credit bureaus' records and yields the same results as your efforts to superimpose two or three credit bureau reports on one another to get a full, accurate, and chronological history of your credit. In addition, the full factual, unlike the credit bureau report, includes information on your place of employment, your income, and your current residence, including the lease or mortgage payment you make to live in that residence. It also

> 66 So far as my coin would stretch; and where it would not, I have used my credit. 99
>
> —William Shakespeare, *King Henry IV, Part I*

produces the composite credit score that determines how much money you can borrow or whether you qualify to borrow.

We strongly advise that you order your own credit report(s) before you visit with a lender and authorize her solicitation of a full factual. There are three reasons for this advice:

- Credit bureaus and creditors make mistakes. Your credit report may include derogatory information that doesn't even apply to you.

- Derogatory credit of which you were unaware may show up in your credit report. If there are mitigating circumstances for this derogatory information, you'll want the chance to write a letter of explanation to the credit bureau to accompany the credit information that goes to your lender.

- You may be able to avoid the embarrassment of showing up for a loan application and being told that there's no way a particular lender can approve you for a loan.

The basic advice here is the same we give you later in Chapter 4. Just as you need to be prepared before you begin your house hunting, you need to be prepared for the mortgage application process.

How to clean up bad credit

Begin by acknowledging the brutal truth. Lenders aren't looking for good character; they're looking for creditworthiness. You may be a lovely person and exemplary citizen. But, if you've experienced a foreclosure in the past seven years, if you've gone bankrupt in the past seven years (and are not planning or cannot for some other reason qualify to get an FHA loan), if you've defaulted on a student loan or car payment, or if you've been more than 90 days late on two or more revolving debts in the past two years, your good character and pristine intentions are irrelevant. Any one of the preceding circumstances may touch off a loan denial. So, don't waste the $50 lenders typically charge for their full factuals if you know that, in the eyes of your lender, you're a credit disaster zone. Use the $50 to pay off debt.

On the other hand, if your credit report contains errors, or if you have only a mildly disturbing history of late payments and

can justify at least some of them on the basis of legitimate mitigating circumstances, you'll want to go ahead with your mortgage application—but not until you do two things:

- Make your own calculations, based on the minimum
  monthly payments on all your debts, and determine that
  you fall within the general limits of the upper ratio for the
  size of the loan you'll need (or have come within several
  percentage points of that upper ratio if your credit history
  is sterling).

- Clear up the errors in your credit report or write letters to
  the reporting credit bureaus giving valid reasons for late
  payments (see Table 2.1).

Table 2.1. Plausible Explanations for Late Payments

Note: Clearly, some of these explanations are more plausible and more
sympathetic than others. But whether or not you can provide a convincing argument for late payments is often determined by how well
you express yourself—not how elaborately, but how succinctly.

1. You were laid off from your job, but have since resumed working.

2. You were ill for an extended period of time and, while you collected disability during the time of your illness, your disability
   payments were insufficient to cover all your debts. You have now
   resumed working and paying your debts.

3. A member of your family was either too ill to work (if that person
   worked in the first place and her income went to pay part of your
   debt) or was laid off.

4. Income normally used to pay debts went to a family member's
   medical expenses not covered by insurance.

5. You were a victim of a natural disaster (earthquake, flood, tornado)
   and had to pay to restore yourself or your property to normal
   conditions.

6. You are an independent contractor who does not earn a regular
   (that is, monthly, biweekly, or weekly) salary. For a period of time,
   your income failed to meet expenses incurred before that income
   dropped. Now you're back on your feet.

continued

Table 2.1. *(continued)*

7. A diagnosed physical or mental disorder has meant that you've had to take on a job with fewer responsibilities and/or tasks at a reduced income.

8. A death in the family meant that you had to pay unexpected funeral expenses.

9. A child's or spouse's illness meant that you had to restrict the number of hours you worked.

10. You can prove that you never received the bill for which you now have recorded late payments.

11. You simply forgot to make payments on one revolving loan. Mea culpa! But the bulk of your credit history is exemplary.

12. You foolishly spent money on a family vacation that should have gone toward paying bills. You're repentant, and you've now established better priorities.

13. You moved residences. You filled out the change of address forms that accompanied your revolving credit bills. For some reason, one of your creditors never acknowledged your change of address and your mail wasn't forwarded. Now you're 60, perhaps 90, days late on that account.

Since we've already discussed how to determine your ratios, here we need to remind you only that as far as your lender is concerned, your upper ratio is based on summing all your minimum monthly payments (except, of course, if they are fixed, such as car payments or student loan payments) and adding them to your intended monthly mortgage payment to come up with your collective anticipated indebtedness.

Clearing up errors in your credit report is a procedural matter. The Fair Credit Billing Act protects you from bills that have been improperly or inaccurately charged to you. The Act specifies that you have rights concerning the correct accounting and billing of accounts such as credit cards, where the amount you pay monthly can vary regularly. Your rights include disputing or asking for clarification of a credit statement. If you feel that an error has been made in the amount you have been billed, you should notify the credit bureaus of your intent to dispute and

Watch Out!

Remember that neither your creditors nor your lenders want to admit their errors. It took acts of Congress (literally) to get them to do so. They may act off-putting when you ask them to correct errors. Don't let them intimidate you! Protect your federally mandated rights.

use receipts or canceled checks to justify your position to the creditor with whom you have the dispute. If you successfully justify your position, it's the creditor's responsibility to acknowledge the error in writing to the credit bureaus and, if necessary, your mortgage lender.

According to the Fair Credit Reporting Act, credit bureaus must accurately report information they supply to your mortgage lender. This act pertains specifically to credit bureaus. They have a history of inaccurately reporting to third-party lenders what creditors have accurately reported to them. If you discover that this has happened to you, it's your responsibility to see that your creditors file new reports to the credit bureaus. It is their responsibility, in turn, to acknowledge their errors to you and change your credit report to reflect the correct information.

Having late payments show up accurately on your credit report and justifying these late payments is far less procedural in nature. You're at the mercy of the credit bureaus and your lender as to whether or not they will accept your written explanation for paying revolving debt late. If, in the past two years, you've had only two or three late payments, and none is over 60 days, you can probably get by without letters of explanation. If you've had four or more late payments, and even one of these is over 60 days, be prepared to compose convincingly or risk a denial.

What works and what doesn't

Interpreting letters of explanation for late payments and determining if your explanation is acceptable is a highly subjective endeavor. What's most important to keep in mind is that credit bureaus don't wipe away bad credit on the basis of your explanations. Instead, they will send your letters of explanation to your mortgage lender along with your credit report and leave it up to your lender to decide whether the mitigating factors off-set the bad credit. Following is a list of explanations for late payments that lenders have sometimes looked upon with an understanding eye in the past.

The best way to handle communication with a credit bureau is to report your circumstances up front. It's better to explain late payments when they're occurring than to wait until you've resumed your normal payment schedule. The quicker you can communicate a circumstance that prevents you from making a regular payment on a debt, the more conscientious and credi-ble you'll appear to a mortgage lender. Think of it this way: Eighteen months ago, you had a string of late payments on your MasterCard account. Your account is now showing current, but if you were fearful that you couldn't make payments 18 months ago, why didn't you work out some kind of reduced payment schedule with your creditor? Creditors listen to such sugges-tions. Why are you waiting until now to explain something that occurred a year and a half ago?

This is the way many lenders think. If you anticipate this response at the time you're experiencing financial difficulties, you can often prevent the difficulties from becoming a stum-bling block to getting a mortgage.

Of course, some people come up with makeshift explana-tions to put a bright sheen on a bad excuse. Early communica-tion with your creditors, or with a credit bureau, or a valid reason for late payments are the best ways to prevent you from

 Bright Idea

In Chapter 1, we explain that mortgage loan officers *want* to provide you with financing. In fact, in their eagerness to make loans work, many of them will help you with your letters of explanation. Take advantage of the offer. Your loan officer is the best person to decide what your lender wants to hear.

being denied a mortgage. Whatever homework you do before you visit a loan officer will pay you the greatest dividends.

The credit counseling rip-off

Many people with credit problems seek the help of nonprofit debt counseling agencies. They purport to be consumer advocates, but in reality, most of them are advocates for your creditors. They advertise extensively on the radio that they can solve problems for you that result from the actions of greedy creditors. Behind the scenes, however, they make arrangements with these same creditors to pay off, say, 80 percent of your debt, spread over a time frame that enables you to make payments lower than the basic minimum indicated on your bills. They make a separate arrangement with you to receive 90 percent of these same payments and then pocket the 10-percent difference.

Such companies, masquerading under names like "Budget and Credit Counseling" or "Consumer Credit Bureau," usually shoulder you with an unbelievable amount of debt. Your total monthly payments may be lower, but they're spread over such a long period of time that, after a while, you feel like Sisyphus rolling the rock up a hill and seeing it fall back as soon as it reaches the top. Moreover, while they might arrange a payment schedule for you that's manageable (even if it seems eternal), these counseling agencies do nothing to resolve the derogatory credit history that sent you to them in the first place.

In fact, their image in the world of creditors is so bad that the creditors themselves, having learned that you've been counseled, may actually have a lower opinion of your seriousness as a borrower, wondering why you couldn't shoulder your debt in the first place. In other words, creditors tend to regard the use of credit counseling bureaus as a sign of personal weakness. In the end, the people who get the most out of your debt restructuring are the credit counselors and creditors. TRW/Experian's credit report often lists Consumer Credit Counseling's 800 number. This should tell you whose side the counselor is on!

In many communities, large law firms have divisions that specialize in credit counseling. They advertise that they'll use all legal means to relieve you of the onerous burden of your bad credit. Their come-on is filled with sweet compassion. They tell you that "you are not alone," that they'll hold your hand as, together, you walk through the minefield of credit. Indeed, many such firms will take on your debt and structure a manageable repayment directly to them for their services—usually at an interest rate that far exceeds what you would have paid your creditor, even on a minimum monthly payment basis. Law firms are not quite as brazen as credit counseling agencies; they don't advertise as non-profit organizations. But then again, lawyers know enough to protect their own interests. When they represent themselves as credit counselors, be assured that their own bills will be the first paid.

So who do you rely on?

In a nutshell, yourself. The best way to handle late payments is to let your creditors know right away that you're experiencing temporary financial problems and, as a result, want to restructure your monthly payment schedule to achieve a lower monthly minimum. Even automobile dealers will extend and, thus, decrease your monthly payments rather than try to repossess your car. Promise to increase your monthly payment once your financial situation improves. In most instances, you'll get an understanding response. Your creditors will prefer to get some kind of payment rather than none at all, and they will appreciate your commitment to upping the monthly payment after you can manage it. Most importantly, they will record your less-than-the-usual minimum monthly payment as an on-time payment, thus saving

 Watch Out!

Remember that it's not the credit bureau's job to remove derogatory credit information. They simply record what your creditors send them. If you can't get your creditors to remove the derogatory notations, however, your own letter(s) of explanation become especially important.

you a negative notation on your credit report. Finally, if you initiate your own debt restructuring, your creditors will appreciate your forthrightness and accommodating spirit—unlike their response to help from a credit counseling service, which invariably incites them to cast aspersion on you.

What if you discover derogatory credit reporting that is in error, or that's the result of circumstances such as those mentioned previously, which were beyond your control? Get angry. Not infrequently, credit bureaus have reported late payments on incorrect accounts. Write a hostile letter to the reporting agency threatening to take legal action if they don't remove the derogatory credit immediately and send you a new credit report proving that the misplaced account has been deleted. If a creditor fails to record your change of address and then sends in a derogatory response on the basis of bills you never received, threaten to take legal action against your creditor if the creditor does not acknowledge the mistake and send a corrected report to the credit bureau immediately.

If you've experienced a setback because of job loss, sickness, or a family tragedy, but didn't realize that the experience had adversely affected your credit until you saw a report, write an irritated letter stating that you're insulted that the credit bureau failed to acknowledge an unavoidable situation and give them the opportunity to acknowledge it now and delete the bad credit that stemmed from that situation. Most credit bureaus will attempt to deflect blame for insensitivity to your creditors. Use this deflection tactic to have them contact your creditors directly and explain your unfortunate circumstance. Whatever the situation that produced derogatory credit notations, however, do your best to correct as much of the derogatory credit as you can before you visit your mortgage loan officer to apply for financing.

Get tough; get honest; get direct

We all tend to feel at least a twinge of guilt any time we discover that someone knows we've experienced a credit problem. If credit is the American way, guilt over bad credit is its lingering specter. We must recognize, however, that our creditors and credit bureau computers don't actually know who we are. Even the composite credit score that determines our mortgage loan-worthiness is generated by a machine, and those of us who want to do so can apply for a mortgage on-line and never speak to a human being. So, our guilt comes from within rather than from without. Our advice to you, therefore, is to cast off guilt. Guilt will make you tiptoe around the edges of your credit problems and not really confront them. Keep in mind that your objective in confronting your credit problems is buying a suitable dwelling for you and your family and that cowardly behavior that stems from guilt will keep you from your objective.

If you've been unfairly notated by a credit bureau, confront your creditors directly. Why should you have to live with some impersonal monolith governing your life? Tell the monolith to back off or risk a lawsuit. If your creditors fail to accept a request for compassionate reduction of your monthly payments in the event of an unfortunate personal situation, be assertive. Put your creditors on the defensive if they reject or fail to acknowledge your request for credit leniency. You'll be pleasantly surprised by how often they'll capitulate.

Remember, above all else, that good credit gets you what you want in our society. Do your best to maintain it. If circumstances force you to lose it for a time, fight your hardest to get your good credit rating back. Don't trust anyone else to fight for you; they're only fighting for whatever is left in your pocket. You can rescue your good credit on your own!

Just the facts

- Know how credit reporting bureaus work and how to confront them.
- Avoid credit counseling agencies. They won't help you restore your good credit.
- Rely on yourself. You're the best qualified person to solve derogatory reporting in your credit files.

Doing Your Homework, Getting Prepared

PART II

GET THE SCOOP ON...
What you need to do before starting the hunt ▪
Coping with mental and physical rigors ▪
Engaging an apathetic partner ▪ Taking control
and managing your experts ▪ Determining what
you need ▪ Coordinating home and lifestyle

Getting Your Act Together

Chapter 3

In buying a home, preparation is everything. Although I realize that you are eager to begin looking at homes, I'm not going to let you go out and play until you've done your homework. As you have no doubt observed, a lot is at stake in purchasing a home. You are committing yourself to an outcome that will have immense personal and financial consequences. So, take a deep breath, listen to your coach, and resign yourself to nothing less than full preparation. Let's do the job right the first time.

Physical and mental preparation

The road to your new front door may be short and smooth or very long and rough. Hope for the former but prepare for the latter. In the best of all situations, you will have adequate time to study and prepare and then to look for a home. Under the most favorable circumstances, you can take advantage of the seasonality of the market and avail yourself of the time to weigh all of your options. Some of you, however, may be operating under tremendous pressure to find a home within a very limited time frame. Almost everyone is constrained by financial limitations, not to mention a narrowly defined set of prerequisites that a new home must satisfy. For those on a tight schedule, we caution against shortcutting the preparatory and introspective tasks that will define what you need and what you can afford. Those with a more relaxed schedule also need to demonstrate patience and not rush the process.

The physical toll

For most folks, house hunting is pretty much a grind. At first, raw enthusiasm and a desire to get going will carry you along on adrenaline. Unless you get lucky and find a home on your first couple of outings, you're going to need the endurance of a distance runner, rather than the speed of a sprinter.

> 66 It is thrifty to prepare today for the wants of tomorrow. 99
>
> —Aesop, c. 550 B.C.

Accept that the process will probably be long, or at least longer than you think, and that a bit of pacing will be necessary. Your agent, likewise, will also probably subscribe to the notion, on any given expedition, that less is more. If you and your agent are judicious and selective in your choices of houses to see, and if you keep your search concentrated in a defined area (as opposed to running back and forth across town), you should be able to keep the fatigue factor in check. Even so, you should bear a few things in mind:

- Remember that every chain has its weakest link. In home hunting, someone is going to get tired first. If that person isn't you, don't push your house-hunting partner beyond his limit. Just accept that we don't all have the same level of stamina and call it a day.
- Don't go hunting on an empty stomach.
- Travel light and keep some bottled water and perhaps some light snacks in the car.

- Even though it eats up time, stop for a soda (or whatever) between every two or so house visits.

- Take time after each inspection to discuss what you have seen. Also collect fact sheets, surveys, and pictures from every house you visit. These practices will reinforce your recollection.

- Be aware that your concentration will flag before you do and that you may develop a bias toward the houses you see later in the day when you're tired.

- If you get tired, don't be reluctant or embarrassed to have your agent reschedule some appointments for another day.

- After a while, houses will start to look alike. We recommend taking photos of any house that you do not immediately reject, as well as keeping a home-hunting logbook.

- If you have been hunting every day or every weekend, give yourself some time off. It will serve to restore your perspective.

Establishing communications

If you are single or do not have to consult with anyone in regard to your home-buying decision, feel free to skip ahead. If, on the other hand, you are buying a home with your spouse, partner, friend, parent, or anyone else whose needs and opinions must be considered, then you must develop some communications guidelines.

Start by determining whether both of you will be equal in the home-buying process. Be aware that just because you're married doesn't mean that equality is necessary. Some individuals abdicate responsibility and authority to their spouse in the interest of saving time, accommodating impossible schedules, or even because of a lack of interest. It's okay for one person to take all, or the lion's share of the responsibility, as long as both parties agree to that arrangement. What's not okay is to load all the responsibility on one person, allow that person to do the work, and then second-guess him or her.

It is all too easy for couples working on a home purchase together to cross their wires if they are not careful. Sometimes, the problem is gender related. Women characteristically are more opinionated than men when shopping for homes and come armed with a more specifically defined set of requirements. Men typically respond more generally to homes and are open to a more diverse range of home designs, styles, and attributes.

For some men, however, this openness stems simply from not having given the subject much thought, as opposed to an absence of taste, interest, or opinion. Men we interviewed became quite animated once they warmed to discussions of house design, size, and function. Many remarked, after the fact, that they were surprised by their level of interest and enthusiasm. Concerning their previous apathy, many believed initially that they didn't have anything of value to offer or contribute.

It doesn't take Freud to see gender bias at work here. Decisions about the home have a long tradition of being squarely planted in the female domain. In the end, however, all of you will live in the house, so it's probably a good idea to push, poke, and prod a bit to get everybody's opinions on the table.

Regarding male/female couples, my recommendation to female readers is to set aside some time to involve your male partner in a structured discussion of what you need and want in a home. Familiarize him with some of the design concepts and considerations explored later in this chapter. More often than not, he will evolve from an apathetic bystander into a fully involved participant. Incidentally, the downside of not tackling this problem up front is that your partner may get his education on the job, in other words, by looking at houses. Although this may be better than no education at all, it's time-consuming, and he won't be fully prepared to join the process until you are fairly far along. The saddest case of all is the man who abdicates responsibility and then discovers he hates the house his wife has her heart set on. When it comes to the home-buying process, it's best to begin participating early on.

If you're sharing the load equally, spell out what that means. Does it mean that you will undertake the entire process together or divide up the work? Or, does equality simply mean that both of you can exercise veto power? Because defining and then finding the right home is such a labor-intensive process, plenty of room exists for ruffled feathers and resentment if one person feels manipulated or overworked.

Active listening

Good communication transcends the eloquent articulation of your own ideas and opinions. It also involves being able to listen to your partner. Active listening allows you to derive meaning beyond the spoken word. It is sort of like listening between the lines, with a focus on what's behind the words. Your wife may ramble on, for example, about having a studio in the new house where she can paint or quilt. On the surface, this might sound like a waste of space. Why, after all, can't she paint or quilt in the family room or den? With active listening, you may recognize that she is not really talking about painting or quilting at all, but rather a personal need for privacy, tranquility, and having a refuge to escape the frenetic activity of the household. Practice by listening carefully to your partner. Then probe beneath the surface with well-considered questions, demonstrating not only that you have been paying attention, but also that you care. When I give you the lowdown on real estate agents and how best to work with them, we'll be discussing active listening again. It's usually the most important personality trait of a good agent.

Emotional bumps in the road

Because new homes are the stuff of dreams, it's critical that you stay grounded in reality. After weeks or even months of searching, you may find the perfect house. Not unexpectedly, this will be an occasion of great joy and perhaps even greater expectations for a happy conclusion to the entire home-buying effort. Finding a home, as you will discover, is a long way from owning it. Literally dozens of variables beyond your control are capable of stopping your dream of buying a particular home. By way of analogy, mountain bikers expect to fall and white-water kayakers expect to turn over; it's part of their sports. Likewise with home buying, upsets and setbacks are all part of the process.

Many homebuyers subscribe to the myth that somewhere there is a perfect home for them. When they find it, as they usually do, it suddenly becomes the *sine qua non* of their existence. From that moment, their behavior is altered in a way that is contrary to their best interests. They are afraid, for example, to negotiate hard for the best price, and they may overlook defects in the house or problems concerning the surrounding neighborhoods. They must have the house because they will never, never find another like it.

Wrong.

My grandfather once had an opportunity to buy stock in Coca-Cola for $1 a share. He passed on the investment and lamented it until his dying day. The truth is, since my grandfather's day thousands of equally good investment opportunities have come and gone. Opportunities arise constantly as a function of change, and that applies to the home market as surely as to the stock market. So, if you find a perfect home and, for one reason or another, see it slip beyond your grasp, take heart. Other homes are just as perfect, and you will find one.

Your job, for as long as it takes, is to stay grounded, to control your emotions, and to proceed carefully and methodically. Believe me, it won't always be easy. Force yourself, regardless of your level of excitement and enthusiasm, to slow down and look for flaws and pitfalls . . . in the house, in the financing, in everything. Don't be hypercritical, just conscientious and thorough. Which brings us to the next topic.

Taking control and setting limits

Many homebuyers are intimidated by the home-buying process because, among other reasons, they are inevitably surrounded by experts in the form of brokers, agents, lenders, and attorneys. Admittedly, it's tough to hold your own when you ostensibly know so little and everyone else knows so much. But the bottom line, quite simply, is that you are the boss.

First, understand that the experts are not doing you any favors. They are earning a living in their profession in a very competitive market. Without you, the homebuyer, they don't even have a market. Quite simply, you are the center of their business world.

If you purchase a ticket to a Broadway show starring, say, Julie Andrews, you have every right to expect her to perform profession-ally and to the best of her ability. If she walked onto the stage and said, "I'm famous and important, and you're a nobody," and then refused to perform, you would be outraged. Regardless of how famous Julie Andrews is, you would want your money back. Same deal in the real estate game. It doesn't matter how cool, smart, powerful, or well connected your experts are. What matters is that you're the one picking up the tab. You have every right to demand performance.

> **66** An expert is one who knows more and more about less and less. **99**
>
> —Nicholas Murray Butler (1862–1947)

Look at the flip side. If you do your homework, network, shop around, check references, and choose wisely, you'll proba-bly end up with some good experts in your camp. How should you use them? For starters, listen to them; they are knowl-edgeable counselors, after all. Ask questions when you don't understand, probe when you don't think you're getting the whole story, and get a second opinion if your experts disagree, or if something doesn't sound right. Think of yourself as the president and of your experts as advisers. Listen to what they have to say and weigh the content carefully but never forget that all of the decision-making power resides with you.

Being in control, and managing your experts well, doesn't mean that you have to monopolize the conversation by making your opinions known. Even if you have a business background or experience in real estate, it's to your advantage to listen more and talk less. Remember that you're not out to impress anyone. So place your emphasis on processing and learning and curb competitive urges and the need to dominate; they're counter-productive.

Your relationship with your real estate agent

Of all the relationships in the home-buying process, your relationship with your agent is the most important and, therefore, the one most likely to cause problems. You will spend more time by far with your agent than with any of the other players. You will get to know each other as people, spend hours together inspecting homes and scarfing down hamburgers in your agent's car. A friendship may actually evolve. But if it does not, the appearance of a friendship certainly will. This intimacy, real or perceived, will make you more vulnerable to manipulation. That is not to say, of course, that your agent will exploit this vulnerability (although some do). You should recognize the potential for exploitation and stay alert. Your agenda and your agent's agenda may not always be congruent.

From your agent's perspective, the best sale is a quick sale. For agents, time is money, and if every client took six months to find and buy a house, they would find themselves investing more time in each client than they could afford. What agents hope, and work toward, is that more sales will be quick and easy than long and hard. It's about averages. If the averages are not in the agent's favor, he or she might try to rush the process. Be alert for statements like, "I don't think you're going to do any better than this"; "I think this one is going to sell quickly";

or "Homes in this area don't become available very often." Although all of these statements could be perfectly true, they could also be warning flags that your agent is rushing you. Bear in mind that you are in charge of the schedule. Take the time you need to get it right, even if you risk missing a time-sensitive deal. Remember the Coca-Cola stock? Tell yourself over and over: "There are many perfect homes out there. I can take my time and be careful."

The other intuitively obvious—but often overlooked—thing you need to know about your agent is that the more you spend on a house, the more he or she makes in sales commission. Thus agents will often try to trade you up—probably not to a level that will bankrupt you or even strap you financially, but all the same, a bit more than you were willing to pay. Our term for this is *agent creep.*

Here's how agent creep works. You complete your analysis and number crunching and figure out how expensive a home you can afford. You tell your agent what your spending cap is. Your agent uses the first few houses she selects to confirm the preferences that you have expressed verbally. Although this is all quite normal and legitimate, your agent is also paying careful attention to what exactly about these initial houses really turns you on. By the end of the first couple of outings, she has a good sense of both what you are looking for and what elicits very positive emotional responses. Maybe not immediately, but soon, the agent does some scouting on her own. The agent finds several houses that roughly meet your requirements and that fall within your spending limit, but that—she anticipates based on prior

 Bright Idea

A sometimes useful strategy is to hedge your bet, providing your agent with a range or cap on price that is somewhat below what you actually are willing to pay. With this option, you are compensating in advance for the probability of being traded up.

Watch Out!

When couples start looking at houses, the agent will assume that whomever sits in the front of the car is the key decision maker. If you don't want to convey this impression, take turns riding in the front.

observation—you will probably reject for one reason or another. The agent also finds a house that will cost, say, 10 percent more than your limit, but which is sure to set off all of your emotional fireworks.

The next time you go house hunting, your agent sets up the schedule so that you see the so-so homes first, and then at the end of a long, hard day, she comes up with something like this: "There's another house that just came on the market, and I need to check it out for some other clients. It's a bit more expensive than what you're looking for, but it might give you some good ideas. Want to see it?"

Well, you know the rest of the story. You fall in love with the house, and when you are already talking about spending $140,000, what's another $10,000 to $15,000? Plus, when you spread it out over your monthly mortgage payments you'll hardly know the difference, right? Wrong. Technically speaking, she got you, although admittedly if you really love the house and can afford the extra $10,000, it's a win/win scenario. The point here is that if you don't want to be set up like this, set strict limits with your agent. Tell her you do not want to see any homes that exceed your limit, or, alternatively, establish a range. Chances are you'll be shown homes mostly at the upper end of the range, but that's to be expected. Finally, concerning agent creep, don't get bent out of shape when it happens. It doesn't mean that your agent is dishonest, only that she is testing your limits.

Your relationship with your lender

This relationship is not as dicey because your exposure to one another will be more limited, and it is far less likely that anything beyond a strict business relationship will develop. The main thing you need to know about the person sitting across the desk at the bank or the mortgage company is that, usually, he or she is a salesperson and not a loan officer. In other words, their job is to bring in business and initiate loan applications. Approving loans is somebody else's job. What this means, among other things, is that in a large lending institution, the person you deal with will not have the authority to negotiate various aspects of your mortgage or closing costs. They will instead announce matter-of-factly that the bank's policy is thus and so . . . as if nothing is negotiable. This is pure baloney. Plenty is open to negotiation when shopping for financing, and we tell you how in chapters 1 and 4. We'll also explain in these chapters who's really in charge of the loan application and approval process.

Children, schools, and the home-buying process

Children and their needs are often at the center of buying a new home. Here, we explore your children's participation in the home-buying process and look at the ways that choosing schools influences your home-buying options.

The role of children in home buying

If you have children, you should give some thought about how best to include them in the home-buying process. Some home-buyers don't consider bringing their children with them when they look at homes. Others insist on bringing the kids to every single home they see. If you have kids, the degree to which you want to involve them in your home search is, of course, up to you. It depends on your own family infrastructure and the age of your kids.

Be forewarned, however, if you take your children house hunting, that children tend either to love or despise every house they see. If you're like some parents, their input can be a source of great distraction and drive you, not to mention your agent, crazy. In the case of young children, it's probably better to show them only the houses that figure into your final selection. Older children, on the other hand, can not only provide you with valuable input, but should rightly have a voice in the matter. Once again, however, you may want to narrow down the field a bit on your own. If you do not include the children in the house-hunting or decision-making process, at least bring them to the home you decide to purchase once or twice before you actually close and move in. This will help them adjust to their new environments.

School choices

If you have children and you're moving to a new community, the school issue will be especially important to you as you choose your home. How do you determine which school system will be best suited to your child or children? More aptly put, how do you find a school system that fits both your kids' needs and your budget? The process can be rather tricky, so it's best to get your priorities straight beforehand.

Do better schools mean costlier houses? Generally speaking, yes. Homes in those neighborhoods generally recognized as having the best public schools will be more expensive per square foot than their counterparts in other neighborhoods.

If you have not already narrowed down the areas with the better school systems, it is easy enough to find out the rankings of local schools. These rankings, which are quite detailed, are customarily published in the local newspaper. You'll find breakdowns by type of standardized test, subject area or area of aptitude, and grade level of those tested. By comparing percentile scores, you can tell which schools have the better average performances among their students. Most good real estate agents also have access to this information and should be willing to share it with you. In fact, agents who specialize in selling houses in a closely circumscribed area may know many of the

Bright Idea

Because most school officials are eager to cooperate, you should have no trouble finding out vital statistics about a particular school. These include average scores on standardized achievement tests and average class size.

teachers and administrators in the schools and be willing to offer introductions.

Some of you will want details on facilities for gifted, handicapped, learning disabled, or emotionally conflicted students. Other areas about which you may want to inquire include educational credentials of teachers and staff; library and media resources; band and other musical facilities; sports, athletic programs, and other extracurricular activities. If you're undecided about neighborhoods, it is a good idea to collect information from several different schools and then compare them.

It's a matter of priorities

Although you will probably find nice (and relatively more expensive) homes in the areas with the best schools, this does not mean that you cannot find your dream home in another area. Or, you may find a superior program for your child with special needs in a school that is not as strong overall. There are, after all, exceptions to every rule.

As in other instances in the home-buying process, you will need to set priorities, weighing the desire for top-quality education against other priorities for your family. After evaluating your options, you may decide on a more expensive home than you had originally anticipated—assuming, of course, that you qualify for a bigger mortgage.

Another option is available, however—private schools. You may find that the public schools in the area or areas you've targeted fall short of your requirements. It may be that you are unwilling to pay the going price for homes in the areas with

Bright Idea

If you are the parent of a child with special needs, it is especially important to comparison-shop for the best school.

desirable schools. Or, perhaps you prefer private or denominational schools.

For whatever reason, if you go the private or parochial school route, you can avoid the higher prices dictated by a particular school system and instead select a home whose price is comparatively low because of the school system. The savings may even make up for the tuition of private school—depending on how many children you have.

If you're being relocated, you should expect your relocation real estate agent to provide you with all the information about schools that we've just discussed. Still, it would be advisable to take a preliminary scouting trip to visit with the guidance counselor at the schools you believe to be most viable. Printed material can provide useful statistics, but only a personal visit can give you a feel for a prospective school. Many a homebuyer has found such a visit reassuring, and others have found it revealing. The school with the highest test scores could, for various reasons, end up being a real turnoff for you and your kids.

A primer on home design

Let's turn now to sizing up what you want and need in a home. By the time we are adults, we have spent most of our lives living in space that someone else has provided for us. From our parents' home, to dorm rooms, to the sorority house, to the barracks, to our first rented apartment, we essentially have moved from one box to another, making it home, but not really paying much attention to its form or how well it functioned.

What we want to stimulate here is some thinking about what your living environment can be. Although you are about to purchase a home, it's very likely that you haven't given much thought to why all of the places you've lived worked or didn't work. In fact, very few of us think about these things because, by and large, the places we live are so amazingly alike.

Trapped inside the box

In America, almost everyone lives in a home that was designed by someone else for someone else, or more accurately, by someone else for everybody. Our homes, from the largest to the most modest, were conceived by architects (occasionally) and builders (usually) who knew nothing about the individual human beings who would inhabit their houses. "One design fits all" was and continues to be the name of the game. Our only choice, one predicated essentially on wealth, is whether we want our house in small, medium, large, or extra-large size.

Dozens of magazines are full of floor plans for dream houses, but it's the same tired story; they are homes created for people that the designers never met. Most of us will never have the opportunity to design and build our own home from the ground up. Even so, no law says we have to live in and use the spaces available to us in the same numbing, clichéd ways to which we have become habituated.

A home should ideally be more than interconnected boxes, although that's the way we have been conditioned to think. When you think about your new home, think outside the box. Think about the things you will do in your home and imagine the best possible environment for doing them.

Every home represents some marriage of form and function. You would think that after hundreds of years of slapping these boxes together, we'd have that function thing licked. But no, we still see houses built with kitchen doors too small to move in the refrigerator, dining rooms a good distance away from the kitchen, bedrooms without closets, and kitchens too tiny to cook in. Although you need a license to fly a plane, practice medicine, or even to drive a car, anyone can design and build a house.

Thinking outside the box

Some basic rules of thumb exist for house design. For now, let's remain on the conceptual plane. This first step in thinking out of the box is to get rid of the box. Stop thinking about your home as a box connected by corridors and stairs. Don't even think of your home as a collection of rooms. Rather, think of your home as space where you live and work. How that space is divided, arranged, and designed begins conceptually with understanding your family, the needs of its individual members, and its collective needs.

Basically, your family's needs fall into three overlapping categories:

- **Psychological**—feeling comfortable and secure.
- **Aesthetic**—the feeling of being pleased and stimulated by your environment.
- **Functional**—having space that allows you to pursue your household tasks efficiently.

Add to these the individual family members' needs for both privacy and community, and you're almost ready to start designing your space.

A critical element of bringing some original and creative thinking to designing space is to chuck old notions, bad habits, and constraining baggage. Don't transfer the design defects of your present home to your new one. Wipe the slate clean and design spaces that really work.

Start by thinking in terms of space relationships and traffic flow. This is not quantum physics. Dining areas should be close to the kitchen, bedrooms should be as far as possible from noisy areas of the house such as the great room or the recreational room. You get the idea.

Balance individual needs for privacy with the amount of space you think you can afford. It would be great, for instance, to isolate your child in a room specifically dedicated to music lessons, but if you can't afford it, he'll have to practice piano in

Bright Idea

For your new home, make a checklist of furniture in your existing living space and the purpose it serves. This will help you pinpoint pieces of furniture—particularly inherited ones—that go unused and take up space.

the living room or family room. Give a lot of thought to space dedicated to functions that are not part of the daily routine. For some reason, Americans have a nutty tendency to set up formal living and dining rooms, rooms that account for 20 to 40 percent of a home's total square footage, but never see use except when special guests are entertained.

List all the activities that will take place in your home, based on your family's interests and lifestyle. Note that some activities may be compatible, others not. Reading and homework require a quiet space, for example, and are usually not compatible with playing the piano or watching television. Spaces can be dedicated to a specific function or can support a wide range of activities. A dining area adjacent to the kitchen, for instance, can be used for eating meals, doing homework, playing board games or cards, or paying bills.

In deciding how to use space, pay attention to each family member's personality and need for privacy. Some people require a quiet environment for reading or doing homework, and others can function perfectly well in a room where the TV or stereo is playing. Your specific intimate knowledge of each family member will allow you to design space that both is efficient and takes into consideration individual needs.

After you have determined the specific functional areas your family requires and their relative size, you can begin exploring the aesthetic dimension. For each space you have identified, decide how that space should ideally look and feel in order for the members of your family to be enriched by it. Should your family room be bright, open, spacious, and dynamic, or should

Bright Idea

Make a list of which features, in which order, are most important to you in a home. By carefully plotting your priorities, you won't waste your time looking at homes that don't measure up.

it be intimate and cozy? Should your main dining area be formal, informal, or designed to accommodate varying levels of formality?

Based once again on your knowledge of your family, attach priorities to each element of your working design, differentiating preferences from absolute needs. You may prefer, for example, to have an informal dining area adjacent to the kitchen, but you could live with an informal dining area in the kitchen. On the other hand, you may decide that you must have a dedicated playroom that can be childproofed for toddlers.

When developing your space, remember that families and their needs vary over time. Design space that is flexible and can be modified to reflect changes in your family's size and lifestyle over the years.

Working conscientiously through these questions and variables will allow you to get a grip on how much space you need, how it will be divided into functional areas, what will go on in those areas, where those areas should be situated (relative to each other), and how they should look and feel. You will find that understanding how your family uses space (and what design best fits that use) translates very directly into specific criteria for buying a home.

Pig's ears, silk purses

Having defined and designed living spaces for your family, most of you will integrate your designs into existing houses (as opposed, say, to building a custom home). The house you buy, therefore, will be the canvas on which you paint your custom designs. Don't expect, realistically, to find a house that matches your designs 100 percent. Expect to make some changes and compromises, to turn the proverbial pig's ear into a silk purse.

If a house is fundamentally flawed, however, whether poorly built or incompetently designed, no amount of effort will permit the implementation of your plans.

To provide some technical guidance in recognizing design flaws, the minimum acceptable dimensions for various elements of a house are listed in Table 3.1.

Table 3.1. Minimum Accepted Standards	
Exterior doors	3' × 7'
Interior doors	2½' × 7'
Ceiling height	8' is standard.
Halls	3' wide—entrance halls should be at least 4' wide.
Stairways	3' wide, with 1' tread and 8" rise per step.
Full baths	5½' × 7'
Bedrooms	8' × 10'
Living room or great room	12' × 15'
Dining room	10' × 10'
Kitchen	8' × 8'

Old versus new versus dirt

Houses come in three versions: old, new, and hypothetical. Your lifestyle and pocket book will have a major impact on which you choose. In a general way, you can make your choice between the three options by answering such questions as:

- Do you like swinging a hammer and sawing wood? If so, an older home is a good bet. It will put your handyman or handywoman skills to the test.

- How much do you expect to be at home? If the answer is very little, or simply if you prefer to do other things besides work on your home a lot, a newer home might be the best choice because it should require less maintenance.

- Do you like neighborhoods with mature trees, sidewalks, and character? If so, you may be attracted to an older home.

- Do you want your home to be a reflection of exactly who you are? Then building from scratch may be your best option.

This old home

An older home tends to appeal to our nostalgic side. The idea of an older home recalls sidewalks, pretty lawns, and tree-lined roads where children play safely and adults visit on front porches. What lies behind the white picket fence and pretty façade, however, can take up a good bit of your free time. Expect an older home to have defects and quirks. Be prepared to fix the first and live with the second.

Among the most common defects of older homes are sagging roofs, cracked foundation walls, poor insulation, outmoded heating and cooling systems, and old plumbing, wiring, and fuse boxes. Most of these defects can be corrected, but only with time and money. If you're at work most of the time or aren't particularly handy, you might want to buy a newer home and wait for some trees to mature and some neighbors to move in around you. If you're staunchly committed to an older home, be sure to have a cash reserve for repairs or plan on setting up an equity line of credit (if your cash down payment is large enough to accommodate one). If you need to get an equity line, the good

 Watch Out!

When you buy an older, or preloved home, make sure to put an inspection contingency in your contract. Most inspection clauses have an "up or out" section enabling you to withdraw your contract if a home is beyond repair or if the seller refuses to make repairs on major systems.

news is that major improvements and additions tend to boost the value of homes considerably. In addition, the interest you pay on a home equity loan is tax-deductible. When you sell, you should be able to recoup much or all of your investment.

Fresh and new

The most important things to have when you buy an older home are the time to live in it and the money and dedication to maintain it. Buying a newer home is a wiser choice if you're a workaholic or traveler, if you're on a tight budget with no room for repairs, or if you simply prefer the pristine quality of a fresh new neighborhood. If you buy new, curb the nostalgia. All but a very few newly built homes are in new subdivisions where the trees were removed to create a grid of streets. It may be that your fellow newcomers to the neighborhood won't have the time or inclination to visit on your front porch (if you have one).

From an economic standpoint, the new home is a wiser choice than the old. In addition to the savings you'll realize by not having to make repairs, your purchase of a new home will mean lower energy costs. New and improved insulation standards and techniques, as well as new construction materials, mean your energy bills will be substantially lower than in an older home. Conversely, newer homes tend to be more thinly framed than older ones. Your long-term future in a new home may mean reinforcing foundation walls and roof support systems. By then, however, you may have acquired friendly neighbors and grown nice, leafy trees.

Starting from scratch

Chapter 7 discusses in detail new construction, so I'll keep our discussion here brief and basic. Finding a lot and contracting to have a home built for you (called a *custom home* in the building trade) is the most complicated of the three types of purchase. First, you will need an architect's or draftsperson's drawing of your planned home, complete with specifications (specs), so that your builder can give you a realistic price. Then you will have to

Bright Idea

Most builders supply a limited, one-year warranty when you close on your home purchase. After you move in, make a *punch list* of repairs or unfinished items for the builder to fix before the year is up. (This one-year warranty may also apply to termite work done at close of escrow, which should be checked on before the warranty runs out.) Also demand that your builder include an extended warranty on foundations.

find a lot that suits your custom home and make sure that it either perks to accommodate a septic tank or can be connected to the local sewer system. If your custom home is to be built in a subdivision, you will need to make sure that it conforms to the covenants, codes, and restrictions of that subdivision.

The lot you like best might come with its own builder assigned to it. You may need to decide whether you want to settle for a builder you don't know or continue your search for an uncommitted lot. Whether you choose an assigned builder or your own, make sure that the builder is a member of the community's Home Builder's Association. Take the time to walk through a few homes your intended builder has already completed.

You probably should avoid having a custom home built for you in another part of the country other than where you currently live, unless you have total faith in your builder. Builders and their subcontractors are notorious for blowing the schedule when no one is around to supervise them. They have been known to take shortcuts and (for them) cost-saving measures. For example, if you're not around to notice, the 12-inch separation of floor joists your flooring specs call for may wind up at 18 inches, and then your house will not be as well supported as it should be.

If you are around to watch and are familiar with the area in which you're building, few things are more pleasurable than seeing the place you want to live in come alive. Buying an older home, or even buying a new one built before you come on the scene, usually involves a fair number of compromises. The custom home, if you plan right, should involve considerably fewer.

An integrated, holistic approach to home buying

As important as it is, your home and its purchase are but single threads in the fabric that makes up your life. It is a terrible and potentially disastrous mistake to make the home-buying decision in a vacuum. The decision to buy a home, and what to pay for it, should be made in the context of your long-term personal, professional, and financial objectives, with particular attention to balance and flexibility.

Over-extending

By way of example, consider the young college grad who, on landing his first job, buys an expensive new car. To make the car payments, the young grad must compromise on the quality of his apartment and may even find himself working a second job. The car, in essence, affects, and to a large extent determines, his

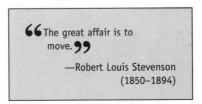

> 66 The great affair is to move. 99
>
> —Robert Louis Stevenson
> (1850–1894)

standard of living, his time, his disposable income, and his ability to invest and save, and the car may even preclude the opportunity to take steps necessary to advance in his job. It's difficult, after all, to study for the CPA exam when you're working two jobs.

Likewise, it's easy to over-extend when buying a home. Over-extension isn't the only consideration in an integrated approach to home buying, however. Does your profession, for instance, require you to maintain an office or entertain clients at home? What is the size of your family? Do you expect the number of family members living in the home to decline or increase? Do you anticipate tuition expenses for your or your children's education? Do you need an automobile or special tools for your work? How much do they cost, of what quality, and how often must they be replaced? Do you, your family, or your aging parents have medical conditions that will require financial support? How much money do you want to invest for retirement or for unexpected contingencies? What about quality-of-life considerations? Do you want to travel, indulge a hobby, or dine out frequently?

We will discuss the rules of thumb that creditors use to determine the maximum amount of money that they are willing to lend you later. That maximum amount, however, can be driven by their own business interests and acceptable levels of risk. What they are willing to lend may have no relevance at all to what you should be willing to borrow. This amount should be a function of a careful personal inventory—a detailed assessment of your overall needs and goals with a view to the future. Comprehensive planning is the only enlightened way to analyze a home-buying decision.

In fairness, an ill-considered home-buying decision is not exactly the end of the world. A home is, of course, a marketable asset, and marketable assets can be sold if the need arises. But, experience has demonstrated that many homeowners, like our young grad with his new car, put themselves and their families through hell before acknowledging that their home-buying decision has crippled them financially. Although the home and the mortgage consume the family's limited resources, how many other needs are going unmet?

Working within your limits

Table 3.2 is a worksheet to assist you in integrating your home-buying decision with your long-term goals and other facets of your life. Your inclination might be to eyeball or skip over it. That would be a mistake. Begin exercising the discipline that is necessary for the successful integrated purchase of a home now.

Make copies of the worksheet and begin with a first draft. If not enough drops out at the bottom to cover the mortgage on a new home, revisit each expenditure category to see whether any belt-tightening is possible. But, be as concrete and realistic as you can. You won't learn much if you fudge the numbers to make the results come out as you wish.

In making projections of your earnings and expenses in the future, be conservative and allow for about 3 to 4 percent average inflation per year. *Family* is defined simply as the group that will share the home regardless of blood relation or marital status—including parents, children, and others.

Table 3.2. Integrated Home-Buying Planning Worksheet

	Now	5 Years from Now	10 Years from Now
Size of my family	_____	_____	_____
Household monthly take-home income (that is, income less payroll taxes)	_____	_____	_____
Less (per month, unless noted)			
Food expenses	_____	_____	_____
Phone, cable TV, newspaper/ magazine subscriptions	_____	_____	_____
Club and membership dues	_____	_____	_____
Car payments	_____	_____	_____
Life, home, liability, auto insurance payments	_____	_____	_____
Health insurance	_____	_____	_____
Nonreimbursed medical (per year ÷ 12)	_____	_____	_____
Payments on existing loans	_____	_____	_____
Recreation, entertainment, and dining out	_____	_____	_____

continued

Table 3.2. *(continued)*

	Now	5 Years from Now	10 Years from Now
Expenditures on hobbies and leisure activities	_____	_____	_____
Contributions to charity and church	_____	_____	_____
Tuition payments	_____	_____	_____
Funds set aside for retirement	_____	_____	_____
Funds set aside for tuition	_____	_____	_____
Funds set aside for investment	_____	_____	_____
Home and auto maintenance and repair (per year ÷ 12)	_____	_____	_____
Vacation and travel expenditures (per year ÷ 12)	_____	_____	_____
Furniture and appliance expenditures (per year ÷ 12)	_____	_____	_____
Clothing expenditures (per year ÷ 12)	_____	_____	_____
Professional equipment expenditures (per year ÷ 12)			
Total monthly expenditures before rent or mortgage	_____	_____	_____
Amount available for housing	_____	_____	_____
(Household monthly take-home income minus total monthly expenditures)	_____	_____	_____

As a final reminder, remember that buying a home is a sequential process that includes and (ideally) integrates almost every facet of your life. Commit to the process, prepare thoroughly for each step, and don't rush things. If your life gets too crazy to do the job right, call a time-out and regroup. Maintain a sense of humor, stay optimistic, communicate with your partner, and anticipate some setbacks along the way. In the end, when you're relaxing comfortably in the living room of your beautiful new home, you'll understand with certainty that it was your dedication and diligence that brought you there.

Just the facts

- Prepare for the physical rigors of house hunting and periodic setbacks.
- Take control, set limits, and manage your experts.
- Take the time to determine what you need in a home.
- Integrate your home purchase into the overall framework of your life.

GET THE SCOOP ON...
How much you can afford ▪ Tax deductions ▪
Using ads effectively ▪ Selling before you buy ▪
Location and timing

Getting a Grip on the Market

H ere's a story about the poet Percy Bysshe Shelley. He asked a friend to teach him to swim, and the friend told him to jump in the lake. "Then what?" Shelley asked. "You'll know what to do when you get in the water," replied his friend. Fully clothed, Shelley jumped in, sank to the bottom, and waited for inspiration. After a minute or so, the friend dove in, only to find Shelley sitting, wide-eyed, on the bottom of the lake. After he pulled Shelley to shore, the gasping poet asked, "Now what?" Shelley never learned how to swim.

Don't make the mistake Shelley did. Buying a home is not a passive or particularly intuitive endeavor. You can't just plunge into it expecting that all the choices and all the steps you should take will suddenly become clear to you. Home buying requires an organized, carefully thought out, and, above all, proactive approach. Don't take the home-buying plunge until you have a plan.

Having read from Chapter 3, you should have a firm handle on why you are buying a home, what kind of home you require, and how responsibility for decision making will be shared. You should also understand how much control to exert and have a realistic sense of what the home-buying process will demand both physically and emotionally. Now it's time to get a good grasp of the marketplace in which you will be conducting your search. In this chapter, you'll learn the basic rule-of-thumb calculations to figure out how much of a mortgage you can get. You'll discover how to use advertising resources, tax deductions, and other financial ploys to your advantage. We'll investigate the two most critical aspects of your search for a home: location and timing. When you have considered all these issues, you'll have a good grip on the real estate market and a plan to enter it with confidence. But first, you need to get a realistic estimate of the price range of homes to consider.

Can you afford it—how do you know?

Bear in mind that although the home-buying process is basically linear, the sequence of steps is not necessarily fixed. You may want to skip some rungs on the ladder and return to them later, and you may want to climb other rungs simultaneously. Take, for example, the subject of your mortgage loan. After you embark on your home-buying journey, it makes sense to get involved in certain aspects of mortgage loan qualification early on. There's no need to make a formal application for a loan until you find the home you want. However, you need to have a good idea of what price of home you can afford before you begin looking in earnest. You also want to thoroughly review your own credit history and financial status to preclude unpleasant surprises and delays later in the process.

So, as with other aspects of looking for and ultimately purchasing a home, you'll most likely turn your attention to your loan application and approval at several points along the way. In Chapter 1, we examine the entire loan application process and your mortgage options in depth. At this point, however, let's look at what you need to know, as well as the basic steps you need to take in order to determine how much home you can afford.

Don't forget insurance and taxes

Although we will examine homeowner's insurance in detail in Chapter 12, a brief word here will suffice for our discussion of how much you can afford to pay for a house. Homeowner's insurance is based on purchase price, structural material of the home, and proximity to a fire district. If you pay $100,000 for a home, expect your annual homeowner's insurance premium to be roughly $400.

However, certain factors can increase the amount of your premium, such as a relatively high crime rate in the area. Moreover, if you plan to insure your house against hazards such as floods or earthquakes, expect your insurance to be at least double the normal rate.

You may be among the homeowners who also have to deal with a totally different type of insurance—private mortgage insurance (PMI). Instead of protecting the homeowner, PMI protects the lender. If you put down less than 20 percent on your home purchase, many lenders will require that you pay PMI, which indemnifies them against foreclosure. Another way of saying this is that if you borrow more than 80 percent of the purchase price of your home, you ordinarily will be required to pay at least some PMI. The PMI can add between 5 and 10 percent to your mortgage payment. Over the last few years, however, lenders have become increasingly more creative in finding ways that you can avoid PMI. Only a small minority of home purchasers can come up with a 20 percent down payment, especially in this age when home prices have for the most part accelerated faster than personal income. To accommodate qualified buyers with less than 20 percent to put down on a home, many lenders offer blended first and second mortgages, the most popular being the 80 percent first loan and a 15 percent second loan at a slightly lower interest rate. The combined rate is still considerably lower than the cost of PMI. For the most

Moneysaver

In addition to homeowner's insurance and, if applicable, PMI, you need to include property taxes—sometimes called *ad valorem* taxes—in the calculation of your monthly mortgage payment. Be aware that property taxes vary significantly from state to state, even from municipality to municipality. They can constitute as much as $\frac{1}{3}$ or as little as $\frac{1}{15}$ of your total monthly mortgage payment.

creditworthy, other non-PMI options include 100-percent financing and 103-percent financing, the latter covering the purchaser's closing costs in addition to the full contract price of a home. Again, although these loans are typically made for a higher interest rate than conventional products, they produce a lower total monthly payment than do loans with PMI attached to them. In Chapter 1, we explored many more options for avoiding PMI, although in some instances you will want to have it as part of your loan.

Get out your calculator!

The simple way to figure out the maximum amount you can spend on a home is to add what you can borrow to the amount of money you have for a down payment. The total is the top price you will be able to pay. Remember, however, that the amount a mortgage company (or other lender) is willing to lend is quite different from what you can actually afford. As discussed in Chapter 1, what you can actually afford is a function of all of the professional, familial, and personal demands on your available financial resources, both now and at least over the short- to intermediate-term.

If you're not familiar with the entire loan application process, for example, you may wonder why your friend or acquaintance who earns less than you do or has less money than you do for a down payment can afford a more expensive home. It is crucial to recognize that lenders take your total debt obligations into account when qualifying you for a certain loan amount. If you are paying $900 a month for your Jaguar, your $50,000 annual salary will not afford you as much buying power as your friend who earns $40,000 and drives a Kia.

To determine how much a lender will permit you to borrow, use the same rule of thumb that Fannie Mae (the Federal National Mortgage Association) recommends: the 28 percent/ 36 percent formula. Bear in mind that this is only a guideline; many lenders and certain types of loans allow some latitude in these percentages. The 28 percent portion of the formula allows you to spend no more than 28 percent of your gross monthly income on your total monthly mortgage payment, which includes principal, interest, taxes, and insurance (collectively abbreviated as PITI) and, if applicable, condominium fees. The 36 percent portion of the formula brings into the picture any long-term debts you may have. Called revolving debts by mortgage lenders, these are debts that require more than 10 months to pay off and would include monthly alimony, total minimum monthly payments toward long-term credit card debt, and the monthly payment amount on any other outstanding loans (cars, furniture, appliances, school, and so on). This latter portion of the formula recommends that you spend no more than 36 percent of your gross monthly income on your total monthly mortgage payment plus any long-term debts.

Although most lenders will increase your upper ratio by several percentage points if your credit history is especially good or if you have what are usually referred to as compensating factors, such as a large savings account or a sizeable amount of money in retirement, they establish the basic ceiling in the belief that you cannot remain economically viable if you are devoting more than 36 percent of your gross monthly income to making payments on debts.

Let's walk through an example. Suppose that your gross monthly income is $3,600. Then, according to the first part of this formula, you could spend no more than 28 percent of this amount, or $1,008, on your monthly mortgage payment

($3,600 × .28 = $1,008). The second part of this lender's rule of thumb stipulates that you should, under normal circumstances (that is, without perfect credit, a large amount of money in savings, or a significant retirement account) spend no more than 36 percent of your gross monthly income, or $1,296, on both your mortgage payment and long-term debt service ($3,600 × .36 = $1,296). If you are one of those rare individuals who does not have any long-term debt, then you could theoretically tolerate a PITI payment of 36 percent of your gross monthly income, or $1,296 monthly. If you do carry long-term debt, of course, your maximum payment will decrease.

At the end of this chapter, we have included a worksheet for you to fill out, applying the 28 percent/36 percent formula, or lender's rule of thumb, to your own income and debt figures. Using it, you can calculate the maximum amount of mortgage payment your lender will allow you to make, even before you formally apply for a loan.

When you actually go to apply for a loan, your lender will ask you to supply a credit history to make sure that you are not late or in default on your credit obligations. Before you make this inevitable visit, and certainly before you get your heart set on a particular house, it is advisable to have a realistic sense of your credit history. Avoid unpleasant surprises! (See Chapter 2 for more on this subject).

What's your interest in this?

You've seen how you can use the 28 percent/36 percent rule to determine the maximum monthly mortgage payment that a lender will approve (see the worksheet that follows). The actual amount of a mortgage, however, is determined by the current interest rate. The profound effect of the interest rate on your home-buying capabilities is illustrated by the "Fixed Rate Monthly P&I (Principal & Interest) Factors" chart in Appendix B. From this chart, you can see that, for example, if the current interest rate is 7 percent, and you have a 30-year loan, you will be paying $6.65 per month for every $1,000 worth of loan that you take out. So, for a $100,000 loan, you will be paying $665.30 per month in principal and interest. If the current interest rate is three percentage points higher, or 10 percent, the same $100,000 loan will cost you $877.57 per month—a difference of $212! Because interest rates play such a key role in the home-buying process, it is important to follow their fluctuations carefully.

Maximum Possible Mortgage Payment Worksheet

Fill in each blank below with the appropriate amount.

1. Gross monthly income from all sources:

    $_____

    $_____

    $_____TOTAL gross monthly income (line 1)

2. Multiply total gross monthly income by .28 to determine maximum monthly mortgage payment, including principal, interest, taxes, insurance (and, if applicable, private mortgage insurance, condominium fees, or co-op fees).

    $_____TOTAL gross monthly income (line 1)

    _____ × .28

    $_____maximum monthly mortgage payment, including PITI, PMI, and other fees if applicable (line 2)

3. List monthly revolving debt amounts or minimum payments due.

    $_____(credit card:_____)

    $_____(credit card:_____)

    $_____(credit card:_____)

    $_____(credit card:_____)

    $_____(car payment)

    $_____(car payment)

    $_____(other:_____)

    $_____(other:_____)

    $_____(other:_____)

    $_____TOTAL monthly revolving debt

continued

Worksheet *(continued)*

NOTE: When calculating your monthly mortgage payment, as in Table 1.1, use as a reminder the acronym PITI—for principal, interest, taxes, and insurance. Also, don't forget to include all additional fees that may apply, such as PMI and any condominium or co-op fees.

4. Add lines 2 and 3.

    $_____(maximum monthly mortgage payment) (line 2)

+ $_____(TOTAL monthly revolving debt) (line 3)

    $_____TOTAL monthly indebtedness (line 4)

5. Divide line 4 by line 1 to determine the ratio of total monthly indebtedness to total gross monthly income. (Express result as a decimal, for example, .29, .33, .36, and so on.)

_____TOTAL indebtedness percentage (line 5)

NOTE: Complete items 6 and 7 only if your answer to line 5 is higher than .36.

6. Multiply your total gross monthly income by .36 to determine the total monthly mortgage payment and revolving monthly debt amount you can qualify to pay.

    $_____gross monthly income (line 1)

_____ × .36

    $_____maximum allowable total monthly indebtedness
(line 6)

7. Subtract line 6 from line 4. What's left is the amount by which you must reduce your monthly debt, your mortgage payment, or both, in order to qualify for a mortgage loan.

    $_____TOTAL monthly indebtedness (line 4)

– $_____maximum total monthly indebtedness you can
afford (line 6)

    $_____amount by which you must reduce your monthly
debt/mortgage payment, etc. (line 4 minus line 6) (line 7)

Remember—the purpose of this worksheet is to figure the amount of mortgage you can obtain and does not take into consideration your down payment. You must, of course, include your down payment when determining the maximum house price under the 28 percent/36 percent rule.

Tax advantages—really!

Understanding how the interest payments on your mortgage, as well as your property taxes, are tax-deductible will further help you zero in on what price home you can afford. The one tax deduction that both the Internal Revenue Service and the U.S. Congress seem to hold sacred is the one for mortgage interest payments. If you're buying your first home, you may need to itemize your tax deductions for the first time. This process will give you leverage with your taxes that you've never had before.

The percentage of your total mortgage interest payments that you can deduct for a given year will correspond to your tax bracket. For example, if your income after deductible expenses puts you in the 30-percent tax bracket on your federal income tax returns, then you can expect a savings on your federal taxes of 30 percent of your annual mortgage interest payments. Let's say that you take out a 30-year mortgage of $150,000 at an interest rate of 7 percent. According to the "Fixed Rate Monthly P&I Factors" chart, your monthly payment (principal and interest) would be $999. In the first few years of your mortgage, about $950 of this $999 per month would be interest. So, over the course of a year, you would have paid 12 times this $950 in monthly interest, for a grand total of $11,400 paid in interest for the year! This means that if you are currently breaking even on your federal income taxes (that is, do not owe any tax beyond the amount withheld or deposited as estimates), 30 percent of this $11,400, or $3,420, would be refunded to you.

 Moneysaver

In the discussion of tax advantages, we focus on federal income taxes. If you live in a state that has state income taxes as well, it's a good idea to consult your accountant to see whether you qualify for any mortgage interest deductions on your state taxes.

Table 4.1 contains examples of potential federal tax refunds, based on tax bracket and total interest paid annually on a mortgage.

Table 4.1. Tax Refund for Mortgage Interest

Federal Tax Bracket	Annual Mortgage Interest	Potential Refund
10 percent	$5,612	$561.20
15 percent	$6,250	$937.50
20 percent	$7,016	$1,403.20
25 percent	$7,962	$1,990.50
30 percent	$8,837	$2,651.10
35 percent	$10,212	$3,574.20
38 percent	$13,616	$5,174.08

Let's go back to the earlier example of the 30-year, $150,000 mortgage at an interest rate of 7 percent and put your hypothetical $3,420 tax deduction to practical use. If, prior to the purchase of your $150,000 home, you were breaking even every April 15—in other words, you didn't owe the IRS, and the IRS didn't owe you—you would now become eligible for a $3,420 tax refund. You would have essentially earned back three and a half months of interest payments!

Here's another way to view your new tax advantage, a way that many people seem to find astounding. When you divide

Bright Idea

The "Fixed Rate Monthly P&I Factors" chart and two sample amortization schedules (Appendix B) help you determine the amount of interest you pay on your mortgage each month. You may, however, want to discuss with your accountant what type of mortgage payments will have the optimum tax advantages for you.

Moneysaver

Property taxes are deductible. As with interest on your mortgage, the amount of the deduction is determined by your federal income tax bracket.

your hypothetical $3,420 tax refund by 12, you get $285. You could call this your "monthly refund allotment." For instance, suppose that prior to purchasing your house, you were renting to the tune of $800 per month. If you subtract the $285 allotment from the $999 you're paying each month in principal and interest on your mortgage, your after-taxes payment comes to $714. So, exclusive of property taxes and your homeowner's insurance, your $150,000 mortgage would "net out" costing you $86 less per month than what you were paying in rent!

Of course, since the portion of your mortgage payment applied to principal increases over time, the amount of your tax refund will decrease slightly every year. If you make payments for six years, however, you will be reducing your mortgage principal by more than $6,000, and increasing your equity by that amount plus whatever amount your home has appreciated in value. On the other hand, if you continue renting for the same six years, chances are that your monthly rent will have gone up considerably.

The conclusion to be drawn from all of this is fairly obvious: Unless interest rates rise sharply, the tax advantages of home ownership can be considerable. Unless you have no savings for even a minimal down payment, your rent payments are dirt-cheap, or you have no interest whatsoever in buying a home (in which case you wouldn't be reading this book), it's fiscally wise to take the plunge.

Finding out what's out there

Whether you're moving across town or across the country, you will find homes advertised in six basic places: in the newspaper; in local supplements or periodicals; in yards via For Sale signs;

on the Internet; on local cable TV channels; and (at least in major cities) at For Sale By Owner offices and in their tabloids. Individually, none of these sources is complete; when used collectively, however, they give you a pretty complete picture of what's available.

Newspaper ads

As you probably know, the vast majority of "Homes for Sale" ads appear in a special real estate section in the Saturday or Sunday paper. In a large metropolitan area, these ads are usually divided into sections that represent different downtown areas, suburbs, and sometimes different subdivisions within suburbs. To take advantage of newspaper ads, you should have some idea of where you want to live. A map is usually included with numbers or names that correspond to the various sections of town. Frequently, ads are divided by type of residence: freestanding homes, town homes, and condominiums.

The typical ad is brief (two to three lines). It usually includes the number of bedrooms and baths and notable features of the living and eating areas, such as sunken den or eat-in kitchen. A FSBO (For Sale by Owner) will give you the owner's telephone number, and agent listings will have the real estate agent's name and number. Most ads simply announce the availability of the home, although a few of them will advertise an open house, indicating the time and date.

Certain platitudes frequent house ads. "Charming" is usually reserved for older homes, while "dazzling" often refers to something newer. Other buzzwords and their translations include "quaint" for run-down; "warm and inviting" or "precious" for minuscule; and "move-in ready" for recently swept.

One important thing to remember about newspaper ads is that they provide only a random selection of a larger inventory. Only open house ads give addresses; the purpose of all other ads is to get you to call a phone number after you're enticed. Going to open houses, however, is a great way to familiarize yourself with what's available in a given area and at what price.

Watch Out!

Most newspapers introduce their real estate sections as "Comprehensive Guides." They're not! Any day's ads are only a partial list of homes available. You might miss your dream home if you rely exclusively on them.

Monthly publications for agent sales

Most communities have a monthly publication in which real estate agents can advertise their inventory. (*Homes and Land* is the most comprehensive and has the largest circulation. It is a national publication with a multitude of regional branches catering to almost every local market.)

These periodicals are free, and you can usually find them in grocery stores and near newspaper vending machines. This type of publication tends to provide more complete information than newspaper ads on houses for sale, along with photographs and agent phone numbers. Because of these extras, you'll wind up with a pretty good idea of which homes to tour—better than you'll get through the newspaper.

The downside of monthly publications is that they're expensive to advertise in, so a lot of agents don't use them. In most communities, only about one in every seven or eight home listings appears in such a publication.

For those of you moving to a new town, periodicals from the grocery store can be quite useful, because they convey the town's character and taste. They will help you get a good sense of neighborhoods. They will also help you if you want to hook up with an agent that specializes in a certain area, or an agent who seems appealing. Because the selection of homes is based solely on which agents have paid to advertise, however, the periodicals shouldn't be used exclusively to help you find a home.

Speaking of moving to a new town, here's a word on the virtues of renting. Before you actually live in a place, it is difficult to know in which neighborhood you are ultimately going to feel most comfortable. Most communities have month-to-month

Bright Idea

If you call the number in a general ad, don't commit to seeing the house. Ask the owner or agent for the address, explaining that you'll drive by the house and call back if you're interested in looking at it. Otherwise, you might waste your time going into a house you won't like and risk being nagged by a persistent owner or agent.

rental facilities precisely for this reason. Unless you have a clear idea of where you want to live in a new town, you may want to consider a short-term rental. This would buy you some time to familiarize yourself with the people and the community, so that you could more precisely pinpoint the areas that would be viable for your home purchase.

Phone home—using yard signs

Until recently, the yard sign was an outmoded advertising vehicle. Now, a new technology has made it a surprisingly good source of home-sales information. The yard sign of today often has a rider with a local phone number you can call to get an extensive description of the home. By dialing the same phone number, you can get descriptions of all the other houses currently listed by the agency. Advertisers have transformed Touch-Tone phone technology into highly useful information menus. In fact, the real estate industry leads the way in using telephone advertising.

The principal advantage of telephone advertising is that you can shop from the comfort of your home or car, without an owner or salesperson tracking you down to solicit your business. It also gives you the freedom to decide to skip the open house for a home with an inflated newspaper ad.

Just as importantly, many real estate agents and FSBO publications provide riders on signs or places in newspaper ads that refer to Web sites where one can learn more about a particular property. Perhaps the hottest advertising strategy in real estate today is the *virtual tour:* an Internet room-by-room visual tour of property.

Surfing the net

More and more agents are advertising homes for sale on the Internet. Many include their e-mail address in their monthly publication ads. Why not e-mail a request for a comprehensive list of the homes they have to offer? You might even be referred to an agent's Web page and get instant professional help.

You will also discover that almost all of the larger real estate companies have their own Web sites, which means that you can shop from the comfort of your own computer. Even if you're moving from one part of the country to another, you can usually find the relevant agency Web sites. The quality of the color graphics is far superior to the Multiple Listing Service (MLS) printed counterpart, which is often in black and white. You will often find interior views of each home, as well as exterior—a big improvement over the traditional one-dimensional photo of the front elevation in an MLS book. It is, thus, possible to discover the nature of a particular community's real estate market while avoiding the cost and inconvenience of travel. We discuss Internet searching in detail in Chapter 5.

For couch potatoes only

You will find more than one real estate company in all but the smallest of communities. Real estate companies are in fierce competition with one another. They compete for a dominant market share in their local communities and use every imaginable technological innovation to achieve such a position. Local cable TV channels have become a key part of that technology. Larger real estate companies have their own home shows with photographs of listings, their price, their major features, and the name and phone number of the listing agent.

After watching a few of these home shows, you will discover that each company tends to have a particular niche in the overall marketplace. For example, some will specialize in condominiums and town homes, others in new construction, and still others exclusively in upper-bracket priced homes. If you decide

Bright Idea

If you're moving from one side of town to another, try placing your own ad in a weekend real estate section describing what you're looking for and using a voice-mail system to collect responses. Someone whose house is not on the market could call with just what you need. That would be worth the $20–$30 expense of the ad.

to look for a home with an agent, you can often choose from among those whose listings most appeal to you. At the very least, you can choose the real estate agency that seems to specialize in the particular market that you find most attractive.

Shopping without an agent

Advertising technology has also made it easier for private individuals to sell houses without the use of a real estate agent and, consequently, to avoid having to pay agent commissions. In larger communities, you will find For Sale By Owner (FSBO) magazines right beside real estate agency publications in supermarkets and drug stores. In fact, in larger cities you may find a FSBO in your prospective marketplace: a company that, for a small fee, provides yard signs, newspaper ads, and even Web sites for owners to advertise their own home.

For Sale By Owner companies can provide benefits to you as well as to sellers. Not only can they give you exposure to a large number of homes, but they also provide contract forms and, in some communities, a list of real estate closing attorneys. Some of the more sophisticated FSBO companies perform nearly all real estate agency functions, but without the agent, and can, therefore, save you the expense of agent fees. If you go down the FSBO road, however, you should understand that real estate agents carry errors and omissions insurance to protect not only themselves, but you as buyers, from legal infractions that can occur in the purchase of a home. When you buy a FSBO, you could find yourself without legal recourse if your home was misrepresented. If you feel the need for a realtor's intervention in the purchase of a FSBO, do not automatically conclude that you're shooting for the moon. Savvy real estate agents can often negotiate a commission with FSBOs.

Coordinating the various advertising media will give you the most comprehensive survey of the homes a community has to offer. Don't rely solely on one advertising source. If you're moving to a new town, you may still be somewhat mystified without a real estate agent. You will want to make one of your first priorities contacting an agent advertising in a monthly publication or by e-mail or Web site. (We'll show you how to pick the best agent in Chapter 8.) If you're technology-shy, write a letter. Finding a pleasant and responsive agent who knows the market well can greatly simplify your home search.

Do you have to sell before you buy?

The preceding discussion of listings applies to everyone searching for a new home. The following comments apply to those of you who are not first-time buyers, currently own a home, and are trying to make decisions about when to sell your home. If you currently own a home, you will probably need to sell it before you buy another one. If you do not sell your current home first, you'll have to write a contingency contract. Chances are good that someone else will also want the house in which you are interested, possibly someone who has either sold their house or doesn't have a house to sell. Odds these days are about two to one against you. This means that two other prospective buyers will be more qualified than you are! Still, if you don't

 Moneysaver

Sellers tend to be more prone to negotiate when they are responding to a noncontingent contract (that is, you don't have to sell your house first). If they know they're going to close with you, they'll be more accommodating on price than if they have to wait for your house to sell.

have the money for a down payment without first selling your home, and you are determined to buy a new home immediately, you will have to try to beat the odds.

Two alternatives are available to help you beat the odds: the bridge loan and the rental agreement.

The bridge loan

A bridge loan is temporary financing that enables you to buy a home while you still own one. Processed by a bank, it is not a mortgage. With a bridge loan, you can finance 100 percent of the purchase price, and then make monthly payments to the bank until you sell your house. You have to show enough income to justify having both a mortgage payment and a bridge loan payment. One disadvantage is that the interest rate on a bridge loan is usually higher than that of a mortgage. But, if you desperately want a particular house, and you have a good chance of quickly selling your current house, a bridge loan gets you through the front door. After you close on your former home, you can pay off your bridge loan with the proceeds from permanent financing (your primary mortgage loan).

Bear in mind, however, that the bridge loan is only for the fortunate few: those who can make both a mortgage and a bridge loan payment. Let's explore another option for being able to offer a noncontingent contract before you sell.

How leasing can make you money

Leasing your present home is a viable option. Make sure that the monthly rent payment you'll receive is equal to or greater than your mortgage payment on your new home. Although you will be making two mortgage payments, you will be reimbursed for one of them, plus you'll be able to take the interest payment tax deduction for both of them. If you have the minimum amount for a down payment on your new home and a valid lease on your previous one, most lenders will offer you permanent financing. Many homebuyers have actually made money in this process.

Certain circumstances must apply. First, you must have bought your current home when interest rates were considerably higher than they are today. Second, the value of your current home must have gone up, or at least remained constant. If both of these circumstances apply to you, you may want to lease your house and use it as an investment with positive cash flow. This last, however, requires refinancing.

Advantages of leasing

Here's an example to illustrate how you can make money by refinancing and leasing your house. Let's say that six years ago you bought a house for $115,000. You borrowed $100,000 for 30 years at a 9-percent interest rate. Your mortgage payment (principal and interest) is $805 per month. After six years, you have reduced your mortgage to $94,000, and your home has appreciated in value to $130,000. Now you want to buy a new house, and you want to put down $16,000.

You can get that $16,000 by taking out a new loan on your current house for $110,000 at an interest rate of 7 percent. Your new monthly mortgage payment (principal and interest) would be $732.60. If you charge $800 per month in rent, which is perfectly reasonable for a $130,000 house, you would be clearing about $67 more than your mortgage payment.

Plus, even though your new mortgage loan is $10,000 higher, your new monthly payment would be more than $72 less than the current $805 per month! So you're netting a total of almost $140 per month by leasing out your home. Table 4.2 shows the math.

 Watch Out!

If you rent your former home for a year or more, the county tax assessor's office will probably take notice and void your homestead tax exemption on it. If this happens, expect your property taxes to double! Still, you will have offset most, if not all, of this increase by refinancing.

Table 4.2. How You Can Make Money by Refinancing and Leasing Your Home

To "get" a down payment on a new home, put

- $110,000 new loan on your current home, and
- ($94,000) payoff on your old mortgage

which gets you

$16,000 realized for a down payment on your new home

Monthly Earnings from Rent	Monthly Savings on New Mortgage
$800.00 rent taken in	$805.00 old monthly payment
($732.60) new mortgage payment	($732.60) new monthly payment
$67.40 cleared each month +	$72.40 monthly savings =

$139.80 TOTAL cleared each month

According to the scenario just described, you have accomplished five very important things by refinancing and leasing out your current home.

- You've generated $16,000 for a down payment on your new home, which may very well be all you need.

- You still have $20,000 of equity in your current home, which you can always sell later if you need the money.

- You've reduced your mortgage payment to an amount lower than you can expect to realize in rent (you could realize a nifty profit here).

- You have gained the tax advantage of two mortgage interest deductions.

- Finally, your mortgage payment will be fixed, whereas there's a real possibility that from time to time you can increase the amount of rent you are receiving, thereby, increasing your profit margin.

Disadvantages of leasing

Look before you leap into leasing. It is important to monitor your tenants regularly to make sure that they are maintaining the old homestead properly. Also, don't underestimate the amount of time it takes to be a conscientious landlord. If renting gets too stressful, you can always sell later.

If you're moving across the state or across the country, it would be wise to avoid the lease option. Although you can usually find a property manager to protect your home, his fees will be high, and you will have to rely on a third party to mail your rent checks. It would be nice to think that the property manager you chose to represent your leased home did more than collect the rent checks, but you have no guarantees, even if you instruct the property manager to perform site visits. In order not to become one of the many horror stories about absentee landlords—tales full of trashed, burned, or neglected homes—sign a contract with your property manager requiring monthly "condition of property" reports and putting the burden on him or her to make the lessee pay for damages or neglect.

To summarize, choose the bridge loan or the lease option if necessary to buy the home you want and then watch out for the pitfalls. Generally, though, the best course of action is to secure a noncontingent contract on your current home before buying another one, unless you can leverage that home in a financially beneficial way, like in our preceding example.

Location, location, location

There is an ongoing debate as to which of two factors, location or timing, is more crucial in the home-buying process. Basically, location is everything, but getting the right location at the right price depends on timing. "Location, location, location" is the most frequently given answer to the question, "What are the three most important issues in buying a house?" Exactly what does "location" mean?

In the real estate business, "good location" is a code for a property with high dollar value and the prospect for substantial appreciation. For the homebuyer, however, location is more subjective. It can mean having easy access to a shopping center. It can mean not driving too far to get to work. It can mean being close to your chosen place of worship. For families with young children, location usually includes a good school system. For most, it means an area with a low crime rate. For some people moving across the country, it means a friendly climate, or a more relaxed style of living. It ideally means a place where property values are increasing and where zoning regulations preserve the integrity of existing neighborhoods.

It is rare for any one home to fit all these definitions. So it's important for you to prioritize your needs relating to location (see the worksheet in the following section), just as you prioritize your other home choice needs, as discussed in Chapter 3. If location needs and desires were the same for everyone, then everyone would desire to live in the same place.

Finding the best part of town for you

When you break cities or towns into sections, neighborhoods, subdivisions, and streets, you quickly discover that some are more desirable, and consequently more expensive, than others. Your task is to balance location with affordability. You might be able to identify the best neighborhood in the city, but that doesn't mean that you can afford to live there. However, you can sometimes buy a nicer house, or one closer to work, by economizing on what it costs to commute.

 Bright Idea

"Location!" is a common tag in real estate ads; it implies a favorable location. But, favorable to who? Before running off to see a home that has a touted location, call and ask what's so special about it. What's special to some may not be special to you.

If you intend to relocate elsewhere in the city where you currently reside, you're probably somewhat familiar with other areas and neighborhoods. This knowledge will certainly facilitate the narrowing of your choices. Watch out—the depth of your knowledge based on a few casual drives may be too superficial to justify a purchase. A little knowledge, as they say, is a dangerous thing. Before choosing a location for your home, you need a lot of knowledge.

Take your time and investigate your prospective neighborhood or subdivision thoroughly.

Prospective Home Location Worksheet

Subdivision or Neighborhood _____

_____

CONVENIENCE   Commuting

                              Miles   Time

Distance to Buyer 1's Work _____

Distance to Buyer 2's Work _____

Distance to
Elementary School _____

Distance to
Junior High School _____

Distance to High School _____

Distance to Day Care _____

Distance to Church _____

Distance to Health Club _____

Distance to Supermarket _____

Distance to Pharmacy _____

Distance to Hospital _____

Distance to Police _____

Distance to Fire Station _____

continued

Worksheet *(continued)*

CONSIDERATIONS

Traffic Assessment: Rush Hour_____

Traffic Assessment: Other Hours_____

Accessibility Assessment_____

Noise Assessment_____

Crime Assessment_____

Age of Subdivision_____

Price Range of Homes_____

Real estate value trend: Last 5 Years_____
Last 10 Years_____

Upkeep & Maintenance Assessment_____

Utilities Available: Electric_____ Gas_____ Cable TV_____ Water_____

Infrastructure: Sidewalks_____ Sewer_____ Street Parking_____

Notes_____

_____

_____

_____

Checking out a subdivision or neighborhood

When you discover a neighborhood or subdivision that appears interesting, check the traffic patterns at rush hour, talk to the folks who live there about crime, or better yet, stop by the nearest police station. Inspect the condition of the infrastructure, including sewers, roads, sidewalks, and parks. Ask how maintenance of, and improvements to, infrastructure are funded, and by whom. Check into subdivision codes, covenants, and restrictions, including the policy on pets. Get the scoop on utilities, garbage collection, and the availability of cable TV. Research the range of selling prices for recently sold homes and then dig deeper to see whether property values over the past five years have increased, decreased, or held steady. Drive around and get

Watch Out!

Be aware that a neighborhood on the rise, particularly one amid an urban renewal or re-gentrification process, may manifest some of the same characteristics as a neighborhood on the decline. Check the trend in property values and the nearby retail picture to ascertain which direction the neighborhood is really headed.

a sense of how the area is maintained. Are the homes in good repair; are the lawns well attended? Come back after dark and see how the streets are lit. If you have school-age children, scrutinize the quality of the schools and inventory the number of suitable parks and playgrounds within walking distance. Take a look at the customers at nearby malls, restaurants, and shops. Do they look like people you would like to have as neighbors?

Beware of areas where rental properties and owner-occupied homes are mixed. Renters are not usually as conscientious as owners about upkeep and appearance. Unfortunately, absentee landlords are not much better.

If you buy in a subdivision, the best lots are the ones most distant from the subdivision entrance, those on cul-de-sacs, and those close to parks, lakes, or golf courses. In addition to investigating the area where you might buy, also pay particular attention to the health and viability of adjoining areas. Their current status may be a harbinger of things to come.

Neighborhoods in transition and urban gentrification

Neighborhoods, like the people who live in them, change over time, sometimes for the better and sometimes not. Changes can occur gradually or almost overnight, as when a major employer shuts down. Your job is to probe and question until you understand what's happening in your prospective neighborhood. A transition from mostly empty nesters to younger couples (with or without children) may not have a noticeable effect on property values or quality of life. Conversely, erosion of the tax base due to a local economic downturn can be seen almost immediately in everything from the quality of schools to the maintenance of highways.

The bottom line is that you do not want to buy into a neighborhood that is on the decline. How can you tell? Look for an unusual number of homes for sale and/or unoccupied, and a trend toward converting single family dwellings into multiple-family units. Be cognizant of poorly maintained homes and infrastructure. Increased crime is often signaled by burglar bars on ground floor windows and doors, as well as by evidence of vandalism, including the presence of graffiti. Empty retail space and attrition among nearby retailers are also indicative of decline.

A word about new subdivisions

The future of a new subdivision rests largely on the reputation and capitalization of the developer, as well as the state of demand in the new home marketplace. When purchasing a home in a brand-new development, you can't be quite sure who will move in as your neighbors, or whether the developer will make enough money to stick around and complete the development. When demand for new homes in the area is high, chances are that the lots will sell out quickly to a fairly economically homogeneous population of buyers. If demand drops off, however, the developer may be forced to liquidate his interest or compromise standards. This last can take the form of less stringent requirements for his builders, building smaller houses than those first constructed, or cutting prices (and profit margins) to attract less-qualified buyers.

 Watch Out!

Be wary of more modest subdivisions built by smaller developers with marginal financing. If a housing slump or a local economic downturn occurs, postpone buying until most of the homes have been completed and you're sure that the development is going to be finished as planned.

The cost of commuting

If you work in a large city, housing close to work may be outrageously expensive or, for a variety of reasons, undesirable. However, long commutes are likewise undesirable, and, as we will demonstrate, expensive.

Excluding holidays and vacations, you probably work about 48 weeks a year. With a five-day work week, that translates into 240 round-trips from home to work and back to home. Calculate the time in minutes of each round-trip commute and multiply it by 240. If, for example, you spend 25 minutes commuting each way, that would add up to a 50-minute round-trip. Fifty minutes a day times 240 round-trips per year equals 12,000 minutes, or 200 hours of commuting per year. If you calculate your hourly wage to place a value on your time, you can figure the opportunity cost of commuting. For example, if you make $10 an hour at your job, your commute is costing you $2,000 per year ($10 × 200 hours = $2,000). And, that's before you factor in transportation costs such as gas, auto maintenance, tolls, train or bus fare, and so on.

So what's the point? If you apply the amount you spend (or forgo) each year commuting to your mortgage, you can probably afford the more expensive home closer to work.

"Timing is everything"

As we mentioned earlier, timing affects whether you can get the location you want at the right price. Consider the following example. In a certain suburb in Illinois—let's call it Suburb X—the schools are the stuff of legend. Sellers know to put their homes up for sale in the spring. This, of course, is the time when many house-hunting families become anxious to buy so that they can get the kids into the prestigious school system the following year. From March through July, home sales are brisk. It is clearly a seller's market. Meanwhile, Mr. and Mrs. Green, who live in a nearby suburb, have always wanted their children to go to the prestigious schools in Suburb X but have never been able to afford a home in the area. Enter the Browns of Suburb X, when Mr. Brown is transferred to another city in November. Although they would have gotten an excellent price on their home a couple of months earlier, there is now only a buyer pool of one—the Greens. Because of fortuitous timing, the Greens are able to buy the Browns' home for 10 percent below the asking price.

For those of you who want to move to a good school system, it is best to have some latitude as to when you can buy, so that you don't become pressured into paying too much for a house or paying a high price for a bad house. Fall is the ideal time to get a good price. Most buyers who are moving for the start of school have already moved in by this time, yet there is often still a large inventory of houses left over. Go ahead and make an offer!

Another aspect of timing for you as a prospective buyer is how long a home has been on the market. A home that has been for sale for six months or more doesn't necessarily have some huge, hidden problem. It may have been poorly marketed, or it may have just had bad luck. However, you may find in such a home a seller who is ready and willing to negotiate. You may just find a bargain basement jewel.

Still another way to take advantage of timing is to keep your ears open and your eyes peeled for contracts that fall through. Contracts can fail for a variety of reasons that have nothing to do with the quality of the home. If you hear of such a contract, it could be that the seller is willing to take less money for the house, just to be certain that it will close. Real estate agents love to talk about "the sale that fell through." If you have an agent,

 Moneysaver

Even if you don't have school-age children, you may want to consider a home in a good school district for resale purposes. Usually communities with the best school systems provide the best services across the board and enjoy a low crime rate to boot.

ask him or her to tell you about dead or dying contracts. Sometimes, you can turn someone else's loss into your gain.

As we have already observed, fluctuation in interest rates can have a dramatic impact on the size of your monthly mortgage payment. Interest rate changes do not follow seasonal or rhythmic patterns. They tend to be tied to small fluctuations in the bond market and move up or down gradually in increments of one-eighth of a percent. Interest rate movement is more dramatic if you take the long view. Down from an all-time high of 18 percent in 1980, the interest rate at the time of this writing is about 5½ percent (a 40-year low!). Since 1992—when interest rates dipped below 7 percent for the first time in 25 years—rates have fluctuated between 5.5 and 10 percent.

Just the facts

- Use insider methods to determine how much you can afford.

- Be sure that you really understand—and use—your tax advantages.

- Don't rule out any of the six main sources of advertising.

- Investigate bridge loans or renting if you own a home and will not be able to sell it before buying a new home.

- Assess your priorities and, if feasible, use strategic timing to get the home that is best for you.

GET THE SCOOP ON...
The pleasures of surfing the Internet ▪
Getting the information you need ▪ What you
can and can't say on e-mail ▪ Avoiding
irrelevant information

Home Shopping on the Internet

In chapters 8 and 9 we look at what real estate agents do for a living, how they conduct their business, and how they shouldn't conduct their business. More specifically, we explore how buyer brokerage gives you unprecedented power and influence in the home-buying process, and how you can use this to your best advantage when you're buying a home. When you look for a home with your agent, you should expect her to demonstrate loyalty to your financial interests and sensitivity to your needs.

If this were a book on the home-selling industry, however, we would talk about real estate agents in a very different way. Another dimension to agency is *marketing* homes effectively so that *other* agents will sell them. As a result of their marketing efforts, agents may develop such a wide customer base that they're able to sell the homes to their own clients. These agents have established a working relationship with sellers by mutual agreement. Sellers contract with them for a certain period of time to represent their homes exclusively: to market them and to sell them for a fee. This process is called *listing*, and for most residential real estate agents, listings are the bread and butter of their businesses.

> 66 An old and venerated saying in the real estate business is 'When you're out of listings, you're out of business.' Unbeknownst to you, your eager buyer's agent is not only helping you to buy a house, but most likely, in that cauldron of listing agents, is competing to sign up sellers. 99

As it happens, the listing side of the real estate business is ferociously competitive. That's because most agents compete to get those prime listings—houses that ooze style and are in what's generally considered to be a great location—in other words, houses that will sell fast. So most agents are looking for that leg up on the competition—something they have that gives them an advantage.

A marketing tool for the agent and a resource for you

In today's real estate world, the leg up is the Internet. Many an agent visits her prospective sellers with laptop in tow, ready to show off a personal or company Web page and to demonstrate the many features of a particular home that can be put on a Web site. "Sign on with me," these agents say, "and you'll get the widest possible exposure to your home." And, they're right! The Internet has become the first important new marketing tool for the real estate industry to appear in years.

The great news is that you can tap into all these listings logged into the Internet from the convenience of your personal computer. If you're on-line, you can find a terrific sample of houses in all price ranges in almost every community in the United States. In fact, you might discover agents' Web sites with three-dimensional photographic mock ups of homes.

If you feel at all comfortable with computers, we recommend that you, as a home buyer, take full advantage of a marketing tool designed to help agents and agencies appeal to sellers. In fact, many good agents promote their Web sites to sellers but actually use them to attract buyers. If they use the Internet resourcefully, you can learn a tremendous amount about available housing in the community where you intend to live, as well as about the quality of schools, the cultural life, or even the tastes and interests of the listing agent. In this chapter, we'll briefly explore how to tap into the Internet and then turn our attention to using the Internet as a critical aspect of your home search.

What? Me surf?

For many of you, the Internet is a way of life. It's how you access the greatest amount of information on every imaginable subject with the greatest speed. For those of you who have a personal computer but have not yet gone on-line, however, we hope this chapter will give you just the excuse you need to get there. If you're already on-line and have the most basic level of computer literacy, you may wish to skip the next several paragraphs.

Getting on-line is a relatively simple and inexpensive process. All you need to do is add a modem and a telephone jack for the modem to your computer hardware and then choose an Internet Service Provider (ISP). Today, a number of well-known multipurpose commercial providers (MSN, Earthlink, and America Online

> ❝ To be a successful real estate agent today, you have to be prepared to spend money to make money. What you need to spend your money on is technology. We're almost at the point where if you're not on-line, you're going to become obsolete in the real estate business. ❞
>
> —Tommy Brigham, President, RealtySouth

are the best known) who take you from the gated communities of electronic newspapers, chat rooms, stock prices, and the like, to the diverse world of the Internet, typically for about $20-25 per month for dial-up service. All these commercial services provide guidance in how to tap into the hundreds of thousands of Web sites available to all browsers by helping you locate and click on your particular area(s) of interest.

What is the Internet?

If you already know, you can skip this section. If you don't, here's a quick summary. Think of the Internet as you would the international telephone system. Telephone service extends all over the world. When you pick up the receiver on your phone and dial another phone, your phone company, which is analogous to an ISP, automatically routes your call through the available phone lines until the phone on the other end rings. If the phone you are calling is connected to a phone system, you can reach it, even if the phone you are calling is serviced by a different provider than the one you use, which is why, for example, people on Prodigy can communicate with people on Mindspring. You can talk to anyone who is there to answer the phone.

Instead of a phone, however, imagine a computer at each end. That's what the Internet is. It's millions of computers, all over the world, serviced by different ISPs, connected in a way that lets other computers call them up and access whatever information has been made available for public viewing. In most cases, the computer uses the same lines the phone system uses, so connections get routed through available lines automatically. That's why you need to at least have a modem and a telephone jack to be on-line, or even better, cable Internet access, which is much faster. If your computer is connected through a modem and a telephone jack to the Internet, you can reach any other computer connected to the Internet—sometimes several at one time, like the old party lines of an earlier telephone era. You can view, retrieve, and, if you have a printer, print any information

Bright Idea

If you need to get Internet information on a particular home, requesting it via e-mail produces a far more rapid response than waiting for an agent to send something to you via the U.S. mail or returning a personal call. It's always best to check with your real estate agent, however; some people prefer communicating via e-mail, and some still prefer using the phone and check their e-mail infrequently.

made available for public viewing on any computer or Web site that someone has made available to the Internet. Even without a printer, you can retrieve the information and save it to a word-processing document.

If you have an Internet connection, you have access to virtually every publicly accessible computer on the Net. You can create your own Web site to convey information about yourself or about some service you provide to the immense cyberspace of the Internet. Indeed, locating a particular kind or piece of information on the Internet is not much more difficult than dialing a phone number correctly. Your initial entry onto the Internet accesses a relatively small number of broad topics. When you click your mouse to open one of them (a hyperlink), you get a narrower subset of topics within the broader one, and so on, until you discover the particular topic you were looking for followed by a link, such as "homes in Memphis . . . Memphishomes.com."

Okay . . . I'm in Memphis. Now what?

After you arrive at a real estate agency's or real estate salesperson's Web site, what can you expect to see and how can you communicate with the person whose listing or listings appeal to you the most?

When you sign up with an ISP, you make up an *e-mail address* and are given a telephone access number for getting on-line and using e-mail. Although most real estate agents' Web sites provide voice-mail numbers, office numbers, or home phone numbers, these numbers tend to work best for the casual buyer who has plenty of time to shop around, wants to compare Web sites, or wants to compare a number of different agents to evaluate the services that each provides.

However, if you're eager to know all the particulars about one or two houses that you see on a Web site, e-mail is the best way to get instant feedback. Most truly assiduous agent Web users have their own e-mail addresses and have their computer turned on at all times, anxious to see how many *hits* or visits they're getting to their Web site; such agents will e-mail you (usually with alacrity) with any information you request. Remember that although these agents are marketing their listings for sellers, they are equally attuned to ways to solicit your business as a buyer. Their credentials will probably appear on their Web site, but what will win you over to them as a customer is their rapid response to your requests for information.

You should also know what e-mail enables your prospective real estate agent to do for you. Through e-mail, your agent can keep you informed of new listings without concern for time of day or whether she is at work or at home. She can even e-mail photos of properties along with extensive descriptions. Also, an agent with a sophisticated Web site can establish hundreds, even thousands, of *links*, which feed information on a daily basis directly to her Web site. For example, many agents now belong to the Internet Real Estate Directory (IRED). Besides other services that we'll examine later, IRED News feeds agents and consumers interest rate quotes from hundreds of lenders on a daily basis. As interest rates change or as new loan products appear on the scene (both tend to be an almost daily occurrence), this information is downloaded into your would-be agent's Web site and is instantly retrievable by you via e-mail.

Although it's extremely handy to have a hard-working, high-tech real estate agent shopping the market for you on a daily basis, you might not want to rely exclusively on her services to meet all your home-buying needs. In this age of heavy, high-speed traffic on the Information Superhighway, your would-be agent is trying desperately to keep up with the flow by adding more and more links to her Web site so that you don't go to another source for information. One of the reasons she has had to enter the arena of fierce competition for listings is that homeowners themselves have become more adept either at using computers to market their own property or at finding an Internet marketing company who will market it for them at a cost significantly lower than the average agent's commission.

Although it's clear that the good real estate agent is by far the best resource for accessing the highest quality of information about the housing market in a particular area, it's also clear that many For Sale By Owners have learned to use the Internet to go directly to you, the homebuyer. *For Sale by Owner* magazine, for example, is actually a Web location where owners can post their own ads, buyers can view listings, and agents themselves can work to transform that FSBO market into a For Sale by Agent market.

Have I found the right agent on the Internet? Here's what to look for

The most important aspect of an agent's, agency's, or community's Web site is clarity. You should see an e-mail address prominently displayed, so that if you need help in navigating through an entire Web site, you can e-mail an agent, company, or city directory to get instructions or clarifications. Directly above or below the e-mail address should be an agent's picture, a company logo, or a municipality's name. The most ambitious and successful agents will have their own Web sites; however, so if you came first to a company or municipality Web site, type in more specific instructions and, unless you're planning on moving to a very small town with just a few agents, you'll eventually come to the following:

- A series of photographs of particular agents

- A catalog of their listings

- Color pictures of their listings

- One catch phrase or a series of catch phrases meant to capture your attention and encapsulate what best embodies the agent's intentions ("we respect the value of your time"; "market knowledge and real estate expertise"; "warm, personal service"; "thoroughness and attention to detail"; and "I succeed where other agents have failed" seem to be the most popular).

Table 5.1. Top Listing Services on the Internet

Listing Service	Web Address	Description
Internet MLS	www.trinet.com.home conn.information.html	Home Connections, lists homes for sale.
On-line Real Estate Auctions	www.valleynet.com/ ~webcity/	The Real Estate Junction, real estate listings by category.
On-line East Coast	www.infi.net/REWeb	Real Estate Web, East Coast listings.
Electronic Realty Services	www.tyrell.net/~ers	Electronic Reality Services. Listings of apartments, houses, agents, commercial properties across the country. Offers both free and paid listings.
RE/Max Realty	www.remaxhq.com/ atlanta	RE/Max North Atlanta's on-line service. Includes local listings and consumer information on buying and selling property in Georgia. Provides direct e-mail to agents, mortgage lenders, home warranty providers, insurance agents, home inspectors, and attorneys.

Listing Service	Web Address	Description
FractalNet	www.fractals.com/realestate.html	FractalNet Real Estate Server, "the most complete ordered listing of residential real estate on the Internet." Fractal gives up-to-date information, on-line real estate listings, and so on. Submit listing link request via e-mail.
Buyer's Agent	www.sover.net/~relo Network	American Relocation Center, offers an array of tools.
National Listings	www.us-digital.com/homeweb	Includes nationwide listings, profiles of real estate companies and agents, financing and mortgage information, and consumer tips. Operated by U.S. Digital Corp., a publisher for the relocation and real estate industries.
For Sale by Owner	www.human.com/mkt/fsbo/	For Sale by Owner magazine. A place where owners can post their own ads, buyers can view listings, and agents can work the FSBO market.
Worldwide Listings	www.wren.com	WRENet, World Real Estate Network, interactive and searchable real estate database, all kinds of property.

 Bright Idea

By using a list of listing services, such as the one we provide in Table 5.1, you will save the bother of having to use a search engine to find these sites.

After you're snagged by a catch phrase and are deeply lodged in a particular Web site, here are the most important additional elements you'll probably find:

- **Areas of specialization.** An agent's personal Web site will indicate the price range of houses she specializes in selling and the particular area of a community where she sells the most. If an agent advertises herself as your "all-purpose agent," watch out! In fact, watch out for any claim you see on a Web page; it's all advertising, and there's no guarantee that you will receive the service promised. The real estate sales industry has become increasingly specialized, and most agents have developed a greater and greater degree of knowledge of a smaller and smaller area of the business.

- **Credentials.** Give the agent whose Web site you've selected room to brag. Their record in sales and their advanced degrees in real estate do make a difference in the person you ultimately select to represent you. Chances are that if you're using the Internet to select a home or an agent in the first place, you're moving from one community to another, and you'll want to have confidence in your agent's knowledge of the marketplace and her skills in conveying that knowledge.

- **Links.** A really thorough Web site will give you avenues for additional information that will ultimately become a crucial part of your home search. These avenues are the *links* we discussed earlier: additional Web pages that carry current interest rates, the names of lenders with unique loan packages, the means to access credit bureaus, lists of customs and conventions for closing homes in various communities, lists of the best places to shop for home designs, home repair equipment and supplies, home furnishings, and so on.

Okay, I want to know more

After you've found a Web site that presents an agent whose credentials and attitudes you like and whose links seem so comprehensive that you feel no need to shop elsewhere, it's your turn to activate a relationship. For many of you, writing to an e-mail address simply won't work. No matter how hard you try, typing in requests for information or making personal introductions on a computer screen will always seem impersonal or awkward. This has nothing to do with your writing skills or your overall ability as a Web surfer. Rather, it's the result of the fact that typing, itself, can sometimes seem like an incomplete or overly formal means of communicating.

If you feel this way, take heart. Any good agent will have provided an office or home phone number and probably a voice mail number along with her e-mail address. If you catch your agent at home or at her office immediately, great! The first question she will ask you is whether you found out about her services on the Internet. If your answer is yes, your agent will (privately, of course) be ecstatic. Statistics indicate that sales prospects who find agents on the Internet have a better than 50-percent chance of using those agents to buy property—about double the percentage of those who locate agents by other means. If you wind up getting an agent's voice mail, leave a time you want the agent to call you back. The agent who calls back when you specify is someone you can most likely depend on to be prompt and efficient in other ways, as well.

Cranking out the e-mail

If you choose to communicate with your prospective agent via her e-mail address, introduce yourself in a simple and direct

Moneysaver

For most people e-mail is a far cheaper way of communicating long distance than the conventional telephone.

Watch Out!

Never share anything over the Internet that you would object to becoming public knowledge.

way. Indicate to the agent the type of home you're looking for and the price range. Then ask the same questions you would ask someone with whom you would be talking face-to-face, only be as succinct as possible. Don't feel bad if you missed a question and only think of it later; you can e-mail anyone as often as you wish; unlimited e-mail usage is part of most fixed monthly payment plans with Internet providers, so you won't be charged extra no matter how often you write.

Communication with your prospective agent via e-mail will certainly be awkward the first few times you try it if this is also your first time using e-mail to make requests. For some of you, no matter how hard you try to overcome the awkwardness you feel, you won't be able to use e-mail as comfortably as if it were the phone; for others, using e-mail will become as easy as entering a casual conversation.

In fact, some of you may feel so conversational and at ease using e-mail that you'll invite an agent to join you in an Internet Relay Chat, which is a multiuser, multichannel chatting network (more generally called a *chat* or *chat room*). Chat rooms allow people all over the world to talk to one another in real time. You can arrange with your agent to enter a particular chat room at a particular time and, with other buyers and perhaps other agents in the room with you, casually review your concerns as a buyer of real estate, and have them addressed immediately.

How far should I go?

How far along can you go toward buying a house if you shop on the Internet? The answer is "all the way!" But, we doubt that this is the right answer for you. Although some agents use pretty sophisticated computer graphics to image their listings in three dimensions and even indicate the square footage and ceiling heights for each room, the reality they create isn't quite as *virtual* as you might be led to believe. There is nothing quite like the feel of actually stepping into a home and imagining yourself living there. You might save the cost of a trip and a few days' time by doing all your home shopping on the Internet, but the savings would hardly make up for the disappointment you would experience in realizing you don't like the house you've just bought.

Of course we're exaggerating . . . we don't expect you to go all the way to and through a closing on the Internet unless, for example, you're buying a one- or two-week vacation in a time-share situation. In fact, we don't expect, or advise, you to do a lot of things solely on the Internet. So just how far can you go? It's a matter of how much control you want to retain in the buying process.

The don'ts

Somewhere along the line you'll discover that using the Internet can be somewhat addictive. Try to keep your enthusiasm for the technology under control. Particularly in shopping for and buying a home, remember that the Internet is a tool, not a universal solution.

- Don't arrange to buy a custom home over the Internet. Without several conversations with a home designer, surveyor, and builder, and without several visits to the building site, you'll have no way of knowing if the builder can produce what you designed. Besides, there are rip-off construction companies who advertise on the Internet that they can build from your designs and who really hope that if you use their services, you'll stay away from the construction site!

- Don't apply for a mortgage over the Internet. First of all, even if you don't have the time or are in the wrong location to see a loan officer, you'll need to use an overnight mail provider and a fax machine to send all the documents you'll need to make a loan application. . .the Internet isn't enough. More important, your loan officer will need to supply you with several critical documents that have your Social Security number on them. Pirates cruise Web sites looking for such information, and the Internet is still far from being thief-proof. Don't send or receive sensitive documents on the Internet unless you are sure the site uses encrypted technology and is safe.

- For reasons of confidentiality, don't compose, negotiate, or execute a contract to buy property over the Internet. Among other sensitive things, contracts have legal descriptions of home purchases. These could be stolen and disreputable people could attach liens to properties based on these legal descriptions.

- Don't expect a home inspector to perform a thorough evaluation of a property you're buying in your absence and then e-mail you a full report of his findings. If you're buying a house with anything that needs fixing, your inspector's personal attention to both you and the seller is the only way to work out any snags that might compromise your purchase or impair a closing.

- Don't close a sale over the Internet. Rarely does a closing occur that last-minute issues don't have to be resolved, some of them possibly requiring the utmost confidentiality. You don't want sudden, personal things about you to go out over the Internet.

Finally, be aware of possible snafus on the Internet. In terms of what you read on the Internet, not only are there deliberately false claims, there is also information inadvertently reported incorrectly. In terms of what you post on the Internet, remember that the misdirecting of your private e-mail is as easy as a single typographical error. For the sake of your privacy, be careful when sending mail, and in turn, do not conduct business with anyone who you doubt can exercise the same care.

The do's

Insofar as home buying is concerned, use the Internet for what it was intended: as a source of information, some of which you'll need to check out with other sources to verify its accuracy. You'll be able to download more information on the home purchase process than you can ever use; so here's a list of what's most important for you to research and use.

- Information about a real estate agent in the community where you intend to buy and a comprehensive list of all properties she can show you in the price range and style of home for which you're looking.

- Everything listed in *For Sale by Owner* magazine within the parameters of your style and price range. (You may want to compare prices with those of agency listings to see whether individual owners have done a good job researching the market.)

- A comprehensive list of home inspectors in the community where you intend to buy. This list should include their qualifications and years of experience.

- Current interest rates for every kind of home loan imaginable. Also, the types of loans offered by all the mortgage companies and banks in the community where you intend to live, along with e-mail addresses and phone numbers for each of these institutions. Remember, when you're making inquiries, not to give out your Social Security number or any credit-history information.

- A list of title companies that have *title plants* (a library of information that traces all liens and encumbrances placed on every home that has ever sold) and can instantly determine whether there are any *clouds* or irregularities in the title to the home you're purchasing.

- Samples of all documents you might have to sign and/or review as part of a real estate closing.

As you can see, you'll need to monitor yourself in your Web search and discard a lot of junk when you download information. Shopping on the Internet really can make you an informed buyer and transform the real estate agent, the loan officer, the inspector, the title company, and the closing attorney into a team. Just remember that you are the captain: know your players well, and surf the Web with enough intelligence and discrimination so that everything merges into a satisfying home search and a pleasant closing. It all begins with you gaining control of your little domain on the Internet and not letting a tidal wave of information sweep you under.

> **❝** The problem with house hunting on the Internet is that in no time flat you'll be awash with so much information you'll be at a loss to determine what's useful and what isn't. Also, if you give out your e-mail address, you'll get a lot of junk e-mail in return. The best way to get only what you want is to be selective in what you ask for. **❞**
>
> —Jerome Newman, Real Estate Agent

Just the facts

- Find out what you need to get on the Internet and what provider will best serve your needs.
- Learn how to use e-mail to your best advantage and be discriminating about when to and not to use it.
- Understand exactly how far you can go in your home search when shopping on the Internet.
- Learn how to discriminate between downloading useful and useless information onto your computer.

Preliminary Choices

PART III

GET THE SCOOP ON...
The rise and fall of interest rates ▪ How and
when home buying is an investment ▪
Adjustable-rate mortgages (ARMs) ▪ The
Taxpayer Relief Act of 1997

Home Buying As an Investment

So far, we've talked about the importance of preparing yourself psychologically for the home-buying process—the soul-searching necessary to discover what you and other family members really want and need in a home. We've reviewed the various lifestyle factors that may impel you to move and how these factors will influence the type, style, and location of homes you will look at. We've discussed strategies for getting a grip on the home marketplace, as well as your personal finances, so that your search for a home will be as productive as possible. We also have reviewed several of the options available to you for financing a home and, more specifically, how to be prepared financially so that when you make a decision to buy, you know you'll be qualified for a loan. We have touched on the idea that we live in an increasingly mobile society, which in turn affects our moving decisions. What we need to examine here is how this same mobility affects our financial decisions as well . . . how it affords us the opportunity to clarify and narrow down our loan choices.

In this chapter, we explore the impact of our greater mobility on home buying as an investment. The increased frequency with which we change our locales and the resulting decrease in the average length of time we stay in a given home has made the investing part of buying a home more important than ever before. Our greater mobility has had a profound effect on the type of financing we choose. Specifically, more of us are choosing adjustable-rate mortgages (ARMs) as a means for achieving the lowest possible mortgage payment. Although the entire spectrum of mortgage financing possibilities was the focus of Chapter 1 (Ready... Set... Finance!), here we focus on the investment aspects of certain low-interest rate, short-term mortgages.

In addition to our greater mobility, a second phenomenon has given a new meaning to the investment aspect of buying a home. Thanks to certain U.S. government actions, culminating in the Taxpayer Relief Act of 1997, we now can move more frequently with impunity. Uncle Sam has made it possible for us to make money from the sale of our homes without having to turn over a sizable chunk of our profits to the Internal Revenue Service. While mortgage interest payments have always been tax-deductible, only since the implementation of this Taxpayer Relief Act have we been able to take all the profits from selling a home, put them into another home, play with them on the stock market, or even buy a vacation home with them without paying a tax penalty. In other words, this act has added a tremendous amount of investment power to the process of buying a home.

Parting is not such sweet sorrow, anymore

There was a time when, as a homebuyer, you would expect to live in your home for a long time, perhaps the rest of your life. Certainly long enough to watch your kids' height lines rise on the door frame over the years, and long enough to know the radiator's hissing song by heart and anticipate the squeaks in the floorboards. Your home would become like an old friend.

Although some sellers still get teary-eyed at their closing because they're leaving their old friend, their ranks are thinning. Today, the purchase of many a home has become part of a larger career plan. In the mind of many purchasers, buying a home is more of an investment than a com-mitment. In fact, it has become increasingly common for home-buyers to anticipate their next move before even completing their current one.

> ❝In these days of the national or interna-tional company, being willing to move from one location to another is often the key to moving up the corpo-rate ladder. . . . The old idea of a stable home has been replaced by vague notions of corpo-rate loyalty ('Big Daddy will take care of you if you travel with him.')❞
>
> —*Real Estate Outlook,*
> August 2001

Throw away the rocking chair!

Here's an exercise that will dramatically illustrate how, as a soci-ety, we are moving around more with each passing generation. First, think about how long your grandparents lived in their house. Next, think about how long your parents lived, or have lived, in their same house. Finally, tally your own duration in the house or houses you've resided in and try to anticipate how long you'll live in the house you're about to buy.

For the majority of us, our duration in a given residence has decreased with each subsequent generation. Certainly, the beginning of this phenomenon can be traced to our country's shift away from a farm culture. Forty-five percent of you between the ages of 25 and 50 had at least one set of grandparents who were farmers and who worked the same acreage for 30 or more years.

But, especially since World War II, we have become less agrarian and more industrial and service-oriented. Fewer than 10 percent of your parents farm or farmed. Hence, they were not as tied to a particular piece of land. Only 25 percent of them lived or will live in the same home for 30 or more years. Still, 90 percent of them stayed in the same line of work and remained in the same town all of their adult lives. Today, on the other hand, career changes have become far more common as more and more of us seek advanced degrees and regularly reassess the best way we can contribute to a rapidly changing society. As we have seen, career advancement frequently requires moving from one community to another.

Between our grandparents' and parents' generations, while we find a significant decrease in farmers and those who've dwelled in the same home for 30 years or more, among individuals, we don't find a significant amount of shift between jobs or towns. Today, career and location changes are the dominant tendencies of most individuals' working lives. As a result, our very perception of the word *home* has less and less to do with the physical and familiar, a specific place, and more and more with a vague notion of psychological "warm feelings," which are themselves subject to constant change. So work makes us move; moving makes us less likely to attach permanent feelings to our dwellings; temporary and vague feelings of well-being make it still easier for us to move!

Like key changes in the nature of our jobs, increases in the speed and simplicity of our travel have greatly reduced the length of time the average homeowner stays put. If we combine these elements, we find that for those of you between the ages of 22 and 50, in stark contrast to your parents, there is less than a 5-percent chance that you will pay off your mortgage before you move! This means that it is unlikely that you will develop a deep emotional attachment to your home. From an aesthetic as well as practical standpoint, you may expect it to serve you well during your tenure, but you will not necessarily be moved to tears when you sell.

Who lives here, anyway?

The phenomenal increase of career-related mobility has had a profound impact not only on what many of us consider as home but also on the composition of households (defined by the Bureau of the Census as an individual or group of people who occupy a housing unit). Frequent career-related moves have often meant deferred marriage, deferred or cancelled child-rearing plans, increased urbanization, decreased family size, and other notable changes in household patterns. Table 6.1 dramatically illustrates many of the ways that the American household has changed.

Note: One of the major implications of the statistics in Table 6.1, when combined, is that the household is a smaller entity than it used to be, but at the same time better equipped to handle change.

Table 6.1. Household and Family Composition, 1970 versus 1995

1970	1995
Married couples with children made up 40 percent of households.	Married couples with children made up 25 percent of households.
There were 3.14 people per household.	There were 2.65 people per household.
One out of every five households had five or more people.	Only one out of every 10 households had five or more people.
People living alone made up one-sixth of all households.	People living alone made up one-fourth of all households.
Two out of every three households were in metropolitan areas.	Four out of every five households were in metropolitan areas.
Forty-four percent of families had no children under age 18 living at home.	Fifty-one percent of families had no children under age 18 living at home.

Real Estate Outlook, March 1997

If you don't find yourself in any of the facts and statistics we've touched upon thus far in this chapter, you're in a tiny minority of the home-buying population. Assuming that you've found yourself somewhere in these facts and statistics, you may want to consider coming up with a strategy for minimizing your mortgage payment and maximizing your ability to select a home by looking at home buying as part of an overall investment strategy.

Developing a strategy

As we have seen, the demands of today's careers, including corporate transfers, as well as the search for better job opportunities, drive us to move more frequently than ever before. Of your five closest neighbors, one will move each year. Obviously, this has created a tremendous surge in the real estate industry. For you personally, it is far less likely than even 10 or 15 years ago that you will have time to develop the same level of attachment to a community as your parents did.

In addition, you may not be staying in your home long enough to experience a significant increase in its value. In the past, investing in a home was much like investing in the stock market has always been: over the long haul, although you experience ups and downs in the market value of your investment, the overall tendency has been toward appreciation of value. As far as a home is concerned, the long-time home dweller who bought in a good location and maintained his or her property could also experience this same kind of appreciation, sometimes of a very sizable amount. In our current, increasingly mobile climate, you may not have the time necessary to experience this appreciation, yet still want to *move up* with each successive relocation. This is where the following discussion of ARMs comes in: You may still be able to make a larger down payment on a more expensive home when you make your next move if you get the right ARM for this home, even if you don't actually make money on its resale.

Many of you will find it advisable to develop a home-buying strategy in accord with the trends discussed here. Let's explore two components of a successful strategy: owning a home with the lowest possible (and practical) monthly payments, and owning a home with the highest rate of return on your investment when you sell. In other words, let's explore home buying as a business.

The short-term mortgage loan

The adjustable-rate mortgage (ARM) emerged out of the frightening rise of interest rates in the late 1970s and early 1980s. An ARM is a loan that starts out at a lower interest rate than the current fixed rate and, after staying fixed for a period that ranges from six months to seven years, adjusts upward or downward every year thereafter. It is paid out over the same length of time as a fixed-rate loan—in other words, your ARM will be amortized over a period of 15, 20, or 30 years, just like a fixed-rate loan—but its variable interest rates after the adjusting period are usually higher than that of their fixed-rate counterparts.

In the early 1980s, homebuyers seeking relief from a whopping 18 percent interest rate could *buy down* their rate as much as 4 or 5 percent by paying points, or prepaid interest, at closing. For example, let's say that you took out a $100,000 mortgage at an 18-percent fixed interest rate but bought it down to 13 percent by paying five points (each point equals 1 percent of the loan amount) at closing. You would have saved $250 or more per month on your payment.

So if you had taken out a three-year ARM, which means that your initial rate—in this case, 13 percent—would have remained constant for three years, you would have saved $9,000 ($4,000 after the cost of points) during that period. If you had opted for a five-year ARM on the same $100,000, you would have saved $15,000 over five years! Smart buyers during the early 1980s set aside some of the money saved by paying points. When interest rates declined, they used the money to refinance their home before the higher annual rate adjustments kicked in.

Relief finally came in 1985, when the fixed rate was 11 percent, down seven percentage points from 1980. A refinancing boom occurred almost overnight, as homeowners with ARMs got new, fixed-rate loans with an interest rate lower than their original loans. The population as a whole was not moving as frequently as it is today. By closing their ARMs and fixing an interest rate, many homeowners were able to live in their homes far more cheaply than they had anticipated.

A second refinancing boom occurred in 1992, when interest rates plummeted to 7 percent. Since that time, interest rates have tended to fluctuate between 7 and 9 percent, although as of this writing (May 19, 2003, a day that may one day be inscribed in mortgage history books), fixed-rate, 30-year mortgage loans have reached a 41-year low of 5 percent! Every time interest rates have been at 7 percent or lower, an astonishing number of individuals have chosen to refinance. Why wouldn't they? A drop in interest rate from 7 percent to 5½ percent on a 30-year mortgage of $100,000 means a savings of $97 per month. We will be bold and speculate that interest rates will not go below 5 percent in the next few decades, even though banks and secondary lenders still make serious money on these unprecedented low rates, because, as we've learned through the process of amortization, a very large chunk of your payments for the first 5 to 10 years of your mortgage is interest (the lender's investment in your principal goes down very slowly).

We may be lead to think that when fixed interest rates are down to 5 or 6 percent it would be pointless to get an adjustable rate loan. In point of fact, the ARM is more popular than ever. Its popularity has nothing to do with *buying down* high fixed rates. Rather, it is a function of the increased mobility we experience in a fluctuating job market and the tendency we've already discussed to move far more frequently than we used to. The ARM is also used by some as an equity builder, a strategy we'll discuss later in this chapter.

How can the ARM help you today?

As a home buyer, you can use the ARM in various ways to maximize your investment. The ARM comes in five varieties, based on the period until adjustment to a fixed rate begins: six months, one year, three years, five years, and seven years. The shorter the period until adjustment, the lower the interest rate paid during that period. Table 6.2 shows what the monthly payment would be on a 30-year loan of $100,000, first with a fixed rate of 6 percent and then with the last four of the five different ARMs. (Monthly payment includes principal and interest.)

Table 6.2. Comparative Monthly Payments Based on a 30-Year, $100,000 Loan

Type of Mortgage	Interest Rate	Monthly Payment
Fixed-rate	6.0 percent	$599.55
One-year ARM	3.75 percent	$467.10
Three-year ARM	4.25 percent	$503.61
Five-year ARM	4.75 percent	$523.21
Seven-year ARM	5.50 percent	$561.47

Given that closing costs are the same for the ARM and the fixed-rate loan (the phenomenon of lenders charging you discount points against the lower interest rate when you get an ARM loan having gone by the wayside in our current low interest-rate climate), when should you get an ARM, and which ARM should you get? In order to answer these questions, we need to know what a lender's motives are for offering what seems on the surface to be the fabulous deal of ARMs in the first place.

Remember that ARMs came into being to help people afford homes when interest rates were at an all-time high. Don't think that a group of benevolent rich people looked down upon our economic plight with sympathy and decided to let us borrow money at a low interest rate and live happily ever after with a modest little mortgage.

Watch Out!

Don't trust ARM lenders to look out for you. They want you to sign up for the highest possible index in order to exact the highest amount of interest from you when your ARM begins to adjust.

The initial interest rate you get with an ARM is, in reality, a teaser rate. It's bound to go up substantially after the fixed-rate period of time of your ARM expires. For example, if you ask your lender what the initial interest rate of a one-year ARM is, he or she may quote 3.75 percent while the market rate for fixed-rate mortgages is 6 percent. What your lender may fail to explain is that your ARM is tied to a margin that can come into play every time your ARM adjusts.

For example, your lender may specify in your ARM mortgage documents that the margin is 2.75 percent. This means that when the index, or current fixed-rate interest, is 6 percent, you can wind up with an effective mortgage interest payment of 8.75 percent! Remember . . . this doesn't happen all at once. Annual caps typically hold the amount your mortgage interest rate can increase in any given year to 2 percent. After two years, however, your one-year ARM could be as high as 7.75 percent; after three years, it could be as high as 9.75 percent. When your lender offers you an ARM, especially a relatively short-term ARM of six months or a year, he is betting on you remaining in your home for at least two or three times longer, so that he will make a lot more money from your interest payments than he would make on a fixed-rate loan! In fact, your lender is also betting that if you stay in your ARM-financed home for longer than you expected and your interest rate exceeds the current fixed rate, you won't get around to, or won't be able to afford, refinancing. So much for benevolence!

With all of these warnings and caveats concerning ARM loans on the table, we can now look at the four dominant types and some possible scenarios for each. What's most important to remember as you consider these types and scenarios is that getting any kind of ARM loan takes discipline. You need to have a fairly certain sense of how long you plan to stay in the home you're buying. Also, you'll need to make sure that your ARM loan has no prepayment penalty: money you would owe your lender if you paid off your loan early for any reason. Moreover, if there's even a halfway decent chance you'll be in your home for longer than the fixed-rate period of your ARM, you'll need to set aside the money saved in the first few years of having your ARM for closing costs on financing a conversion to a fixed-rate mortgage.

The one-year ARM

Table 6.2 shows that, compared to the monthly payment on a current fixed rate of 6 percent, the payment on a one-year ARM is about $140 lower—for the first year of your mortgage. If you're planning to buy a house for the sole purpose of renovating it and reselling it within a year, a one-year ARM is an ideal loan for you.

Make sure that you buy a home in a desirable neighborhood where sales are brisk, because a vast majority of one-year ARMs adjust upward after the first year. (There's still is a cap to prevent increases of more than 2 percent in a given year and 5 to 6 percent over the lifetime of your loan.) If you're still paying the mortgage into the second year, you'll start eating into your profits. So, there is a certain amount of risk involved.

In another scenario the one-year ARM might be advisable, but as a means to an end rather than an investment. If your income-to-debt ratio (explained in Chapter 4) does not qualify

 Bright Idea

If you're buying to renovate and resell, put a lid on any urges to do something unique or unusual. Adhere to general standards of taste, so that the home will attract a larger pool of prospective buyers.

Watch Out!

If you have an adjustable-rate mortgage, beware of the dangers of the earlier-than-expected sale. Chances are greater than 90 percent that a real estate agent will be involved. If so, the agent's 5 to 7 percent commission would erode most, if not all, of the savings realized by your ARM!

you for monthly payments over a certain amount, a one-year ARM could enable you to purchase a home that would otherwise be beyond your reach (that is, at a fixed interest rate).

But, be careful. Choose this option only if you're sure that your income level will increase or your debt load will decrease. The only constant in a one-year ARM is that, after that one year, the interest rate will go up! It's true that because of the increase cap of two points, the maximum rate you would be paying in the second year is 5.75 percent, but after that, it's anybody's guess. You could wind up owning more house than you can afford.

It would be extremely rare for anyone to keep a one-year ARM for more than three years, because chances are that after the third year, your interest rate will be much higher than the going fixed rate. If you stay in your home longer than you anticipated when you opted for a one-year ARM, you'll probably want to refinance within two or three years of buying your home. If this should be the case, make sure that you've set aside enough cash for a new set of closing costs!

The three-year ARM

Are you an M.D. resident or intern? Are you just starting law school? Have you taken an out-of-town job with a three-year contract? Are you a college football coach? If you're in a situation where relocating in the next three years is likely, or if you expect to experience a big jump in income as the result of earning a degree, a three-year ARM can make good business sense.

As Table 6.2 indicates, on a 30-year, $100,000 mortgage, your monthly payment would be about $80 lower than the payment on the fixed-rate loan. You would be saving $2,880 over three years (about the cost of a one-week vacation in Europe, including air fare, or a nice start on the down payment for your next home). Even if you stay in the home for five years, the total amount you will have paid with a three-year ARM is still very likely to be less than you would have paid in five years with a fixed-rate mortgage.

The risk element in the three-year ARM stems from the often capricious nature of life. What if you drop out of law school and decide to move to Bangladesh, or, you get caught in downsizing at work? If you have to sell prematurely, you'll most likely lose money. Even in the most desirable of neighborhoods, a home probably would not appreciate enough in under three years to earn you any real money.

However, what if you want to stay longer in your home than originally planned because you've fallen in love with the community? In this case, the three-year ARM won't hurt you much; although you'll have to pay closing costs when you refinance your home, they will probably amount to less than the money you saved by getting the three-year ARM.

The five-year ARM

This loan can be a real gem. Using our same example, it would save you $40 per month over a fixed-rate loan and a total of $2,400 by the end of five years. With a five-year ARM, even if you remain in your home for a sixth year, you will have saved money. Even if you stay a lot longer, chances are that your income will have increased sufficiently to cover a larger monthly payment or that you will have saved enough money to refinance at a fixed rate.

The main risk with the five-year ARM is the possibility that interest rates will climb so steeply during the five years that your new monthly payments will increase dramatically when you refinance. The five-year ARM won't amass you a fortune, but it is a fairly painless way to conserve money if you reside in your home close to five years, which, after all, is the new average for home-buyers. Statistically, 92 percent of homes bought in any given year sell for at least 9 percent more than their original purchase price after five years. In some neighborhoods, homes have been known to go up in value over 50 percent in the same five-year period. Although you're not saving quite as much money on a year-by-year basis, as you would with a three-year ARM, you're building more than enough equity to pay a realtor's fee when you sell, and you will have money left over for a down payment on your next home purchase, even if you haven't set aside additional funds.

The seven-year ARM

The difference in monthly payments between a fixed rate of 6 percent and the corresponding seven-year ARM rate of 5.75 percent (again, on a 30-year loan of $100,000) comes to only about $16. Because the difference between a fixed-rate loan and a seven-year ARM is only one-fourth of a percent or less, this is the least used of the four basic ARMs. It is sometimes recommended by a lender when buyers need to qualify for a slightly more expensive home than they otherwise could. In other words, your lender may recommend a seven-year ARM so that you can stay within the proper ratios on your monthly payment. Another seven-year loan product addresses a slightly more universal need and could save real money. Remember that seven years is now considered a longer-than-average time to stay in one home. For those who can safely commit to the same home for *more* than five years, lenders provide the seven-year balloon note. The interest rate is usually about three-fourths of a percentage point under the fixed rate; but the entire unpaid principle balance (after seven years) becomes due and payable. The expectation is that you'll refinance this outstanding principal after the seven-year period; but, of course, you risk the possibility that interest rates will be so high that refinancing will strangle your financial resources. On the whole, the uses of a seven-year ARM are fairly limited; yet in certain circumstances, this ARM may fit your personal needs.

Watch Out!

The *balloon* loan starts out at a lower interest rate than a fixed-rate loan, but cannot be extended after the initial fixed-rate period ends. Instead, it *balloons*, with the outstanding principal payable in full. The balloon note typically runs from 7 to 10 years—longer than most ARMs.

We have thus far discussed only one basic type of mortgage loan—the ARM. Remember, this is not the principal chapter on financing. In Chapter 1, we covered the whole array of financing options available to you.

As you can see, the short-term (five years or less) home purchase is an ever increasing phenomenon. This is a function of modern demographics and places an unprecedented emphasis on home buying as a business proposition, or as a way to save money during your brief tenure as the owner of a particular home. If you know in advance of your purchase how long you will be living in your new home, you can comfortably choose the optimum mode of ARM financing. You can transform the business of financing into a relatively stress-free and even pleasurable experience.

Another ARM-like loan is the Libor, which some high-end buyers find attractive. The Libor is an interest-only loan that is tied to a particular British index based on the interest rates the government charges banks to borrow money. They can range in length from one month(!) to five years, with the interest rate going up accordingly after the fixed period ends but always lower than the interest rate on ARMs. Obviously, however, the only equity you achieve through a Libor is in the appreciation of your home. Most Libor borrowers, therefore, try to use their savings to pay additional principal along with their monthly interest payment.

You should know in advance of applying for any ARM, however, that an element of risk is involved. If your timing is off, you could find yourself with escalating interest rates and mortgage payments. While the timing of your purchase is important, as we saw in Chapter 4, the timing of your sale is crucial also. Do not seek out an ARM just to save money in the short run unless you are confident that it will save you money in the long run as well.

The Taxpayer Relief Act of 1997

Since 1997, buying a home as an investment has taken on a new meaning. This is due to the passage of the Taxpayer Relief Act of 1997, the largest tax relief bill passed by Congress since 1981. The bill is far-reaching in its impact on most Americans, but especially on current homeowners and first-time buyers.

The current homeowner's relief

Until the passage of the Taxpayer Relief Act, profits made on the sale of any home were taxed unless you, the taxpayer, bought another home of equal or greater value. The only way to avoid this taxation was for you to wait until you were age 55 or older, at which point you would be allowed to exclude a profit, or *capital gain*, of up to $125,000. You could do this once in your lifetime.

The new law allows you as a single homeowner to make profits of up to $250,000, and you as a couple filing a joint income tax return to make profits of up to $500,000, on the sale of your primary residence without having to pay any capital gains taxes, even if you should choose not to reinvest your profits in the purchase of another home. This is not a one-time option! You are allowed to sell once every two years and still avoid the capital gains tax on your profit.

The new law applies to people of all ages. You may be among the many empty nesters that planned to wait until they were 55 to move out of their large, expensive homes into a smaller one. Or, your current home may have gone up in value, but you still want to make a small down payment on your next home and keep some spare cash handy. You can now take the profit from the sale of your current home without having to invest it in the purchase of a new one.

Moneysaver

Don't overlook the enormous savings possibilities in the Taxpayer Relief Act of 1997. Previously, if you made $50,000 on the sale of your home and chose not to put your profits into the purchase of your next home, you would forfeit 20 percent, or $10,000 to the IRS. You now would forfeit nothing.

Additionally, faced with the prospect of selling your home and taking a huge hit in taxes, some of you may have felt forced to buy another large, expensive home and invest all your profits in it to avoid this hit. This scenario has been virtually eliminated by the Taxpayer Relief Act. For that matter, if you're a retiree for whom it makes economic sense (to say nothing of spatial sense!) to scale down, you can now buy your smaller home without experiencing tax liabilities.

If you are among the fortunate few who will have a capital gain of more than $500,000 from the sale of your home, you, too, will experience some relief when you sell. Of course, your first $250,000 or $500,000 will come to you tax-free. The percentages for taxing additional capital gains have also changed. Before the passage of the new tax bill, the top capital gains rate for any assets held for more than a year was 28 percent; the top rate is now 20 percent. This change means, in effect, that the taxed portion of your profits greater than $500,000 is reduced by $8,000 for every $100,000 of additional money you realize from the sale of your home.

A new opportunity for first-time buyers

The new tax law contains advantages for first-time homebuyers as well. If you have an Individual Retirement Account (IRA), you may now withdraw money from it tax-free for use as a down payment on a home and the closing costs connected with its purchase. The only stipulation that may impede you from taking advantage of this opportunity is a requirement that you must have held your IRA for a minimum of five years in order to withdraw funds from it without penalty.

For those of you beginning a new IRA this year, the tax- and penalty-free withdrawal feature will not take effect for five years. If you do plan to start a new IRA, you may want to explore the Roth IRA, one of the provisions of the new tax act. The Roth IRA, now available through banks, investment services, and accountants, allows you to withdraw up to $10,000 for a home purchase once you've held the account for five years.

Whether you're buying for the first time (and plan eventually to resell) or you're a veteran homebuyer, the Taxpayer Relief Act of 1997 holds still another major advantage for you. Until now, it was necessary for homeowners to keep careful records of all home improvements so that any expenses could be deducted from the profits realized in the sale of a home. Because the new ceilings on taxable profits are so high, and because these profits can be accessed without tax consequences as often as every two years, there's little need to be so assiduous. For all but a few homeowners, the $500,000 capital gains exclusions virtually eliminate the necessity for home improvement record-keeping.

Just the facts

- If you are among the homebuyers who change jobs or work locations frequently, you should recognize the ways in which home buying is more of a business proposition than a lifetime commitment.

- Study the new loan products that have become available to accommodate the short-term purchases.

- If you can tolerate some risk and will most likely be living in your home for seven years or less, investigate the variety of ARMs available as alternatives to a fixed-rate mortgage.

- Understand how the Taxpayer Relief Act of 1997 has created many new opportunities for buying and selling homes as an investment strategy.

GET THE SCOOP ON...
The horrors and joys of building ▪ How to avoid
the most common mistakes ▪ Getting it right the
first time ▪ What your lender won't tell you
about financing ▪ Picking the best loan for you

The Truth About New Construction

I n Chapter 3, we briefly touched upon the option
of buying a newly constructed house. This chapter is devoted entirely to the subject of new construction. However, our focus will be on building a
home that meets your exact specifications from the
ground up, rather than one that has already been
built. The made-to-order aspect of a custom home
distinguishes it from a home that is prebuilt on the
speculation that it will find a buyer. It is exactly what
you want, not something that is built to someone
else's generic notions of what an individual or a family might need.

Admittedly, we've held back on this subject, but
for good reason: You need to know all your financing
options, how to choose the right realtor for your
needs, and how to negotiate, especially with a custom builder, before you even consider the possibility
of employing someone to build your home according to your own plans and specs.

143

In this chapter, we examine the unique challenges and opportunities that confront you if you decide to build the home that meets your exact needs . . . your dream home, as it were. We've talked to individuals at both ends of the custom-home building experience, from the most despairing to the relatively ecstatic. From their comments, we've compiled a series of constructive lessons on what to avoid as well as what to pursue, should you choose to hire a builder and get the house you've always wanted custom-made for you. We've also outlined the financing options for building a custom house, so that you can choose the one that makes the most sense for you. You'll find tips on how to steer clear of the scams and rip-offs that can victimize the uninformed. By the time you finish this chapter, you'll know whether or not—from not only a financial perspective, but also a personal one—you're ready to take on the awesome responsibility of what could be one of the major projects of your life. And, quite possibly, one of the best.

Spec houses versus custom houses

As already mentioned, there is a world of difference between the spec house and the custom house. Anyone who tells you otherwise is wrong.

A spec house is a house built with the builder's money on the builder's speculation that there will be a buyer—in other words, that there is a market for the house. A spec house can be located in a variety of settings, for example, in an established neighborhood, amidst older homes, or in a previously vacant lot that has become available for sale. Or, a site can become available due to a fire that has virtually destroyed the original home, if the owners of the original home don't want to rebuild on the same spot. Finally, a spec home or homes—even an entire spec neighborhood— might spring up in a previously undeveloped area.

Sometimes, rezoning is involved. In the case of a whole neighborhood of new spec homes, it is likely that a single entity owns the development rights. Often this entity will be a real estate company, but it could also be a developer, group of developers, or a builder or building group. These areas are marked by those perennially pleasing names like Glen, Cove, or Highlands, typically preceded by something that grows (Cedar, Fern, Azalea), babbles (Brook, River), or otherwise appeals to our inherent love of nature (Mountain, Meadow, Eagle). New neighborhoods such as these tend to be marketed aggressively.

From your standpoint as a buyer, zeroing in on a spec house is not really very different from buying any other home that is not new. Despite its pristine condition, it has more in common with a used home than it does with a custom home. As with a used home, you carefully go through it, inside and out, to see what needs to be fixed. However, instead of negotiating repairs with the owner, you meet with the builder and formulate a *punch list* of items needing attention. These might include scratches on paint or wood, dings and nicks, leaky faucet seals, and so forth. Typically, the builder agrees to fix or finish these usually minor items. Then, at closing, instead of signing off on an inspection report, the builder or builder's agent provides you with a builder's standard one-year limited home warranty policy. Finally, assuming that you've worked out a contract and met all loan and inspection provisions, you're a homeowner.

This brief and tidy rundown is not intended to give short shrift to or dismiss spec houses. New homes built on spec have many appealing qualities, the foremost of these being their newness! We simply want to stress that, in contrast to buying a custom home, buying a spec home is in most respects no different from buying any other existing home. Both processes start with picking out something you really like that meets the criteria you've already established as part of your home search. The main difference is that one of your criteria is that your home be new.

Table 7.1 outlines distinguishing features of custom versus spec homes. We hope this table will help you consider whether having the home of your dreams custom-built is a realistic possibility.

Table 7.1. Custom Homes versus Spec Homes	
The Custom Home	**The Spec Home**
Designed and planned by you.	Plans chosen by a builder or your architect/draughtsman on the speculation that someone will want the home.
Built under your supervision, or under the supervision of a contractor or subcontractors you've appointed.	Built by a "spec" builder, typically under his/her occasional supervision.
Built with materials of your choice.	Constructed with builder choice grade materials (to maximize profit by minimizing building expenses).
Usually built on a lot you've picked out and possibly purchased.	Constructed on a builder's lot or by a builder for a land developer and/or real estate company.
Custom home financing available after the home is complete and deemed ready for occupancy.	Ordinary financing available upon review of your plans and specs
Builder warrants work at start of construction.	Builder provides one-year limited home warranty at end of job.

Note: Building a custom home involves establishing a relationship with your builder at the very outset of the project. In contrast, buying a spec home—while it may be just as new as a custom home—involves a less personal association with a builder, whom you usually meet for the first time only when his or her house is complete and ready to sell.

The pros and cons of a tailor-made home

Buying, which actually boils down to building, a custom home is in most respects a more arduous undertaking than buying a used or a spec house. Without a doubt, building your home from scratch comes with its own unique set of challenges.

Conversely, it has its own rewards, too. According to some, building your own home requires a greater degree of knowledge. Most agree that it requires a greater commitment. Make no mistake . . . what it requires more than anything else is a greater degree of patience!

Some ambitious souls design their own custom home, but the vast majority hire an architect or draughtsman to design a home that meets their needs and desires. Some people have very definite ideas about layout, style, and materials; others want recommendations from professionals. Many people choose an architect and/or builder on the basis of completed homes they have seen. Others select a pre-existing design from a book, magazine, or computer. A custom home is, of course, supposedly designed solely for you, but most folks are actually seeking more of a personalized variation than something that is completely and utterly unique in terms of look, materials, floor plan, and so on.

As you move through this chapter, you'll run head-on into a few of the pitfalls associated with having a custom home built. However, you'll also discover the satisfaction that you can derive from starting at the drawing board, finding and transforming the lot that suits your intended home, watching your vision take shape, and finally experiencing how your design concepts in your head and on paper look and feel in real life.

A generally satisfied buyer of a custom home may report that having his or her home designed and built was like a telescoped version of a marriage. There were the usual small irritations and disappointments, but also times of true ecstasy.

 Moneysaver

Customizing an existing home can be far more costly than building a custom home from scratch. Whereas a new custom home builder's profits run around 10 percent, a remodeler's profits tend to be in the 30 to 50 percent range! Also, it is very difficult to recoup the expense of remodeling when you sell your house unless you can wait long enough for the local market to catch up with your renovated home's new value.

Over the years, we've heard many stories from custom home owners . . . some disarmingly frank; most loaded with cautionary tales and suggestions. We've included three very different narratives here as illustrative case studies: "Grudgingly pleased (but $16,500 poorer)," "The contractor from hell," and "The happy young man." In these true stories, you'll find three very different sets of custom homeowners. Read them and ruminate.

Grudgingly pleased (but $16,500 poorer)

Here is the story of George, a physician in Detroit, Michigan, and his wife, Janine, an advertising executive. They ran into some unpleasant surprises and upsets in their quest for a tailor-made home. Perhaps some of the unpleasantness could have been avoided had they shown better judgment.

George begins, "Janine and I like most things about our custom-built home, now that we're finally settled in. But it took us several months to get over the frustration we felt as the process of building it got out of control time-wise and money-wise. Our first mistake was picking out a lot on our own. We bought it with nothing in our hands but an old survey and little in our minds but a vague notion of what we wanted in a house."

Janine continues, "We chose a Home Builder's Association member named Ron who had built a home for a woman we know, right in the area we wanted to build in. This woman reported that she was extremely satisfied with Ron's work."

First, the bad news: What George and Janine didn't know was that Ron owned the lot on which he had built the house for their acquaintance and that he had established a line of credit to build it. Also, their acquaintance selected a house plan that Ron said would fit perfectly on the lot. He gave her a fixed price to build the house, which included a 10-percent profit for his labor. In return, she had to do two things: sign a contract with Ron that included paying $5,000 in nonrefundable earnest money; and get her financing in order for a closing date five months hence.

Watch Out!

When you are looking for a lot to buy and build on, always find out up front if it is connected to a sewer line. Don't ever assume that it already is, or even that it is possible to connect a sewer to the property.

But George and Janine didn't have the same smooth sailing that their acquaintance had. First of all, they learned that the lot they had purchased had not been connected to the city sewer line, which was over 500 feet from the proposed house. Suddenly they needed to set aside $8,000 to connect their house to a sanitary sewer. This was not the only surprise.

Now, the worse news: "Things got worse before they got better," explains George. "We had a local architect draw up plans for our house. But when we brought the plans to Ron, he sympathetically explained that the design we had paid for wouldn't fit inside the 'setback lines.' (Setback lines are imaginary lines that indicate the minimum distance that a residence must be set back, on all sides, from the property lines and the street.) "We discovered that setback lines had never been drawn onto our survey!"

Ron went on to explain that the zoning board would never approve the variance, or exception to these setback codes, to accommodate the floor plan the couple wanted. So it was back to the architect. One week and $2,500 later, George and Janine had a compromise house plan that they could live with. More importantly, the revised plan had a "footprint," as the positioning of the house on the lot is called, that fit within the setbacks.

"As we struggled to stay afloat," Janine observes, "we wondered in horror what else we had failed to anticipate. "Setback lines". . ."variances". . ."footprints". . . they seemed such a total mystery. To Ron's credit," she goes on, "he suggested that he buy the lot from us at that point and proceed to build the house using his own line of credit. He said that we should go ahead and get permanent financing, as our friend had."

"Unfortunately," George interjects, "we took the advice of another friend, who insisted that it would be better for us to keep control of our lot. We applied for a construction loan on the basis of Ron's plans and specs. We then paid Ron on a 'draw' basis as invoices came in for him and his subcontractors' labor and materials."

"Taking out a construction loan was our dumbest decision!" George continues. "Suddenly, Janine and I—both with full-time jobs—had to find time to study itemized invoices . . . balance funds in a special account . . . pay monthly interest on our accumulating construction loan . . . and, as the bills mounted, run over to check the progress of our developing house. As for Ron, he was being paid for his labor as part of his biweekly invoices; he seemed to be in no particular hurry to finish our house, and in fact, it took him nearly eight months rather than the expected five to complete it. Meanwhile, during those extra three months, we paid over $6,000 in construction loan interest!"

> 66 The number one reason people end up getting burned by paying more for their custom home than they should is that they failed to check out the credentials and track record of their builder. 99
>
> —Don Ryan, Custom Home Builder

"We're finally beginning to experience the pleasures of living in a custom home," concedes Janine, "now that we've almost recovered from the emotional and financial stress of building it!"

Where did George and Janine go wrong? First, they went out and purchased their own lot without a survey done by a registered engineer. They didn't even think to check on a sewer line, which ended up costing them $8,000 for the connection. Second, they didn't include setback line restrictions in their instructions to the architect, which cost them another $2,500 for the revised house plans. Third, taking out their own construction loan instead of letting Ron bear the financial burden was foolhardy. Acting as their own building supervisors caused a lot of unnecessary anxiety. Finally, because Ron was not sufficiently motivated to complete the job quickly, they had to pay $6,000 in interest, as well as suffer a three-month delay. As it ended up, George and Janine had to pay a total of $16,500 more than they had expected, for a house different and slightly smaller than the one they had originally hoped to build.

The contractor from hell

Courtney, a registered nurse in Birmingham, Alabama, and her husband, Bob, a CPA, made the mistake of being too trusting. Courtney ignored her gut feeling that something fishy was going on . . . until it was too late.

"For Bob and me," Courtney explains sadly, "building our dream house turned into a nightmare." Bob and Courtney had owned their lot for a few years and had saved enough money to make a down payment on a construction loan. "We also had a great set of plans for our intended home, and our architect walked our lot with us and assured us that our plan would fit perfectly on it." All the couple needed to do was find a builder, and they would be ready to start making their house dreams come true.

"I called several of our friends who had built new homes in order to get recommendations," says Bob. "Every one of them had some complaint or other about their builder! 'So-and-so was sloppy,' or 'So-and-so went way over his bid price.' 'So-and-so took twice as long as he promised to build our house.' Finally, we decided to call the contractor who had inspected our last house and see whether he had any suggestions. 'Terry Steel,' he said without hesitation. 'He just did a big addition on the back of our house, and he did a fabulous job! Do you want me to call him for you?'"

"Two days later," Bob continues, "a big, friendly guy was at our door ready to look at our plans and then ride out with

Courtney and me to walk our lot. He was very excited over the prospect of building our house." Courtney and Bob gave him a set of plans, and he promised to return them in a week along with specs (how much everything would cost, "broken down to the last nail") and a bid. Their architect had already told them approximately how much the house would cost, so they were pleased when the bid came back only a few thousand dollars over his figure. (Terry explained that the difference was because lumber prices had gone up.)

A fixed-price what?

Courtney picks up the story: "Terry presented us with what he called a 'fixed-price contract' for $325,000, which included a 12 percent markup, clearly indicated, for his fee as the general contractor. He told us that he would present us with invoices 'every two weeks or so' as the job progressed. Barring long periods of inclement weather, he assured us that he would be finished with the house in six months. I was about to say that we wanted to look at a few houses he had built and maybe get another estimate or two. But he seemed so nice, eager, and, yes, honest. When Bob jumped in and said, 'Let's do it!' I didn't protest."

The contract was signed. The very next day the couple visited their bank, took out a 180-day note for the amount Terry said it would cost to build the house and made plans to get permanent financing as soon as the house was complete.

Bob continues, "The only thing about which Terry scrupulously stuck to his word was the part about bringing us invoices. He brought them constantly!" The first one came after he'd removed a few trees from the lot and leveled it with a few truckloads of fill dirt. The next one arrived after he poured footings and prepared the mold for the poured concrete foundation. Less than a week later, he brought a third one to pay for the foundation itself and for the subflooring on the main level. In less than three weeks, Terry had been paid more than $50,000!

Moneysaver

When your builder provides you with the specs for your custom home, make absolutely sure that he or she also gives you a schedule for completion of each phase of construction, along with the price for each phase. This way, you can guard against paying for work that is not yet done.

Courtney says quickly, "I started getting worried. I half-jokingly asked Bob if maybe Terry didn't have his own line of credit and had to pay his subcontractors as soon as they completed each task. Bob weakly assured me that it was too soon to worry. I remember him saying, 'at least our house is getting built in a hurry.' But my worry intensified when Terry's wife came by with the fourth invoice, which was for the framing contractor's work. She explained that this money would take us all the way through the 'black-in' stage, which she said was when the house was completely framed and the first layer of insulation was put on the outside."

Terry's wife seemed anxious and uncomfortable. Courtney wrote the check for the framing just to get rid of her. The problems they had only suspected before became all too apparent when she and Bob rode over to the building site the next day and discovered that only the first floor of the house had been framed. Also, from what they could tell, the floor joists were 18 inches apart. Their plans clearly called for 12-inch separations between joists.

"I wanted to kick myself for not following my instincts earlier," Courtney laments. "I should have clearly voiced my misgivings to Bob all along. All we had to do was see our half-framed house that day to figure out what was going on. Good old friendly Terry was using our money to pay subcontractors for other jobs by invoicing us ahead of schedule rather than after a particular job was completed." The couple called their attorney and asked whether they had any recourse. At that point, she explained, there was nothing they could do except refuse to pay the next invoice until they made sure the particular job it specified had been completed.

"Well, we didn't want to wait," continues Courtney. "We called that night and left a message on Terry's answering machine. In an uncharacteristically gruff voice, Bob insisted that when Terry brought us our next invoice, we wanted to go over to the house site with him and make sure that it was completely framed and that every other item on the invoice has been completed. He ended with, 'You won't get another penny from us until we're satisfied that we're getting what we're paying for!'"

The vanishing act

"That's when Terry disappeared," explains Bob, "leaving us with a half-framed house and an inferior floor joist system. Strangely, we were relieved when, a few days after Bob left his message, he called again and was told by that eerie computerized voice that the number had been disconnected. We called our attorney again and told her we had paid a total of $95,000 to a contractor who had now skipped town. She suggested that we get a building appraiser to look at the house and estimate the actual cost of the work that had been done to that point. The estimate was $60,000. We knew right then and there that we'd never recover that $35,000."

As it turned out, no other general contractor was willing to touch a house started by someone else.

Suddenly, Bob and Courtney were their own general contractors, poring over confusing and often contradictory books on how to build one's own house.

It took nearly a year to finally get their house built. Subcontractors are not too quick to respond to private individuals with whom they haven't established a business relationship. (None of the ones Terry Steel had contracted with would even talk to them.) They spent a lot of time on the telephone, begging people to come to the house and do various tasks.

"Of course we couldn't get builder prices on anything," says Bob. "As it turned out, we didn't have the money to finish our house in the way we had intended. We had to eliminate many of the features that would have really personalized it for us. Now here we are, trying to sell what we had planned as our dream home."

The only good news is that the real estate market is pretty good right now. Courtney and Bob should come close to breaking even on their blood, sweat, and tears investment when they find a buyer.

What's to be learned from this painful story? At least three things:

- Even if you get a fixed-price contract, which you should always insist on, make sure that the expenses are itemized.

- Always check your contractor's invoices to make sure that the subcontractors have been paid, before you pay.

- Finally, personally verify that any work you are being billed for has actually been completed.

The happy young man

Our third and final story is of a young man who demonstrates that building a home from scratch is occasionally an enjoyable experience. Lorenzo, an enterprising 30-year-old, runs his own small graphic design company in Tucson, Arizona.

"From what I've heard others say, I was lucky in my home-building experience. I'd always wanted to live in a home I built myself. But I'm no carpenter, so I knew I'd have to settle for planning my dream home while getting someone else to do the actual building. When I had saved enough money to buy the lot I'd always wanted, I went to my local home plan center and really did some research. After a few weeks, I picked out a great design—a New England style, two-story clapboard house that I knew would look terrific on my pretty wooded lot. I copied the plans."

The home design book that Lorenzo used suggested that people call a surveyor after picking out their favorite house plan. So that's what he did. When Lorenzo met the surveyor on his lot, he had with him something called a "plot plan" that

Moneysaver

Architects tend to charge three or four times as much as draughtsmen to draw up a set of house plans. You probably need an architect for an especially large house; but for those of you who have a good idea of the under $1,500,000 home you want to build, a draughtsman will serve your needs as well an architect.

had the setback lines for the lot. He also had a copy of the "covenants, codes, and restrictions" that essentially explained what size and style of house he could build that was consistent with the rest of the neighborhood. The surveyor took the plot plan with him and called back a few days later saying he'd drawn a "footprint" of the house onto the lot.

"He said it fit just fine," says Lorenzo, "but that he would have to change the roofline a bit to conform to neighborhood standards. As it turned out, the small change actually made my house look more attractive."

"The surveyor told me that I didn't need the services of an architect to draw the final plans. He said that a draughtsman could do the job for about one-fourth the price and that a good builder could then review the plans and draw up specs. Finally, the surveyor suggested that I drive around in a few subdivisions, look at new houses I liked, find out who built them, and call a builder whose work I liked. I really appreciated the style and workmanship of a house built by Marcia Johnston."

After easily locating her phone number in the Yellow Pages under "Home Builders," Lorenzo gave her a call to ask whether he could see a few other houses she had built. The next day he was riding around in Marcia's car and dropping in with her to visit some very happy folks who had bought three of her homes. He showed her his plans and asked her whether she was interested in drawing up specs and building it. She was very interested. "Her enthusiasm was contagious," adds Lorenzo.

"About a week later, Marcia called to let me know that she had attached her specs to the draughtsman's plans. She suggested that I go to a local lender, arrange permanent financing, and get an appraisal based on the plans and specs she would provide. 'How much will it cost me for the house?' I asked her. '$193,500,' Marcia replied, 'though if it appraises for less than $193,500 plus the value of the lot, I'll build the house for the lower price.'"

Lorenzo did just as Marcia instructed. He was happy to hear from his mortgage company that he could use the equity in his lot ($38,000) as a down payment and finance the full $193,500 of the build job. The loan officer suggested that he get something called a "construction perm" loan. That way, he would only have one set of closing costs—whereas if he got a regular construction loan immediately and permanent financing when the house was done, he would have two sets of closing costs. Like Marcia, the loan officer said he should go ahead and get an appraisal.

"Marcia certainly knows what she's talking about!" states Lorenzo. "The appraisal came back at $231,500, exactly what I had paid for the lot plus the quote she had given me to build the house. We signed a regular real estate contract, which assigned my lot over to her while she built the house. Marcia explained that by doing things that way, her builder's risk insurance would cover any injuries or unforeseeable acts of nature that could interfere with building the house." The loan officer had already explained to Lorenzo that Marcia could take her draws directly from the mortgage company. Meanwhile, Marcia invited Lorenzo to come visit the job site any time he wanted to.

"In half a year I was in my new home," says Lorenzo, "and I've been pleased with it ever since. Not that there weren't a few hairy moments—like the times I asked for what are called 'change orders' that Marcia said would cost me a few thousand extra dollars. She explained that I would have to redo my entire loan if I was going to make the changes, and that this would cost me more than the change orders were worth. Marcia said that unless I could pay for the changes in cash, she didn't advise doing them. Well, I didn't have the extra cash, and I realize now that the changes were unnecessary anyway."

Given the fact that he didn't have any previous experience or special knowledge when he first went to the home design center to look for house plans, Lorenzo claims he is "fortunate." He says, "I got good advice from the start; I had a thoroughly reliable builder; and now I live in a house that's perfect for me!"

How to get it right (the first time)

You've gotten three insider views of the tribulations and joys of building a custom home. Notice carefully those traits and behaviors that distinguish the one truly happy buyer from the others. What did Lorenzo do differently?

He credits his success to being lucky, and admittedly, Lorenzo was blessed with apparently honorable and bright professionals. But, Lorenzo also did his homework. He researched; he read; he investigated; he paid attention. Too much is at stake to do otherwise when you custom build.

Doing your research and seeking good advice

Certainly the couples in the first two stories had a clearer idea of what they wanted in a home. In addition, they seemed more connected in their communities than Lorenzo. In fact, we could assume that, respectively, George and Janine and Courtney and Bob had more resources for getting their dream home built correctly and within budget than Lorenzo did.

But our third buyer did three things that set him apart and made him a "winner."

- First, he was willing to do the research necessary to get a clear idea of what he wanted in a custom home.
- Second, he placed great value on the quality and reputation of a builder's work, and insisted on seeing it firsthand.
- Third, throughout his entire custom-home experience, he had the good sense to seek out and use expert advice.

Bright Idea

When you enlist a surveyor to walk your lot, insist on getting a topographical survey, called a *topo*, as well as the schematic flat plane drawing of your lot and its setbacks. Topographical maps are readily available for nearly every inch of land in the United States. They should cost you little or nothing.

Notice that before spending a lot of money on an architect, Lorenzo simply found a design plan he liked in a book and copied it. He had the sense to contact a surveyor (someone who would know the topography and setback lines of his lot) and make sure that the house he liked would fit on his lot before spending money to have a draughtsman draw up formal plans (a good tip from the surveyor). Because Lorenzo had a basic plan and a footprint for his house provided by the surveyor, he probably saved a few thousand dollars in architect's fees. Importantly, he sought out direct recommendations from homeowners regarding Marcia's talents as a builder.

Another smart move—permanent financing

Lorenzo did something else that showed his good sense. He got permanent financing on the basis of a fixed contract price before any changes were made to the lot and before the first footing was poured. This move was especially strategic: Because Marcia built the house on a lot she owned, she incurred her own risk of loss. She could only fulfill the contract (and, thus, be fully paid) by completing the house according to the original plans and specs. In addition, she had incentive to complete the buyer's house in a timely fashion because her only way of getting paid was to get her percentage of what she paid her subcontractors.

Meanwhile, the first two stories show the drawbacks, indeed the horrors, of getting a custom home built using the wrong series of steps. Perhaps the most valuable lesson to be learned from these stories is that a pivotal wrong step early on can plunge you into the abyss: Having taken such a step, it is extremely difficult to right it with subsequent steps. Don't let an early mistake precipitate a whole series of them.

Ways to get it wrong

Unfortunately, you can err in many ways when you set out to have a custom home built. Keep this list close for easy reference. It recounts some of the more common mistakes committed by buyers building a custom home.

- Buying a lot without ascertaining that it's close to a sewer line you can tap into or that it percolates for a septic system.

- Buying a lot before having it surveyed, or reviewing an existing survey, with the setback lines drawn onto the survey.

- Going to an architect or draughtsman to have a house plan drawn up before the architect or draughtsman has had a chance to walk your lot, review the setbacks, and study the neighborhood's covenants, codes, and restrictions.

- Not getting an appraisal based on a site review of your lot and an evaluation of your plans and specs.

- Not interviewing several builders, looking at homes already built by those builders, and getting references.

- Not getting permanent financing lined up before you start your home, even if you plan to pay your builder yourself on a draw basis.

 Watch Out!

Don't even think about starting a custom home unless you secure a contract with your builder that has a fixed price for the house plus the lot and a firm completion date. Even if you're experienced, don't pay your builder yourself unless you're close enough to the job site and have enough time to oversee the work regularly.

- Not executing a formal real estate contract with your builder, which establishes a completion date and has a clause outlining the builder's risk.

- Not making sure that your builder has the proper municipal inspections done at every step in the building process: foundation inspection, framing inspection, plumbing rough, electrical rough, plumbing final, and electrical final.

- Not having a copy of your builder's permits.

- Making constant change orders that impcdc the builder's progress or create expenses that exceed the dollar limits of your contract.

Ways to get it right

On the other hand, you can do many right things. Here's an even more important list to keep handy. It recaps the right steps to take as you plan and build your custom home.

- Choose the right lot for your house. Determine that you can get water on and off the lot, establish where the setback lines are, and, if the lot is in a newer subdivision, review the covenants, codes, and restrictions that determine what you can build, including size, material, and minimum distance of your intended home from the others on either side of it.

- Examine your lot with a licensed surveyor who can answer any questions you may have about the setback lines, covenants, codes, and restrictions, and also show you any easements that are designed to accommodate utilities or the needs of adjoining neighbors. Have the surveyor draw a "footprint," or foundation sketch, onto your survey.

- Choose a house plan to which you're committed only after you've carefully studied your lot with the surveyor.

- Check out several potential builders for your home before you choose one you like. Look at what these builders have built before, getting testimonials on your own from a few of their homeowners. Give two or three of these builders a copy of your plans and have them draw up specs for you to compare.

- Check with your local Better Business Bureau to make sure that no complaints have been lodged against any of the builders with whom you may be working.

- Choose a builder who doesn't mind if you visit your building site from time to time to check on the progress of your build job and to ask questions.

- Have the builder "buy back" your lot from you and own it during the time he or she is building your house so that you're not liable for accidents or catastrophes that may occur during the building period.

- Make sure that your builder provides you with a standard one-year home warranty policy that ensures his or her return to your home to make any repairs of flaws you uncover during your first year in your new home.

- Draw up a sales contract with both a fixed price and fixed date on which your home will be completed and you will be ready to close. The standard name for this type of contract is "contract for proposed construction on a builder's lot."

- Perform a walk-through a few days prior to closing to make sure that your home corresponds to all the builder's specs and to review the builder's paid invoices to make sure that, after closing, there will be no unpaid bills or assessments on your home that you might be responsible for paying later.

 Moneysaver

Have all of your design plans and specs worked out before you begin building your custom home. Any changes you make in midstream will not only cost money, but they will significantly slow down the building process.

How are you going to pay for it? (The straight scoop on new construction financing)

As we've already said, the first blunder made in the process of building your custom home can precipitate several more. Watch out for the domino effect. An intelligent sequencing of events is crucial to a smooth process. Before you even begin to consider the custom home option, it is essential that you prequalify yourself for financing. To do this, apply the 28 percent/36 percent formula we outlined in Chapter 4 as a means of determining how much you can afford to borrow. There's no point in picking out a lot and developing a set of house plans unless you're confident that you can afford the lot, as well as a house of the scope you have in mind.

So, you've applied the 28 percent/36 percent formula to determine how much house you can finance/afford. Next, you've found the lot you want, picked out house plans, and determined with a surveyor that your home will fit properly on your lot and comply with the neighborhood covenants, codes, and restrictions. The next step is to have the builder you have decided to use price your home, together with the value of your lot.

After you have a survey, plans, and specs, you're ready to visit your lender. The most important aspect of this visit is to listen carefully. You'll be given a series of options on how to finance your custom home, but perhaps few, if any, opinions about which of the options is best for you. As we review the various financing options, we'll share with you some of the more familiar hazards involved. Your lender will provide you with three basic options.

The personal construction loan

The first option is a personal short-term loan, usually for either 180 days or 90 days, with a one-time renewal option. This loan is a personal line of credit in the form of a note, which indicates

Bright Idea

The more business you do with a particular bank, the closer that bank will come to making the prime rate available to you for a custom home construction loan. Banks pay attention to repeat customers, unlike mortgage lenders, who, as part of a large anonymous group, wouldn't even know if you had borrowed with them before.

your interest rate and requires full repayment within the designated period of time. If you choose this financing option, you'll be serving as the business manager for the building of your home.

To secure such a note, take a copy of your plans and specs to the bank and ask for enough working capital to buy your lot (if you don't own it already) and build your home. Your banker will require that you have already accumulated enough cash for a down payment to hold in reserve until you get permanent financing. If you do own your lot, you can often use your equity in it (the fair market value of the lot minus any existing financing on it) as a substitute for a cash down payment.

Your banker will issue you a line of credit against which you can write checks to your builder (general contractor), who will in turn take out her profit and pay her subcontractors as work on your house progresses. This line of credit cannot exceed the appraised value of your home less the amount of equity you have for the purpose of a down payment.

Interest rates for personal construction loans are usually tied to the prime rate, which is the rate banks charge their best customers. Let's say the current prime rate is 5.5 percent. If you're planning to take out your first construction loan, expect to pay between "prime plus one" (6.5 percent) and "prime plus one and one-half" (7 percent) for the use of the bank's money. The actual amount of interest you end up repaying the bank will be determined by how quickly your builder completes your house.

Four possible drawbacks are connected with this first financing option:

- First, although it's in your best interest (pardon the pun) for your builder to finish your home quickly, it is not necessarily in her best interest. Your builder simply won't be motivated to move as expeditiously as you would want.

- Second, you become your own building supervisor. If you choose this option, be prepared to check invoices regularly, write a lot of checks, balance the figures, and frequently visit the building site. You'll need to review your builder's invoices as soon as she presents them to you in order to make sure that you're staying within your budget. You'll also have to compare each individual item on each invoice to make sure that the specs and materials outlined in your original plans are the ones your builder has used. It takes a lot of time and a certain amount of expertise to visit the building site regularly and make sure not only that your builder is doing the proper job the proper way, but also that the invoices match the work performed and that you're staying within budget.

- Third, you own and are responsible for the lot on which your builder is building. This means that you are incurring the risk if an accident happens to one of her subcontractors, or, for example, if a child happens to wander onto the construction site and suffer an injury.

- Fourth and finally, with this type of loan, you'll end up paying two sets of closing costs. One set is for the bank loan. This will probably include a loan origination fee, which is usually 1 percent of the total amount of the note; an appraisal fee; a closing attorney's fee; a title policy fee; and several other administrative fees. The second set of closing costs is for your permanent financing, which will include all of the previously listed items except the title policy and appraisal fees.

Our opinion of the personal construction loan should be obvious. Unless you're a control fanatic with a lot of time on your hands, it's not your best option. However, if you thrive on

Watch Out!

Even if you enjoy being closely involved in the building process, you're going to feel frustrated and angry whenever your builder underestimates a particular subcontractor's work (be assured that this will happen—more than once) or hasn't made the kind of progress you had hoped for.

control, have the time to visit the job site regularly, and enjoy devotion to detailed paperwork, go for it.

Admittedly, for some people, the feeling of control outweighs the frustrations. But, we have heard far more complaints from people taking out personal construction loans to build their home than from people taking either of the other two loan options we're about to review.

Better luck with the builder loan

In this second financing option, it is your builder rather than you who gets a line of credit from a bank and makes draws when needed to pay subcontractors. But, you can expect to sign on the dotted line as well . . . as an underwriter. Being an underwriter means that if your builder turns out to be a Terry Steel—disappearing into the sunset after spending more than the job entailed—it is your responsibility to pay back the builder's note after you complete the job and put

> **❝**If you're the underwriter [of a builder's construction loan], you're responsible for whatever debt your builder incurs if he or she fails to make payment or defaults.**❞**
>
> —Paul Schabacker, Construction Lender, First Commercial Bank

your permanent financing in place. The builder loan is, on the whole, a better choice for most custom homeowners-to-be than the personal construction loan. Before we examine its benefits, let's address the Terry Steel phenomenon.

You have ways to protect yourself from getting ripped off by a builder like Terry Steel. Make sure that the builder you've chosen has established lines of credit with suppliers and sub-contractors. Ask your builder to show you evidence of these lines and proof that he or she has a record of paying subcontractors in a timely fashion. Many notorious cases abound of builders drawing from one customer's job to pay overrides on another job, or even getting into a financial bind and using a construction loan (one you've underwritten, perhaps?) to pay personal bills. (*Note:* You should also require current proof of liability and workers compensation insurance as well as check the builder's license status with the state contractors license bureau.)

On the other hand, if you have sufficient references for your builder, and if she has a track record of staying within budget and adhering to a timely schedule, then the builder's construction loan may fit your needs well. Why? First, your builder, and not you, will be responsible for paying any closing costs associated with the loan. Second, your builder, and not you, will be paying the monthly interest on the loan. This should be a motivation to keep costs down and ultimately come in with a completed home at or under budget. Third, your builder will be functioning as the businessperson she is most likely trained to be. This businessperson will keep careful records so that you won't have to; pay both herself and the subcontractors; and coordinate the sometimes complicated schedule of which sub-contractors appear on the job site in what order.

The construction perm loan—your best bet?

Unlike the personal construction loan, the construction perm (for *permanent*) loan involves only one closing and, therefore, only one set of closing costs. You apply for permanent financing on the basis of a down payment (usually nonrefundable, because your builder will be customizing your home for you at the outset of construction). You make your loan application with a survey and set of plans, which are in turn appraised the same way that an existing home is appraised to determine its fair market value.

In Chapter 1, we outlined all the steps involved in applying for a mortgage loan. Suffice it to say here that, unlike the personal construction loan and the builder's construction loan, the construction perm loan is a mortgage (a long-term repayment instrument) rather than a bank loan (a short-term loan repaid from proceeds taken from a mortgage that you put into place as soon as your custom home is completed).

When you apply for a mortgage loan to buy an existing home, you usually commit to closing within a period of between 15 and 60 days from the execution date of your sales contract. At the time of the loan application, you lock in an interest rate so that, even if rates should go up from the application day to the time of closing, you're guaranteed the rate quoted to you at the time of application. The shorter the period of time from application to closing, the lower the interest rate you will be quoted.

In the case of the construction perm loan, however, your lender can commit only to a fixed, low interest rate with a built-in means of recouping a loss if rates rise from the time of loan application until the time your house is complete and you begin making regular mortgage payments. Because it will no doubt take between six months and a year to build your custom home, you will be asked to pay points (a form of prepaid interest) at the time of closing to protect your lender from any loss incurred from rising interest rates. By paying points, you lock your interest rate just as other homebuyers do . . . it's just that you have to pay money up front (at your construction perm loan closing) to get this lock.

After you've closed your construction perm loan, your builder will be able to take draws on your loan whenever necessary to build your house, but only after your lender has examined the progress your builder has made. You will pay interest on your builder's accumulating draws until your home is completed. But because you have a contract with your builder that specifies not only the price of your custom home but the completion date as well, your builder will be motivated to complete your home in a timely fashion.

Moneysaver

If interest rates don't go up from the time you close on your construction perm loan to the time your new home is complete, you can apply for at least a partial refund of the points you've paid to protect the lender against rising rates. Some lenders provide this option, called a *float-down option*; none wants to. That's why you'll have to ask about it up front!

When should you choose the construction perm loan over the personal construction loan or the builder's construction loan? Certainly, you should choose the construction perm loan if you're not available regularly to watch your new home come out of the ground or to check invoices. If the building of your custom home is part of a move across state or across the country, you certainly won't be in a position to make draws or to review your builder's draws. The construction perm loan may be the only choice you have!

Additionally, the construction perm loan may be your least expensive option. Even though you will be asked to pay points to fix your interest rate, you will have only one set of closing costs (with the personal construction loan, you'll probably have a 1-percent loan origination fee—that is, 1 percent of your mortgage loan amount—and another loan origination fee at the closing of your permanent financing). Even if you're building in the community where you currently live, if you completely trust your builder, the construction perm loan may be your best option. It will free you from a lot of paperwork but still enable you to visit the building site on a regular basis.

Making the choice that's right for you

We've moved through the three basic new construction financing options, from the one considered to be most risky—the personal construction loan—to the one that's generally the least risky—the construction perm loan. The middle ground is the builder loan. Table 7.2 recaps the main features of each loan option.

Bright Idea!

One of these loans is right for you. If you have doubts, then the least hazardous—the construction perm loan—is probably your best choice.

Table 7.2. The Three Basic Types of New Construction Loans

	Personal Construction Loan	Builder Loan	Construction Perm Loan
Lender	Bank	Bank	Mortgage company or bank (as mortgage broker)
Liable party	You	Your builder, but you underwrite	You
Duration	90–180 days	90–180 days	Long-term (mortgage)
Set-up	Line of credit, you supervise and write checks	Line of credit, builder supervises, writes checks	Builder takes draws, supervises, writes checks
Interest rate	Prime or higher	Prime or higher	Going rate, or fixed—you pay points to protect lender against flux

Just the facts

- Learn the difference between spec and custom homes.
- Familiarize yourself with the classic errors often associated with contracts and contractors.
- Carefully research your lot selection, home design, and means of financing.
- After weighing the advantages and drawbacks of each, choose the financing option that's best for you.

GET THE SCOOP ON...
Real estate in the new millennium ▪ Having
a meaningful agent relationship ▪ What's your
type, anyway? ▪ Who pays? ▪ An agent's
responsibilities

The Lowdown on Real Estate Agents

"Cut out the Middle Man and Save!" We find this slogan on everything from mail-order vitamins to the railroad salvage furniture warehouse. In real estate jargon, the common translation is "For Sale by Owner!" For you as buyer, we could go a step further and add "Ditch the Agent . . . Deal Directly with the Seller and Save!" But will you save? We'll address that question in this chapter.

The new rules governing agents in today's real estate market make it a better climate in which to look for a home, possibly better than when you bought your last one. In the last several years, the emergence of the buyer agency—which we'll explain—has been accompanied by more rigorous standards in the profession. The National Association of Realtors requires agents to take continuing education courses, including a mandatory course in state law. Agents who want to work successfully under the blanket of the law must conduct their business in

171

a legal and ethical fashion. They are mandated to full disclosure. Because of the myriad details an agent must now know to sell a home, a decrease has occurred in the number of agents who sell homes only part-time or occasionally.

The vast majority of home buyers work with a real estate agent . . . before, during, and after their search for a home. Understandably, most people would rather appoint a professional to do the kind of research, legwork, and paperwork typically involved. (Of course, using an agent doesn't mean there won't be any hassles.) However, just as some people prefer to be their own contractor when building a home, some intrepid individuals prefer to buy a house on their own. If you think you're among them, this chapter will help you decide for sure. If you've already decided that you want to purchase a home without out the help of an agent, don't skip this chapter. You'll find much here that is useful to know about the industry and the process.

> 66 Let every eye negotiate for itself And trust no agent. 99
>
> —William Shakespeare, *Much Ado About Nothing*

Our intent in the pages that follow is to give you a fundamental understanding of what an agent is, what an agent does, and how it all relates to you as a homebuyer. We'll discuss how agent-client relationships work in today's real estate market so that you can pick an agent and work comfortably with one, or, if you prefer, work around them. We'll review the way agents get paid and how this affects you. When you finish this chapter, you'll have a good grasp of just how agents fit into the overall picture. You'll get a rundown of the various types of agent-client relationships, the various ways in which an agent should protect your interests, and the three types of agent specialties. At the very least, you'll come away with a clear understanding of what an agent is supposed to do and a sense of what makes a good one.

What is a real estate agent, anyway?

A *real estate agent* is an individual who, after scoring well on a rigorous examination, is licensed in a particular state (no such thing as a national license exists) to sell property for a fee, usually called a *commission*. You may have heard the term *real estate broker* used interchangeably with real estate agent. In fact, a broker is someone who, after practicing as a licensed agent for at least two years, passes the broker's exam, which focuses more heavily on issues of finance. A licensed broker may manage a real estate agency, a capacity in which he or she advises, consults with, and sometimes arbitrates disagreements between agents working under his or her supervision. Virtually every real estate agency has a managing broker. Some brokers, however, prefer to use their additional expertise to enhance their service to their clients, rather than manage the service of others. If the agent you select has his or her broker's license, you should expect especially useful advice on the financial aspects of buying a home.

Exactly who do they represent?

At one time all agents focused on the expectations and demands of the seller. On the buying side as well as the selling side, they would seek the highest purchase price and best terms for the seller, while giving the least possible amount of disclosure—and protection—to the buyer. This seller-oriented approach created a whole layer of subagents, who buyers believed worked for them, but who really worked for the seller. Although absolutely legal, it was confusing at best, duplicitous at worst.

Fortunately, the era of subagency is over. The various state Real Estate Agency and Disclosure guidelines/acts established during the last decade brought equal rights, so to speak, to the buyer. This means in current practice that your agent works exclusively for you and that you can obtain the sort of expert representation that was formerly reserved solely for the seller.

Meanwhile, in all but a few instances, your agent's commission is paid from the seller's proceeds at closing, so that, although your agent will in all likelihood be working exclusively in your best interests, you will not need to pay your agent's commission. In today's market, if you are a purchaser working with an agent, that agent has a legal obligation to represent your interests. This relationship is called *buyer agency*. (Meanwhile, the seller is represented by a *listing agent*, who works for the seller's best interests.)

However, in one instance the buyer agency relationship between you and your agent changes — if you were to buy a home listed by your agent or someone else in your agent's firm. In such an instance, with your written permission, your agent will represent both you and the seller as a *dual agent*, rather than as a buyer agent. A dual agent represents both the buyer's position to the seller and the seller's position to the buyer. Industry protocol dictates that agent and client must formally document their working relationship. The two main types of relationship you can enter into with an agent are a Buyer Exclusive Agency Agreement and a Consensual Dual Agency (see representative samples of these agreements in Appendix C).

If you decide to use an agent, it is a wise (and in most states legally mandated) precaution to sign this Buyer Exclusive Agency Agreement with the agent you've chosen before you begin looking at houses.

If, as just mentioned, you ultimately buy a home listed by your agent or your agent's company, you'll be asked to sign a second and a third form: a change of agency status and something on the order of Consensual Dual Agency Addendum. This latter form authorizes your agent to serve in a *consensual dual agency* capacity. Unlike the Buyer Exclusive Agency Agreement, which establishes an exclusive relationship between you and your agent for a specific period of time, the Consensual Dual Agency Addendum relates only to the specific property you are about to purchase. It pertains only to the role your agent plays

Bright Idea

State and local guidelines determine the type and level of agent service and disclosure. Ask your local Association of Realtors for a copy of its guidelines. Likewise, every state publishes its own license law booklet, which you can order through your state's Real Estate Commission.

in the sale of that particular property. Whether you sign one, two, or three forms, their purpose is to clarify three things:

- For whom is the agent working?
- For how long?
- Who is paying the commission (buyer, seller, or both)?

It is not necessarily a bad thing if you end up buying a home for which your buyer agent is also the listing agent. As Ronald Reagan said, "Trust, but verify!" It is important that you always know whom your agent will be working for in advance of seeing a home.

Ahem! Who's picking up their tab?

If you use a real estate agent, he will be paid a commission for selling you a home. Who actually pays your agent's commission? In most cases, as we have already indicated, the seller of the home pays. (The exception is some For Sale By Owners, which we'll discuss later.) When a real estate agent lists a person's home for sale, he reaches an agreement with that person to be awarded a percentage of the sales price as a commission. Three basic scenarios can occur from that point:

1. The agent can sell the home to his own client, in which case the entire commission would be paid to the agent's company at closing. The agent would be the only agent to receive any proceeds.

2. The agent can sell the home he has listed to the client of another agent in his own firm. A single commission check will be issued, and the firm will in turn pay each agent his

share of the proceeds. (They may not get an equal share, depending on each agent's pre-agreed "split.")

3. Finally—and this is by far the most common occurrence— the agent could sell a home listed with another real estate agency, in which case each real estate agency will receive a check for one-half of the total commission. Each agency will then remit the appropriate portion of its proceeds to the respective agents.

Let's now take a moment to review the preceding scenarios from your point of view if you're using an agent.

Scenario One—Your agent sells you one of his own listings. He would get commission on the selling end and on the listing end. If a home listed by your buyer agent happens to be the home you want, there's no reason not to buy it. Just be aware of the potential for conflict of interest, because your agent will make more money than if the commission has to be shared. However, a reputable agent with even a modicum of concern for his reputation would not try to push a home on you. Often, an agent showing you houses in a particular neighborhood will have listings in that neighborhood, so it's neither unusual nor unethical for him to show them to you. It is always refreshing, however, to hear an agent tell you that she has no vested interest in any home she shows you.

A competent and honest agent will learn more about your taste and preferences with every home you view. This enhanced knowledge allows him to be more selective in his choice of homes for you to view. Like a marksman zeroing in on a bull's eye, he will be able to come closer and closer to what you want

 Watch Out!

Remember always that an agent can exert a subtle influence on the outcome of the home-buying process by ordering the sequence of the houses you see. In other words, he can set you up to fall in love with one of his listings after showing you several so-so houses.

on each successive outing. An agent who fails to zero in is an agent that you should zero out.

Scenario Two—Your agent sells you a home listed by a colleague in his real estate firm. Should this occur, less potential for conflict of interest exists than in the first scenario, although you should recognize that it's not unknown for colleagues to pressure an agent to favor their listings.

Scenario Three—Your agent sells you a home listed with another real estate company. (This is the most likely to occur of the three scenarios.) Obviously, no conflict of interest exists in this scenario.

The agent's portion, or *split*, of the commission comes from the *gross commission*, which is the total amount of commission paid to your agent's company, usually at the closing after all documents are signed. No standard commission split is in place. Each agent contracts with his or her company to be paid a certain percentage of each dollar of gross commission. New agents and agents who don't sell as much tend to get smaller splits (say, 40 to 50 percent of the gross commission), and agents with a good track records usually command the larger splits (in the 60 to 85 percent range—in some cases even higher). Occasionally, the very top producers negotiate a 100-percent split with their company. They, in turn, pay a flat monthly or annual fee to cover administrative costs (office space, computer use, secretarial and copier services, and so on). Technically, a real estate agent is not an employee at all, but an *independent contractor*—in other words, someone who has enlisted the aid of a company to provide services in exchange for fees (what the real estate company gets after paying the agent's split). Regardless of the commission split your agent has arranged, no money changes hands until a sale closes.

Whoops! The seller isn't offering a commission

What about those cases when the seller does not offer a commission to the agent who brings the contract? Although it rarely happens, it could be that the seller only authorizes payment to the listing agent. How will your agent be paid? It could be by you. Read with utmost care the buyer brokerage agreement you sign with your agent. It contains a provision that, in the event that the seller will not pay your agent a commission, you will.

Almost all buyer agency forms you will be asked to sign give you the choice of only looking at properties on which commissions are offered by the listing broker. However, if you do wish to view a property on which commissions are not offered by the listing broker, you will be given the option of agreeing to the provision just mentioned. Notice that it is only an option—you don't have to agree to it. This fee can come out of your own pocket at closing, or you can cover it by adding money to the sales price of what you buy. (A commission check would then be cut to your agent's company at closing.) Again, in the vast majority of instances, the seller will be paying your agent's commission. Your paying it simply won't be an issue. But, be prepared. It may be a good idea to tell your agent that you want to see only property for which the seller has agreed to pay a commission. You also could strike any clause in your buyer broker agreement that might put you in a position of having to pay your agent.

What about the "For Sale By Owner"?

Let's say that you stumble upon an irresistible For Sale By Owner (FSBO, often called a "Fisbo" in the trade) that has all the features you're looking for in a house. If you're working with an agent, should you ditch that agent to save money? This

---

 Watch Out!

Any agreement for representation that you sign with an agent runs for a specified period of time. If you sign one, add a clause stipulating that you may, at your sole discretion, terminate the agreement. If, however, your agent has already successfully negotiated a contract for you, you and your agent should then strike this clause.

is a commonly asked question and a situation that occurs quite often. Granted, you probably can save money by going it on your own. Perhaps the most commonly heard complaint among realtors goes something like this: "I've been working with John Doe for 5 months and showed him more than 50 houses. When I called him yesterday to see more houses, he informed me that he just bought a Fisbo . . . without even consulting with me!" Frankly, that's a risk all realtors take, and even though it can have dire consequences for the realtor, any competent one will accept the risk. Although all realtors would like to bat 1,000 and sell a home to every client who gets in her car, realtor bat- ting averages are more like Major League baseball players' averages. With most Fisbos, the seller does not reduce the asking price by the amount he is sav- ing on agent commission. Rather, the seller usually pads the ask- ing price somewhat in hopes of making a little extra on the sale. You don't have to fall for this scheme. If you're on your own, chances are excellent that a Fisbo seller will accept an offer 5 to 7 percent under the asking price and still feel that he got fair market value for the home.

> ❝O world! world! world! Thus is the poor agent despised. ❞
>
> —William Shakespeare, *Troilus and Cressida*

Which brings up an important question on For Sale By Owner homes: How do you know what the fair market value of a Fisbo is? You may be in a bit of a Catch-22: If you choose to work on your own, you may very well not know the fair market value; yet if you choose to work with an agent, you won't be able to offer a reduced price quite as confidently. You can travel a middle ground, although few people are aware of it. You can hire a real estate agent for a significantly reduced fee, who will do the research, tell you the fair market value, and then help you to pre- pare a contract. An agency relationship has recently come into being expressly for this specific situation, called a *contract agency*

> **Moneysaver**
>
> Most buyer agency agreements ask you to pay a brokerage fee if a seller refuses to do so, but no law requires you to pay one. If you choose not to pay a buyer brokerage fee to your agent, however, do not ask or expect your agent to show you Fisbos. That would be a monumental insult.

or *transaction agency*. If you have been working with an agent all along, you would sign some type of change of agency status form and proceed from there. (Although your agent's commission will probably be reduced, at least he or she will get some commission.) Otherwise, you would hire an agent for this single transaction. This arrangement allows an agent to be a vehicle of information without representing your point of view over the seller's, or vice versa. In other words, the agent is a neutral party. You'll find that most real estate agents will agree to serve as a contract or transaction agent for a few thousand dollars or less.

Here's why. An agent who agrees to be your contract agent is under no obligation to show you property, even the property you want to buy, so they don't have to invest a lot of time showing you homes. Their only obligations are to show you the comparable sales that determine fair market value of the home you want and to fill in the blanks of a standard real estate contract as you instruct. If you want to go this route, you sign a 24-hour contract with the agent that stipulates that your relationship is limited to carrying out these two duties. The contract further stipulates that these duties are connected only with the sale of the home you plan to buy. After you close on the house with the Fisbo seller, you make out a check for the contract agent's fee. (Remember, all real estate agents must place their license with an agency, so the fee must, by law, be paid to the agency, not the agent.)

Choices, choices, choices . . .

Like members of any profession, agents come in every imaginable personality package. Remember, the process of searching for and selecting a home usually takes several weeks. Because it will probably take several more weeks to go from contract signing to closing, it's important to choose an agent with whom you'll enjoy spending time. The house-hunting process is quite intimate. A good agent will go beyond the basics of size and style of a home you want and will ask you about your income and other traditionally confidential matters.

Prequalifying your choice of an agent

After networking and soliciting the advice of friends, you will develop a short list of possible agents. You can begin the prequalification process by eliminating those who do not conform to specific personal preferences. I know a female physician, for example, who insists that her agent be a woman. Another friend refuses to work with any agent who smokes. Next, arrange to interview the finalists. During your interview ask the agent how long he has been in practice and whether he has a particular area of specialization. Assess personal compatibility and gauge how well the agent listens. Verify the agent's knowledge about the areas of town in which you are interested by inquiring about schools, traffic, public services, shopping, and real estate value trends. Determine whether the agent is available to look at homes at times convenient to you. Finally, ask the agent for the names of the last five individuals he represented. Call each of them and inquire about the agent's responsiveness, competence, and ability to organize the search. Draw them out on what it's like to spend time with this agent. Ask whether they would recommend this agent and whether they would use the agent again.

 Bright Idea

Friends' recommendations are tried and true ways to find suitable and trustworthy agents. In fact, the vast majority of successful agents get most of their business from personal referrals.

Should you use a friend?

It's quite possible that you have a friend who is a real estate agent. Because, on average, a metropolitan area with a population of one million will have about 2,000 agents specializing in residential sales, you may in fact have several agent friends vying for your business. Should you choose one of them? It depends. If your friend is new in the real estate business, you may want to pause before enlisting his services. Of course, just because someone is new does not necessarily mean he is incompetent; everyone has to start somewhere. Nearly one-third of all new real estate licensees bail out before the end of their first year. To put the matter bluntly: Do you really want to let a new agent cut his teeth on you?

On the other hand, if you are friends with an individual who is experienced in real estate and whose judgment you respect, you may well find that working with him beats working with a stranger. Just remember that at some point you will be asked to disclose your finances—your income, your partner's income, your debts, and so on—to your agent. Perhaps, it will be necessary to review your credit report as well. Make sure that you will not be uncomfortable sharing and discussing such delicate information with someone you have known in another context. What it boils down to is a matter of preference. Some folks will always prefer going to a friend when they need a doctor, a lawyer, or a real estate agent. Others always feel more comfortable with the neutrality of a stranger.

> **❝** Everyone thinks they can sell real estate. My first year was brutal. I must have written a thousand letters and banged on what seemed like as many doors. I was down to my last $1,000 in savings when I finally made my first sale. **❞**
>
> —Anonymous, Real Estate Agent

You may have two or more friends who are real estate agents. How do you choose between them? Bear in mind that word of

Watch Out!

Never call the number of a name you see on a For Sale sign and ask that agent to meet you at a house. The agent you meet there will most likely have an exclusive agreement with the seller and may not be able to discuss the price or condition of the property. Therefore, you could find yourself in an awkward and annoying situation.

your hunt for a house will get out fast! No sooner will you start seeing houses with one friend than two or three more will call to solicit your business. They may ask you why you chose Friend One over them. When you give an answer, don't expect these friends to be understanding. If you want to avoid all discomfort of this sort, you are, of course, free to work without an agent, or you can choose an experienced stranger as your agent and explain to your agent friends that you wanted to avoid conflict. This tactic could produce a genuine appreciation that you didn't choose one over the rest. On the other hand, it could make all of them mad at you!

Deciding whether to use an agent

As mentioned earlier, although the majority of home buyers choose to work with a real estate agent, there's no law that says you have to. The more you know about how agents work, however, the better equipped you'll be to decide whether or not to use one in your search for a home. At this point, you've been introduced to the various types of agency relationships that are available to you. You've learned about how agents get paid. All

Moneysaver

If you engage the services of a real estate agent, you lower your risk of losing money and/or being the object of a legal action. Unlike you, a private citizen, your agent carries *errors and omissions* insurance to protect him or her against such hazards.

of this background information can help you decide whether or not you want to employ the services of an agent or go solo.

If you're not sure whether to use an agent or not, see how many of the following conditions apply to you.

- You're unprepared to deal all by yourself with mortgage loan officers, home inspectors, appraisers, surveyors, closing attorneys, and others.

- You're unfamiliar with the conditions and conventions of contracts and contract negotiations in the community where you intend to live.

- You don't know whether the homes in the area in which you're interested in buying are fairly priced or what type or size of home you can buy in a particular neighborhood with the amount of funds you have available.

- You're new in town and have no idea about the character of particular neighborhoods, their schools, their cultural activities, or their public services.

- You don't have access to licensed home inspectors.

- You don't know where to go to get the best loans and the best loan processing service.

- You're unfamiliar with the closing process in the state where you'll be buying.

If any of these conditions apply to you, seriously consider using an agent.

Choosing the type that's right

If you've decided to use an agent, you'll soon observe that a wide range of experience and expertise exists among them. You'll want to zero in on the type that's right for you. Here are the major categories of agents out there.

The all-purpose agent

The first type is the all-purpose agent. Like a Renaissance man, this type of agent is knowledgeable on a broad scale. She is not limited to a particular price range of home, or a particular neighborhood. This person knows what's for sale in a wide range of areas and can use a computer to quickly get a great deal of information about any home you might want to see, including a picture. The real estate equivalent of a utility infielder in baseball, she is used to driving all over town to help clients find what they want.

The location specialist

This type is found especially in larger cities, where there are not only more houses and neighborhoods, but also more types of housing, such as condominiums, co-ops, and town homes, as well as single-family, detached dwellings. If you already know which area of town you want to live in and which type of housing you prefer, really grill any prospective agent to determine her level of experience and expertise in that area and type.

The on-site specialist

The flight from inner cities, a good economy, and a phenomenal increase in new home building have helped to create a third type of real estate agent: the on-site specialist. This is an agent who is permitted to sell only in a particular subdivision. She represents one or more home builders who have an exclusive agency agreement with a real estate company. With an on-site agent, you can usually be confident that you'll pay a fair price, because there's relatively little room to negotiate on newly constructed homes. Also, the on-site specialist should know more about the property than anyone else.

Although the all-purpose agent or location specialist can help you find a home in the on-site specialist's subdivision (through a cooperative brokerage agreement), it's rare for an on-site specialist to leave a subdivision to sell you anything else. If you're not fully committed to buying a new home in a particular subdivision, you should work with an all-purpose agent.

The relocation specialist

If you are relocating, this is the single instance in which you should unequivocally use an agent to help you find a home. The exception would be if you don't want to buy a house in your new community until you've lived there several months. However, many corporate transferees prefer to get into a house right away simply because their company will help defray some of the immediate expenses associated with the move. Use a relocation specialist.

This specialist can be found either at a firm that also serves local clients or at a real estate company that deals exclusively in the relocation business. In the former case, large national relocation organizations seek out the most highly regarded real estate companies and establish a network of agents to handle corporate transferees in different communities. The real estate companies pay the relocation firm's referral fees, which come out of agent commissions. It is the responsibility of the real estate company to meet sales quotas established by the relocation organizations. These relocation organizations expedite the sale of properties and instruct corporations on how to offer incentives to transferred employees, such as help with moving expenses, closing costs, and agent commissions.

Most real estate companies provide special training for agents participating in their corporate transfer business. These agents are taught to be sensitive to *relocation trauma*—the sudden transplanting of a family from one community to another. They are expected to know the home-buying customs and considerations in the community you're coming from and to

 Moneysaver

Relocation specialists can save you time, money, and energy in house hunting by obtaining extensive information about your housing needs from your company and its referring agent and then working with you at your point of departure.

explain the transitions you'll need to make to feel comfortable in your new hometown.

If you are among the 20 percent of the home-buying population who experiences a corporate transfer each year, your company should have you screened by a relocation organization and then assigned a relocation specialist in your new community. If you are relocating independent of a company, contact the most reputable real estate firm in the area where you now reside. They can put you in contact with a relocation specialist, and you can proceed from there.

What to expect of your agent

If you use an agent, regardless of how you find him, what type you select, or which kind of agency relationship you enter into, your first order of business before you begin seeing houses is to make sure that your agent plans to work with and for you only. The only way to accomplish this is for you to review and sign a buyer exclusive agency agreement.

After you understand this vital legal relationship with your agent, you can begin to discuss the size and style of the home you want, the character of neighborhood, and the price range in which you will be shopping. A good agent is a good listener. If you describe your ideal as a three-bedroom, two-bath Cape Cod in the $200,000 range in a quiet neighborhood, and your agent shows you a five-bedroom, three-bath English Tudor for $300,000 sitting next to a shopping center, you may want to start your agent search again!

If nothing even approximating your ideal home is on the market, your agent shouldn't waste your time showing you inappropriate properties. It's obnoxious to show you houses above your stated price range, even if you can afford them. If your agent has listened well, and if both the style and location you want is available, you shouldn't have to take any wasted or false steps.

Watch Out!

Most buyer agency agreements are *exclusive agreements*—both you and your agent are obligated to its terms. If you want to discontinue working with your agent, remember to terminate your original agency agreement. Otherwise, you may be obligated to pay a commission to your original agent even if he does-n't sell you a home.

Plugging into the information highway

The Multiple Listing Service (MLS) is a computerized information network. Through MLS, all agents of participating real estate firms make available to agents of other participating firms information on the homes they have listed, including pictures. Participating agents give other agents the opportunity to share any commission on the closing of a sale, usually on a 50/50 split. Any minute of the day, an agent who participates in MLS can *pull* from the online resource via a computer the listings that may suit your needs.

MLS publishes a biweekly or monthly book (depending on the size of your community) with all its listings. However, as agents have become increasingly computer-literate, the book has become a vestige of the real estate past. If your agent depends on the MLS book, he will be relying on information that could be weeks or even months old. If you find yourself riding in your agent's car thumbing through the MLS book and asking whether a home is available, you've found an unprepared agent. If your agent says, "Let's call Fandango Real Estate Company and find out," perhaps you should rethink your choice of agents. A good agent should have an itinerary based on the latest findings of available homes and their current prices. This means using the computer.

What your agent can do for you

As your chosen representative, your agent can, and should, do the following toward your mutual goal of finding you a house:

- Disclose that he is working solely for you in conducting your real estate business. As noted earlier, 10 years ago, you would most likely have been your agent's *customer* (someone to whom someone else is trying to sell something) rather than *client* (someone whose trust is respected and who is entitled to exclusive representation).

- Talk fully about the nature of the real estate market in the community in which you plan to live. This includes whether property in that community is appreciating or depreciating, crime statistics, and quality of schools (test scores, national rankings, and so on).

- Get tax records that show what an owner paid for the house you might buy and when they paid it.

- Compare the cost of the home you are considering buying with the selling price of other, similar homes in the neighborhood and give you an informed opinion of real value.

- Recommend an offering price on the basis of the information derived from the tax records and comparables.

- Discuss with the listing agent and/or seller your concerns over the home you plan to buy.

- Negotiate a contract on your behalf.

- Attend inspections and appraisals as your representative.

- Help move your loan application along.

- Arrange for and attend a closing as your representative.

Now . . . what are you supposed to do?

We've reviewed the various types of agency relationships, the main agent specialties, and the services you should expect from an agent. What demands should you place upon yourself if you use an agent?

First, understand the nature of your agency agreement. After all, it is a contract, and you should become thoroughly familiar with anything to which it obligates you. We've already pointed out that in most instances, a seller will have already agreed, through the listing of their home for sale, that they will pay an agent's fee (commission) to a buyer agent who sells their home. If the house you wish to buy is a For Sale by Owner (FSBO) or a house on which the seller has not agreed to pay a buyer agent's fee, you will be asked to pay a commission to the buyer-broker, the agency for which your agent sells houses.

Second, use your real estate agent as a repository for information about the marketplace in a community. How much of this stored information you will be able to retrieve depends on you to a large extent. Unless you have a clear idea of what you want and need in a home and can communicate your desires and needs effectively, even the most knowledgeable and competent of agents may not be able to help you. So do your homework!

Third, be discriminating! Look at houses with someone who makes you feel comfortable, someone whose honesty, advice, and experience give you peace of mind—someone you would like to see again after you've moved into your home. Don't be afraid to trust your instincts.

Finally, choose an agent whose expertise corresponds to the type of home and location you want and the agency relationship you expect to establish.

In the next chapter, we will discuss further what your agent will expect of you, and vice versa, but specifically during the house-hunting process. Having gotten over that hurdle, you will be ready to head toward the finish line.

As part of your agency agreement, you can expect help from your agent in many areas. (If you're on your own, you'll perhaps need to take more initiative to educate yourself.) If you choose a truly competent agent, then all other aspects of the home-buying process—selecting a mortgage, negotiating a contract, getting your chosen home inspected, and finally, closing the sale—will fall into place. Of course, you should not put blind trust in your agent or shirk your own responsibilities: You are,

Bright Idea

Remember that your agent is a person, too. Be willing to demand that he fulfill his duties, of course. But, also be sure to thank him when he acts professionally, makes extra efforts on your behalf, and gives unusually keen advice.

after all, the one spending the money. If you have a good agent,
however, he won't let you go too far astray.

So, finding a good agent to work with is half the battle. Of
course, the battle doesn't end there. After you've chosen an
agent, you must know how to use that agent to your best advantage as you look at houses and ultimately decide to purchase
one of them. Looking at houses with your agent will be the
focus of our next chapter.

Just the facts

- Enter into the agent relationship that best suits your
  needs—exclusive buyer, dual agent, or transaction agent.

- Always know whom your real estate agent represents, how
  he will get paid, and what it means to you.

- Zero in on the agent specialty that corresponds with the
  type and location of home you plan to buy.

- Expect your real estate agent to help you move through
  the critical steps from contract negotiation to closing.

The Process Begins: Looking for and Getting the Home You Want

GET THE SCOOP ON...
Your agent's responsibilities ▪ Buying locally versus relocating ▪ Getting what you need from
your agent ▪ What you shouldn't forget to do ▪
The right questions to ask

The Search Is On: Looking at Houses with Your Agent

If you have committed to working with a real estate agent, you have entered the most intimate part of your home-buying endeavor. As you look at houses with your agent, you'll be regularly exposed to the work aspect of his or her personality—something even the agent's own family might never see. On occasion, you will see your agent's social self. You, in turn, will be revealing aspects of yourself, some that you may not even know about. In short, you'll be developing a unique relationship that may even continue long after you move into your new home.

In this chapter, we are going to examine the various dynamics of the agent–client relationship. You'll discover in the following pages the essential steps your agent should take in preparing you to look at houses and then guiding you through the sometimes arduous process of looking. We will also outline the various courtesies and considerations you should expect of your agent during the process, and vice versa. Finally, we'll talk about what your agent can and should do for you after you have picked out the home you want to buy.

Expect the best—reject the rest

Remember that you've signed an agreement in which your agent has pledged his or her trust, loyalty, and confidentiality. This pledge calls for a certain ethical standard on your agent's part, but a frank, open personality doesn't hurt either. Your agent will in all likelihood be able to offer opinions on everything from neighborhoods to schools, shopping, driving—even the salient points of local restaurants. She will also inevitably comment on the quality and style of the houses you tour together. After a while, you may form a mental picture of your agent's own home. You will certainly get a sense of her personal life.

Meanwhile, your own personality will come forth in expressions of taste. If you're direct with your agent about the features of the homes you see—about what excites you or turns you off— you'll be giving your agent important signals about your lifestyle that will help focus your mutual search. You may wind up being quite surprised to find out what you really like. As in therapy, you may consequently discover hidden elements in your own personality. Many people end up astonished, but happy, at having bought a house quite different from the one they originally imagined.

> ❝Our agent couldn't keep his mouth shut. He had a lot to say about what he liked and didn't like in the houses we saw but never asked us about what we liked. He couldn't ever narrow anything down, and he simply couldn't listen. We dropped him after a few days of looking and some precious time wasted.❞
>
> —Anonymous, Lexington, KY

Don't think your agent/therapist isn't sizing you up through this whole process of self-revelation. A good agent is always looking for your soft, vulnerable side—the emotional expressions that will signal that a particular home gives you those warm fuzzies. You'll need to be expressive to narrow down your search for a home. You may be openly charmed by the features of a home; just be aware that your agent will try to bring you back to such beguiling moments when trying to get you to commit.

So, as we explore the process of looking at houses with your agent, keep in mind that you are about to enter a very subjective, intense phase in the home-buying process. If it is to be a successful and productive phase for you, it should be characterized by your agent's attentiveness, resourcefulness, and diligence, as well as your own openness and frankness. Quite simply, it will require sharing and understanding from both of you. So, are you ready to bare your soul?

Keeping you tuned in to the market

Your agent will be successful only if she finds the house you want and accompanies you to a closing. As we explained in the last chapter, that's the only way she will get paid. So, it's up to your agent to keep you apprised regularly of houses that come on the market; to mail or fax you printouts and photographs (or, if appropriate, a newcomer package); to give you business cards to leave at open houses when you look on your own; to work around your busy schedule; and to be prompt, diligent, and attentive.

The agent from hell

If you prequalified, screened, and interviewed prospective agents and checked their references as suggested in the previous chapter, it is very unlikely that you have chosen a "bad" agent. Still, it's possible. We've all met people who can breeze through an interview but who fail on the job. Like every other business, in real estate, some agencies are run efficiently, and others are not. Likewise some agents are diligent, perceptive,

Watch Out!

As most of these Agent from Hell items suggest (see Table 9.1), if there's no basis for you to trust your agent, you'll only feel as though you've wasted your time working with her. Ultimately, as you're fed misleading information, you'll feel betrayed.

and know how to close a deal, and others just wing it. Just as in any other business, an individual's length of tenure as a real estate agent is no guarantee of top-notch or keen performance.

Later in this chapter, we'll examine the many ways a good real estate agent can facilitate your home search by starting as a good listener and ending as a shrewd but honest negotiator. First you should learn how to avoid the ugly struggle on the battlefield of bad agents by recognizing the weapons commonly in their arsenal. If, when working with an agent, you detect any one of the following characteristics of the "Agent from Hell" (see Table 9.1), run—don't walk—away before you become part of the walking wounded. Terminate your agency agreement and use your negative experience as a tool for finding someone better equipped to help you.

Table 9.1. Signs of the Agent from Hell

1. Upon first meeting your agent, you realize that he has failed to disclose, in writing, the party for whom he is working. Problems: First, you could wind up later writing a contract with an agent whose primary allegiance is with the seller and, therefore, pay too much for a house; second, your agent could ask you for a commission, even though you had an unwritten understanding that sellers were responsible for any agency commissions paid.

2. Your agent fails to have you sign an agency agreement that specifies who is responsible for agency commissions if you buy a home with the help of that agent. Problem: You'll have no idea for whom your agent is actually working.

3. You have a seemingly fruitful session with your agent in which you spell out both your home needs and what you can afford. A few days pass by, and your agent hasn't called to tell you what's available or set appointments to show you homes. Problem: Your agent has higher priorities than your needs.

4. You explain in great detail the type of home that best meets your needs and how much you plan to pay for what you buy. Your agent shows you homes that are inappropriate or over-priced. Problem: You're burdened with a bad listener who could ultimately waste a great deal of your time.

5. Your agent seems more interested in talking about himself or about extraneous issues than in focusing on your home search. Problem: Your agent's job is to feel out your needs, not to use you to sympathize with his own.

6. You find an ad of a listing in a newspaper, see a yard sign, or discover an entry on a Web site before your agent has found the listing for you. Problem: How do you know that your agent is keeping up with the marketplace if you've found something to look at that he has not?

7. Your agent makes inappropriate remarks of a sexist, racist, or otherwise vulgar nature. Problem: You may be personally offended, and your agent is probably in violation of Equal Opportunity legislation. In any case, this shows overall poor judgment.

8. You've found the home you want and have asked your agent to write a contract on your behalf. Your agent puts you off until another time. Problem: When you're buying a home in a brisk market, you need to seize the first opportunity to write an offer.

9. Your agent fails to prepare a "purchaser's estimated settlement charges" form for you indicating the down payment, closing costs, and mortgage payment you'll be making on the home on which you're writing a contract. Problem: The unpleasant surprises you could experience later, after you've talked to a loan officer, are almost too ugly to contemplate.

10. You've made a written offer and now find that you're waiting an inordinately long period of time for an acceptance or a counteroffer. Problem: Your agent has a responsibility to inform you exactly when he delivered your offer to the seller or the seller's agent and exactly when you should receive a written response. If your agent dawdles, the home you want could get away from you.

11. You've found the house you want and are prepared to write an offer. Your agent says something like: "Gee, that's kind of low. Let me just convey this orally to the seller before we waste anyone's time." Problem: Your agent should be prepared to deliver, in writing, any offer you choose to make and, whatever the offer, has a fiduciary responsibility to disclose all its contents to the seller. How a seller responds should not be a guessing game for your agent.

(continued)

Table 9.1. *(continued)*

12. You've worked out a contract with a seller, and now your agent seems to have disappeared, as if with the intent only of showing up at a closing and collecting a commission check. Problem: Your agent should be prepared to work with you through all the many important phases, including a property inspection and a title search, that take you to the closing table. Consider anything short of such work abandonment. Tell your agent's managing broker that the agent has not earned his or her commission.

On your first outing together, you will probably look at several properties. Your agent should show you a fairly broad range of possibilities, within your specifications, to educate you about the marketplace. So, as soon as you sign your agency agreement, give your agent a schedule of times when it is most convenient for you to house-hunt. A good agent will call you in advance and give you an itinerary and an estimate of how long it will take to complete it.

A sample call from your agent would sound like this: "There are several houses that I want you to see. It should take us about two hours to look at them. I noticed that Thursday afternoons are a good time for you—can we meet at my office at two o'clock?"

When you show up at your agent's office, you'll be given MLS printouts for each house, perhaps some photographs, and maybe a community map with the area around each house highlighted.

From time to time, however, you might get a call like this: "A really special house just came on the market—I think it's going

---

 Watch Out!

Any one of these Agent from Hell behaviors (see Table 9.1) could seriously jeopardize your home purchase. A few of them could even put you in legal hot water. Be prepared to terminate your agency agreement by contacting your agent's managing broker. No matter what your agent has told you, an agency agreement is an employment contract. You are the employer.

to sell quickly. Can you find any time today or tomorrow to go look at it?" Be flexible. A good agent is too focused and too busy to send you on a wild goose chase. Occasionally, you may have to skip lunch and hop in your car to see a house. The reward for your flexibility and responsiveness may be finding the house you've always wanted.

Let your agent make relocating easy

If you don't already live in the town where you'll be buying, expect your agent in that town to mail you a newcomer's package—the larger real estate companies will put together their own, but all banks have them—with maps, a list of schools, restaurants, places of worship, and special features. The agent will also send pictures and printouts of homes that meet your needs, his business cards, and a schedule of times he can devote to you when you come to look.

If you must fly to your new community, think of your agent as a travel guide. Let your guide arrange hotel accommodations. Don't be too shy to ask your agent to pick you up at the airport. Above all, expect your agent's undivided attention after you've arrived.

If you find yourself on your own

Your agent doesn't have to be a control freak to keep your loyalty. It may be that you want to look at houses at a time when he is unavailable. For example, you might find yourself with a free Sunday afternoon when your agent is out of town or holding an open house. You may see a few open house ads in the newspaper and want to have a look.

As we've mentioned, your agent should have given you some business cards to take with you when you're on your own. This will avoid the embarrassment or irritation of other agents soliciting your business when you visit. If you're relocating, however, you should make arrangements with your agent far enough in advance to know that he will be available to you.

Bright Idea

Your agent should be plugged in to the latest timesaving technology. If your agent is out of town, he should be quickly reachable by voice mail. If you find the home you want to buy when your agent is away, you should be able to negotiate a contract by fax. More often, when busy agents are away, they appoint stand-ins to take any pressing calls.

When you're ready to deal

When you are with your agent looking at houses, expect him to have all the tools of the trade, so that when you're ready to make an offer, you can do so immediately. These *tools* include more than just contract forms; they also include a calculator (for figuring closing costs and mortgage payments) and an "Estimated Cash Required to Purchase" form.

Above all else, expect the unexpected when you're with your agent. You might wind up sitting at the kitchen table of the house you want to buy. You have decided you want it so badly that you can't leave. You find yourself writing an offer with your agent. Because the vast majority of sales offers require that you put up earnest money, it's a good idea to have your checkbook with you at all times. Remember, too, that a good agent can tell you whether you can qualify for the loan you'll need and give you a list of mortgage companies and the name of loan officers who will prequalify you for financing at a moment's notice. As we indicated in Chapter 3, however, it is always a good idea to get prequalified before you begin the search process. In short, expect your agent to be responsive, even if it means sticking with you when he had other plans. Don't feel guilty. Your agent will happily accommodate a change of plans if a commission check is on the horizon. It's also incumbent upon you to show some flexibility as well. Don't leave your agent and a possible purchase in the lurch to run off to a hairdresser's appointment. Keep your home-buying priorities in the forefront because chances are good that if you're desperate to own a particular home, some other buyer is desperate as well.

Remember, too, that your agent is sizing you up for the sale the whole time you're together. In the parlance of the real estate business, your agent is closing the sale with you constantly, trying whenever possible to find out your objections and also doing whatever is possible to help you overcome them. If you are indecisive or conflicted about committing, do not be surprised when your agent calls this to your attention. It is perfectly legitimate in light of your waffling that he wants to verify that the possibility of selling you something is real.

Closing questions can run from mild to brutally frank. If you and your agent have established a positive relationship, they may also be imperative. For example, you may find just the right condominium for your needs but object to how high the monthly maintenance fee is. Your agent may respond by explaining that the maintenance fee not only covers care of the common grounds, but also water, cable TV, and use of an elegant clubhouse. You may like everything in a house but the carpet over plywood subflooring and just assume that the cost of installing hardwood floors would be prohibitive. Don't be surprised to find an agent saying that you could buy a comparable house with hardwoods for $15,000 more but have them installed in the home you like for half that cost. A really good agent should know this kind of information.

> **❝**Listen, I'm in the business to feed my family. I don't have the time to drive around uncommitted nebishes who are willing to look at everything and just say 'I know what will be right when I see it.' If a client can't be precise about wants and needs or looks dumbfounded when I ask closing questions, I've got to write them off.**❞**
>
> —Anonymous, Real Estate Agent

Usually, when agents invoke their closing strategies, they have enough knowledge of the marketplace to justify their use. In fact, if they don't use them, they're usually doing you a disservice. As we've indicated, sometimes there's a need for an agent's closing strategy to be very frank and direct. This is typically a function of the particular market in which you are looking. You could find yourself in a situation where the home you want has just come on the market, is a popular style, and is in a location or community that's very much in demand. In the next chapter, we give you negotiating strategies to deal with such a situation, but a good agent can help.

In some parts of the country, housing is in such demand that it's not unusual for a home to come on the market on a particular day and prompt multiple offers by evening, several of them for over list price. Your agent should know enough about supply and demand that if you've picked out the house you want he can: 1) frankly advise you to offer as much as you can afford; 2) prepare you to write a large earnest money check; and 3) be prepared to close on the day the seller wants you to close. Be grateful for such advice. If your agent really knows his marketplace, such a strategy is invoked in the interest of getting you the home you want.

It's because of the issue of supply and demand more than any other that your trust in your agent is essential and that you should be looking for a different agent if you haven't developed it. The brutal truth is that your search may not be as casual as you would like. You may be under job pressure to settle down in a new home before you're completely ready. Or, you may need to compromise on a home to get children enrolled in a school district by a certain time. There's even a greater possibility that you'll want a home that a lot of other people might want as well. In this situation, your agent's sense of the future value of the house you want may be critical to your overall buying strategy. That sense of the future comes from having a firm grasp of trends in the marketplace.

Bright Idea

If you're moving to or within a large city, have your agent provide vacancy rates for condominiums and co-ops. Like the amount of available land in the suburbs, vacancy rates in cities determine housing prices: the lower the rate, the higher the prices.

The matchbox and the mansion

Although market conditions can change rapidly in response to the shape of the economy in general, you should keep a few constants in mind that pertain to the particular location where you will be conducting your home search. Let's say that you find yourself in Scarsdale, New York, looking at an adorable post–World War II three-bedroom, two-bath, 1,600-square-foot bungalow with a list price of $550,000. You're astonished, not only by the price, but by the fact that every other house-hunter in the world seems to be looking at the same house.

Meanwhile, eight miles down the road in the new Glen Oaks subdivision of White Plains, New York, four-bedroom, three-and-one-half bath homes with about 3,000 square feet are selling for about $425,000. All of these houses sell eventually, and they gradually appreciate in value; but when you go inside one of them, you won't feel like you are a bit player in a circus of eager lookers. The house is bigger, better, cheaper . . . and available.

What determines the astronomical difference in price? First, Scarsdale is landlocked. Every available lot has a home on it. You can't get into Scarsdale unless someone moves out. Also, by every imaginable standard, Scarsdale has an excellent school system; nearly 100 percent of high school students attend college, most of them the college of their choice. Finally, the median family income in Scarsdale is well over $100,000. Scarsdalians can pretty much determine whatever they want to charge for their houses. Meanwhile, the very fact that new subdivisions are coming out of the ground in White Plains means that, at least in the near future, there will be a plentiful supply of houses. Because housing prices fall into a larger spectrum of the population's affordability index, more people with families can buy homes in White Plains than in Scarsdale. Precisely because of this fact, the student/teacher ratio in White Plains is higher, and academic standards are, therefore, slightly lower.

> **❝** You know why I can continue to offer these new homes for the same price year after year? Just look at all this land—enough to keep me building another 25 years. As long as I keep absorbing lots at a constant rate and those darned agents don't ask for higher commissions, I can keep my prices pretty much constant. **❞**
>
> —Arthur Howard, Home Builder

Given conditions in White Plains, which is still, after all, a prosperous community, home prices must be kept in line with demand and with the townspeople's median income. Whether you're looking in Scarsdale, White Plains, Hoboken (New Jersey), or wherever, your agent should know about these market conditions and, when you're ready to buy, help you make your decision about what to offer on the basis of these conditions.

Ask not what your agent can do for you, but . . .

What can you do for your agent? Lots of things. Your agent's time and dedication should be reciprocated by you. Together, you can reach a clear understanding of the size, style, and price range of the house you want. We cannot emphasize enough how important it is for you to have a plan. The last thing either you or your agent wants when looking at houses is a disorganized, scattershot approach.

The following are key behaviors you can exhibit to make your agent successful on your behalf:

Bright Idea

As far as your agent is concerned, time is money. Waiting on you when you're late could mean the loss of a listing or another sale. Agents have to punch their own time clock. If they're not selling, they're not getting paid. Be respectful of your agent's time.

Be prompt for appointments

Show up at your agent's office on time. If you're running unavoidably late, call to let your agent know. Assume that your itinerary has been carefully arranged. If you're late for the first house, you may create a chain reaction that can be fixed only with a lot of phone calls and irritation to the respective home-owners. For instance, what if a seller has left home to accommodate your appointment, returns to find your agent's car still in the driveway, and ends up having to drive around and around the block?

Even though neither you nor your agent owes the seller the same legal allegiance you owe one another, you nevertheless want to be courteous. Practically speaking, your promptness may later make the difference between presenting an offer to a responsive seller or an irritated one. Your promptness also affects your agent's calendar. It is probable that when your agent called you with an itinerary and a time frame to complete it, he had other appointments to schedule as well. If you run late, you could end up disturbing not only your own itinerary, but also your agent's entire daily calendar.

If possible, leave the kids behind

In Chapter 3, we discuss the possibly negative impact of bringing your children on house tours. If you make your appointment to see houses far enough in advance, you will be able to choose a time when the kids are in school or otherwise cared for.

Having your children with you when you're house hunting can not only diminish both your own ability to look at homes carefully, but also your agent's. Think about how much your agent might be distracted by the flying french fries and spilled drinks (in his car!) and the bickering. You'll have plenty of time to show your kids the house you buy before you move in. It's not your agent's job to baby sit while you look. You need your agent's total attention. Unless you're the parent of a genuine angel, leave your little angel at home.

Be frank with your agent

On the first day you tour houses, a good agent will probably explain that he has no vested interest in any of the houses you'll see. What this means is that he will not try to convince you to buy any particular house because of monetary gain or commission incentives.

Take this statement as an open invitation to be frank with your agent. Sometimes, it will only take stepping inside the front door for you to decide you don't like a house. If this happens, don't be too shy to say it's time to leave, and why. Your forthrightness will not insult your agent; he will see it as a positive signal. By telling him immediately what you don't like, you help narrow down your search to houses you do like.

Your frankness will be rewarded in another way, as well. As we've said, looking at houses with your agent is the most intimate part of the home-buying process. Your frankness will only stimulate your agent's frankness, and that could save you both time and missteps. You may end up joking over the hideous lava lamp, or orange shag carpet, or the black velvet Elvis on the wall. This can help to put you and your agent on friendlier

 Watch Out!

If your agent's house is on the market, and you want to buy it, what should your agent do? Rescind your buyer agency agreement and suggest that you find another agent to sell it to you. An agent must disclose his license status in any offer to purchase a self-owned property and can act on his own behalf only in such a sale, not yours.

terms and might have the added benefit of making your agent a more committed ally in the negotiating process.

What can you do for yourself?

So much for what you can do for your agent. This is, after all, your prospective house, so don't neglect yourself! Here are some reminders or areas to pay particular attention to. First, assuming that you don't have to take the plunge into buying the first home you look at, Table 9.2 contains a checklist of what you should bring with you when you go house hunting. You'll need most of these items only for the few homes you really like; but for these few, the items are invaluable.

Table 9.2. Essential Equipment for the Home Search

Note: Items 1–7 in this checklist are essential. They may give you enough information to decide in favor of or against a house without having to make a return trip. This is especially crucial if you're visiting a new town and have to return to your old community before your permanent move.

For You to Have:

1. A general list of what you want and need in a house.

2. A notebook in which you can write your general impressions of what you like and dislike about the houses you take seriously.

3. A tape measure or, even better, a sonar measurer (hardware stores sell them for about $30) that you can hold up to walls to get measurements for each room.

4. A cheap camera. It's best to use a Polaroid or digital camera so you can be immediately sure that you have the shots that will be useful to review later.

5. A list of the most essential pieces of furniture you will be moving into your new home. For sofas and refrigerators, make sure that you've written down their width and length.

6. Graph paper so that you can draw these pieces of furniture into the configurations of the rooms where they might ultimately go.

(continued)

Table 9.2. *(continued)*

7. A street map of the community you plan to live in, so you can make sure that the houses you like are close to the conveniences you plan to use on a regular basis.

8. Cash or a credit card, so that if you're looking at homes during a dining period, you can offer to take your agent out for lunch or dinner. (Your agent should eat with you and offer to pay as well, not only out of courtesy, but because he will deduct both meals as a business expense.)

9. A small flashlight so that you can examine nooks and crannies carefully or investigate dark basement foundation walls.

10. A checkbook—just in case you do have to make that sudden plunge to get what you want.

For Your Agent to Have

1. Multiple listing printouts for every home you plan to see.

2. A clean, comfortable automobile, or, if you're looking at condominiums or co-ops in a specific area of a city, cab fare.

3. Showing instructions for every home you'll be seeing, so there is no need to scurry about frantically to find a lock box or hidden key.

4. Business cards.

5. Items 1, 3, 7, 8, and 9, from the buyer's list of necessities.

 Bright Idea

If you are fairly literate technologically, you might want to bring along a digital camera and upload your photographs later for more careful consideration. (A video camera may also be convenient.) Most digital cameras allow you to view the captured photos (small format) immediately and can help you keep track of which house came first (order of photos) or which house had a particular feature. If you rule out a house completely, you can delete its photos. Eventually, you will probably narrow down the pictures on the "chip" to only 2 houses, which then makes the decision easier (we hope!).

Try to remain calm (and realistic)

Today's computer technology and fax machines mean that it's possible to find the home of your dreams, execute a contract, and be approved for a loan all on the same day! You can order an inspection for a day or two later and be ready to close and take possession almost instantly. Perhaps the house you decide on is vacant, and the seller's executor/executrix can show up to close right away. However, a major step is missing from this picture.

No matter how much you've fallen in love with a house, you should take the time to study the best financing plan for you and to write a home inspection contingency into your contract. This contingency enables you to rescind the offer and receive a refund of your earnest money if your inspector finds something wrong with the home you want that is beyond remediation. The time from contract execution to closing doesn't have to be inordinately long, but it should be long enough for you to be on top of everything involved in getting to closing. If you rush too much, you could lose control of the situation, with disastrous consequences. Buyers have sometimes been rushed into committing to a home after a general inspection but before having had the opportunity to evaluate the inspector's written report. In one case, the inspector's on-site, oral evaluation was positive; but a few days later, after the buyer rushed to remove the inspection contingency from her contract, the written evaluation disclosed a soil defect that could later compromise the strength of the home's foundation.

Unless you've procrastinated until a week before your lease runs out to start looking at houses, let the home-buying process play itself out naturally. Otherwise, you might make an impetuous (and possibly dumb) decision.

In any event, chances are pretty good that you'll buy a house that is still occupied. Don't try to force a seller out of a home before he is ready. Although it's true that sellers like to hear

Moneysaver

When a home you like seems overpriced, you can benefit from your agent's research on comparable houses. If this research reveals that the price tag is indeed too high, the comparables will justify your writing an offer for fair market value.

about loan approval and inspection results quickly, they won't like your determination to make them move faster than they expected. It is entirely possible that they still need to find a place to live.

Don't overdo the visits to your future home

Don't drive yourself and everyone else crazy by visiting your prospective home too much. After you've worked out a contract, limit visits intended to show it off to friends and relatives, preferably until you've moved in. If you're dying to show it to Mom, who just flew in from Des Moines, perhaps you can do this at the time of the inspection, when you would be there anyway. Remember, if you show it before it's really yours, you're inviting opinions that may be better left unexpressed. Like the one from your father-in-law, huffy because you didn't let him help choose, who remarks, "How much did you say you were paying for this crackerbox?"

Overcome your shyness

The most important thing you can do for yourself is to look at houses carefully. To do this, you may have to overcome your basic shyness or reluctance to look in a stranger's closet or to flush their toilet. You may have been taught that it's rude to turn on someone's stove, or to open the oven door and smell the pot roast. You may be mortified at the thought of looking in a stranger's refrigerator. Take heart! Keep in mind that the seller wants to sell his house and that it has been left wide-open for scrutiny. So, if it doesn't have tape over it, or a sawed-off shotgun propped against it, go ahead and look inside.

Other things you should find out

Nosiness pays off in other areas. Here are several important questions to ask:

- Where's the fact sheet? (This is usually supplied by the listing agent.) Make sure that there is a fact sheet and that it tells you the age of the roof, the age and type of the appliances and basic systems, and other pertinent information.

- How often has the house been shown? If the answer is a lot, suggest that your agent find out why others haven't made an offer. Do they know something about the house you don't?

- How long has the house been on the market? Although many variables can affect the length of time a house has been on the market, timing means a lot. Maybe the seller is more ready to negotiate now than he was several months ago.

- What are the seller's reasons for selling? If your sellers have their home on the market simply to upgrade or downsize, they may not be in any hurry to sell and may not want to negotiate on price. On the other hand, if they've been transferred or have some other deadline for being elsewhere, they may be eager to negotiate. Knowing their motivations puts you in a more knowledgeable position from which to make an offer.

- What has been improved recently? Try to get a good sense of which elements or features in a home have been renovated or improved. If possible, find out the cost of the

 Bright Idea

Often owners keep lists and receipts for major repairs and items they replaced. If the sellers do not readily make these receipts available to you, then ask your agent to get them. They could provide valuable financial and contact information for the future.

renovations and/or improvements. You'll gain a better sense of what may need to be repaired or upgraded in the future. Also, a continuous pattern of home improvement may indicate that the previous owners took good care of the home.

- How much are the utility bills? The average home's three bills—gas, electricity, and water—can equal one-fourth of your mortgage payment, or more. A bit more insulation or a new plumbing line could cut utility costs significantly.

- What appliances stay? Usually stoves, ovens, and built-in dishwashers remain. Look at the condition of these appliances. Do those staying add material value to the home? Will you have to replace them soon?

- Which comparable sales (commonly referred to as *comparables*) can be used to justify the list price of this house?

Your agent should be able to pull up on her computer information all recent sales of homes that are comparable (in price, approximate number of square feet, neighborhood, and so on). She can tell you the sales price and sales dates of these homes. The critical point here is that your agent should be able to put this information to practical advantage for you. How? By comparing the list price of the home in which you are interested with the average sales price of the comparable homes.

To illustrate, let's say that you are interested in buying 123 Bland Street, which is on the market for $149,900. However, the average list price of the comparables in the area indicate that 123 Bland Street is priced $5,000 too high. Because your agent is working on your behalf as a buyer broker, she can confidently defend your offer of, say, $145,000 with objective data. Conversely, it could be that the house you want is underpriced. In such a case, using data on the comparables, your agent can urge you to make an offer quickly and at nearly the full list price.

Bright Idea

Real estate agents and appraisers closely study the comparable sales of houses to a "subject property" you may be interested in buying. It's through comps that agents determine the prices of the homes they list. If you ask for the comps for a particular home and your agent gives you a blank stare, reconsider with whom you want to work.

I've chosen a house—but did I look at enough?

You may experience a twinge of remorse immediately after picking out the house you want to buy. This usually springs from the question, "How do I know I've seen enough houses to make this decision?" The answer is that there is no answer. You could go on looking forever and make house hunting your profession. The reality for most hunters, however, is that you'll know the house you want. It may be the first house you see, or the thirtieth. (If your agent's been a good listener, there should seldom be that many.) When you arrive, you won't want to leave.

In fact, "love at first sight" has a better chance of defining your reaction to your house than to your significant other! Suddenly, you'll be ready to negotiate an offer. Before you plunge in, read Chapter 10.

Just the facts

- Be sure that your agent makes your house hunt easier and more focused, whether you're buying locally or relocating. Learn how to avoid the Agent from Hell.

- You can help your agent work to your best advantage by being prompt and flexible, and leaving the kids at home.

- As you search for your home, be frank with your agent and overcome your shyness.

- When you find the house you want, find out as much as you can about its condition and background.

# Chapter 10

GET THE SCOOP ON...
Negotiating like a pro ▪ Things you should never
do ▪ Removing the loan contingency ▪ The
inspection contingency

Removing the Barriers: The Art of Negotiating

You've looked and looked—whether with an agent or on your own—and you've found it at last! The home of your choice . . . the home for which you really want to make an offer. Now the suspense begins, as you enter the negotiating stage of the home-buying process. This is the part where you'll confront various contingencies and conditions that you'll need to remove, or have removed, in order to close on the sale of your home.

In this chapter we'll take you through the negotiation of your contract, including coming to terms on price, removal of the financing and inspection contingencies, and agreement on any conditions in the contract. In other words, we'll take you all the way up to the point of closing. Two major steps fall in between negotiating and closing: financing your home and having it professionally inspected. The first of these steps was covered in Chapters 1 and 4 (hopefully, you'll know what kind of financing program is best for you before you or your agent compose an offer); the second is covered in Chapter 11.

As mentioned previously, on the pathway from contract negotiation to closing you will run into contingencies and conditions. Think of them as parts of an obstacle course. As you successfully get around, over, or through each obstacle, you get closer to the finish line: closing and home ownership. This obstacle course has two basic types of components:

- The human players in the real estate game
- The terms and conditions of your contract

Whatever you can learn about these components in advance of writing a contract will help you negotiate with a seller to your best advantage. Before you get out your pen and begin to fill in the blanks of a real estate contract, let's take a good look at the obstacle course. If you know it before you run it, you'll fly over the hurdles with ease.

Playing with the players

A lot of invisible or barely visible people with big appetites are waiting to enter the real estate game as soon as you write an offer on a home. They will gradually take on a palpable form as you move through the steps from contract negotiation to closing. Assuming that you aren't paying in cash, let's introduce all the remaining players, in the order that they'll most likely appear before you: the loan officer and the loan processor. You are not required to have an appraisal; however, it's the only objective way to determine fair market value. See Table 10.1 for a complete list of players.

Table 10.1. The Players and Their Roles

The Players	The Roles
The buyer (you)	To make an offer to the seller to purchase a home—gets the game in motion
The buyer's agent (sometimes called the ("selling agent")	To advise you on what to offer and help you negotiate with the seller to secure the home (if you have one)

The Players	The Roles
The seller	To negotiate with you in response to your offer
The seller's agent (usually called the "listing agent")	To help negotiate a contract on the seller's behalf
The loan officer	To help you secure the best loan for your financial situation
The loan processor	To do the paperwork that puts your loan in place
The home inspector	To determine the overall condition of the home and advise you as to what repairs to request of the seller
The appraiser	To assess the market value of the home you plan to purchase
The surveyor	To make sure that the home falls within property lines and setback lines (unless you buy a condo or co-op)
The title company	To insure your homestead against any liens or claims by past owners of the home you have under contract
The closing attorney (in some states the "settlement" or "escrow" agent)	To close the purchase of the home for you and the sale of it for the seller—in other words, to transfer the deed; also (only if you're buying without an agent) to hold your earnest money check and apply it to your down payment at closing

The spectral seller

In the great majority of cases, you will not have met the seller of the home you plan to buy until after you've negotiated a contract (your agent or the seller's agent will have stood between you and the seller until this point). It may be hard for you to get a feel for the mysterious, invisible person from whom you're buying your house. For many of us, this makes the seller seem larger than life; for some of us, the seller's invisibility makes him the enemy. The most important thing you have to remember about the seller as you negotiate your contract and, later, a repair addendum, is that he wants to sell what you want to buy.

The image of the enemy will serve only to keep your wants and the seller's wants apart.

> 66 Real estate selling is the one game in which the old cliché of the 'win/win situation' truly applies. Buyers and sellers both want to feel good about the price and terms they've negotiated all the way through to the closing. 99
>
> —David Emory, Real Estate Agent

Of course, the seller is your competitor. Each of you is trying to secure the best terms for yourself. This is the game. The fewer illusions you carry into it, the better chance you have of winning. If both you and the seller have real estate agents, their job is in part to deflect and ultimately defuse any suspicions either you or the seller have about each other's motivations or attitudes.

Judge and jury: The loan officer

If you're getting a loan as part of your home purchase, you should have engaged your loan officer as a player very early in the game. It's possible that your being able to purchase a certain home depends not only on the amount of money you borrow, but on the interest rate attached to that money.

Your loan officer many need to advise you against acting quickly on a home if interest rates drive it out of your range of affordability. If your loan officer says it's a good time to buy, however, he may be able to advise you on how much you can actually pay, and in this sense, be the determining player in your march toward a contract. Moreover, when you make an *official* application for a loan—when you've decided which home you're going to buy—your loan officer will probably tell you that

Watch Out!

If you can't close your loan within the lock period, that period automatically expires, and you'll have to renegotiate a new interest rate (although in a time of declining interest rates, this could play to your advantage).

the your interest rate is determined by the length of the *lock* you have on your loan. Fixing a rate for 30 days, say, usually results in an interest rate between one-eighth and one-quarter of a percentage point lower than fixing a rate for 60 days, because the lender is taking a lesser risk on interest rate volatility affecting its capital return on the shorter locked period.

Next to your real estate agent (if you use one), your loan officer will be the most visible player on the field; for it's his job not only to help you buy your home, but also to communicate your progress toward loan approval to the seller or his agent.

Investigation day: The home inspector

We examine all the elements of a good home inspection in Chapter 11. At this point, however, we need to stress the fact that a home inspector is someone you hire to make sure that the home you plan to buy is basically sound or to discourage you from buying it if your future safety and well-being could be compromised. The magnitude of the inspector's role as a player is exemplified by the fact that it puts a contingency in your contract that is removed only when

- You are satisfied with the results of the inspection and want to proceed toward a closing.

- You and the seller agree to repairs the seller will either make or pay for.

- You are dissatisfied with the results of the inspection and decide to withdraw your contract and have your earnest money refunded to you.

Watch Out!

The inspection is the area of the buying process over which you as a purchaser exercise the most control. Some homebuyers allow themselves to be intimidated by the inspection, as if it's *their* house that's being inspected. Always remember that it's the *seller*, who is challenged in an inspection, and not you.

What's it really worth? The appraiser

After you have a contract on a home and make your official application for a mortgage loan, your loan officer will ask you to pay for a credit report (discussed in Chapter 2 and later in this chapter) and an appraisal. The purpose of the appraisal, which usually costs about $350, is to determine fair market value of the home you have under contract.

Lenders perform appraisals to protect their money. What if you should move, need to sell your home, and discover you can't realize sufficient proceeds from its sale to pay off your mortgage? What if you fail to make your mortgage payments, your home goes into foreclosure, and must be sold (literally!) on the courthouse steps? How does the lender know that its funds are safe and will be recouped in the event of material loss? The purpose of the appraisal is to demonstrate to the lender that none of these events will happen by determining

- That there's sufficient value in the home to pay off your mortgage and return your initial equity.

- That there's enough economic stability in the area where you're buying to sustain or increase value over the foreseeable future.

The appraisal also gives you certain implied rights. If the home you plan to buy appraises for *less than* you are paying for it, your lender may not finance the home to the extent you need. This will give you the opportunity either to withdraw your contract and have your earnest money returned (because financing is a contingency in your contract) or to renegotiate your contract with the seller so that your intended home's sales price falls within the limits of your appraisal.

Many people assume that the appraiser acts as an inspector. Nothing could be further from the truth! The tape measure, not the flashlight, is the appraiser's basic tool. He determines fair market value only, and this by the size of the home you plan to buy and the relative stability of the neighborhood in which it's located exclusively.

> **❝**I blew $350 for an appraisal on a house that turned out to have a cracked foundation and a hole in the heat chamber the size of a fist! If I'd thought more about the implications of buying an old house, I would have waited until after the inspection before I committed to paying for an appraisal.**❞**
>
> —Unhappy Homebuyer

Sitting pretty: The survey

If you purchase your home with cash, you do not need to have a survey in order to close. A survey may be a lender's requirement or a title company's requirement meant to demonstrate that your intended home sits within the boundary lines and, more specifically, the setback lines, of the lot. A survey also shows any encroachments or easements that might devalue the property or cause you to have to enter legal action sometime after buying your home. Your lender may need to know in advance whether your mortgage, equity position, or both, could be compromised by such things as shared driveways, easements that allow utilities to be run above or underneath your property, or an imposition of something from a neighboring property (a fence, for example, or a retaining wall) onto your own.

Even if you buy with cash, you should still consider having a survey performed, because this is the only way you'll know for

Moneysaver

Within the last few years, many lenders have accepted surveys as old as five or six years on an existing home. Surveys typically cost between $200 and $600. If you can get an acceptable survey from a seller, you could save as much as 10 to 15 percent in closing costs!

sure that your lot is not compromised in some manner. Moreover, a survey may be your only way of knowing your intended home occupies the lot the seller says it occupies.

Entitled to what? Title insurance

Having title insurance is mandatory when you purchase a home. The basic purpose of title insurance is threefold:

- It protects you against any liens or encumbrances that may have been placed on the property you are buying due to actions of (or actions against) any previous owner. This protection applies not only to the purchase of an existing home, but also to a new spec or custom home, in the sense that the builder is the owner, and in that capacity, may have unpaid bills or disputes with subcontractors.

- It recites the legal description of the property you're buying, including any easements or encroachments that may have shown up on the survey. Importantly, it insures you against any legal action taken by a neighbor because of such easements or encroachments.

- Your title insurance policy generates your deed, which specifies the type of ownership you have chosen.

In Chapter 12, we examine title insurance from top to bottom. You'll discover exactly what kind of protection it provides and how that protection differs from the protection afforded you by your hazard insurance policy.

Lawyers, lawyers everywhere

As in most other acts with legal consequences, buying a home puts one or more attorneys in play. Title insurance companies are often owned, and invariably supervised, by attorneys. An attorney must verify the accuracy of the legal description on the survey of the home you plan to buy and make sure that you can take title in the manner indicated on the contract. An attorney is also the "settlement agent" or "escrow agent" who directs the closing on your home. Note that an escrow agent in states such as California is not an attorney and as such is prohibited from giving legal or other transaction-related advice such as how to hold title.

If you are getting a loan, the closing attorney will ask you and the seller to sign a statement explaining that he represents the lender at closing and, therefore, cannot take sides in a dispute between you and the seller. If you buy with cash, the closing attorney's responsibility is to close the sale according to the terms of the contract. Because a cash closing tends to be much quicker and simpler than a financed-sale closing, the closing attorney usually charges less for his services.

Terms of confusion

After you've found the home you want, you should be ready to write an *offer*. Because the form you'll be writing the offer on is called a contract, you may experience some confusion. An offer is a formal, written proposal from you to the seller expressing what you're willing to pay for the home and the terms under which you'll buy it. Terms usually include the following:

- The amount of earnest money you agree to put up to secure the property (this money ultimately becomes part of your down payment) and how you will finance the purchase.
- How you will be taking "title" to the property.
- When you plan to close and move in ("take possession").

- How you'll have the property inspected as well as the length of time in which this must be performed.

- Which appliances, light fixtures, window treatments, and items of furniture, if any, remain with the home.

- If you have an agent, who pays the commission and how much (in California, the buyer usually does not see the amount in the contract).

- Who closes the sale and who the closing or settlement agent will represent.

- Who provides title or pest control (termite) services?

A contract is a fully executed document (that is, signed by all buyers and sellers) in which agreement has been reached on price and all terms. It is usually the same form as the offer, only amended as appropriate to show resolution of the terms and conditions.

If you're working with an agent who represents you, don't hesitate to review the market analysis of comparable sales, as we discussed previously, to help you determine an offering price. If you're buying without an agent, you may want to get an appraisal performed so that you know whether or not the seller's asking price is reasonable. Because the Multiple Listing System has gone public, even if you're buying a Fisbo, you should be able to generate enough closed sales from your computer, including price and square footage, to determine a reasonable offer. It's a good idea to decide the maximum amount you'll pay for your new home in advance. This will help you and your agent set realistic goals and expectations.

 Bright Idea

The offer you write will include not only terms governing you as buyer, but also terms applying to the seller. The two most important of these are the seller's commitment to deliver clear title to the property and to keep sufficient hazard insurance on the property to cover all risk of loss through closing. Chapter 12 examines title policies and hazard insurance in detail.

Things you shouldn't do

First, do not think of the terms as secondary to the price. Often such issues as the condition of the home, when you can close and move in, which appliances remain, and how you'll be permitted to take title will determine whether or not you'll complete your purchase. For example, if your inspector discovers unsatisfactory conditions that either cannot be fixed or that the seller refuses to fix, you may want to withdraw your contract and get your earnest money back.

For another example, you may need to move into your new home on a particular date that the sellers can't accommodate. In fact, it is not uncommon for a contract to expire because the issue of possession—the day you must actually move into the home you're trying to buy—can't be resolved to either your or the seller's satisfaction. For this reason, we advise you to be flexible about the possession issue. You may need to close on a certain date to take advantage of a good lock on your interest rate, but the seller might need additional time to give you possession. It's pretty normal in the real estate industry to give a seller four days to a week between closing and possession (after all, what if a seller is packed up and ready to leave the day before closing only to discover that, for some unavoidable reason, you can't close?). But occasionally, even longer periods of time might be needed between closing and possession, especially if you have a place to live until you take possession, but the seller would be homeless if you took possession too soon. In such an instance, your agent can prepare an *occupancy agreement* for you stating the financial terms under which you'll allow the seller to remain in the home you will soon be owning for a clearly specified period of time.

Another possible impediment to buying or negotiating the sale of any property is a problem with gaining clear title to it. You might wind up purchasing a home in bankruptcy or one with some other "cloud" on the title and discover that your request for a "general warranty deed" showing your intended

Watch Out!

If you try to buy a house with any kind of cloud on the title, your agent can be a big help. Your agent is trained to read a title policy correctly and can alert you to any hurdles to taking clear title at closing. Occasionally, obtaining clear title is impossible. This is not something you want to find out at the closing table!

home to be "free of all liens and encumbrances" cannot be filled. It's actually possible for a bankrupt seller to retain a one-year "right of redemption."

Second, don't expect your agent to know a seller's motivation for selling or to second-guess the seller's decision to make a counteroffer with which you're unhappy. And, don't theorize on the seller's motivations yourself. You'll simply be letting suspicion cloud your ultimate goal: buying the house on terms agreeable to you.

Do not expect your initial offer to be accepted. This rarely happens. It is equally unusual for your initial offer to be rejected. Most likely you'll receive a counteroffer that may address both price and terms. The offer may go back and forth between you and the seller several times before you reach full agreement (a *contract*).

Key questions you should ask

Before you enter the offer/counteroffer phase of buying a home, you want to be as educated as you possibly can. Knowledge is power. Try to find out as much as you can about the seller's reasons for putting his house on the market. For example, has the seller been transferred to a new community? If so, when must he actually be in that community? Also, has his company helped with moving expenses, agent commissions, or closing costs? The answer to these questions will give you valuable insight into how negotiable the seller is likely to be on timing and price.

In the case of a local move, why is the seller moving? Has the seller found another home to live in? Is the purchase of the seller's new home contingent upon his selling and closing the current home? Is he merely testing the market for interest in his current home in order to determine whether moving to a new one is feasible? Is the school year about to begin? Is the birth of a child imminent? Knowing as much as possible about the seller's mindset, without engaging in paranoiac speculation of the seller's character, will be useful in your negotiations.

If the seller's home is being marketed by a real estate agent, has that agent been realistic in setting a price? Can you get a list of comparable sales that the agent used to set the price? If so, what is the difference between the average list price and the average sales price of the comparable homes? This information, which is readily available on both your and your agent's MLS computer system, could become an especially powerful negotiating tool.

Because of the widespread use of buyer brokerage (discussed in Chapter 8), you can expect your own agent to give honest, thorough answers to these very practical questions. The answers will help you determine how much to offer and perhaps give you some insight into what kind of counteroffer you can expect. If you and your agent both feel that a home is overpriced, you may decide not only to make a low offer but also to have your agent compile a list of comparable sales to submit with it, in order to justify your offer.

 Moneysaver

Another vital question to ask in anticipation of negotiation is: How extensive is the inventory of homes for sale in the community where you intend to buy? This question should let you know whether you're in a buyer's or seller's market. In other words, according to the laws of supply and demand, does the buyer or the seller have the upper hand?

Bright Idea

It may happen that you write an offer on a *corporate* home, that is, a home bought by a relocation company from a transferred employee (to help the employee buy another house). There is no sense in guessing what an impersonal company will take for a house. Offer what you and your agent think the house is worth and then hold the line.

As we've said, it's futile to speculate on a seller's motivations for responding to your offer in a surprising or unexpected way. Mysterious, sometimes unfathomable forces are often at work when people buy and sell houses. However, if you make an offer based on objective information provided by your agent, including the current state of the marketplace, you can negotiate from a position of knowledge.

A knowledgeable approach will be far more productive than speculating (probably misguidedly and with a bit of paranoia) as to why the seller is trying to squeeze you for your last available penny. Negotiating with a hostile attitude rarely produces anything but the seller's resolve to stick to a certain price. Keep in mind that your objective is to get the seller to say yes to an offer or counteroffer you can live with!

The fine art of negotiating

The following scenarios will show you some of the ins and outs of the all-important negotiation process. You might find yourself in a situation similar to one of the first two scenarios. We hope we can help you avoid altogether the third scenario, which deals with buyer's remorse.

"I've gotta have it!"

You've found it! The house of your dreams! However, your agent tells you, or you figure out on your own, that it's the dream house of many other buyers as well. In an area of town where inventory is low and an extremely attractive home comes on the market, it's not uncommon for the seller to look at several offers. What should you do in order to beat the competition? If you can afford to, offer more than list price. If the house you want is in such demand, several offers may be over list price, so you'll need to do something else to distinguish your offer from all the rest: Write a larger-than-customary earnest money check (real estate agents usually recommend that buyers put up between 1 and 2 percent of the sales price as earnest money, although the actual amount is usually determined by the custom in the community where you're buying), and, if you plan to get a mortgage, make sure to provide a *qualification letter.*

A qualification letter is a statement written to you by your lender documenting that you are creditworthy. It indicates that your income will support the debt you will be taking on with the purchase of your new home. It should take your lender only a few minutes to receive your credit report via fax, verify your income from pay stubs, and prepare the letter. The seller may find the qualification letter so reassuring that he may choose to accept your offer over a higher one simply to be certain of a closing.

If you find yourself in this situation, it's also a useful negotiating strategy to make your contract contingent upon the home being appraised for contract price or higher. This may serve not only to distinguish your offer but may give the seller, dazzled by multiple offers, a valuable reality check. In some instances, the sale of a very popular house has fallen through because of an appraisal that comes in under contract price. Usually, this unfortunate turn of events occurs not because the seller's agent exaggerated the home's worth, but because the seller demanded too much money.

"Look at all the For Sale signs!"

From time to time, a single neighborhood, sometimes even a single street, will have numerous homes come on the market at the same time. If all these For Sale signs were the product of a growing crime rate, a decline in the quality of schools or basic services, or an obnoxious neighbor, your agent should tell you as much. However, sometimes there is no reason for all the signs other than the fact that a lot of people happen to be moving at the same time.

If that's the case, you may have stumbled into a rare opportunity to buy below market value. If you pick out a home from a number of possibilities in the same neighborhood, you can have your agent use the glutted marketplace as a rationale for a low offer. If you do make such an offer, you may want to soften the blow somewhat by indicating your willingness to close quickly and by having your agent present a lender's qualification letter along with your offer. The seller might be so relieved to have a quick and certain closing that he will accept your low offer with gratitude.

> ❝I've seen cases where I thought a house was worth, say, $200,000, and it was listed for $200,000. But it sold for $220,000! Why? Because the house had multiple offers on it! As far as the appraisal, I argued that the demand for this house was so intense that its real market value was $220,000.❞
>
> Mike Cordell, Real Estate Appraiser

In this scenario, your negotiating tactics put the burden on the seller's agent to argue on behalf of your contract. A good listing agent would say something along these lines to the seller: "Look, I know this is a low offer, but you can close on the house in two weeks. With this qualification letter, you can be certain that a closing will take place and that you won't have to make another mortgage payment! With all the other houses for sale around here, it could take three or four months to get another offer. Your additional mortgage payments in the meantime could end up costing you more than you'll lose by accepting this offer and closing in 14 days!"

Since much of the persuasion here is left to the seller's agent, you may see your role as potential buyer as less active than in the first scenario. This particular brand of inaction—waiting for the

Bright Idea

The offer to close quickly is a great bargaining chip, even if you don't actually move in for a month or two. First, your first mortgage payment will not be due until at least after closing. Second, as long as you execute an occupancy agreement with the seller, you can count on your house staying in the same shape as when you first saw it.

other person to make the next move—can indicate a position of strength. Playing your cards right often means not saying too much.

"Oh, dear, I'm just not sure . . ."

Which brings us to a phenomenon that is the bane of real estate agents' existence and the cause of many a sale's demise: *buyer's remorse.* Tales abound in all real estate offices about those conflicted buyers who chickened out just as their offer was about to be accepted by the seller. Don't discount your agent's hard work, and your own hard work as well, in getting to the offer-writing stage. Your agent's work involved not only making appointments for you and showing you houses but also a serious consideration of your stated needs and expectations.

Two common brands of buyer's remorse are "Gee, maybe I shouldn't spend so much after all," and "Am I going to like it as much in a year or two?" If you think you're going to experience it, you may want to forgo buying until you feel that you can cope with negotiating.

Sellers and sellers' agents seem to have a sixth sense when it comes to buyer ambivalence. If you show any hesitation, the seller may question the level of your sincerity and your motivation to close. Ultimately, the seller may hold firm on a higher counteroffer than he would even make if you had come into the negotiation showing confidence. So even if you overcome your remorse and proceed with the negotiation, the seed of doubt has been planted. The seller may well have hardened his position, and you may have lost a potentially great deal.

As you think about all the negotiating strategies that can work for you, remember one perpetual truth about sellers: Their risk is typically greater than yours. If you lose a particular house to another buyer, chances are excellent that you'll find one you like even better and be relieved that the first deal fell through. Sellers, on the other hand, upon failing to work out a particular offer, wonder when, or if, they'll ever get another one. Meanwhile, a large part of their economic destiny could be tied into making a sale work. The confidence you demonstrate in negotiations—in showing that you have every intention of closing on a seller's house—may be just the assurance he needs to accept a deal that you will love!

> 66 Who never deeply felt,
> nor clearly willed . . .
> Who hesitate and falter
> life away,
> And lose tomorrow
> the ground won
> today . . . 99
>
> —Matthew Arnold (1822–1888)

Buyer's remorse can occur for several different reasons. It's usually expressed either as, "I guess this just isn't the house we want after all," or "When I look at this mortgage payment, I get sick to my stomach." Regardless of what the remorseful buyer says, the real cause of buyer's remorse is not having your act together. You as a buyer simply have not developed a clear picture of what you want and what you feel comfortable paying before you began shopping.

Assuming that you haven't fallen prey to buyer's remorse and you're ready to proceed with the purchase of your home, if you have a real estate agent, it's that agent's responsibility to represent your interests during the entire offer/counteroffer phase. Your agent will put your requests and demands before the seller or the seller's agent without breaching any responsibilities of duty, obedience, and confidentiality to you.

After you reach full agreement, you'll be "under contract." Don't celebrate too soon. Among the terms you agreed to are two contingencies: conditions under which you can withdraw your contract and receive a full refund of your earnest money. These contingencies are the financing clause and the inspection clause.

Getting your contract to a lender

Getting financing on the home you have chosen is the first contingency you need to address. If you're paying cash for your new home, you may want to skip this section because you won't have a financing contingency in your contract, but don't skip the discussion of financing your home in Chapter 1. There, we show you why there are compelling reasons for taking out a loan on your home sometime after closing, even if you choose to buy with cash.

Here's a typical finance contingency clause:

> "This contract is contingent upon the purchaser obtaining a [type of loan] in the amount of $_____ amortized over a period of ____ years at an interest rate of ___%. Purchaser agrees to apply for said loan immediately."

By now you should have discussed with your agent or your lender the type of financing that best suits your needs. Make your finance contingency as realistic as possible. It's always best to be up-front with a seller. Even if you should change your loan terms later, it's only fair to a seller to let him know how you intend to finance the home. This builds the kind of trust that helps lead to an amicable closing.

If you've hired a real estate agent, one of that person's responsibilities is to communicate regularly with your lender in order to tell the listing agent or seller that you have been pre-qualified from the outset of negotiations and that you are now actively involved in the loan application process. Your agent is the communications link between you and the seller. If you're buying without an agent, make sure that a closing attorney or escrow agent has your earnest money on deposit in anticipation of a closing and tell your lender who that person is! It's illegal in most states for the seller to hold earnest money, either check or cash.

If you fulfill the terms of your contract, your earnest money will be part of your down payment. Your loan officer will need to see acknowledgment that your earnest money has been deposited in an escrow account.

When you visit your loan officer with your contract to purchase, he will explain to you all available loan options and literally customize a loan that matches your financial profile and the length of time you plan to live in your prospective home. If you work with a tax or trust accountant, discuss with that person the investment consequences of your potential purchase as part of an overall estate plan. Whatever you do, take the "estate" part of real estate seriously. It's something to which you'll be holding "title" as part of an investment portfolio reflecting your "real" estate.

Goodbye to fear and trembling

Do not be intimidated by the serious and often stern examination your loan application will be given. Because all but the most unusual of loan applications will require a credit report, examination of income tax returns, and a salary evaluation, many people regard their visit to a loan officer as somewhat like an IRS audit. Some applicants have reported feeling "stripped naked," "put under a microscope," or "outright humiliated" by disclosures that are essential in order to obtain financing. In addition, because they have been told that the purchase of their home may be the largest investment they'll ever make, they sometimes emerge from their visit to a loan officer full of fear and trembling.

Don't let the loan application process leave you with these feelings. Your loan officer has a vested interest in making your mortgage work. Normally, he is paid part of the lender's fees (loan origination fee, processing fees, and so on) that are attached to your loan as closing costs. In addition, the officer must meet a quota of successfully processed loans to earn a base salary.

The loan officer's request for documentation is not meant to suggest that you aren't creditworthy, but to give your loan officer an opportunity to justify your creditworthiness to an outside underwriter. The application process is not a personality test or a moral measure. Think of it as a neutral process designed to give you the best resources for making your home purchase a reality.

Finally, the latest national statistics tell us that first-time home buyers make a down payment that is smaller than the average person pays in cash to purchase a car or pay for a funeral. If you buy when interest rates are fairly low in an area where home prices are stable or moving upward, you should be able to get a handsome return on your initial investment plus the proceeds realized from the reduction of your loan principal when you sell. Therefore, the idea that you will be tied to some insurmountable burden when you buy a house only introduces extraneous emotional issues. Go to your loan officer prepared to learn—not to tremble.

> **❝** I am often amazed at how scared some of my applicants seem to be. I try to reassure them right away by explaining that the only reason I'm here is to help them get the house they want. **❞**
>
> —Tony Robbins, President, A.M. Robbins Mortgage Company

Meeting with your loan officer

As mentioned earlier in this chapter, when you have your formal meeting with your loan officer (the meeting that occurs when you have a fully executed contract in hand), you'll be asked to pay for a credit report and an appraisal. As we discussed in

detail in Chapter 2, you may want to prepare for this meeting by
ordering a personal credit report beforehand. This will allow
you to find any mistakes and prepare to discuss any blemishes.
If you suspect that something negative may come up on your
credit report, tell your loan officer. He may recommend that
you wait to pay for an appraisal—as we've said, a typical
appraisal costs about $350—until your credit passes muster,
your ratios work for the type and amount of loan you'll be getting, and your intended home has passed an inspection. There's
no point withholding any information about your credit history.
Remember, again, that your loan officer wants to provide financing to you.

Before your loan officer can approve you for a loan based on
a home you've already put under contract, she will want to see
the following documentation:

- A copy of your sales contract, signed by all parties
- A residence history of your past two years
- An employment history
- Tax returns—the two previous years' federal tax returns
  and all of your schedules if you're self-employed; a 1099
  employee; employed in a family business; receiving all or
  part of your income from bonuses, commissions, trusts, or
  partnerships; an owner of rental properties; or receiving
  income from nonverifiable sources such as tips or installment sales

Your loan officer will also want to review the following:

- Your checking and savings account numbers (copies of the
  last 2 months of bank statements often help)
- Stocks, bonds, and other investment account information
- Your life insurance policies, to determine face value (via
  statements from the insurer)
- Your IRA/retirement plan accounts, verified by a recent
  statement

- A list of automobiles you own—their make and model and current market value—and evidence of clear title if you own the car(s) free and clear
- Any other assets (that is, personal property)
- Credit information, including, for each account, creditor name, account number, and monthly payment amount and current balance

If you bring all this information with you to your first meeting with your loan officer, it may be your last! He should be able to tell you right away what type of loan package best suits your needs and may provide approval quickly, sometimes within hours! If your credit and your ratios look acceptable, you'll be able to sign a "Truth in Lending" statement and move on to your next big project: getting your new home closed!

The inspection

This is the second contingency in your contract. Some people make the mistake of not having their new home inspected if the seller will only accept an "as is" contract. Even if the seller is unwilling to make repairs, you still want to know what kind of a house you're getting into. In fact, the inspection contingency may be the only way for you to get out of a contract on a house that an inspector looks upon negatively.

In your contract, you will have specified a certain date, usually about 7 to 10 days after execution, by which you'll have your home inspected. The contingency gives you the chance to withdraw your contract if the inspector finds a serious and irreparable condition or any serious condition that the seller refuses to correct. In most cases, you'll wind up negotiating repairs just as you negotiated price. You'll certainly want to ask the seller to repair the defects that concern you the most. Perhaps you can see your way clear to pass on some of the minor ones.

A good inspector should be able to tell you approximately how much repairs will cost and which ones should be performed

Bright Idea

Most inspection clauses in real estate contracts state that it will be the responsibility of the seller to deliver the heating, cooling, plumbing, and electrical systems and any built-in appliances in normal operating condition at the time of closing. But, you'll need to walk through your new home just prior to closing to make sure that the seller has met that responsibility.

before you move in. (See the sample inspection report in Appendix C.) His or her advice should help you ask the seller to make the most important repairs, or at least to fund them. You will then draw up a list in the form of an addendum and go back and forth with the seller until you reach an agreement. The signed addendum will then become part of your contract.

How will you know that the seller has made the repairs he or she agreed to make? In most states, it's customary for you to conduct a walk-through a day or two before closing. At that time, you will also want to make sure that the major systems are operating properly. If the repairs have been extensive, it's a good idea to have your inspector join you during the walk through to make sure they've been done correctly. You should also ask the listing agent or the seller to provide receipts for any work performed as a response to your inspection addendum. If there's a listing agent involved in your purchase, you'll probably be asked to sign a form stating that you're satisfied with the results of the walk-through and are prepared to close as scheduled. If you're dealing directly with a seller, it's a courtesy to let the seller know that you're satisfied and ready to close.

The last hurdle (hang in there!)

After you've removed the loan and inspection contingencies, and you are satisfied that the seller can deliver clear title and has performed all repairs in an acceptable manner, you'll be ready to close. The last hurdle you have to face is making sure that the settlement statement you will sign at closing accords with the terms of your contract:

- That the purchase price is correct
- That your earnest money has been added to your down payment or refunded to you if you're getting 100-percent financing
- That your closing costs line up with what your loan officer told you
- That fees split between you and the seller have been divided correctly
- That property taxes have been prorated accurately

If your loan package has arrived at the settlement agent's office in time, you should have the opportunity to review the settlement statement (called a HUD 1) a day or two before closing. This will give you time to make corrections if there are any errors or to ask your loan officer to clarify anything you find confusing. The settlement statement is a very important document (see Chapter 13 for a further discussion of HUD 1). Understand what's in it before you close. Once you do, you're ready to be a homeowner.

A final thought: Negotiating is a fine art. It's fun to do it with finesse. More importantly, it's gratifying to do it profitably!

Just the facts

- Do not prepare an offer to purchase a home until you know the players involved in turning that offer into a viable contract.
- Know the strategies involved in the process of successfully negotiating an offer into a contract.
- To remove the loan contingency, make a formal application with a mortgage loan officer as soon as possible and inform the seller as soon as you're notified of loan approval.

- To remove the inspection contingency, negotiate what repairs the seller will perform and their cost, just as you negotiated the contract price of the home.

- Review the settlement statement, which itemizes your closing costs, to know exactly what you'll be paying at closing.

Wrapping Up

GET THE SCOOP ON...
The three inspection options ▪ Negotiating
repairs ▪ Inspection? Who needs it? ▪
Who should do the job ▪ The walk-through

The Inspection

S ome of the worst real estate horror stories concern people who failed to get their home inspected. People have died from carbon monoxide emissions that came from uninspected furnaces in recently purchased homes. Others have experienced the collapse of inadequately supported roofs or fires that started in faulty fuse boxes or breaker boxes. The list goes on. Presumably, you will have spent a fair amount of time in the home you decide to buy before you actually move in. But, if you're like most buyers, you will spend the majority of that time convincing yourself that you want the home and not considering whether or not the home has defects.

You may have overlooked those dings, nicks, and other charming features that make a house a home. You may have entirely missed the slanted door frames, cracks in the marble hearth of the fireplace, and creaks in the floors. You may have missed any number of things that could compromise your personal safety or empty your pocketbook as you listened to the sellers describe their love for the home and how assiduously they have maintained it. Meanwhile, your real estate agent, glowing over a possible sale, might have complimented your excellent taste or marveled at the house's charm, all the while helping you place furniture. A seller or a listing agent may be busy telling you about all the wonderful improvements the seller has recently made, claiming that your home-to-be is in "absolutely mint condition." Your own excitement, fueled by the enthusiasm of those around you, may prompt you to pass on the idea of an inspection. This would be a terrible mistake.

> 66 Don't view me with a critic's eye, but pass my imperfections by. 99
>
> —David Everett, New Ipswich, NH, 1791

In truth, it's hard to imagine a circumstance in which a competent real estate agent would not allow you *not* to have the house you're about to buy inspected. But, we don't want you to find out otherwise! So in this chapter, we focus on all aspects of the inspection of your desired home, from why you should have one, to what your choices are, to how you choose an inspector. In short, we'll review everything you need to know about this critical component in your home-buying experience.

What are my inspection options?

If you're buying without the services of a real estate agent, chances are that the contract you write will not have special language regarding an inspection. If this is the case, we urge you to select one of the inspection clauses we're about to review and put it into the contract. If you buy with a real estate agent,

 Watch Out!

Most sellers who are not represented by real estate agents hate to hear about inspection clauses and fear the idea of an inspection itself. If you come across a FSBO seller who refuses to allow her house to be inspected, walk away from the house and don't come back!

however, your contract will have specific clauses containing various inspection options. That's because agency contracts also have disclaimers that you'll be asked to initial. Here is a typically worded disclaimer from an agency contract:

> Seller and purchaser acknowledge that they have not relied upon the advice or representations of a broker or broker's associated salesperson relative to the structural condition of the property, including condition of the roof and basement; construction materials; the nature and operating condition of the electrical, heating, air-conditioning, plumbing, water heating systems and appliances.

Essentially this disclaimer means that your agent has made no claims about the condition of the property you've bought and cannot be held accountable for any defects revealed during an inspection or discovered after you've moved into your home. If you initial such a disclaimer without having your home inspected, you're hanging out on a limb (over a cliff and in a very high wind, we might add). In short, you're without recourse if something is wrong with the property you've just bought.

Let's look at the three most common inspection clauses, or options, in agency-produced contracts. Again, if you're buying on your own and use a contract form without an inspection clause, be sure that you write one of them in.

The "as is" option

The first of the three possible inspection clauses that you may be presented with states that you'll buy your home in "as is" condition. It typically reads like this:

> The seller shall not be required to make any repairs to the property whatsoever under this contract. The purchaser has inspected the property, either personally or through others of the purchaser's choosing, and accepts the property in its present, 'as is' condition, including wear and tear to the closing.

If the sellers have already disclosed that they have no intention of making or paying for any repairs, you might be tempted
to initial this clause. You would be amazed at how many buyers
do this unwittingly. Don't do it, unless by some chance you've
already had an inspection done. (It's very rare that you would
have an opportunity to get a home inspected prior to executing
a contract.) That's why we call the inspection a *contingency*:
You're not required to close on an already executed contract
unless you're satisfied with the results of the inspection.

You may, in fact, find yourself buying a home in "as is" condition: some sellers will give you no choice. Assuming that you
haven't had an inspection done prior to executing the contract,
if you do initial this clause, you're essentially saying that you've
decided not to get your home inspected: that either you're comfortable with things as they are or you would prefer to save
the few hundred dollars that an inspection costs. You've put
yourself in a *caveat emptor* (buyer beware!) situation: If you're
approved for your loan and the seller can deliver clear title, you
may have just taken on what could turn out to be the biggest
financial and safety risk of your life. If a seller refuses to make
repairs, but your inspection reveals conditions unsatisfactory to
you or capable of putting your health and safety at risk, you have
every right to cancel your contract even if you've bought a home
"as is." Once again, however, if you actually sign an "as is" clause
that *waives* your right to an inspection, you're stuck with what
you get and have no legal recourse with which to back out.

The middle ground

The second inspection clause is far better than the first and can
be adequate in certain circumstances. In the rare case that you
have had the home you want inspected prior to executing a
sales contract, which does happen in a small minority of communities, you are requesting that the seller make and/or pay for

Bright Idea

As we've already discussed, it's up to you to do a walk-through immediately prior to closing to make sure that the major systems are in normal operating condition. If you simply take the seller's word that the systems are okay, you have no recourse if they're not. If you initial the third clause you can have your inspector attend the walk-through with you.

certain repairs, which you then itemize on an addendum. The typical second clause reads like this:

Purchaser has inspected the property, either personally or through others of purchaser's choosing, and, without relying on any representation or warranty from seller or broker or any salesperson or any written description of the property, accepts the property in its present 'as is' condition, including ordinary wear and tear to closing, except that seller agrees (subject to any dollar limits below) to 1) make any repairs required by the lending institution; 2) deliver the heating, cooling, plumbing, and electrical systems, and any built-in appliances in normal operating condition at the time of closing; and 3) perform the following: _____.
Repairs required of seller under this paragraph shall not exceed $_____.

If you have made your inspection into a vehicle for negotiating a contract, this clause could have its advantages. As a courtesy to the seller, it establishes a ceiling of how much she might be expected to pay for repairs. If by some rare chance your lender's appraiser does find something needing repair, the seller has agreed to perform that repair. Finally, unlike in the first clause, here the seller agrees to deliver the major systems in "normal operating condition" at the time of closing.

The most protective option

The third inspection clause option is the only real, comprehensive contingency clause among the three. This is because you've already executed a contract, and now you're going to have your home inspected:

Purchaser requires additional inspections of the property at purchaser's expense. Promptly after seller's acceptance of this contract, purchaser shall either personally, or through others of purchaser's choosing, inspect and investigate the property. If such inspections reveal conditions unsatisfactory to the purchaser ('defects'), purchaser may, at purchaser's option, 1) terminate this contract; or 2) request seller to correct the defects. Purchaser shall exercise this option by written notice to seller on or before _____, which notice shall specify the defects seller is asked to repair or that caused purchaser to elect to terminate this contract. If purchaser elects to terminate this contract, seller shall promptly refund the earnest money. If purchaser requests seller to correct the defects, seller shall notify purchaser within ____ days of receipt of such request whether seller will correct the defects. If seller elects not to correct the defects, purchaser shall notify seller by written notice, within ____ hours of receipt of seller's refusal to correct the defects, that purchaser elects to terminate this contract or waive the defects and proceed to close the sale. Purchaser's failure to notify seller of any such defects or to terminate this contract shall conclusively be deemed acceptance of the property 'as is.'

In most agency-generated contracts, there's a very important second part to this clause, which says something like:

In addition to any repairs agreed to by seller and purchaser, seller agrees to make any repairs required by the lending institution and deliver the heating, cooling, plumbing, and electrical systems, and any built-in appliances, in normal operating condition at the time of closing.

Apropos of the previous clause, "repairs required by the lending institution" would actually be based on written recommendations from an appraiser. However, such recommendations are rarely made, except in the case of older homes in serious disrepair, when the purchaser's quality of life might be adversely affected. It is precisely because an appraiser's recommendations for repairs are so unusual that we so strongly endorse the inspection process.

What's in clause three for me?

There are several issues involved in the lengthy, rather complicated third clause that we've cited. First, if your inspector does find defects, you must notify the seller in writing with a request to repair them or pay to repair them, or you must void your contract by a certain date and time. If you fail to respond by that date, it will be assumed that you're buying your home "as is." Do not fail to respond!

The virtues of this clause are:

- If your inspector finds irreparable defects, you can withdraw your contract and receive a full refund of your earnest money.

- If the seller refuses to correct all or even some of the defects, you can also withdraw from the contract.

- You can negotiate repairs. The most common approach is for you to draw up and present to the seller an addendum to your contract, based on your inspector's written report, stipulating repairs you want the seller to make or simply to pay for. Let's say that you write an addendum with 10 repair items and the seller elects to fix or pay for seven of them. You still have the opportunity to accept the seller's counteroffer, make your own counteroffer, or withdraw. However, in the

> 66 I can't tell you how many times home buyers have showed up as I was appraising the house they're about to close on and ask me if I was the inspector. If there's one thing I wish buyers would understand, it's the limits on what I do. 99
>
> —Carol Zanaty, Real Estate Appraiser

great majority of cases, the third clause ultimately produces a written, executed agreement, typically including the seller's acquiescence in making or paying for the repairs you find most important, and you've removed a barrier as you move further on your way toward closing.

Even though it's by far the most stringent, sellers tend to like this latter clause the best. If you've had a full inspection, the seller is relieved of the specter of litigation down the road. Moreover, the inspector might uncover a defect the seller was unaware of. For example, it's rather common for inspections of older homes, especially those with forced-air gas furnaces, to discover pits or holes in the flue pipe leading from the furnace to the chimney, from which the effluvia from heated air escapes. These pits or holes allow carbon monoxide to escape from the flue pipe into the house because of incomplete discharge. Most sellers who plan to stay in their homes for a few weeks or more after the inspection would *want* to correct this defect on their own, if only to protect their personal safety during this relatively short period. If you close *without* an inspection and later discover a defect, you're entirely without recourse to anything but your own foolishness.

Finally, you should always check to make sure that the repairs you've requested have been done by the seller. If you don't trust that the seller will do the repairs satisfactorily, or if you have your own contractors whom you would prefer to make the repairs and have consulted with them about how much these repairs will cost, you may want to reach a cash settlement. As an alternative, you could ask your inspector the approximate cost of the needed repairs. Then you can request that the seller either reduce the contract price accordingly or provide cash at closing for these repairs. (We prefer the latter; all too often, buyers that ask that their new home's purchase price be reduced to account for needed repairs never perform these repairs, because they don't have the cash in hand to do so.)

Who needs an inspection?

In a word, everyone. If you're buying an older home—in fact, any home that someone else has lived in—it's bound to have defects. Perhaps the 50-year-old cottage you've fallen in love with has had the central heat and air-conditioning systems replaced. How do you know they were installed properly? Or, that the roof decking adequately supports the three layers of shingles that have been placed on it over the years? Perhaps the light fixtures are operating properly. How do you know that the old-fashioned fuse box that runs the electrical system hasn't been double-lugged to accommodate new appliances? You could move in, plug in your computer, and start a fire!

Don't give safety short shrift

Is that slanted door frame just a charming feature of an older home? Or, has the main girder supporting the home been hollowed out by termites, causing the flooring system to weaken? Are the squeaky floors a pleasant reminder of the quirks of a home, or an indication that its floor joist system is inadequate?

The litany can be endless. But, these questions have one element in common: They all involve your personal safety. A good inspector will provide you with a written report that you can use to generate a repair addendum. Even if everything in your new home checks out to be sound, or even if the seller refuses to make any repairs and you decide to buy anyway, you still have a useful guidebook for future maintenance issues. For example, your inspector may note that the 10-year-old roof shingles have a few more years of life in them. It would be inappropriate to ask a seller to replace them. But, you can budget for your own shingle replacement later on.

 Moneysaver

There are excellent home warranty products on the market for buyers of older homes. They work like insurance policies. The average payment for one year's coverage is about $400. There's a $50 deductible for each call for repairs. If, for example, your furnace breaks down, your $450 investment could get you a $2,500 furnace! In many communities today, agency-generated contracts have boiler-plate language giving you the opportunity to request that the seller provide you with a one-year home warranty at closing.

Inspect your new home, too

Do not think of the inspection as appropriate for used homes only. You may buy a home that's newly built. If you do, there's an excellent chance your builder will provide you with a "builder's limited home warranty agreement" like the one in Appendix C. Because of this warranty, your builder will return to your home to fix anything covered in it that doesn't work properly. As mentioned before, you may also generate a punch list of minor items that need repair or touch-up. Your builder will return to fix these as well.

But, who will have noticed the hairline crack in the brick running in a jagged pattern along the back of your new home— a crack that widens after you've lived there a few years because a foundation footing was improperly poured? Who will have noticed the absence of a roof rafter, which a few years later has caused the roof itself to sag?

If the builder had noticed these problems, she would have fixed them before you ever decided to buy the house. If you have your new home inspected, there will be time to have them fixed prior to closing. You may even discover that your new home was built improperly (such things don't become obvious to the layperson until years after closing). Because of your inspection clause, you have the right to withdraw from your contract.

It's possible that you've decided to buy a vacant lot with the intention of building a custom home rather than buying an older or newer home. If that's the case, you will want to know in advance of buying the lot that it *perks* for a septic tank system or that a sewer can be run to the place on your lot the house will occupy. You will want to have the subsurface soil tested to make sure a shelf of rock won't impede the pouring of footings and building a foundation. You will want an expert to examine the "covenants, codes, and restrictions" if your lot is in a subdivision, to make sure that you can build the style and size home that you want. In short, there's no buying situation for which an inspection is inappropriate.

Watch Out!

We don't know of a single subdivision that doesn't have at least one of what builders call *dog lots*—lots full of rock, lots that don't perk, lots needing too much fill dirt, and so on. An inspection can save you from the inevitable grief of having a home built on such a lot.

But what, exactly, are home inspections meant to accomplish? What are an inspector's highest priorities? What does he examine most closely? What do inspectors not examine, and who do you get to evaluate what they don't examine?

What to expect from your inspection?

First of all, any homebuyer must acknowledge what an inspector can't do. Inspectors don't have X-ray vision. Moreover, they don't have the tools to take anything apart or the license to make any repairs. A home inspection is essentially a visual process meant to uncover glaring problems and help you reduce any risks you might encounter by moving into a home. Your personal safety is your inspector's primary concern.

Despite these limitations, an inspector can perform the following important tasks:

- Make observations: Observations can itemize particular areas of concern and generalize a home's condition relative to properties of the same age built with similar construction materials.

- Consider implications: What might be accomplished by making repairs.

- Weigh risks and possibilities: Risks and possibilities are the long-term effects of living in a home in which an inspector has found defects and include whether or not the repair of defects should be an immediate or long-range objective.

Bright Idea

If you know prior to having an inspection performed that you have a problem with one or more of a home's systems, it may be wise to have a specialist come with the inspector to evaluate the specific nature of the problem.

- Draw reasonable conclusions: Conclusions involve whether defects are so serious that their repair needs to be undertaken.

- Make recommendations: Recommendations are written descriptions of how a particular repair can be performed most effectively and predictions of what kinds of maintenance issues may come up in the future. Typically, these recommendations fall into three classes of findings that get an inspector's highest priority of attention: 1) things that are dangerous; 2) things causing rapid or costly damage (termites or fungus are good examples); and 3) essential things that don't work (electrical outlets, the heating and cooling system, appliances, and so on).

Inspectors perform these tasks by completing a visual inspection of your house, both inside and out, focusing on the critical issues indicated here in Table 11.1.

Table 11.1. What's Looked at in a Good Inspection

1. The foundation

2. Heating and air-conditioning systems

3. Plumbing and plumbing supply lines

4. The electrical setup and the condition and type of the wiring

5. Roof shingles, decking, and rafters

6. Siding (the external covering of a home, in other words, brick, wood, stucco, aluminum or vinyl siding, etc.)

7. Attic

8. Garage

Because the home inspection process is essentially visual, the typical inspector will not evaluate or report on house components that aren't readily visible or accessible, such as insulation hidden behind a wall cavity. There are some more specialized inspections, however, which you can request from experts for an additional fee. These include the evaluation of

- Water wells
- Septic systems
- Swimming pools
- Water quality testing
- Radon testing
- Termite and fungus issues
- Boundary and property line issues
- Value of property

Despite the limitations of an inspector's purview, the services that he performs are invaluable. A good inspector is always asking questions such as: What's different here? What's holding this or that floor system up? What surprises are waiting? How do the air, moisture, and people move in this house? How does this or that system work? Where do the wires go and why? What was changed here and why? Did the change work? What is this little oddity? Could it point to something important? Within a few days, all these questions, as well as any other observations your inspector makes, will be encapsulated in a 12- to 20-page report that you can use both as a safety and reference guide to your new home and as the springboard for negotiating repairs with a seller.

 Moneysaver

If the home you're buying is on a septic system (rather than a sewer system), you may want to ask your lender to make a septic tank cleaning and evaluation a requirement for the seller to perform. This could not only provide peace of mind, but save you a few hundred dollars.

Some inspectors work from a standard form that includes a list of all the working components of a home and marks the condition of each "satisfactory," "marginal," or "unsatisfactory." These inspectors often provide a summary of defects and/or warnings at the conclusion of their inspection. Either way, you should make every effort to attend your inspection and follow your inspector as he moves from component to component. His off-handed comments might later be invaluable to helping you know what to service in your home and why. If you are working with a real estate agent, that person should also attend the inspection. After all, you'll be enlisting her aid in preparing a repair addendum for presentation to the seller. Given how invaluable your inspection report can be, the one outstanding question you should have is: Who am I going to call to conduct the inspection?

Who you gonna call?

Home inspector is not a job that requires a special degree or license. You can put up a shingle and promote yourself as a home inspector with a piece of wood, hammer, nails, and some money to advertise. Many home inspectors are former builders who have grown tired of managing subcontractors. Some are brick masons who've picked up a bit of knowledge about foundations over the years. A few are frustrated former real estate agents. So, how do you ensure that you've found a professional inspector?

First, the individual should be licensed in one of three trades. An inspector may be a licensed Heating, Ventilating, and Air Conditioning (HVAC) technician, a licensed plumber, or a licensed electrician. You can practice as an inspector without a license, but it takes one or more of these licenses to show that you can do the job. Second, your inspector should belong to a national organization of home inspectors (the three major home inspection organizations are ASHI, American Society of Home Inspectors; NAHI, National Association of Home Inspectors; and AIA, American Inspectors Association).

A member in good standing of such an organization will have taken courses in home inspecting at some central location and will have evidence of completing a certain number of inspections, without pay, in order to become certified. That person will have an inspector's license.

If you buy through a real estate agent, that person should be able to supply you with a list of the most qualified home inspectors in your community. Don't expect your agent to give you one name. That would look like collusion. And, it would mean that you've given up control of a critical aspect of your buying process to someone else. If you need to hire an inspector on your own, consult the local Yellow Pages for a list of names, and then call the Better Business Bureau in your town to make sure that no complaints have been filed against the inspector you might choose. If you're simply moving from one side of town to the other, ask satisfied homebuyer friends who they used for an inspector.

After you find an inspector, don't simply arrange a time for that person to meet you at the home you've bought. Ask the right questions in a telephone interview. What are the inspector's qualifications? How many inspections has the inspector performed, and how long has he been in business? Does he do inspections full-time? Does the inspector object to your accompanying him during the inspection process? How long will the inspection take? Will the inspector produce a written report so that, if necessary, you can negotiate repairs with the seller?

Be sure to ask how long it will take to get the written report. Because inspection reports nowadays are generated on a computer, it should only take a day or two for your inspector to provide you with a written report. And, as we have said, many very good inspectors provide written reports immediately at the end of the inspection. Time is of the essence here. You'll probably be dealing with an anxious seller who has given you a deadline for any requests for repairs.

Finally, you should ask how much the inspection will cost. Concerning this last question, don't haggle over price. The best

Bright Idea

If your inspector shows up only with a flashlight and a legal pad, send that person away. A professional inspector should have all the tools of the trade.

inspectors tend to be the more expensive ones. They've paid for a lot of equipment and a lot of education. Their expertise is worth something!

There's one other question—a critical one—that you should ask your would-be inspector: "If you find defects, can you fix them?" If the answer is "yes," hang up the phone. Nothing is more unethical than an inspector rigging his inspection so that he can get repair work from it.

The inspection report

After you've chosen an inspector, arrange an inspection time when you can be present. Your real estate agent will attend the inspection, too, but not to represent you (remember the disclaimer) so much as to provide security and help you prepare a repair addendum. As we've said, your inspector should be happy for you to tour the house as all its systems are being evaluated and should be willing to address any particular concerns you have along the way.

It's not uncommon for the seller to attend the inspection as well. This isn't a bad thing. Sometimes a diplomatic inspector can point out problems that need attention, so some repair items can get resolved even before you've been given a written report or composed a formal addendum. In addition, a seller who has been present during an inspection and can see defects verified will be a lot more receptive to your repair addendum, because the surprise element will have been removed.

Some inspectors generate their written evaluations from a laptop computer and give them to you on site. Others have a check-off system "grading" the various features of the home; they may turn this checklist over to you immediately. Others take their laptop data and generate a full report a day or so after completing the inspection. The most important thing you need to know is what to do when the inspection is completed and you have the report in hand.

The repair addendum

Make sure that you've completed the inspection, received a written report, made a copy of the written report for the seller to review, and prepared a repair addendum to deliver to the seller within the deadlines specified in your contract. Remember, if you fail to meet these deadlines, you could be forced to buy your home "as is"!

If you're working with a real estate agent, compose the repair addendum together. Your agent will tell you not to nit-pick. Any home will have some superficial defects. As a buyer, you should know that you'll always have some maintenance issues to address. If you're writing the addendum on your own, be realistic. Choose those items that are of serious concern to you. Your priorities should be similar to your inspector's priorities. Ask the seller to repair them, or if you're more comfortable doing things your own way, ask the seller to provide enough cash at closing for you to make the repairs yourself.

If you don't reach an agreement on either the extent of repairs or how they'll be paid for, you can always withdraw your contract and get your earnest money back. That's why you chose the most stringent inspection contingency clause in the first place!

The walk-through . . . or is it time to walk?

If you have chosen to let the seller make the repairs, how will you know that they have been done properly? How will you know that the basic systems have remained in normal operating condition from the time of the inspection to the time of the closing? "Trust" is the worst answer you can give to these questions.

At your inspection, ask your inspector to return to the home with you a day or two before closing for a walk-through. Make sure that you have your checklist of items that the seller has

agreed to repair. Put the burden on an expert to tell you that
the repairs have been done properly and that nothing has happened recently to compromise the basic systems. Ask to see
receipts for all work for which the seller has paid. If your inspector finds something wrong, you have a much better chance of
delaying the closing until it's repaired than if you simply offer
your own opinion. If everything is fine, the seller's agent will
probably ask you to sign a satisfaction form.

If you have bought on your own or if there's no seller's
agent, offer the courtesy of signing off on the repairs. You and
the seller will be meeting again at the closing table in a day or
two. If you feel that the seller has been cooperative, why not
take another step toward an amicable closing? Whether you've
bought on your own or with the help of an agent, make sure
that you've achieved peace of mind about the condition of your
future home before you come to the closing table.

Just the facts

- If you execute a contract to purchase with a real estate
  agent, you should initial one of three inspection clauses.
  If you execute a contract on your own, you should include
  an appropriate, fully protective inspection clause.

- No matter what kind of home you're buying, or even if
  you purchase a vacant lot with the intention of building,
  you should have an inspection.

- You should choose an inspector who, through licenses and
  training, is well-qualified to do a good job and will provide
  a written report outlining her findings.

- If the seller has agreed to make repairs, you should do a
  final walk-through prior to closing to make sure that the
  repairs were done properly. During the walk-through, you
  should also make sure that your home's basic systems are
  in normal operating condition.

GET THE SCOOP ON...
What to do between the inspection and closing
■ Title insurance ■ Homeowner's insurance—
what it covers, what it doesn't ■ Insidious
exceptions ■ Mudslides and floods: Why should
they concern you?

Before Coming to the Closing Table

Chapter 12

After you've had an inspection completed on your new home and have successfully negotiated any necessary repairs, you will probably have a short waiting period before closing on your purchase. During that time, you'll most likely be scurrying around attending to furniture, drapes, packing, painting, and the like. In short, you'll be busily doing the things necessary to make the house you're about to move into a home. Our main concern in this chapter is to ensure that, in your scurrying, you do not overlook the crucial technical measures necessary to protect what is soon to be your homestead. (In Chapter 14, we'll go over other important issues that you need to consider just before you move into your new home, as well as immediately thereafter.)

The word *homestead* is a significant one. It refers to what is usually the major part of your estate; it is your claim to ownership, secured by a deed that is underwritten by a title policy. In most states, evidence of your homestead significantly reduces your property taxes. Called a *freehold estate*, your ownership position entitles you to tax relief you don't enjoy by having a *leasehold*, or a home or other property that is rented rather than occupied by the owner. The title policy you will receive at closing serves to protect your deed to the property. What protects the property itself is your homeowner's insurance (often called *hazard insurance*). Homeowner's insurance indemnifies your home against loss or damage.

In this chapter, we'll review the steps you must take in order to fully protect your home and your homestead. First, we'll examine title insurance. Title insurance comes in the form of a commitment that protects both you and, if there is one, the mortgagee (the lender or maker of your mortgage), against any challenges to your full ownership of a property. We'll also explore the relationship between your title insurance policy and the deed it underwrites.

Second, we'll discuss the nature and intent of homeowner's insurance. In most cases, the final step you'll take before closing will be to visit with or call an insurance agent of your choice to make sure that an insurance policy accompanies all your other closing documents. Often, ordering homeowner's insurance is done in a perfunctory manner—as an obligation to be handled quickly—when it is in fact a critical final step toward closing. After all, the policy you order determines the extent to which you are protected from loss or damage to your property.

Just what is title insurance?

Title insurance protects the *fee simple* (wholly owned), or freehold, estate or interest in a legally described parcel of land and the dwellings that stand upon that parcel of land. It exists to protect you against any liens, encumbrances, or adverse claims that may have been filed against the property and/or its current or previous owners. It serves to protect you from inheriting anyone else's legal problems. Without proper title insurance, you could be vulnerable to any claims by or against any previous owners of the property you purchase.

Bright Idea

If you do not already have a will, we strongly suggest that you have one drawn up immediately before or after closing to protect your homestead by naming an inheritor if you should die or become incompetent. Should you die *intestate*—without a will—you may lose the choice of inheritor.

Title insurance cannot be put in place, however, until a series of conditions, spelled out in the title policy, are met. Traditionally, the title policy is ordered by the listing agent for the property you buy or, if you buy a For Sale By Owner, by the seller. The process of ordering and conveying your title policy should be handled with the care and diligence that the document merits.

Rarely are you given the opportunity to review your title policy at closing. Typically, it is just another document in the loan package that you receive at the end of the closing. You will, of course, be signing the deed to your property, along with a "name affidavit" proving that you have no outstanding legal judgments against you. In other words, you'll review the essential material that your title policy generates, but not the policy itself. Because so much of importance is generated by your title policy, we want you to have the straight scoop on what it is and what it does.

Entitled to what?

So exactly what are you entitled to? In three words: full, unencumbered ownership. You would not, for example, be encumbered by a tax lien placed on the house by the IRS 10 years ago when Don Deadbeat failed to pay his taxes. As someone with equity, without free and clear title, you could be held accountable for Don's tax debt. To offer a second example, your title policy would protect you from a mechanic's lien put on the home some years back, when Stephanie Slacker failed to pay Chris the carpenter for some work he did for her.

These are not idle examples. Homebuyers have ordered title policies from companies without title plants and discovered much later that existing liens and encumbrances were not noted. Many people have experienced major economic hardship due to these omissions. You can go back and sue the title company for any errors or omissions in a title, which have caused you hardship. Doing so, however, can be a difficult and time-consuming process that you can easily avoid by getting your title policy right the first time.

In a somewhat different vein, your title policy says that you are free from obligation on any pending assessments not disclosed in your contract—for example, an assessment to pay for the installation of a sanitary sewer system. Simply put, you are entitled to full protection against financial damage caused by any prior and/or undisclosed claims against what is now your rightful property.

In Appendix C, you'll find a sample "Commitment for Title Insurance." It includes all the elements that make up a complete title policy. Let's review the key elements here:

- "Payment to or for the account of the grantors or mortgagors of the full consideration for the estate or interest to be insured." Put more simply, your title policy acknowledges that the current owners of your home will be paid the full amount (that is, consideration) of the contract price as the means of foregoing their own entitlement.

- "Proper instrument(s) creating the estate or interest to be insured must be executed and duly filed. . . ." These "proper instruments" consist of two items. The first is the warranty deed that the current owners of the home you're buying will convey to you at closing. The second is the mortgagee policy, which applies only if you're getting a loan. The lender is the mortgagee, while you are the mortgagor. Just as the warranty deed protects your interest in your property, the mortgagee policy protects the lender's interest. They are both part of the same overall title policy.

Bright Idea

You can impress your agent by asking whether your title policy was written by a company that has a *title plant*, which is a compendious microfiche library that includes everything recorded on every parcel property in the county where the title company has its office. There's always the possibility of error by title representatives if they research from incomplete files.

- "Judgments, bankruptcies, and tax liens. . . ." If you have a name that is even remotely common, chances are good that someone with your name will have had a lien, bankruptcy, or judgment filed against him or her. Therefore, during the process of applying for your mortgage loan, it is entirely possible that judgments filed against another individual with your name could appear on your credit report. If these judgments are serious, they could keep you from qualifying for a mortgage loan. During closing you'll be asked to sign a "name affidavit" stating that you're not the same "John Doe" or "Henrietta Squibblemeier" who has a particular judgment or series of judgments recorded against him or her. You'll be disclosing this through the signing of the affidavit.

- "Satisfaction. . . ." At the closing, part of the money you pay for your home will go to pay off any existing loans that currently exist on it. The closing attorney or the listing agent for the home you've bought will have ordered *pay-offs* of these loans and will *satisfy* them immediately after closing.

- "Taxes" and "Assessments" spelled out in "Schedule B." Your title policy will alert the closing attorney of any taxes, dues, or assessments that need to be paid in order for you to have clear title. These may include fire dues, garbage pick-up dues, library dues, neighborhood association fees, lines of credit, sewer installation assessments, and the like.

Apropos of this item, you may be inclined to think when you leave your closing that the closing attorney was paid an inordinate amount of money for the time it took to turn over to you a copy of your deed and have you sign a bunch of papers. In fact, however, most of the closing attorney's work goes on behind the scenes, before the closing, when she is tracking down all the possible payoffs that need to be made and satisfying all the requirements spelled out in your title policy—most of which also need to be recorded.

> 66 These days, payoffs are often handled by couriers who take a check directly from the closing to the lending institution. That's why the seller often finds a "courier fee" listed in the closing costs. If we're paying off a seller's loan, the interest clock is ticking! So we need the check to be delivered quickly. 99
>
> —John Randolph,
> Real Estate Attorney

- "Easements, Restrictions and Right of Ways. . . ." After the recitation of your name and the name of the seller(s), the first major element of your title insurance policy is the legal description of the property you're about to buy. If you buy in a newer subdivision, the legal description will be brief and simple, for example, "Lot 3, Block 5, Fernwood Estates, 4th Sector, as recorded in Map Book 5, Page 12." However, if you buy in an older, established subdivision or in an unincorporated county village, your title policy will likely include a "metes and bounds" legal description that can be up to several pages in length. A metes and bounds survey literally "walks" the lot, citing every curve and every angle by geometric "minutes."

The legal description also recites any setback lines within which your home must lie. It is from the legal description in the title policy that a survey of your property is drawn by a registered surveyor. That survey includes a footprint of your intended home. It's the closing attorney's responsibility to determine that your home stands within the setback lines. It's also her responsibility to alert you in advance if it does not and to instruct you on how to apply for a variance so that you're not in violation of the covenants, codes, and restrictions set out in the title.

Since the legal description recited in the title policy generates the survey, the closing attorney will go over the survey with you in some detail. Almost all single-family home lots include easements. These are rights of access granted to your local utilities so that, say, Oshkosh Power Company or Beulah Vista Gas can get onto your property to repair or improve their services. The attorney will also examine the boundary lines set out on your survey to make sure that there are no encroachments. These occur when something of yours (a fence, for example) encroaches onto your neighbor's property, or, conversely, something on your neighbor's property encroaches onto yours.

The formality and indeed the legality of the terminology surrounding title insurance policy may seem forbidding. Every element in your title policy is important, however, and serves to protect your estate. In the material world, your estate is most likely the biggest, and very probably the most valuable, thing you can own and have the pleasure of passing along, to whomever you choose.

Who conveys the title?

A title policy is conveyed to you by a title insurance company. Most of these corporations are immense and have a national headquarters while maintaining a regional office in every

---

 Watch Out!

If you buy in an older neighborhood, expect to see an encroachment or two on your survey. In the distant past, people rarely called surveyors before erecting fences or even garages. Such encroachments are usually harmless, but if your survey contains an encroachment, your lender will have you hold XYZ Mortgage Company *harmless* if you get into a dispute with your neighbor.

county in the United States large enough to conduct regular real estate transactions.

Title insurance corporations consist of three basic types of employees: managers, attorneys, and account executives. The attorneys review every aspect of a title insurance policy before it's issued to make sure that it is accurate and inclusive. The account executives actually sell the policies. They do this either by regularly visiting real estate sales offices and soliciting business from agents or by going directly to mortgage brokers or to closing attorneys and soliciting their business.

Most experienced real estate agents usually call on one or two account executives on a regular basis. They choose executives that provide quick, accurate service and who alert them to any problems in a policy that need to be solved prior to closing. Hence, the title policy account executive is a vital player in the whole real estate transaction process.

The account executive not only takes orders from agents or attorneys, but also returns to the title plant and conducts the research necessary to draw up the policy. Title company account executives are usually paid a salary for meeting a quota of policies sold, as well as a significant bonus for exceeding that quota. Because their work is what clears the way for the closing attorney to convey the title, their professionalism must be above reproach.

Who underwrites the title?

Your title insurance policy is underwritten by the title company that produces it, but only after it is examined by a title examiner for authenticity and accuracy. As in the sample title policy in Appendix C, the title examiner's signature usually appears at the bottom of the face page of the policy.

For those rare individuals among you who wish to interact with title policies more than you have been able to do by reading this chapter . . . you cannot only examine your title policy in great detail before you close, but you can also make notes and

> ### Watch Out!
>
> Make sure that your real estate or listing agent (or attorney, if you don't have an agent) has read the title insurance policy several days prior to closing and that no clouds complicate or prevent that final and most important event in your home purchase.

queries on any portion of it that you find puzzling or cryptic. There should be a title examiner available to answer your questions. A lawyer by background, he can explain all the legal consequences of every recitation in the policy.

The actual underwriter of your title policy, however, is the title company itself, which places its rather considerable financial holdings behind the veracity of each policy it issues. You've no doubt seen or heard commercials in which homeowners insurance companies state how they "stand behind" every policy they issue. What this essentially means is that they have the capital resources to protect you against loss. In underwriting your title policy, the issuer stands behind you and protects you against any hostile claim made against your homestead.

Title policy protection *after* the closing

The importance of title insurance is best underscored by this frightening and true story about a prominent real estate attorney in a major city. We'll call him the Abominable Attorney. His devious machinations are worth understanding.

Suffering from a personal financial crisis, the Abominable Attorney decided to capitalize on his privileged position by making countless times more money from his closings than he was entitled to make. His scheme was ingenious, and for a terrifyingly long while, it worked. As we have said, an owner's title policy notes seller's loans that need to be paid off at the time of closing. Typically, a closing attorney takes that part of a seller's proceeds realized from the initiation of the purchaser's new loan, his cash down payment, or both and *immediately* pays off any real estate loans currently existing on the property. In most states, sellers are charged a courier fee to have these payoffs hand-delivered or sent overnight to the lender so that the seller has no obligation for payments beyond the date of closing.

The Abominable Attorney came up with a scheme to use this process to his financial advantage. How? In 1998 and 1999, when the stock market was soaring to astronomical heights, he invested the checks he received from purchasers and/or their lenders in the stock market rather than send the money realized from these proceeds back to the lenders to satisfy sellers' loans and other commitments. In other words, he became a day trader acting fraudulently with other people's money. Within a few weeks of each closing, he had made far more money in the stock market than he needed to pay off sellers' loans plus the *per-diem* interest charged by the lender until the date of satisfaction and, for nearly two years, he was able to pay off each loan without any of hundreds of sellers knowing that their money had been withheld.

A successful closing attorney handles tens to hundreds of millions of dollars a month, all of this money placed in an escrow account to pay off liens and encumbrances. So, even by withholding money for a few weeks and investing it in a wildly successful time for the stock market, he netted nearly three million dollars in a period of less than two years. Then greed overtook him (not that it didn't drive him in the first place!). He let a few loans pass without a payoff for more than two weeks, provoking lenders to let their clients know they were delinquent. "How could this be?" thought the sellers. "We closed on our home weeks ago! We have the settlement statements to prove it!" They immediately contacted their (supposedly former) lenders and sent along copies of their settlement statements. This prompted an FBI investigation, but the Abominable Attorney had already fled the country by the time the yellow ribbon of a crime scene investigation was wrapped around the outside of his office.

Of course, meanwhile, the sellers no longer had the money to satisfy their obligations; the Abominable Attorney was enjoying their money, along with millions of other dollars made over the two-year period, at a private Colombian resort. Here's where the title companies, which had underwritten and insured the sellers' loans, came to the rescue. It was their responsibility by law to pay off the sellers' obligations and restore their creditworthiness. It was also their obligation to help lawful authorities track down the Abominable Attorney and make sure that he lived the rest of his life in an environment suitable to his way of making a living.

We have not told this tale to warn you against using closing attorneys—999 out of 1,000 are entirely trustworthy. They conduct their affairs, which involve the handling of huge amounts of money, conscientiously and accurately. We have told this tale, however, to underscore the importance of a title company's commitments and their absolute obligation to honor them. Do not, under any circumstances, regard your new title policy as just another casual document to be perfunctorily reviewed at closing.

The truth about homeowner's insurance

There are two pre-eminent truths about homeowner's insurance. The first is that you can't take out a mortgage to buy a home without it. The second, no less eloquent, is that you would have to be pretty dumb to pay cash for a home and then fail to insure it.

Even if you were to think your home did not need to be protected against hazards, your mortgage company would think differently. If you should suffer a catastrophic loss, your mortgage company's investors would want their money back or want to know that you would receive a large enough insurance settlement to rebuild your home and, at the same time, keep making your payments.

Homeowner's insurance policies insure your home and structures attached to it against loss or damage. "Attached structures" include porches, garages, and any surrounding buildings, attached or unattached, that are not used for business or rented to other parties. These policies also cover personal property in your home, such as clothes and furniture. Certain valuables, such as expensive jewelry, furs, firearms, cash, and antiques, are usually covered by riders that are attached to your regular policy.

Note: Even if you pay for your home with cash, you will be recording a deed homesteading your property to you. In most states, it's a legal requirement that your homestead be insured against loss.

Homeowner's policies include liability insurance. If Uncle Max falls down your stairs and breaks his leg, or if you or anyone else who lives in your home is injured by an explosion, fire, collapse, or any other unforeseeable mishap, the liability portion of your homeowner's insurance provides coverage. This coverage takes care of your legal liability for bodily injury, up to the limits of the policy. It also covers medical expenses up to the limits of the policy for anyone who is accidentally injured while on your premises with your permission. The broader your liability coverage, the higher your homeowner's insurance premiums will be.

If a home catastrophe damages your home to the extent that you need to move to temporary living quarters while it is being rebuilt or repaired, your homeowner's insurance will cover that expense, as well. It will even provide you and your family a meal allowance for the time that you must live away from your home.

Of course, the actual extent of all your coverage depends upon how much you pay for your homeowner's insurance. Every claim has a deductible, which is the specified amount you must pay before your insurance policy money kicks in. The amount of the deductible applies separately to each and every claim. In other words, you cannot accumulate damages toward a deductible, from claim to claim.

Watch Out!

All homeowner's insurance policies set limits on liability as it pertains to personal property. Make sure to consult the "personal property" fine print of your policy to ascertain the various levels of liability for items such as bank notes, jewelry, and rugs. If your valuables exceed the liability limits, you may need to add additional riders to your policy.

The cost

The higher your deductible, the less expensive your homeowner's insurance. For example, with a $1,500 deductible, the policy on a $100,000 home might be $350 per year. With a $250 deductible, the same policy could be as high as $475 per year. What accounts for the difference? Your insurance company knows that the lower the amount of your deductible, the more likely you are to make a claim. (Obviously, with a lower deductible, you will have to pay less toward the damages, while your insurance company will have to pay more.) Most insurance companies would rather you pay less for a policy, have a high deductible, and make fewer claims.

The coverage

What exactly do the dwelling and personal property portions of your homeowner's insurance cover? They usually cover loss caused by

- Fire or lightning
- Damage cause by weight of ice, snow, or sleet
- Explosion
- Aircraft and other vehicles
- Smoke
- Sudden and accidental tearing or bulging of heating and cooling systems
- Windstorm or hail
- Theft

- Riot or civil commotion
- Falling objects
- Vandalism and malicious mischief
- Freezing of plumbing systems
- Sudden and accidental water discharge from plumbing or appliances

You may think that nothing catastrophic could happen that is not covered by your insurance—in other words, that your insurance coverage is comprehensive. Think again. We've examined a lot of homeowner's policies, and we've found the same exceptions listed in every one of them. These are

- Water damage caused by flood or underground water
- Earth movement, including earthquake and mudslides
- Damage caused by settling or deterioration of structural components
- Damage caused by birds, rodents, insects, or domestic animals

It's really quite logical that your insurance company will not cover damage that results from the settling or deterioration of structural components. After all, nothing can really protect your home from aging or from structural defects created by faulty construction. Moreover, if you buy an existing home, most insurance companies would expect that you would have the home inspected and, if any structural damage has been found, either you or your lender will have made sure that it is repaired prior to closing. In fact, if such damage is reported to, or found

 Bright Idea

Certain kinds of damage are more prevalent in some states and locations than other types. For example, freezing of plumbing systems rarely happens in Florida. Make sure that your insurance coverage emphasizes the type of damage you're most likely to experience where you'll be living.

by, an appraiser, your lender will usually require that the appraiser reinspect the property to make sure that the repairs have been done correctly before allowing an attorney to proceed with a clean closing.

It's also logical that your insurance company won't protect your home from birds, rodents, and insects. Upon the purchase of your home, you're given the opportunity to buy pest protection, which at least guards against the latter two types of creature. As to your dogs, cats, ferrets, gerbils, and the like . . . their presence in your home is your choice and not the responsibility of your insurance company.

What seems less logical to many people is that homeowner's policies do not cover water damage caused by flood or underground springs, or earth movement, including earthquakes or mudslides. Let's look into the insurance companies' rationale.

The great mudslide

People purchasing homes along or near fault lines are usually required to purchase special earthquake insurance along with their regular homeowner's insurance. Most of the larger insurance carriers will not provide earthquake coverage. To the smaller carriers who do, you can expect to pay about the same amount of money for special earthquake insurance that you pay for your regular homeowner's insurance. Your earthquake insurance carrier will notify your primary insurance company that you have protection.

What if the top of a mountain behind your home is peeled away to accommodate the construction of a shopping center?

 Moneysaver

Read the fine print in the homeowner's insurance policy you're contemplating buying. There may be exceptions that we haven't covered in this chapter. Your homeowner's insurance is a critical part of your home purchase. Taking it seriously may save you a lot of money down the road.

And, what if, after the peeling and the grading, but before the installation of curbs and gutters, a torrential rainstorm produces a mudslide that destroys your home? Because your insurance company will not indemnify the loss, what kind of recourse do you have?

If your home is one among others in a subdivision that would also be damaged by the mudslide, chances are that you'll have a wonderful class action suit against the developers of the shopping center. A good attorney taking the case on the behalf of you and your neighbors will provide you with living expenses and charge them against the developer as part of the suit. On the other hand, if you're the solitary type who lives far from neighbors and would suffer an isolated loss, you need to find out in advance of buying your home exactly what covenants and restrictions prevent Mt. Pleasant from being developed and turning into a moving wall of mud!

Note: The possibility of a commercial development causing unexpected damages such as a mudslide points to how closely title insurance can be related to homeowner's insurance. Your title policy will show the covenants and restrictions regarding commercial development. It will provide you with coverage against loss stemming from violations of these covenants and restrictions.

There's water in the basement!

Your homeowner's insurance will not cover damage caused by flooding or underground water. However, if the home you intend to buy is located in a Federal Flood Zone, that fact will be disclosed in your survey, and your insurer will require you to purchase special flood insurance. Like earthquake insurance, flood insurance will cost about the same as your regular homeowner's insurance. Therefore, you can expect your total insurance payment to double.

The problem, however, is that many disastrous floods have occurred in areas that are not in a Federal Flood Zone. If you should happen to live in a home outside of the flood zone and suffer a loss due to flooding, your only recourse is for Federal authorities to declare your area eligible for Disaster Relief so that you can rebuild your home. In fact, in recent decades, it's the capricious occurrence of floods outside of Federal Flood Zones that has caused insurance companies to exclude flooding from their regular homeowner's policies.

What if, after a heavy rainstorm, you find your basement covered in water—indeed, your water heater floating on its side? Once again, your insurer will not cover any loss you experience due to water in your basement. At this point, however, we can see various aspects of the home-buying process dovetail. A good home inspector will have pointed out the probability of your basement flooding and will have suggested a remedy such as a sump pump, an underground drainage system, a wall water-proofing system, or a downspout diverter system. Any one of these could obviate the possibility of a flooded basement. In addition, if you have a newly built home, you should have received a builder's warranty that includes protection from water incursion, at least for one year, and in some instances, for as much as 10 years.

We hope we've made a convincing case that your title insurance and homeowner's insurance are essential elements of the home-buying process, and that you should understand the nature and extent of both policies thoroughly before you go to the closing table. When you're in front of the closing attorney or settlement agent, it will be too late to reconsider your coverage. Things simply happen too quickly. Think back to our discussion of the hazards of the "I don't know anything" syndrome, when you abdicate your own responsibility, letting others take control. Title and homeowner's policies are places where you can exercise a great deal of control—prior to the occasion when you'll have very little, which is the real estate closing.

Watch Out!

Comparison shop for homeowner's insurance. Don't assume that the insurer who protects your car will also have the best home insurance rates. Learn about your deductibles and exceptions, and above all else, ask your potential insurer to guarantee the average length of time between an insurable incident and the visit of a claims adjuster!

Just the facts

- Use the time between your home inspection and your closing to evaluate the title policy and homeowner's insurance policy you'll receive; make sure that your homestead is fully protected.

- Make sure that your title insurance policy protects you and your lender by disclosing any liens and/or encumbrances on the property you intend to buy.

- To close the purchase of your home, you'll need to have proof of homeowner's insurance, which protects you against personal injury occurring in your home, as well as loss due to fire, theft, vandalism, storms, and many other natural and man-made disasters.

- Know about the exceptions in your homeowner's insurance policy before you close.

- Realize that the closing is the wrong place to have second thoughts about the extent of your title or homeowner's coverage.

GET THE SCOOP ON...
The closing . . . what is it and who does it? ▪
Avoiding unpleasant surprises ▪ What to expect
on closing day ▪ Tying up loose ends

The Closing

The closing is the appointed time for a settlement agent to affirm that she can deliver "good marketable title" from the seller to you. The closing date is stipulated in your contract as the time when a settlement agent would deliver a deed to you showing your ownership in your new home. (Actually, it will be a copy of the deed—the settlement agent will either record the deed in your own name and mail you the original or instruct you on how to record the deed in your local county courthouse, whereupon the original will be mailed to you within a few weeks.)

Several things will have happened by now. You will have removed all contingencies in your contract. If you borrowed money, your loan package will have arrived at the settlement agent's office, along with instructions from your lender on how to close. If you've bought with cash, the settlement agent will have determined that the seller can give good marketable title so that you can write a check and receive a copy of the deed that will be recorded in your name. In this chapter, we'll examine the legal elements of the closing itself, the paperwork you'll be signing at the closing, and the roles of the individuals who usually attend the closing.

What is a closing?

Closing is a generic term referring to the completion of a sale. The actual event is handled differently in different states. Although the broad term *settlement agent* refers to the person closing the sale, the person authorized can have varying titles and roles from state to state. The federal government does not regulate laws of conveyance. Each state determines the type of individual who, in that state, is authorized to *convey* property, or transfer it from one owner to another. Each state determines exactly how the property you buy will be transferred.

Note: Because laws of conveyance are devised by states, we'll discuss the closing in broad, generic terms. To find out the principal parties involved in a closing in your state, call your local Board of Realtors and ask a representative to send you the real estate law book that governs your particular state.

In some states, an escrow agent—a designated holder of funds—closes a home sale by transferring these funds as necessary in order to convey a deed. In this instance, if there's a mortgage involved in the purchase, the settlement agent closes according to instructions provided by the lender. In other states, title companies, having determined that there are no liens or encumbrances of record on a property, convey a deed to the buyer. If there's a loan involved, the buyer signs all the loan documents before the actual closing, usually at the mortgage brokerage office of the lender or an escrow office. In most states, the settlement agent is an attorney or escrow officer. Referred to as the *closing attorney*, or escrow officer, she closes a sale according to the terms of the contract, the lender's instructions if a loan is involved, and an affirmation of marketable title.

In a majority of cases, if you close with an attorney as a settlement agent, you and the seller, along with your real estate

Watch Out!

The number of attorneys at a closing can also be determined by how complicated the deed transfer becomes. For example, if the title search on a very old
home reveals dozens of owners, old deed restrictions, or ancient liens and/or
encumbrances, it may take a room full of lawyers to work out the title transfer.

agent and the seller's agent (if you both have them), attend
the closing. These days, when competition for loans among
mortgage companies is fierce, it's not uncommon for your
loan officer to attend the closing as well—if not to explain
unclear instructions to the closing attorney or to explain to you
why you're signing each of the myriad documents with which
you'll be afflicted, at least to get some good PR by being a
hand-holder.

The settlement agent does not represent you and cannot
resolve a dispute between you and the seller if there is one. You
can have your personal attorney attend the closing, as can the
seller. On rare occasions, an agent's attorney will attend if
there's a dispute over commissions. In some cases, you'll be
walking into a room full of lawyers. In New York and New Jersey,
for example, tradition calls for both buyers and sellers to be represented by an attorney. In addition, you'll find yourself in the
presence of a closing attorney and a representative of a title
company. In most states, however, the settlement agent can easily perform all the necessary functions to complete the closing.
Because all contingencies have been removed from your contract, your closing will usually be friendly, or at least calm and
businesslike. Legal representation for anyone but the lender
and title company will be unnecessary.

Everyone loves surprises, but . . .

What you don't want at your closing is a surprise. For example,
a seller who cannot deliver clear title, a survey that shows an
encroachment of your property onto a neighbor's or vice versa,

Bright Idea

If selling your present home is a prerequisite to buying your new one, make sure to review your owner's title policy and check with the settlement agent if you have questions or find defects. Also, make sure that you have an updated termite bond, if your state requires one, which you can present to the purchaser of your old home.

or the inability of a termite treatment company to transfer a clean bond on a home when the contract calls for one. If you're getting a mortgage, it's usually your lender's responsibility, as part of a process called *discovery*, to find any clouds in a title, any deed restrictions, any survey problems (such as encroachments), or any pest or fungus infestation, which might compromise a successful closing. Lenders undertake this responsibility because, if they find something awry, they might want to refuse to complete the conveyance. They look askance at anything that could tarnish their mortgagee's title policy and deed. Moreover, lenders need to make sure that that they're underwriting a fully marketable property in the event that a purchaser experiences a foreclosure.

Things can slip through the cracks during the mortgage underwriting process, however, and some pretty frightening surprises can occur. Here are scenarios depicting several such surprises. Fortunately, they are all avoidable. In fact, if you take the opportunity to review your title policy prior to closing, as we've suggested, there should be no surprises.

1. Sally arrives at the closing attorney's office. She is about to become the proud owner of a house now owned by Joe, a widower. The closing attorney asks, "Joe, where's your wife?" "She died two years ago," Joe replies. "But," says the attorney, "this didn't show up in the title!"

   How had this happened? As it turns out, Joe and his wife had bought their home 25 years ago as "tenants in common," rather than as "joint tenants with the right of survivorship." This means that in the event of a sale, the court would have to probate half of Joe's money. "I wouldn't have sold it if I had known that," insists Joe. He doesn't want to close, and Sally is about to leave the closing table homeless.

Well . . . not exactly homeless! If Joe refuses to close, Sally will no doubt file a lawsuit against Joe, Joe's real estate agent, the title company, and anyone else she can get a hold of, for breach of contract and fraud. She would contend, rightly, that Joe fraudulently marketed a home he wasn't in a position to sell. And, most likely, she would win more money in the suit than she would have had to pay for the house. Given this probability, Joe would most likely settle for the half of the proceeds from the sale of the house to which he is immediately entitled, and go to probate court to try to retrieve the other half. Even in this case, however, their closing would have to be delayed while Sally consulted an attorney to devise a plan that would achieve a legal outcome in her favor.

2. When Richard put a contract on his home-to-be, he had no idea that the front right corner overlapped onto the neighbor's property (an encroachment). Richard has a cash contract and never thought to have the lot on which his home sits surveyed. No encroachments showed up in the title policy, which was as cloud-free as the most exquisite summer day. When he first learns of the encroachment at the closing (his attorney uncovered an old survey just

Moneysaver

As a homebuyer, you can use the escrow process to real advantage. If anything comes up at a walk-through or a closing that compromises the condition of your property or your title to it, you can have the closing attorney (who then also becomes an escrow agent) hold funds from the seller until this condition is removed.

before closing), Richard insists that he won't be comfortable owning the home unless the neighbor grants an easement allowing the encroachment. The closing attorney calls the neighbor and asks whether he'll provide an easement. The neighbor refuses to do so on such short notice. Richard is, at least briefly, in a bind. Thankfully, a compliant seller agrees to escrow a few thousand dollars from his net proceeds to help Richard resolve the inevitable upcoming dispute with his neighbor.

3. Rhonda and Lee's contract to purchase called for the transfer of an existing termite bond or the supplying of a new one. The seller, Max, had called ABC Pest Control to transfer his existing termite bond to Rhonda and Lee. ABC comes out to Max's house, treats it for termites as required by law, and officially transfers the bond to Rhonda and Lee. ABC also points out, on the graph-paper layout of the house that usually accompanies the transfer of a termite bond, that there's old termite damage that might have weakened the central girder of the house. ABC treats the girder, but because their contract with Max constitutes a treatment termite bond rather than a repair bond, ABC is under no obligation to repair the weakened girder. Meanwhile, Rhonda and Lee's lender is willing to close their loan as long as the sweet young couple is willing to hold the lender harmless if the girder should ever need replacement.

    Rhonda and Lee don't know quite what to do! Here's the closing attorney, who represents the lender, asking them to sign a paper holding their lender harmless in the event of any future repairs. Here's Rhonda and Lee, who are not at all sure that they want to go through with the purchase of Max's house if termites have been its principal residents. They can choose not to sign the hold harmless agreement, which will have the effect of voiding their mortgage. In such a case, however, can they get a full and

Bright Idea

Many states' real estate contracts now give you the option of asking the seller to provide a standard wood infestation report along with the transfer of a termite bond. If your state doesn't require one, or if such a request is not in the boiler-plate language of your contract, write the request in!

immediate refund of their earnest money? In the future, will they be able to spend the thousands of dollars it would cost to repair the damage to the girder? Of course, they don't have to buy the house, but what a disappointment!

Ultimately, Rhonda and Lee have the good sense to call their lawyer from the closing table to complain that they feel that Max, their mortgage company, and the closing attorney are trying to put them over a barrel. They ask their lawyer to come up with the most appropriate solution. Once again, the principle of escrowing comes to their rescue. At their lawyer's suggestion, Max agrees to let the closing attorney hold $3,000 from his net proceeds until a professional contractor can provide an estimate for the repair or replacement of the damaged girder. The escrowed funds will later be used to pay the contractor for his work, and any remaining funds will be promptly returned to Max. All is saved, but only after much aggravation and an almost totally botched closing.

The seller does the heavy lifting

These examples demonstrate some of the more common types of surprises that can occur. Interestingly, they're all problems or failures of the seller: an inability to deliver good marketable title in the first example, an inability to provide a clean survey in the second, and an inability to supply a bond required in the third.

Up through the time of the inspection, however, each of the respective buyers in these scenarios felt that they had all the hard work to do, while the seller was only waiting for their

Bright Idea

As a seller, even if you have a real estate agent, have a checklist of items that will have to be at the settlement agent's office prior to closing. The most essential items on the checklist are clear title, payoff letters for all loans you have on the house, a survey, termite bond, and any warranties you have on the appliances, HVAC systems, and roof.

money and a chance to move. In fact, however, except for loan approval, which is the buyer's responsibility, all the other terms and conditions in a contract are ones that the seller has to meet.

How can you avoid similar unpleasant surprises? Even seemingly insurmountable obstacles can usually be overcome in time for a closing if you are represented by a truly competent real estate agent. Your agent would review the title policy, the survey, and the termite bond before they are delivered to the settlement agent. A good agent, knowing that Joe's wife had died, would have made sure all the proper signatures were solicited so that Joe could have delivered clear title and collected his full proceeds. A competent agent would have reviewed the survey and alerted Richard well in advance of closing to visit his future neighbor and explain that an easement wouldn't diminish the neighbor's ownership rights. Finally, an agent delivering an offer on behalf of Rhonda and Lee that required a termite bond would have found out quickly that Max's house had old termite damage and would have warned Rhonda and Lee how to handle the lender's presentation of the hold harmless agreement.

What exactly happens at the closing?

Assuming that your closing will be free of any nasty surprises such as those just described—and the vast majority of closings are free of nasty surprises—what should you expect to happen? The answer depends on whether you're paying with cash or, like the majority of us, getting a mortgage.

If you're paying with cash

Your closing should be brief but ecstatic. The seller will have delivered clear title, and either you will be given an original deed to file in the county courthouse or the settlement agent will do the filing for you. Perhaps the seller will have a loan to pay off with money you'll be providing through your purchase. In all likelihood the settlement agent will have ordered the pay-off, subtracted it and any seller's closing costs from your payment, and turned over the remainder to the seller.

At the closing, you'll be reviewing and signing a settlement statement called HUD 1. This is to make sure that the few closing costs associated with the sale have been properly appropriated. The outside column of figures is for the seller; the inside column is for you.

In most states, your normal expenses in a cash closing are an equal split of the settlement agent's and title policy fees, a tax proration, and, if you worked with a real estate agent to whom you agreed to pay commission, your agent's fee. Your signature hand will hardly be warmed up when you'll be asked to write a check, and the closing will have ended. You'll probably spend most of your time chatting with the seller about move-in day.

If you're taking out a new loan

In this case, your signature hand will ache from all the exercise it gets. Here's a list of the documents you will be initialing or signing. These are the basic minimum:

 Watch Out!

If you're closing with cash, you won't have a lender to protect your interests, nor, more than likely, an attorney to arbitrate on your behalf. No one is telling the seller to provide a survey; no one is reviewing the termite bond to be transferred. Examine both carefully and, if you have any confusion, hire a lawyer to represent you.

- The HUD 1 (settlement statement), which adds together your loan amount and closing costs and deducts your down payment to arrive at the amount of cash you'll need to close. Next to your note and mortgage, it's the most important document you'll sign at your closing. Make sure that you understand how your money has been spent. The typical closing costs itemized on the HUD 1 are listed in Table 13.1:

Table 13.1. Possible Purchaser's Costs on a HUD 1

1. Loan origination fee (usually 1 percent of the loan amount)

2. If you're getting a VA loan, the VA funding fee, usually folded into the loan

3. Appraisal fee (often marked P.O.C. for "paid outside closing")

4. Credit report fee (often marked P.O.C.)

5. Settlement or escrow agent's fee

6. Title policy fee (If the settlement agent is opening a loan for you and closing one for the seller, this fee is usually split 50/50.)

7. Survey

8. Fee to record the mortgage

9. Fee to record the deed (based on your equity position in your new home)

10. Underwriting fee (The underwriter reviews your loan package and gives final approval to close to the lender.)

11. Document preparation fees

12. Tax service fee (to start a tax payment escrow account)

13. Flood certification fee

14. Express fees (to return your signed loan package and your endorsed loan check to the lender) or wire fees if money is wired to payoff seller

15. Prepaid items (homeowner's insurance premium, property taxes, interest on your loan from day of closing to the end of the month)

Bright Idea

Your HUD 1 should be kept in perpetuity. Your loan origination fee may be tax-deductible, along with any "points" you pay at closing to lower your interest rate and any prorated property taxes. During the closing, you will give the settlement agent your Social Security number. This is so your lender can report your tax-deductible interest payments to the IRS.

- A disclosure that the settlement agent is closing for the lender and cannot resolve disputes between you and the seller
- A survey or acknowledgment of receipt of a survey
- In most states, a termite bond
- A note
- A mortgage
- An adjustable-rate rider to the note if you're getting an ARM
- A Federal Truth-in-Lending Disclosure Statement
- A name affidavit (If you have a fairly common name, you may need to show that you're not some other person with your name who is a defendant in a lawsuit or who is bankrupt.)
- A typed version of your original credit application, itemizing all your assets and debts
- A statement that neither your credit nor your job situation has changed since you made your loan application
- A form to be filed with the IRS with your Social Security number on it entitling you to claim your mortgage loan interest payments as a deduction
- A form saying that you'll cooperate with the lender or settlement agent if any documents from the closing need correcting

- A check for your down payment and closing costs
- Endorsement of the check for the mortgage from your lender

After you've reviewed and signed all these documents and the seller has signed a lien waiver affidavit and the deed, you're a homeowner!

In the next chapter, we'll discuss your move-in day and what to expect from your new home. But, before we do so, let's return briefly to one last item in your contract: the dates of closing and possession.

Tying up loose ends

In your contract, you and your seller agreed to a closing and possession date. You did this by filling out a statement that reads something like this:

> The sale shall be closed and the deed delivered on or before _____.
> Possession is to be given on delivery of deed if property is vacant; otherwise, possession shall be delivered on _____.

In most cases, your seller will have had time to pack up and move out by the day of closing. Some circumstances can delay possession, however. It may be that you were able to obtain an unusually low interest rate on your loan by making a commitment to close a week or two before your seller could give possession. Because of this, the seller will be living in your home, covered by your homeowner's insurance. It may be that construction on the seller's new home has been delayed a few weeks by bad weather. You still have a lease on your apartment, so you agree to let the seller stay until your lease runs out.

Once again, the seller is living in your house. If for any reason there's a gap between closing and possession, you should work out a written "occupancy agreement" with the seller that

Watch Out!

The contract words "on or before" are meant to give the seller time to tend to home selling–related circumstances. It could leave you in a state of uncertainty! Always change the phrase to "on or before" and get the seller to agree to the change.

determines who is responsible for paying for damages that occur during that gap. An occupancy agreement is a formal statement that your settlement agent can compose and have you and the seller sign. A sample agreement is as follows:

During their period of occupancy in the purchasers' home, the sellers agree to maintain the home in the same condition as it was in when the walk-through was conducted immediately prior to closing. The sellers are responsible for repairing any damage they create or incur during their period of occupancy.

If the occupancy period is two weeks or more, and it's because of the seller's situation that you can't move in, you should probably ask for rent on a *per-diem* basis (in California, the *per diem* is typically for any time after closing as prices are so much higher), equivalent to your mortgage payment, including a pro-rated share of property taxes and homeowner's insurance. Don't forget that you did a walk-through immediately before the closing. Both you and the seller should sign the walk-through form as an acknowledgment of the condition of the property. If there's a long wait between closing and possession, you can meet with your seller again right before moving in to make sure that your checklist is still accurate.

If possession is delayed, we also recommend that you work out with the seller the best day to transfer utilities (normally, gas, electricity, telephone service, and water) into your name. It's best to ask the seller to take the utilities out of their names on a certain day and for you to notify the various services to bill you from that day forward. This will eliminate the possibility of an interruption in services. It can also save you money. Utility companies usually require a deposit or "turn-on fee" if you start a new account.

Because a closing addresses so many legalities, it's easier than you may think to overlook simple logistical issues involved in the transfer of home ownership. We even know of a case where new homeowners left a closing without keys. The seller had already moved out of town, and the homeowners found themselves having to break into their own house!

There may be other considerations to address, as well. Do you know how to work the security system? The sprinkler system? The fireplace dampers? Do you know how to start your furnace pilot light? Do you have all the manuals and warranties on appliances? Is there an especially reliable neighbor who can pick up your newspapers or mail if you're out of town? What are the phone numbers for the local police and fire stations? Don't think that you have to rush away from the closing table just because the setting seems formal. Ask the seller questions you may have forgotten to ask at the walk-through and try to get their address/phone to ask about any unanswered questions, as well as assist in forwarding their mail (as a smart buyer, *you* will have already filled out change of address forms from your local post office!). Take the time to tie up loose ends.

 Watch Out!

In a surprisingly large number of contract negotiations, possession date is the primary stumbling block to successful completion of a sale. Make sure that you and your seller have worked out a mutually agreeable possession date and, if necessary, terms governing the period between closing and possession, before coming to the closing table.

Just the facts

- Understand that a closing is a formal meeting between you and the seller when a settlement agent confirms that she can deliver from the seller to you "good marketable title."

- Read as many of the closing documents as you can prior to that event to minimize surprises or a delay of the closing itself.

- Study the normal procedure that a closing follows in the signing of documents. A cash closing is brief; a closing involving a new loan takes longer.

- If there's a delay between closing and possession, make sure that you execute an occupancy agreement with the seller.

- After the closing, take the time to tie up all loose ends with the seller before you actually leave the closing table.

# PART VI

Taking It a Step Further

GET THE SCOOP ON...
Selecting the right movers ▪ Where to put the
furniture ▪ Checking the systems ▪ Finding out
about your neighborhood services ▪ Meeting your
neighbors ▪ Finding your home's real potential

Moving Into and Living in Your New Home

Chapter 14

Y ou have left the closing, keys securely in hand. Your head is spinning from all the paperwork and activity of the past few weeks—getting loan documents together, negotiating an inspection addendum, investigating documents you will be signing at closing, and a hundred other details. You've hardly had time to think about moving into, much less actually living in your new home.

Before you know it, the day will come when the furniture is finally in place. You'll be sitting in the soft glow of your lamp with your shoes kicked off, listening to the chimes of your grandmother's clock and thinking, "Yep. It's mine." Just as suddenly as you knew you wanted this house, you feel at home in it. What has occurred to transform you from homebuyer to homeowner?

In this chapter, we'll backtrack a bit to that moment when all the obstacles in the way of closing were removed and you first knew that you would really be moving. We'll go from there to the moving

> **❝**It takes a heap o' livin'
> in a house t' make it
> home.**❞**
> —Edgar A. Guest, "Home"

day itself, offering suggestions that will help you avoid spending a night on the floor with a sputtering candle as your only heat. Then, we'll move ahead still further and help you get situated in your new neighborhood and your new home. Finally, we'll help get you ready to plan for the future.

Getting ready to move in

As soon as the last contingency in your contract has been satisfied, you should call a mover and arrange an appointment at your current residence. If you're young and your belongings are still a bit sparse, arranging your move might be simple. For most of you, however, the moving process will be more complicated, and you'll need to choose a reliable mover and discuss a number of crucial issues with that mover first.

Choosing an interstate mover

There are two basic types of movers: interstate and local. If your move is interstate and you're being relocated by your company, chances are quite good that your company will pay moving expenses. If this is the case, get the full-blown treatment—not just a load-up and a drop-off, but a packing service to wrap and box your china and other breakables and valuables. Your employers will expect you to order the full treatment. Don't disappoint them!

On the other hand, if your move is interstate, you're not being relocated, and no one is telling you who your mover has to be, you should invite two or three movers to visit you separately and discuss their rates. These rates are calculated on a dollar amount per thousand pounds and on how long your furniture will be on the truck.

You may be surprised at how much the rates for various movers will vary. You will probably be even more surprised,

Watch Out!

Make sure that you're fully insured by your movers. Some have a maximum insurable rate of, say, 50¢ per pound. If you want to use such a mover, make sure to move your antiques and other valuables by yourself. If you can't, find a mover whose liability insurance coverage is unlimited and who has had demonstrable experience in moving antiques.

however, at what a sophisticated business the moving industry has become. It is likely that you'll be given a presentation (many moving companies now use videocassettes or CDs), an estimate, and a formal, written proposal describing exactly what services each moving company provides.

Invariably, you'll be told by any reliable company that your furniture and your valuables, as well as their movers, will be insured and that any damages you find will be paid for by the company. You'll be told how many workers will be involved. You'll get a packing time and an unpacking time, as well as a route time. By evaluating the degree of their professionalism, the price you are quoted, and their schedule for delivering and unloading your goods, you'll ultimately choose the moving company that best meets your needs.

The big three interstate movers are Allied, United, and Mayflower. They all quote different rates based on their travel maps with routes from one city to another. For example, even though the trip from Denver to Detroit is 1,200 miles and the trip from Biloxi to Hannibal is only 550, the Biloxi–Hannibal route may be more expensive for one mover, less expensive for another, based on two factors—where their truck hubs are and how frequently a particular route is traveled in their schedule.

Using local movers

Unlike the interstate moving companies, the local companies are legion. A local move is typically described as one of 50 miles or less, although if that 50 miles means going from one state to another, it may require the services of an interstate mover; more

Moneysaver

It helps to tell each mover you interview what another mover's estimate was. No mover wants to be underbid. If you play your cards right, you might get moved professionally and efficiently for less than you thought.

and more local companies, however, now hold interstate licenses. Finding a local mover is in many ways comparable to selecting a real estate agent when you already live in town. Typically, when you ask friends who have recently moved for a recommendation, you'll get a wide range of opinions about the movers they chose. Comments will range all the way from, "My furniture showed up in my front yard, looking as if it were dropped from the moon!" to "All my furniture showed up looking perfect, and the packers and loaders were so polite." If you hear two or more people voice the latter opinion, hire those movers!

Barring this occurrence, go to the Yellow Pages, look under "movers," and call six or seven phone numbers. Three or four of the people you talk to will have the smell of stale cigars and utter boredom in their voices. Thank them and hang up before asking too many questions. Invite the two or three polite ones (making sure, first, that they're insured) to visit you and give estimates. Interestingly, there will be less of a variance of rates among local movers. Most of them charge an hourly rate, based on the number of movers arriving with the moving truck. Most local movers will also tell you how many hours they estimate your move will take, from the time they begin to load their truck at one location to the time they drop off and, if you ask them to do so, arrange your furniture at your new location. Your choice of local movers will be based on their level of professionalism and how you fit into their schedule on the day you have to move.

Moving in, at last!

There's nothing quite so depressing in a move as watching your furniture pile up in the center of a few rooms. You get overwhelmed by the feeling that as soon as your movers leave, you'll have to work to place that heavy furniture where your movers could have placed it to begin with. It's like moving all over again! You can keep this from happening.

Let's back up to the day when the last contingency was removed from your contract. Most likely, you've kept your fact sheet with all your new home's room measurements. If not, get a new one. Why not return to your prospective home with the fact sheet, perhaps during the time of your pre-closing walk-through, and draw the shapes of each room on graph paper, designating each square as equal to six inches, or a foot? Next, bring your drawings back to your old place with you for some major plotting and planning. First, measure the length and width of each piece of your furniture. Then you can place everything in the appropriate location in the appropriate room, as drawn to scale on your graph paper.

Some people even cut out little blocks as scale models of their furniture and other large items and try out a variety of arrangements. Either way, with a little planning on your part, as your movers carry your furniture into your new house, you can tell them exactly where to put each item. Your movers will appreciate not having to roam from room to room with heavy furniture. And, you'll find that your move goes much more swiftly and efficiently.

Apply similar forethought and planning to your packed items. You can save time and aggravation by indicating on each box what's in it and in which room or area the box should be deposited.

 Bright Idea

When your movers are loading up the truck, have them load your beds last! That way, your beds will come off the truck and into your house first. If you have a lot of furniture, or if your movers arrive at your new house too late to unload everything, at least you're assured of having something on which to sleep.

Don't expect that the furniture arrangement you have on moving-in day will necessarily be permanent. If you're like most folks, as you become more comfortable with your new house, you'll inevitably make changes. On the whole, however, it is certainly more enjoyable to paint the walls, install new light fixtures or paddle fans, or hang up pictures during those first few weeks than lug heavy furniture up or down stairs or from room to room.

Making sure everything works

While you're decorating your home to make it look and feel like your own, take some time to check the basic systems. Your first few days in residence are a great time to find out some of the following basics. These are the ones rarely included in a walk-through checklist or observed by your home inspector:

- Who serviced the heating and air-conditioning systems and when?
- How much electrical capacity is still unused in the breaker or fuse system?
- How strong is your water pressure?
- How well has the attic been insulated?

If possible, ask the seller to supply the names of the contractors who have checked out the house in the past: plumbers, HVAC technicians, electricians. Many sellers keep detailed service records. If you can't get them, or if the seller didn't collect them, chances are pretty good that the furnace and breaker and/or fuse boxes have labels on them with the servicer's name and the date of the most recent servicing.

If you can't find the information, hire a licensed HVAC technician to service your systems right after you move in and tell you how to maintain them at peak efficiency. Make sure to have the technician show you where heat ducts and cold-air returns are located so you know the size of air filters you'll be using and where they need to be replaced. If your new house has an attic, make sure that it has at least nine inches of insulation.

Moneysaver

Blowing insulation into your attic can, in one year, save you more money on your power bills than the cost of the installation itself.

(Insulation will have been either laid in batts or blown in, in which case your attic floor will look like a sea of cotton.)

If you're moving in late fall or spring, the best way to prepare for very cold or hot weather is to make an appointment with an HVAC technician and an insulation specialist. It's extremely important that your heating and air-conditioning systems operate at maximum efficiency. Also, check that no excessive amount of heat or cold is escaping through porous insulation or poorly caulked windows. You may be about to enter the times of the year when the HVAC system and insulation are put to their severest test. Your utility bills will be a lot lower if these systems are operating at peak efficiency.

Your neighbors and your new lifestyle

In all likelihood, your new home won't be an isolated blip on a panorama of empty land. You'll be in a neighborhood, and you'll gradually feel that you're part of an integrated network of people. Some of you will be living in condominium complexes or town homes where, while you are achieving home ownership, will require many of the same adjustments and accommodations as far as neighbor relationships that you experienced while living in an apartment building.

Chances are that some neighborhood folks will show up at your doorstep on move-in day or shortly thereafter. (*Note:* Almost inevitably, you'll run into the neighborhood *authority:* a garrulous, self-important person who'll be all too willing to supply most of the answers to these questions just to show off!) If they don't show up at your door, seek them out. Take the opportunity to ask some basic questions. These questions, several examples of which follow in Table 14.1, can usually be broken down into two categories:

- Those that have to do with the character of the neighborhood.

- Those that have to do with basic services.

Table 14.1. Questions to Ask Your New Neighbors

1. Are there kids in the neighborhood who baby-sit?

2. Are there lots of pets?

3. Is there a leash law?

4. (Speaking of dogs . . .) Who is the neighborhood watchdog?

5. Who doesn't work during the day?

6. Who carpools to school?

7. Where's the local post office?

8. Where's the local satellite courthouse?

9. Where's the nearest DMV?

10. What is the procedure and day for garbage pickup?

The character of your neighborhood

As you'll soon learn, some of your neighbors will be nosy, some will be downright friendly, and some will keep utterly to themselves. Even the most private of neighbors contributes to the mythology of a place. You'll find out that your neighborhood is a collection of retold stories.

It's up to you to decide the degree to which you want to fit into the neighborhood dynamic. If you move into a condominium or co-op, you may want to become active in the association that manages maintenance fees and determines improvements and repairs. Some larger condominium associations even have social clubs. Belonging in some way gives you a measure of influence in a condo or co-op arrangement. This can be of significant benefit to you if you want your new setting to be a reflection of your lifestyle needs.

Bright Idea

Keep a record of what your neighbors' homes sell for from the day you move in to the day you contemplate moving out. This will give you a good sense both of how much your home appreciates in value over time and what improvements to make for the highest resale value in your neighborhood.

If you move into a new or newer subdivision, you'll probably become part of, and be a paying participant of, a neighborhood association that's responsible for everything from organizing block parties to making sure that the streetlights work. In an older, established neighborhood, you'll discover a special combination of characters. No matter what kind of neighborhood you enter, it will be up to you to determine the extent to which you want to become a participant.

One thing you may observe right away is that your new neighborhood seems quite fluid, in other words, ever-changing. As we have seen, people nowadays move much more frequently than they used to, so you should begin to feel like a part of your community very quickly. In six months to a year, you'll begin to lose that "I'm new" feeling, as you watch For Sale and Sold signs going up around you. In the sense that you've come to stay, at least for the short run, you'll start to feel like a neighborhood veteran when you see old neighbors moving out and new ones moving in.

Knowing your neighborhood services

There are always a few last-minute items that you will have forgotten to check before you move. Not the least important among these is neighborhood services. You may find answers to some of the questions that follow in the relocation packet supplied by your real estate agent; or between the White and Yellow Pages in your new local phone book; or from your local town hall, most of which have packages on town recreation facilities and services. At any rate, here's a checklist of the things you'll need to know so that your life can quickly return to normal.

1. **Garbage pickup:** What day or days of the week is your garbage picked up? Do you have to take garbage cans to the street, or will your service empty them from where you normally leave them? Are you supposed to have standardized cans, or will what you currently use be okay?

2. **Recycling:** Does your neighborhood have a recycling service? Does the service provide a standard bin? What types of items are collected? Do you have to separate cans and bottles and newspapers, or plastic, metal, and glass items? Where do you put your recycling bin for pickup?

3. **Fire service:** Where's the nearest fire hydrant? Where's your local fire station? Do you have to pay for fire service? How much? How often? Where do you send your payments?

4. **Water service:** How often are you billed for water usage? If you're on a sewer system, do you get a separate bill for service? Where is your water meter? Where are your turnoffs if something overflows or springs a leak?

5. **Medical services:** Where's your health insurance policy? Do you have a list of doctors and hospitals in your new community? If you're covered under an HMO, what doctors in your new town are eligible under your new coverage?

6. **Electrical service:** Is your wiring underground, or does it come from poles? Where's your electrical meter? Where is your breaker/fuse box? What do you flip if your power goes out in order to turn it back on? Do you have a backup system if all your power goes out?

7. **Police protection:** Where's the local police precinct, and what kind of police protection do you have? If you have a security system in your new house, is it connected to the local police precinct and fire station?

8. **Recreation facilities:** Where are the most comfortable places to work out? What type of equipment or amenities do they provide? What are their monthly membership rates?

It's always a good idea to make a neat list of the names, phone numbers, and locations of all your local services, your doctors and dentists, and your insurance agent. Keep the list posted near your most frequently used phone. The sooner you know the answers to all of the preceding questions and have a list, the sooner you'll feel relaxed in your new neighborhood.

Looking for potential: a very brief homeowner's guide

You're home. But beyond all the legal and contractual issues you've encountered lies a house. Sure, after the first rush of enthusiasm has died down, you'll find some imperfections and minor inconveniences. There's the toilet that makes a funny noise, the sink that clogs, the eaves that whistle in a storm. But, you've chosen your home carefully, and overall, you like it quite a bit.

Still, unless you had your home custom built, it may not be too long before you see hidden potential—the possibilities for making it even better. It could be said that in each house lies the potential for making it the ideal place to live. There is always room for change.

This doesn't have to mean the daunting prospect of total renovation. You may, for example, have the sense that you're not making the best use of the living space available to you. You want to make improvements. But, you can't exactly decide how you should improve the existing layout, or space, in your house. The following exercise may help you pinpoint the direction you want to take. If you can budget sensibly and carefully schedule the work you want done, you can make inexpensive changes

Moneysaver

The three most popular and cost-recouping areas of a home to remodel, according to research by the National Association of the Remodeling Industry, are kitchens, additions, and baths (in order of popularity).

that will improve the quality of your home life. They may also increase the resale value of your home.

Improving the quality of life in your new home

To put yourself in the right frame of mind, imagine showing your home to a real estate agent or a prospective buyer— anyone with an open mind who may have an ownership interest in your home. From such an objective, disinterested point of view, identify what needs changing by asking yourself some basic questions (Table 14.2):

Table 14.2. Checklist for Change

1. What is annoying or inconvenient about my house?

2. Have I already incurred repair bills on the basic systems?

3. Are there tight spots and bottlenecks where people are always running into one another?

4. Is my home physically comfortable both summer and winter? Is the temperature uniform in all rooms?

5. Are there enough power outlets?

6. Are there enough hose bibcocks?

7. Does the house have enough natural light? Is the artificial light diffuse, yet bright enough so that you can read everywhere? Is everything that should be on a rheostat (adjustable-intensity light switch) on a rheostat?

8. Do the grounds, shrubs, trees, outside lights, and other outdoor features integrate well with the house itself? After you've completed this exercise as part of an objective assessment of your home, move to a more purely personal plane for evaluation.

9. What feature pleases me the most about my house?

10. What feature most displeases me?

11. Is there a room that is used only infrequently? Could it be put to better use?

12. Which room do I feel most comfortable in?

13. Which rooms do family and friends naturally congregate in?

14. Does the current use of space really reflect and fit my lifestyle?

15. Is there a room that needs to be bigger? What would it take to enlarge it?

16. Which room is used for which activity? Is there a logical pattern here? Would alterations improve the pattern?

17. Does the outside patio or deck integrate well with the rest of the house, and vice versa?

18. Should I install an outdoor gas line for putting in a barbecue, or is my "portable" just fine?

19. Would a change of floor covering in a selected room or rooms improve the house?

20. What about the paint, wallpaper, and accessories? Are they appropriate to the various rooms, as well as to the way I live?

You can respond to these questions without having to envision major alterations. The best answers come from visualizing both the functional and the beautiful in your surroundings: those things that are best-suited to the styles and preferences of you and your family. List every obstacle currently standing in the way of your achieving the goal of both practical and beautiful space utilization. The best time to look at your house dispassionately is after you've lived there a short time—before you develop unnecessary habits to compensate for any poor uses of space. Or, perhaps before you've made excuses for, or become inured to, any inadequacies in the operation of the basic systems.

Checklists for change!

You should find that the questions on your checklist for change fall into two categories: 1) cosmetic/surface and 2) fundamental. The first category comprises features that are relatively inexpensive to change and easy to manage—such as redecoration,

 Bright Idea

Make sure to keep receipts and/or invoices in connection with selling your old house and buying your new one. Certain repair costs may be tax-deductible. For purposes of a resale down the road, you should keep these records indefinitely.

minor repair work, and reorganization. You'll be amazed at how moving a few pieces of furniture, painting an accent wall, building and installing some bookshelves, or slicking a blown ceiling can turn space of previously questionable purpose, value, or beauty into something both functional and aesthetically pleasing.

The second category on our checklist for change—fundamental—tends to require a greater expenditure of money and time. Its three most common forms include changing systems, altering existing space, and adding new space. If you change systems—the heating, air-conditioning, water heater, or electrical wiring or circuitry—it's probably best to find out how each of these systems is integrated into a functioning whole. For example, there's no point replacing your gas furnace and leaving your 40-gallon, 15-year-old water heater to chug along, allowing only two showers before it needs a break to heat more water.

Altering space, we're pleased to report, is easier to accomplish than it used to be. Newer homes have far fewer bearing walls than older homes do, making it easier to move or even completely tear out walls than it is in their older counterparts. In very old homes, each stud or framing member supports a roof or second story. Modular walls (walls that don't go all the way up to the ceiling, but still serve to partition off, or divide space) can transform some of your underutilized space into a library, a reading nook, a sleeping loft, or storage closets. The list goes on and on.

Finally, adding new space is, of course, the most expensive enterprise you can undertake. Before you do it, you need to ask yourself two critical questions:

1. Will I be living in my house long enough to take full advantage of my added space?

2. Will I be over-building for my neighborhood, thereby putting my house beyond the price range of the houses around me in the event that I resell?

Moneysaver

Lots of additional storage can be provided by simple closet reorganization. The "let's get organized" and "California closet" movements provide inexpensive reinforced plastic modular boxes, racks, and shelves that can really enhance your storage space and unclutter your living space.

Whether you alter existing space or add new space, keep in mind current trends in taste and design so that your house will be popular with the next wave of buyers. Try to avoid doing anything *perverse*, like adding a cupola on the top of a brick ranch house or putting Gothic arches in the doorways of a house with eight-foot ceilings. These bizarre expressions might compromise the value of your home for another buyer down the road. The tendency today is toward openness—this includes a kitchen with a wide-cased opening into the den, allowing the family to function as an integrated unit. Another marked trend is to have a master bedroom with a vaulted or trayed ceiling. And many newer houses have balconies projected over high-ceilinged living areas below.

If you add on to, or expand your kitchen, which is the hub of many homes, you will usually be able to command a good resale price. In your kitchen, work toward achieving the maximum amount of counter space and natural light. Fresh bathrooms with nicely tiled floors and skylights come in a close second in terms of resale. Of course, additions always add value to a home, but they're beyond many people's reach financially. As far as simpler, less expensive remodeling is concerned, the addition of fireplaces comes in third. Whatever major work you undertake, think not only about making your house as comfortable and practical as you can, but also about the next homeowner's comfort and sense of practicality. That's why we recommend doing your renovation homework early along in your ownership, when you can be more objective.

Bright Idea

Any room that has adequate attic space above it can have its ceiling trayed relatively inexpensively but with positive aesthetic consequences. Currently, ceilings of a height greater than eight feet are in vogue. Adding cubic space in one or several rooms of your home tends to create a feeling of airiness and expansiveness, even if you don't increase the actual square footage of the living space.

A parting thought

Well . . . you're home, and we're happy about any help we've been in getting you there. What we've tried to give you, above all else, is an orderly process for buying a home. All too often, people plunge headlong into the process, without adequate thought or preparation. Invariably, these same people find home buying to be a real ordeal. They come away battle-scarred, with bad memories of what they've gone through and regrets about what they've bought.

In this unofficial guide to buying a home, we've tried to provide you with sound advice, practical insider information, and a logical pattern to follow. We've tried to outline and explain the key components of a successful home search. Although you have two more chapters left to read in this book, we're making the following request now: If you find that we've missed something, we would like to hear from you so that others can benefit. We want you to come away from this book prepared to make your home search a pleasurable experience. Above all, we want you to come away prepared to make your personal search a success.

Just the facts

- Interview two or more moving companies before choosing one.
- Make a detailed scheme of where to place your furniture and other items.

- Check out your home's basic operating systems shortly after you move in.
- Get to know your new neighbors and learn how to access and use the local services.
- Before you get too settled in your new home, think about any changes that could improve your use of space, the operation of your systems, or the overall quality of living in your new home.

GET THE SCOOP ON...
Laws governing real estate transactions ▪
Anticipating legal land mines ▪ Contract language to save your skin ▪ Legal challenges of
new construction

Nobody Knows the Trouble I've Seen—A Real Estate Law Primer

Chapter 15

This chapter was written by John N. Randolph, practicing attorney for 30 years; formerly, partner and residential real estate attorney with Sirote & Permutt, P.C.

If homebuyers, lenders, agents, and closing attorneys all attended the same summer camp, these are the stories they would tell under star-filled skies sitting around a blazing fire. Although, unofficially speaking, the lessons to be learned from each story are pretty apparent, and some have been explored in previous chapters, we're not above beating a dead horse. Thus, we will explain each tale, emphasizing the fine points.

Caveat emptor, let the buyer beware!

Tim and Martha had found just the house they wanted: plenty of storage space, room for more kids, a large kitchen, and a low-maintenance yard. Austin,

317

the owner, was delighted to have gotten a quick contract, as he had already committed with a builder to construct a new residence on a lot he had recently purchased.

In preparation for closing, the termite bonding company made a routine inspection of Austin's house, and reported to him that there was "water" in the crawl space, which was accessed through a trap door in the floor of a hallway. Austin went to a local builder's supply house and purchased a large quantity of sand, which he poured into the crawl space to cover the water. After closing, Tim and Martha detected a stench coming from the trap door and discovered that the crawl space was awash in raw sewage.

The diagnosis was a hopelessly defective septic tank. After being cited by the local health department, Tim and Martha paid the fines and the cost to connect to the public sewer, and sued Austin to recoup their losses. "Caveat emptor," said the judge, "You had the opportunity to inspect the property yourself and learn of its deficiencies before you closed, and now it's too late to complain."

And yet, the same court, in the same term, decided a similar case with an entirely different outcome:

James and Cathy's offer to purchase John's home was accepted with the following contract provision: "House being sold 'as is,'" except Seller warrants heating and air-conditioning to be in working order at the time of closing." John asked Brasher, his agent, to contact a local heating contractor to "get the system running." The contractor reported to John and Brasher that the system was unsafe, and gave them a written report stating, "The furnace has a cracked combustion chamber and the vent is undersized. The furnace, vent, and evaporation coil need replacing for safe operation of the furnace."

"Well," said Brasher, "all we have to do is get the system running." Accordingly, the contractor replaced the thermostat so that the furnace would seem to be operating normally when James and Cathy did their walk-through inspection prior to closing. The inevitable discovery of the cracked combustion chamber led to the inevitable lawsuit, and in this case, the court ruled in favor of James and Cathy.

The difference between the results in these two lawsuits lies in the fact that the cracked combustion chamber presented a potentially grave hazard to the health and safety of the purchasers, James and Cathy, invoking a duty of disclosure upon John and his agent. The heating contractor testified at the trial: "I told (John and Brasher) that they had a pretty serious problem and I was surprised that somebody hadn't gotten hurt or killed." This provided the prime justification for the judgment in favor of the buyers.

As we'll see, today's trend, even in the most staunch Caveat Emptor jurisdictions, is away from the harsh results that Tim and Martha suffered, instead punishing those sellers and real estate agents alike who deliberately conceal material facts about the condition of the property being sold. But these legal conundrums and trends are of little interest or comfort for the average homebuyer, who is far more concerned about a problem-free purchase than providing two teams of lawyers with a year or so of sustenance.

The real lesson to be learned in the cases of Tim and Martha and James and Cathy is that their problems, and, consequently, their litigation, could easily have been avoided with the proper contract provisions and follow-up. Thus, the purpose of this chapter is to touch on a variety of legal issues crucial to a buyer's interest, and to offer a few simple contract suggestions that may keep you and your local trial judge blissfully unacquainted. Finally, we'll explore some of the more recent court decisions in search of remedies for those purchasers who, despite their best efforts to avoid it, find themselves in litigation.

The statute of frauds

Virtually every jurisdiction adheres in some degree to the ancient common law precept, codified in modern times into

Moneysaver

Don't shop for bargains when hiring an attorney. Network, check references, and hire the best available. In the long run you'll save money.

state legislation known as the Statute of Frauds, that agreements for the sale and purchase of real estate are unenforceable unless in writing and signed by the parties involved. Many are the cases in which a purchaser has given an owner an earnest money check on an oral promise to sell, only to have the owner turn around and accept a higher offer from someone else.

Of course, this does not mean that transactions do not occur every day in which no contract has been signed, but the complexity of modern law and the many issues involved in real estate matters dictate that a homebuyer insist upon a competently drafted realty purchase contract. And it is through the use of contingencies that purchasers can avoid experiences such as those suffered by folks like James and Cathy. Here are some of the more important issues that contingencies can address:

Financing

Most people are unable to buy a home without financing, and it is customary in the industry to allow purchasers to break their contracts if, through no fault of their own, their financing falls through. While there are as many different approaches to financing clauses as there are people who write them, our experience is that simplicity is always preferable, and we opt in favor of, "This purchase is expressly contingent upon the purchasers obtaining financing on terms and conditions satisfactory to them."

Confronted by such directness, it is not unreasonable for sellers to counter with a requirement that the buyer provide evidence of at least preliminary approval for a loan within a certain period of time.

Inspections

This is where Tim, Martha, James, and Cathy all shared fault for the fates they suffered, and in fact their omission reveals much of the rationale behind Caveat Emptor. Buyers have every right to fully inspect the residence they want to buy. Indeed, Caveat Emptor dictates that they must do so, and any agent or lawyer who writes a contract offer without an inspection contingency is, in a word, incompetent. Again, our preference for simplicity induces us to use the following language: "This purchase is expressly contingent upon the purchasers performing at their expense such inspections of the property and the residence, its structures and systems, as the purchasers may desire, with results satisfactory to them."

There are many ways in which the Statute of Frauds can apply to inspections that go beyond cases such as that of James and Cathy. Most buyers who work with agents ask them for a recommendation for a competent inspector. Some agents simply tell their clients to shop in The Yellow Pages and call a few inspectors, determine the person in whom they have the most confidence, and hire that person to proceed with a formal inspection. Many agents provide lists of inspectors they have used before to other clients' satisfaction. A few unethical agents, however, have been known to select one inspector for their clients, sing his or her praises, and even make claims about that inspector's qualifications, including verbal affirmations that the inspector is licensed, bonded, insured, or all three. If the inspector botches the job—let's say he misses the crack in the combustion chamber and the purchaser who hired him suffers material damage, physical damage, or both, the real estate agent could be found guilty under the Statute of Frauds.

However, even the most brilliantly written contingency clause is worthless unless the buyers actually perform the inspections they have requested. One of the major justifications for the court's conclusion in the concealed sewage leak case was that Tim had actually been in the construction business with his father for a number of years and should have known what to look for, had he bothered to look.

Wood infestation reports

In our practice, we have had more problems arise in connection with residential infestation of wood-destroying organisms than any other single issue. Most states in regions blessed with termites and other wood-consuming varmints provide for pest control agencies to perform residential inspections and produce an "official" Wood Infestation Report, detailing evidence of both active and previous infestation, and resulting damage. One approach that we commonly use on behalf of buyers is a contingency clause stating, "This purchase is expressly contingent upon the sellers, at their expense, providing to the purchasers at closing a termite bond (and/or powder post beetle bond, or fungus bond, etc.), paid and in force for a year after closing, together with a Wood Infestation Report covering all structures on the property, reflecting no infestation of wood-destroying organisms and no damage therefrom."

Because of the frequency of problems in this field, and because many residential home inspectors do not include wood-destroying organisms in their reports, we usually address this in a separate contingency, even though it is also contemplated by the inspection contingency language.

Federal Residential Lead-Based Paint Hazard Reduction Act of 1995

Federal law now places an affirmative burden, upon both sellers and their agents, to disclose information relating to the existence of lead-based paint in residential housing constructed prior to 1978 (called "target housing" by the Act). Significantly, the purpose of the Act is to require disclosure of known lead-paint hazards, not abatement. In other words, the Act does not require that a seller do anything about lead paint in the housing he owns, but simply to disclose any known hazard.

Watch Out!

Especially frightening to realty agents is the 1995 Hazard Reduction Act's stipulation that it is "his/her duty to ensure (the seller's) compliance" with the act. The agent's or seller's failure to abide by the law may subject them to both criminal and civil sanctions, as well as a potential award of "treble damages" to purchasers who suffer harm from lead paint poisoning.

Simply stated, the seller must

1. Give the prospective purchasers an approved brochure, such as a pamphlet developed by the federal Environmental Protection Agency entitled, "Protect Your Family From Lead In Your Home";

2 Give the purchasers (or have the purchaser waive in writing) a 10-day contingency in which to perform a lead assessment at their expense, and to cancel the contract if they are dissatisfied with the results; and

3. Complete certain written disclosures regarding the seller's knowledge and records relating to the existence of lead-based paint.

While the primary focus of the Lead-Based Paint Hazard Reduction Act is to protect low-income families living in old, poorly maintained residences, there is nothing to prevent a toddler born into a wealthier class from putting paint flakes in his mouth. Very simply, any purchaser with a concern about this potential hazard should take advantage of the 10-day assessment contingency permitted by the federal law.

Survey and appraisal

Purchasers (and sellers, for that matter) frequently confuse surveys with appraisals. An appraisal is a written report, usually performed by an individual licensed specifically for the purpose, comparing the condition and amenities of a particular property with others of a similar nature, for the purpose of producing a professional estimate or opinion as to the market value of the residence being purchased. With a few exceptions, virtually every mortgage lender requires that a prospective borrower's property appraise for at least the amount of the purchase price, or the lender will not extend the financing. In fact, among the first things a lender will normally request of a mortgage loan applicant is a copy of a signed contract to purchase and a check to pay for an appraisal.

If a buyer's contract has a properly drafted financing contingency in it, then she is protected if the house fails to appraise, since she cannot then obtain her mortgage loan; but careful purchasers and those who pay cash for their new home often feel safer with a specific appraisal contingency, and here is our language for it:

> This purchase is expressly contingent upon the property appraising for no less than the amount of the purchase price,

or,

> This purchase is expressly contingent upon purchasers performing at their expense an appraisal of the property with results satisfactory to them.

By comparison, a survey is a drawing of the specific property being bought, performed by a licensed engineer according to certain technical standards dictated by the profession and/or particular laws and regulations. It depicts the property boundaries, the location of the residence and other improvements on the property, fence lines, the existence of established easements for public utilities, drainage, and the like, and the means of ingress to and egress from the property to a public right of way. Regardless of whether a mortgage lender or title insurer requires a new survey, we always recommend to purchasers that their contract contain a survey contingency:

> This purchase is expressly contingent upon the purchasers performing at their expense a survey of the property reflecting conditions satisfactory to them.

While the overwhelming majority of surveys of lots in established residential subdivisions may disclose few significant problems, the exceptions can give people fits. Some of the more common conditions that surveys reveal include shared driveways for which there may be no joint-use easement; violations of building set-back lines, which are especially important in the case of new construction; shared or encroaching fences that raise the possibility of disputes between adjoining property owners as to the location of boundaries; and the lack of access to a public right of way. A buyer simply cannot be informed regarding this condition unless she has access to an accurate, up-to-date survey.

Title exceptions

These include formal, dedicated rights-of-way for ingress and egress, reservations of mineral rights, easements for utilities, and restrictions governing the use of the property being bought. Generally speaking, these matters are already in place and cannot be changed by a purchaser shopping for a new home, but they most certainly impact the way the buyer will be permitted to use the property, and no one, especially those looking at a vacant lot for new construction, should enter into a transaction without the opportunity to cancel the deal if a review of the title exceptions reveals unacceptable conditions.

We may best illustrate problems that title exceptions pose in the case of vacant lots by relating the facts of a case in which we were personally involved. José was a very successful physician and was ready to build a new home for his family consistent with his professional station. He and his wife badly wanted to build in a particular established, upscale residential area, but very few

Watch Out!

Make discreet inquiries to determine if any of your prospective neighbors are malcontent, overly fastidious, belligerent, or litigious.

lots there remained undeveloped, and those that became occasionally available were usually carved out of larger estate properties after the deaths of longtime residents. And it was one of these upon which José ultimately placed an offer.

A title insurance company issued a commitment to insure the lot, but during its examination of the public records, it discovered that the property under contract was once part of a five-acre estate lot established in the 1920s that was subject to a recorded restriction imposed by the original developer that specifically prohibited more than one residence per estate lot, and subdivision into smaller parcels. Investigation revealed that over the decades since the 1920s, most of the original estate lots in the neighborhood had been subdivided more than 50 times, all in violation of the original restrictions, and that in each instance, the subdivisions had received the approval of the city planning authority. José elected to close his purchase of the lot, even though the title insurer told him that they would not cover him against loss if someone attempted to enforce the restrictions.

What José did not count on was that his future next-door neighbor, whom he knew personally, bore him a grudge from a past experience and had the resources and the inclination to give him fits. The neighbor sued José to prevent construction of the new home. Although José ultimately prevailed in court (the restrictions had been violated so many times that they were, in the eyes of the law, terminated by abandonment and nonenforcement), he was embroiled in years of litigation, at substantial expense, and he never did build his new house. José rolled the dice when he closed on the lot and suffered for it, but a more careful purchaser might have refused to close until fully informed of the risks.

There are a number of other issues relating to vacant lots that we'll explore later, but one of the most common involving title exceptions may be found in a covenant contained in a planned subdivision's formal restrictions granting the original developer the right to repurchase the lot if the owner offers it for sale before constructing a residence upon it. We have seen courts issue injunctions against lot owners who have failed to comply with such a limitation, but these were granted in cases where the transfer of title to the new owner had not yet occurred. We have our doubts that a court would, in fairness, set aside a title transfer where the new owner was not actually aware of the repurchase restriction, and had expended substantial sums to construct a new residence. But that new owner might find, as did José, that people can be vindictive and find themselves beating back a forced repurchase attempt in court.

Turning to problems resulting from title exceptions in the case of existing residences, we find that,

> 66 If your neighbors play fast and loose with the subdivision restrictions, that doesn't mean you should. On the other hand, if you go by the book, you might get your neighbors in hot water. 99
>
> —Peter Ford, Contractor

although less dramatic than those suffered by José, they can be significant. The most common derive from extensive restrictions, sometimes taking book length and form, that are routinely imposed these days in more expensive subdivisions. These may strictly regulate everything from exterior color to woodpiles in the back yard and impose fines and liens against offending properties.

A friend was once sued by her homeowners' association for erecting a weathervane on her roof without prior approval by the neighborhood "restriction police." She won her case—we speculate that the judge was influenced by the association's trite and dictatorial behavior. But many purchasers would be appalled by the prospect of having their personal lives and properties so strictly regulated. Contingency language that gives buyers the opportunity to at least become informed of the existence and content of title exceptions before closing might read,

> This purchase is expressly contingent upon the purchaser's approval of the title insurance commitment issued with respect to the property, and of the exceptions, restrictions, easements and reservations it discloses.

Vacant lots for new construction

Lot purchasers must also think about the developer of the subdivision, its stage of construction (when will the roads be finished, the utilities installed?), and particular issues related to actually building on the chosen lot. Several of these issues arose in connection with another matter in which we were involved, described here.

Frank and his wife were attracted to a new subdivision being constructed in a wooded area. The stage of development was only partial, with utility installation and road paving incomplete. Although the developer was reputable, no one (especially in the real estate business) is exempt from financial difficulty, and Frank asked me what provisions we could include in his contract offer that might protect him if the developer was unable to complete the subdivision's infrastructure.

"Don't close until he does," is what we told him, and here is the contingency language we used for his contract:

> This purchase is expressly contingent upon the seller completing construction of all permanent roads providing ingress to and egress from the property, and all storm sewers and drains associated with those roads and with the development, and the seller installing all public utilities, including electricity, telephone, water, sewerage, and cable television, to the boundary of the property so as to enable the purchaser to connect to them at no cost to the purchaser.

In the case of the lot chosen by Frank and his wife, the developer, in establishing required utility easements by means of the

Watch Out!

Language relating to a subdivision's infrastructure seeks to place the burden upon the developer to pay the public utilities' impact or connection fees for the purchaser. But you never know what concessions a developer might be willing to make until you propose them in your offer.

subdivision's record map or plat, created and dedicated an easement for drainage that ran right through the site where Frank wanted to build. Although the lay of the land easily permitted a relocation of the drain to another part of the lot, the problem lay in the fact that the dedicated easement for the drain had, in effect, been legally cast in stone by approval of the record map for the subdivision by the local planning authorities, and to move it would require the same formal consent, which might take months.

To address the problem, we used this language in Frank's offer:

> This purchase is expressly contingent upon the Seller and Purchasers entering into a written agreement, which shall survive the closing, providing for the Seller, at its expense, to relocate the drainage easement upon the Property to a location that is satisfactory to the Purchasers, and providing further for the Seller to obtain, at its expense, approval for such amendments to the Declaration of Covenants and Restrictions, and for any amendments to the recorded plat of the 5th Sector of Old Greenback Estates required by any governmental agency having jurisdiction, as may be necessary to accomplish the vacation of the existing drainage easement and its removal to the location satisfactory to the Purchasers.

The offer went on to say that if the required approvals were not obtained within a certain time, the developer would repurchase the lot.

Frank's wife was also concerned by the fact that this was a new subdivision, located in a relatively remote wooded area, and that because she and Frank were among the first purchasers, years might pass before other homes were built and

Bright Idea

While repurchase provisions may work fine in the case of financially stable developers, no agreement to repurchase is effectual if a developer has failed, gone out of business, and has no assets. Check out a developer before you buy, and be wary of new developers or developers without a local history.

their lot would become less isolated. Accordingly, we included in the contract offer another repurchase provision, triggered in the event that a certain minimum number of building permits for lots in the immediate area were not issued within a year.

With these preliminary concerns addressed, we needed only to ensure that the specific residence that Frank's architect had designed could, in fact, be built on the lot. Accordingly, we concluded Frank's offer with this contingency language, which we always use even in the most uncomplicated of lot purchases:

> This purchase is expressly contingent upon the purchasers satisfying themselves that they can construct the residence and other improvements that they desire upon the property, at a price, and upon terms and conditions, that are satisfactory to them.

"Time is of the essence"

Roger and Jane were fortunate to own an extremely attractive home in a desirable neighborhood, so that when they decided to sell and move, they were inundated with prospective purchasers. In a matter of a few days, they had accepted a contract offer from John, which contained this clause: "The sale shall be closed and the deed delivered to the Purchaser on or before February 17, 1998." Still, so many prospects remained interested in buying the home that Roger and Jane began to feel that they may have acted too hastily in accepting John's offer. Their suspicions were confirmed when Roy submitted to them an offer at a substantially larger price, cash on the line, no contingencies. On their agent's advice, they accepted Roy's offer as a "back up" contract, providing that it would become effective in the event that John failed to close.

February 16th arrived, and John's mortgage broker told him that, through no fault of John's, his lender would be unable to complete the processing of his mortgage loan until sometime the week of February 23rd. "Aha!" said Roger and Jane, "Now we can break this contract and sell to Roy at a much higher profit!" They asked their agent to refund John's earnest money and to set up a closing date with Roy. The agent, after consulting her broker, told them that they needed to talk to a lawyer before taking any further action. Puzzled, they did so, asking, "The contact plainly says that John had to close by the 17th. Why can't we sell to Roy?"

Why, indeed? Because the contract with John did not say that "time is of the essence" with respect to the closing date. While this may seem an unfair technicality, most modern courts have adopted the view that if the parties to a contract intended performance by a particular date to be so important, they would have specifically said so; and that, absent any fault for a delay by the party who is seeking an extension, he should have a "reasonable time" in which to perform his obligations.

It is easier to understand this rationale by considering some of the issues involved if time, is, in fact, "of the essence" to a particular party. In our example, let's assume that Roger and Jane were suffering serious financial difficulty, and that the primary motivation for their decision to sell their house was that Roger had a very large business loan coming due on February 18th, and that he would be subjected to substantial late charges and

Bright Idea

Our examples of when a "time is of the essence" clause is appropriate are not inclusive. If for any reason your demand for a response to an offer is well-served by such a clause, we recommend that you write one into your offer at the very outset.

penalties if he were unable to pay on time. Faced with such difficulties, it is reasonable to expect him to make his prospective purchaser aware that the closing date was of critical importance to him, and that if he, the purchaser, was unable to close on time, then Roger simply had to sell it to someone else.

Or, look at the issue from a purchaser's perspective. Let's say that a buyer, Maury, had been transferred by his employer into the city and had nowhere to live other than the house he had contracted to purchase. Moreover, he had already closed the sale of his previous home and had agreed to vacate by a particular date. In fact, the movers were scheduled to clear the prior residence and to deliver all of the furniture to the new home on the date after the scheduled closing in the new city. One would reasonably expect Maury to have told his sellers of this problem and, if competently advised, to insure that "time is of the essence" language was included in his contract.

Of course, both of these examples raise the question, "If time is, in fact, of the essence, then what happens if a party fails to perform?" A competently written contract will contain the answer. For example, in Maury's case, it would have been straightforward to provide that, "Time being of the essence, the sale must be closed and the deed delivered by no later than July 12, 1999; if the sellers fail to close as herein provided, they agree to pay to the purchaser at closing his reasonable expenses for hotel accommodations and for storing his furniture and furnishings until possession is delivered, and his reasonable expenses in moving his furniture and furnishings from storage to the property."

The example of Roger and Jane's situation does not readily lend itself to providing monetary reimbursement for losses. It is unlikely that John would have ever signed a contract in the first place if it tried to shift the burden for loan penalties and late charges to him. But Roger and Jane's contract could easily have stated that, "Time being of the essence, in the event that the sale is not closed and the deed delivered by no later than February 17,

1998, then the Sellers may, at their option, cancel this contract by refunding the earnest money to the purchaser in full, in which event this contract shall be null and void."

These issues related to time of performance are not restricted to dates of closing. Indeed, every date in a contract for completing inspections, for providing proof of acceptance for financing, and for vacating the property are all considered to be only target dates under the law unless "time is of the essence" is specifically provided, or the parties have a reasonable time under the circumstances in which to perform their obligations. Some lazy drafters, or those who have not thought through the issues involved, will include in their contracts a separate paragraph saying simply that, "Time is of the essence in the performance of this agreement," with unintended consequences.

For example, a day before the contract closing date, a seller may have an automobile accident or other health problem rendering them physically unable to close as scheduled. There are many a cold-footed purchaser who would welcome the opportunity to break a contract in this way. The sellers would then have to resort to litigation, and the case histories are replete with contradictory results on the issue of whom the blanket "time is of the essence" clause was actually intended to protect.

Note: Litigation should be a last resort. Aside from being expensive and stressful, there is rarely any certainty regarding the outcome. More and more, lawyers who close real estate sales are asking buyers and sellers to sign a statement that all parties in the sale agree to arbitrate rather than, or at least before, they litigate.

Our personal preference is to include "time is of the essence" provisions only with respect to specific issues that clearly must be performed by a specific date, and to craft remedies for nonperformance that are not so onerous that the other party would never sign the contract in the first place. Otherwise, we are generally content to leave the "reasonable time" doctrine to run its course, almost always with satisfactory results.

Possession dates

All of the considerations regarding "time is of the essence" apply to the date that parties write into contracts for delivery of possession to the purchaser, but it has been our experience that buyers typically have more problems with what happens to the house between the closing date and the possession date than with when possession is actually delivered.

It is extremely common for contracts to contain a 3-, 4-, 7-, or even 14-day period between the date the sale is closed and the date possession is to be delivered to the buyer, and it is just as common for the parties to fail to address issues such as responsibility for damages to the property and payment of utilities while the sellers remain in possession. Purchasers often have these concerns dawn upon them the day before closing, and call the closing agent asking for an elaborate lease arrangement to be written and, as it were, shoved under the sellers' faces at closing.

Our standard solution to this problem is a contract provision stating that, "The sellers agree to deliver possession of the property to the purchasers in the same condition as at the time of closing, and with the heating, cooling, plumbing, sanitary, telephone, cable television, and electrical systems operating in normal condition; the purchasers shall have the right to a 'walk-through' inspection of the property, immediately prior to both closing and delivery of possession, to determine its condition."

In the case of an extended gap between closing and possession, it is also not unreasonable for the purchasers to ask that the sellers pay them a reasonable rent—for example, at a rate equivalent to that of the purchasers' monthly mortgage payment, including escrows for taxes and insurance. Payment of utilities for the period is also a common agreement. For truly extended periods, months at a time, the parties should enter into a formal lease agreement.

However, the primary point to be retained from all this is that these concerns must be resolved at the stage of negotiating

Watch Out!

Subdivision developers often specify special warranty deeds in their contracts for the plain purpose of limiting their liability.

the contract, not at closing. Otherwise, sellers can legitimately take the position that since repairs or rent or utilities were not addressed by the contract, their obligation is limited to exercising reasonable care during their hold-over period, and should the air-conditioning or other systems fail as the result of ordinary wear and tear, then that's the purchasers' problem.

Conveyances and title assurance

Virtually every purchaser in modern times fully expects the seller to convey clear title to the property being sold, and most stock contract forms do contain provisions to that effect, "subject only to reservations, easements, rights of way, covenants, and restrictions of record." Generally, the highest form of title that one may receive is expressed by an old English common law term, "fee simple," which is defined by Black's Law Dictionary as an estate "in which the owner is entitled to the entire property, with unconditional power of disposition during his life, and descending to his heirs and legal representatives upon his death..."

Interestingly, it is possible for a seller to convey a fee simple title, but to limit his personal liability for possible defects in that title, by specifying in the sales contract that he will give the purchaser at closing what is known as a special warranty deed. The usual impact of such a warranty is that the seller is saying to the purchaser, in effect, "I warrant to you that I have personally done nothing to impair the title to this property while I have owned it, but I make no guarantees about what my predecessors may have done."

Other types of limited conveyances include a special warranty deed given by a decedent's personal representative, confining

Bright Idea

There is no excuse for you, as the purchaser, not reading the contracts and forms that document your real estate transaction. To save time and enhance understanding, request specimen contracts and forms in advance.

the extent of liability for title defects to the assets in the estate, and a quitclaim deed, through which the grantor is saying, simply, "I make no guarantees whether I have a title interest in this property, but if I do, it's yours."

A buyer, quite naturally, will want his seller to give him the highest form of title warranty available, and in most jurisdictions, this is known as the general warranty deed. This encompasses all defects in title, whenever and by whoever created, and, of course, it is the best practice to specify a general warranty deed in a contract offer. But as a practical matter, these warranties are no better than the people who give them. A general warranty deed given by an insolvent may very well transfer title, but it will not give the purchaser any relief if a title defect must be cured.

For this reason, modern transactions are protected by policies of title insurance, which, ideally, place the burden for rectifying title problems upon a national, well-capitalized institution, rather than upon local individuals or businesses of limited means. The title insurance company seeks to limit both title problems and its liability for them in two ways. First, it maintains a modern, computerized title plant with records of all properties within its business area. If, when asked to insure a property, it encounters a title defect, it will require that the defect be cured before the policy can be issued. This reduces the risk of a later claim to nearly nothing.

Second, like all insurance, it spreads the risk of loss among millions of policyholders nationwide. For these reasons, the title insurance company can offer the protection that both sellers and purchasers desire for a relatively small, one-time premium, paid at closing. Of course, who pays for the title insurance is a matter of negotiation and custom in the local area. Keep in mind that a mortgage lender will always require title insurance, injecting another element into the issue of who pays.

New construction and warranties of fitness

Buying or building a brand-new residence introduces a range of issues that differ from those of the "pre-loved home" (our favorite realty agent's euphemism for a used home). Most of these involve getting the builder to finish the construction, finish it on time, and to stand by his work after the closing. But others arise virtually at the outset, and may lead buyers into adventures in bankruptcy and litigation.

To illustrate the latter, we'll examine this too-frequently repeated scenario, which usually involves purchasers of modest means. James and Carla, young, newlywed, and without an established banking relationship, are given a lot by their parents as a joint wedding gift. Inquiring into builders, they are wooed by Seat of the Pants Construction, Inc., Smilin' Sam Smith, President, who tells them, "Now you kids know that you don't have the credit to get a construction loan, but I can. All you need to do is to transfer title of your lot to me, so that I can pledge it as security to the lender, and I'll get the construction loan. I'll deed the property back to you when we're through."

We'll give Smilin' Sam the benefit of the doubt and say that this is what he really did intend to do, but like so many builders, Seat of the Pants Construction, Inc., like other contractors we've mentioned in this book, had a habit of using funds drawn from one project to pay off subcontractors and suppliers on another, with the result that Smilin' Sam became hopelessly behind in paying for James and Carla's new home.

His subcontractors refused to work and they and his suppliers filed liens against the lot. His construction lender threatened to declare his loan in default. His lawyer told Smilin' Sam

Moneysaver

Remember that your ownership of the lot you're building on may comprise the down payment for your construction loan. You forfeit this option if you convey your lot to your builder.

to put Seat of the Pants Construction, Inc., into bankruptcy, and he did. Just as soon as he could get away with it, Smilin' Sam left town. James and Carla found themselves petitioning the bankruptcy court for return of title to the lot to them, which left them with unpaid liens against the property, a defaulted construction mortgage, and an unfinished house.

Suffice it to say again, as we did in Chapter 7, that lot owners should convey their property to a builder only if the lot owners get their own construction financing and have hired a builder to build a custom home.

If it meant that James and Carla had to wait a few years to work on establishing banking relationships so that they could get their own construction loan, they should have done so, for then they would have had some control over the flow of the money and could have minimized their losses when Seat of the Pants Construction, Inc. began to show signs of failure. And they would have retained title to their lot. Better still, they would not have felt compelled to use a builder like Smilin' Sam in the first place.

Controlling the flow of the money is the key to both avoiding legal problems with builders and with getting them to complete the construction as they agreed to do. Again, the solution must start at the contract stage. As we have learned, most builders expect to get paid in installments due at varying stages of construction, and lenders usually structure the "draws" on the loan funds in a similar manner. Buyers can ensure that their builders will finish the job by providing in their contracts for a meaningful "retainage" at the end of the project: "The Builder shall be paid for the work performed according to the attached schedule of payments, but in no event shall the final installment be paid until the Builder has completed construction of the residence to the satisfaction of the Buyers."

Sophisticated builders try to preempt this approach by including in the stock contracts they present their customers language that says that the builder is entitled to close and to be paid in full upon "substantial completion" of the residence, even though there may be numerous incomplete components, which are to be addressed by a "punch list" of items to be accomplished by the builder within a certain time after closing. Once, faced with this provision in a client's contract, we took a calculated risk and told the builder that he simply wouldn't be paid until he finished the job. He fumed and threatened, but knowing that it was the quickest and easiest way for him to be paid, he got busy and completed the house.

In passing, we'll mention that home builders are generally more inclined than individual sellers to accept a "time is of the essence" requirement for completion. This is especially true and is particularly appropriate in situations involving construction loans obtained by the homeowner rather than the builder. The builder understands that the owner is paying sometimes hundreds of dollars in interest for each day that the house remains unfinished, and can be induced to accept that daily figure as the measure of the penalty for late completion. The key to making this work for both the builder and the owner is for them to adopt a realistic schedule for completion at the outset, so that the time and cost overruns can be avoided.

So, now, the new house is complete, you've moved in, and surprise, things start going wrong. The builder shows up for the

Moneysaver

Most builders these days, as a competitive marketing tool, offer in their contracts to extend a warranty on their work and materials for a limited time, generally one to five years, depending on the competitive situation.

first couple of complaints, but as your list gets longer, the builder gets more and more scarce and ultimately refuses to return your calls. Your remedies, once again, are governed by the contract you signed back when you first embarked upon your adventure in home building.

The National Association of Home Builders administers a uniform warranty program for builders around the country who enroll and qualify. But in several states, courts have recognized implied warranties of fitness (for habitation as a residence, for sound workmanship and proper construction, etc.) extended by operation of law from the builder to the first owner, for so long as the latter owns the property. In other states, where no such implied warranty has been established by the courts, legislatures have enacted laws to similar effect. The theory behind these warranties is that a failure to construct a habitable residence violates a special relationship between builder and buyer, in which the buyer places his reliance upon the builder's particular expertise.

Home builders, of course, prefer not to give such a blanket guarantee, and most now provide in their contracts that the limited, one- to five-year warranty that they give will supercede any warranties implied by law. When representing a purchaser in writing a contract, we always replace this provision with one that reads, "The warranty extended by the Builder to the Purchasers pursuant to this contract shall be in addition to, and not in lieu of, all implied warranties provided by the laws of this state." Our experience with getting builders to accept this change has been about 50–50.

Finally, for those with a large construction budget, it may be useful to know that there exist foundation and other structural component warranty policies that may be purchased from national vendors, including those administered through the National Association of Home Builders. These are in the nature of insurance contracts and can cost several thousand dollars. If you ask your builder for this, keep in mind that he will, of course, simply add its cost to your contract price.

The closing

Virtually without exception, our experience has been that if the contract between the parties has been properly prepared, and everyone has abided by their agreements, the closing is a routine and pleasant event. However, when a seller has, in fact, failed to do something that he agreed to do, our advice to the purchaser is always to not close until the seller performs. This often is easier said than done, of course, because buyers are facing deadlines for loan commitment expiration, the need to vacate their present homes, movers are on the way from out of state with the furniture, and so on.

Therefore, any agreements for post-closing performance should be reduced to writing. Lawyers like to insert the phrase, "This agreement will survive the closing," in order to confront a principle of law, recognized in varying degrees by most states, known as merger. The idea is that once a transaction is closed, all of the agreements of the parties become "merged" into and supplanted by the warranties in the deed, and that nothing else "survives."

Beyond performance issues, however, most closing problems result from the parties' misunderstanding of the law's requirements for making a valid title transfer. These can take several forms: Aunt Josie died, survived by three children, and left no will. Who has to sign the deed to sell the property? Or, the seller is an out-of-state corporation. Who is authorized to sign a deed for it?

But more commonly, the problem arises from the state of holy matrimony. Most jurisdictions grant to both spouses certain

 Bright Idea

Although the merger doctrine has taken a battering in several jurisdictions and the Uniform Land Transactions Act rejects it outright, it is still best to memorialize any post-closing agreements by written instrument. It is also not uncommon to induce prompt performance by having the closing agent hold funds in escrow until all obligations are met.

interests in the homestead, or personal residence, of the couple, and mandate that those interests cannot be conveyed away by the other spouse. Speaking plainly, this means simply that both spouses must sign any deed or mortgage upon the property that is their primary residence.

"But," said George to me the other day, "I'm buying the house in my name only! Why does my wife have to sign the mortgage?"

"Is she going to live in the house? As her personal, primary residence?"

"Yes."

"Where is she?"

"Dayton, Ohio."

End of closing.

This kind of problem is usually resolved through the use of "powers of attorney." In the case of mortgage loans, purchasers must obtain their lender's approval for a power of attorney closing, and most require that a close family member, preferably the other spouse, be given the authority. Both lenders and title insurers uniformly require that such powers of attorney be "durable," in other words, unaffected by the incompetence or other disability of the principal; and "specific," i.e., identifying the precise transaction in which it is to be used. They also must be in writing, conform in all respects to the same formality in execution as the deed or mortgage, and be placed on public record.

Obviously, if one is facing a closing deadline, this is not the kind of thing to wait until closing to bring up. In George's case, his mortgage loan officer compounded the problem by telling him erroneously that his wife did not have to attend closing. If a purchaser has any doubt about the matter, he should contact the closing agent as soon as the closing is scheduled.

Sue the bastards

We maintain, as we have throughout this chapter, that buyers whose contracts have been properly written, and who take advantage of all the opportunities given to them by their contract contingencies (called in the trade exercising "due diligence"), should have no meaningful post-closing problems. But those purchasers who, despite all of their best efforts, find themselves with a significant financial loss from a condition in their home discovered after closing, may take heart from a few examples in which smart litigators have been able to defeat "let the buyer beware" limitations and obtain relief for their clients in court.

- New Jersey has been in the forefront of the war on Caveat Emptor. In one case, the sellers of a relatively new home not only failed to disclose, but deliberately concealed, the fact that the house was seriously infested by roaches. "Under modern concepts of justice and fair dealing," said the court, the sellers were under a duty to disclose material latent defects "known to them but unknown and unobservable by the buyer."

- In California, a court allowed a lawsuit against a seller who concealed the fact that the property had been the site of a grisly murder, because its notoriety had negatively impacted the value of the land.

- Back in New Jersey, skirting the issues raised by limited and implied warranties, a court held a builder liable when a small child was badly scalded by hot tap water supplied through a unique water heating system it had installed for the entire development. This court decided this case by employing modern theories of product liability, stating that the builder was under a "standard of reasonable care for the protection of anyone who might foreseeably (sic) be endangered by their negligence."

- New Jersey even held a developer liable for failing to disclose to purchasers that a closed, leaking, former toxic waste dump existed next to their neighborhood.

But the most common litigation nowadays involves allegations that sellers and their agents deliberately concealed, misrepresented, or suppressed facts about the residence that ultimately harmed the buyers.

In a recent decision, the Alabama Supreme Court stated that:

> ... to establish fraudulent concealment, a plaintiff must show 1) that the defendant had a duty to disclose a material fact; 2) that the defendant either failed to disclose or concealed that material fact; 3) that the defendant's failure to disclose or his concealment of that material fact induced the plaintiff to act or to refrain from acting; and 4) that the plaintiff suffered damage as a result...

In that case, Chris and Debbie purchased a "pre-loved" home from Heidi that proved to have significant termite infestation and substantial termite damage. The evidence showed that although the buyers had employed a residential inspector to examine the home before closing, no separate termite inspection was performed. (Yes, Chris and Debbie should have had a wood infestation report contingency in their contact, and, had they acted upon it, they would not have been in this fix.)

In preparation for closing, a termite company performed a routine inspection of the home and issued a written report stating that the house contained "old termite damage," which, together with a letter stating that no active infestation existed and a copy of the termite bond, was left with Heidi. There was evidence before the court that Heidi destroyed the report regarding the "old damage." Heidi denied it, but it was uncontested that, at closing, she personally handed to Chris and Debbie only the copy of the termite bond and the letter stating that no active infestation existed. The purchasers testified that had they seen the old damage report, they would not have consummated the closing.

The state Supreme Court said that these facts met all four of the above tests, because 1) the evidence of Heidi's suppression of the termite damage report from the purchasers, in itself, established an obligation for her to disclose it to them (in other words, one can't commit an act of fraud and be relieved of the consequences simply by keeping it a secret); 2) the infestation report was a "material fact" because Chris and Debbie would not have purchased the house had they known of the problem; 3) Chris and Debbie were "induced to act" by closing on the house; and 4) they suffered damage due to the extensive repair work they were forced to undertake.

Now, go back to the beginning of this chapter and read again the case of the concealed sewage leak. It was also decided by a state Supreme Court, only several years earlier. Can you reconcile that result with Chris and Debbie's experience? No? Neither can we. We think that the only logical conclusion that can be reached is that courts are gradually seeking to eliminate the injustices caused by strict adherence to Caveat Emptor, and sometimes they trip over their facts along the way.

For now, we submit that there are only two ways in which buyers can produce stability in their relationships with sellers vis-à-vis defective conditions in the home they buy:

- They can lobby their state legislatures to adopt real property disclosure legislation, as some 25 states have done so far.

- They can protect themselves by employing the contingencies and other "due diligence" methods we have suggested in this chapter. Lest you believe, however, that our opinion is worth more than anyone else, or that our solutions are infallible, let us conclude with the following disclaimer mandated by our state Bar Association:

> No representation is made that the quality of the legal services to be performed is greater than the quality of legal services performed by other lawyers.

Just the facts

- Exercise all due diligence in thoroughly inspecting your prospective home. Caveat emptor!

- Insist upon a competently drafted realty purchase contract covering numerous contingencies.

- In a contract without a "time is of the essence" clause, the party who is seeking an extension of the date should have a "reasonable time" in which to perform his obligations.

- Use foresight and preventative contract language to cover most potential situations at closing.

- If you have your home built, seek the counsel of a good attorney who specializes in real estate and new construction law.

GET THE SCOOP ON...
The burgeoning industry called relocation ▪
Using the experts ▪ The psychology of relocation
▪ Dotting the i's, crossing the t's

The Art of Relocation

In our age of extraordinary mobility, many of you may be moving because your company has transferred you to a new location. Others may have found more lucrative and attractive employment elsewhere. In either case, your relocation move will have many unique and important elements. Knowing about them in advance will give you control over buying a home in your new community.

The burgeoning industry called relocation

The selling of a home in one location and the buying of a home in another location for the same individual or family often involves a transfer within a company or group of companies. To coordinate such a move, almost all large employers call upon the services of national or international relocation companies (by far the largest today are Cendant Mobility and GMAC Relocation) to assist in what is usually called the "corporate transfer." These companies in turn call upon large real estate firms (most often, the big chains, such as ReMax, ERA, Century 21, and

Coldwell Banker) to provide brokerage services at both ends of the move.

In many areas of the country, real estate firms recruit agents with the promise of their becoming part of a relocation team, which guarantees referrals on a regular basis. This gives agents, who otherwise would have to go out on their own to solicit listings or persuade buyer-clients to work with them, the chance to have a regular source of income. Because most agents live on the edge, having to compete all the time with other agents for a limited volume of business, the prospect of a guaranteed income is not only attractive, but a terrific release from the stress. We've asked many phenomenally successful and wealthy agents if they would trade some of their income for regular relocation business at a smaller commission per sale. Almost all of them would accept the trade for its accompanying reduction of stress.

If you are involved in a corporate transfer, you many have no choice but to cooperate with a relocation transfer network. If you *do* have a choice, especially as a seller, you may want to consider your new employer's motive for inserting you into this network in the first place: The employer wants you on the job at your new location pronto! If you hire a real estate agent who is outside the corporate structure to list your home, she will come up with a suggested price that accords with fair market value in your neighborhood. If you have a corporate relocation company coordinate the listing of your home through a local real estate agent, the company will send two or three appraisers whom, typically, you will not know, to do appraisals that are subsumed under a BME (broker's market evaluation). Then the relocation

---

 Watch Out!

The competition between real estate companies for relocation company business is ferocious. Even though agents at both ends of the corporate transfer give up a substantial percentage of their commissions to the relocation company (on the average, 25 to 40 percent), for the relocation expert, this is often the sole source of her income.

Watch Out!

For you as a seller or a buyer, the greatest danger of the relocation transfer is loss of control. Our suggestions in this chapter are to help you maintain control over an inevitably disorienting experience.

company will set the price for which your home should be listed. Because your employer is in a hurry to relocate you and find you a home in your location, the list price recommended will often be below fair market value and will reduce your potential equity.

As a savvy seller, you can take at least some control of this scary situation by insisting on letting a local agent who knows your market list your home for a short period of time (most relocation companies will allow up to 90 days, as long as your agent is working through them) at fair market value. In exchange for doing this, your agent will agree to give up the listing, and you will agree to allow the relocation company to buy your home at *its* valuation and then try to sell it with one of *its* agents if you and your original agent fail to produce a satisfactory contract. Almost invariably, the agent you choose will sell your home for more money than a corporation-assigned agent will, and you will realize more equity for your new purchase.

As a buyer at the other end of the transfer, one of two things will happen. If you haven't sold your home at the point of origin, your employer or its relocation representative in your new location will either put you up in corporate housing free of charge until your house sells or put up the equity for your new purchase, expecting to be reimbursed from the proceeds of your original home after it closes. If you arrive at your new location ready to buy, a network of relocation experts will be ready to help you with your purchase.

Using the experts

Let's begin by looking at whom you can turn to for help during the various stages of your relocation. Because corporate transfers have become so common, there are now a variety of specialists whose job is to make your move as stress-free as possible. Here are the key players among these specialists.

The relocation director

The title may differ from one company to another, but this expert is usually part of a personnel department. It's the relocation director's responsibility to counsel you on your company's relocation policies, for example, what type of expertise your company will provide in finding you a residence in your new community and what financial incentives you will be offered. The financial incentives may include moving expenses, closing costs on the home you buy at your new location, and commissions for a broker to sell your current home if you're already a homeowner.

The relocation specialist

Relocation centers, real estate firms specializing in relocation, and some moving companies have people ready to furnish you with detailed information about your new community and to give you home-finding tips. Banks in larger communities usually furnish "newcomer packets" that you will want to review with your relocation specialist to make sure that you know whatever is necessary about neighborhoods, schools, and public services.

The real estate agent

If you're being relocated by your company, you probably will be assigned to a real estate agent who specializes in relocation— someone with a large firm that represents a major national relocation organization. The agent already will have received basic information about your home-buying prerequisites. If you're moving on your own to join a new employer, find out from your employer what real estate companies specialize in relocation and explain your needs. You should be able to find someone specially trained to meet them.

Moving companies

Moving companies are an invaluable source for time- and money-saving tips on how to get ready to move and how to schedule your move. If you're moving to a community that's a major drop-off point for a particular moving company, that company will also have a "newcomer packet" that will be particularly helpful in location shopping centers, police and fire services, libraries, and places of entertainment.

Other professionals

Your real estate relocation specialist should be able to put you in touch with qualified home inspectors, pest inspectors, builders (if you're daring enough to build in a new community), closing attorneys, tax accountants, and mortgage lenders. Above all else, remember that relocation is a major specialty in the real estate business. Make sure that you have been assigned an agent who has not only been fully apprised of your needs, but who also knows professionals in all these other areas. That way, your home-buying experience will be fully serviced from beginning to end.

The psychology of relocation

We've touched upon the roles and services of people who can provide you with practical help when you relocate. Because it involves change, relocation is also an emotional process. Here are a few ways that you can help yourself and your family prepare for some of the changes you will face.

Arranging a school transfer for children

Before you begin looking at homes, research the schools in your new community and find the ones that most clearly match your children's needs and your own expectations. If you plan to choose a private school, make sure to look at houses within easy driving distance of the school.

Whether choosing a public or private school, meet with a guidance counselor and seek a level of personal comfort on how well the school matches your children's current level of academic and extracurricular achievement. Learn what the teacher–pupil ratio is and what the disciplinary standards are. Most schools have both curriculum and code-of-conduct handbooks. Review them carefully with your children. Doing so will smooth everyone's transition from one school to another.

Leaving old friends/making new friends

Make sure that you have the addresses and phone numbers for the friends you're leaving behind. One of the best ways of getting used to a new community is talking about it with old friends or inviting them to visit and showing off the sights. Old friends will help you define your roles in your new hometown.

Also, make a list of your favorite activities and give it to your real estate agent. He should get back to you with a list of the places that cater to these activities. This is the best way to find the common ground out of which new friendships grow and mature.

If you're moving with children, their most natural point of resistance will involve leaving friends behind. The best thing to do is focus on the positives. If your move is a step upward, tell your children that moving will mean more family income, a better home, and more opportunities for travel. If your move is lateral, focus on what your children have to look forward to—what unique activities your new community will provide and how they'll be the center of attention as newcomers. If loss of friendship is your children's main concern, remind them of all the friends they've made in the past and point out that now they'll have a chance to make new friends. Although you need to show compassion for the real losses your children will suffer, you should focus on the extraordinary gains they can achieve. Give your children the chance to see themselves as explorers, as pioneers.

Dotting the i's, crossing the t's

You'll probably be shuttling back and forth from your current hometown to your prospective one to look at houses and talk with a lender. What time you don't spend traveling and looking will be spent near a fax machine. Via fax, you can negotiate a contract on your new home, coordinate plans with a mover, write up a repair addendum, and send information to your lender. Despite all the help you've received from experts, only you can choose your new home, work with a lender, and hire an inspector.

Making a moving calendar

In the midst of all this activity, you could neglect the move itself. Don't get whacked from behind by forgetting about moving day. We know of many people who have become so busy buying that they forgot about moving and suddenly had to telescope several weeks of planning into a week or less of frantic phoning, pleading, and praying. Of course, every family's moving schedule will be unique. You can take much of the chaos out of moving day by establishing a timetable in the form of a calendar, arranged in an order that takes you from three or four weeks away from your move to moving day itself. Here are some crucial things to put on the calendar:

1. Change your address at the post office (effective on moving day). Change magazine subscriptions and other computer-addressed mail as far in advance as possible, because they often take at least six weeks to catch up.

2. Make a file of the vital papers you'll need to have with you at all times—the important information you won't want to put on the moving truck. An accordion file is best for this material.

3. Get estimates from moving companies. If you're moving between June 1 and September 30—movers' peak season—expect rates to be a bit higher than off-season rates.

4. Select a moving company, confirm your moving date, and decide whether you'll pack yourself or have the movers do it. If yours is a relocation move, make sure to give your movers' estimate to your employer.

5. Start sorting. Decide what to put on the truck, what to sell, what to give away, and what to discard. Be ruthless—your moving estimate involves the weight of your belongings. That old, clunky sofa you'll never really use may add significantly to your moving costs.

6. Sketch the floor plan of your new home and decide on furniture placement so that you'll be prepared when you meet your movers at your destination.

7. Start do-it-yourself packing of seldom-used dishes, books, workshop and garden tools, hobby equipment, and so on. Empty oil and gas from lawn equipment, motorcycles, or lanterns.

8. Transfer all your insurance policies to your new town.

9. Find a bank and take out a safety deposit box for wills, trusts, and other legal or financial matters.

10. Get your new address to your employer.

11. Arrange for children's medical and dental records and birth certificates to be sent to you. Ask your doctors and dentists to recommend colleagues in your new hometown.

12. Fill all prescriptions.

13. Drop off any last-minute cleaning . . . and remember to pick it up!

14. If you're flying to your new destination, make reservations. If you're driving, have your car serviced.

15. Collect children's games and activities for the trip.

16. Start packing oft-used belongings.

17. Plan any farewell parties and visits.

18. Return any borrowed items such as garden tools and library books. Collect anything borrowed from you.

19. Cancel newspaper delivery. Schedule the day to have utilities transferred out of your name. Arrange to have the utilities in your new home transferred into your name.

20. Pack everything in your kitchen you can do without until move-in day.

21. On the day before your move: a) Empty and defrost your refrigerator. Leave the refrigerator door open; b) Pack a suitcase with your personal belongings; c) Pack a special carton of essentials (toiletries, coffee pot, canned food, can opener, light bulbs, trash bags, and so on) to be loaded last and unloaded first; d) Empty your safe-deposit box and get enough cash for your trip. Close all bank accounts; e) If you're driving to your new destination, load your car. If you're flying, arrange for a taxi to pick you up and have all your personal belongings and the carton of essentials in the front hall to load into the taxi.

22. On the day of the move: a) Strip the beds; b) Make any last-minute suggestions to your movers. Be sure they know how to contact you en route. Give them a map to your new house; c) Sweep and vacuum; d) Lock up and take off!

Keeping records of your move

If you're making a company-paid move, make sure that you know what records you'll need to keep for reimbursements. Chances are that you will not be reimbursed for travel expenses and tips, so keep a trip journal for any expenses you can deduct from your taxes. Remember that any receipts you collect must be dated.

Just the facts

- Use the corporate transfer to your advantage by knowing the players and what they do.
- Learn what you can about schools and neighbors in your new location, but keep in touch with old friends.
- Make a detailed schedule of all the steps in your transfer.

Appendices

PART VII

The Nine Most Popular Home Styles

Cape Cod

Colonial

Condominium

Contemporary

Country

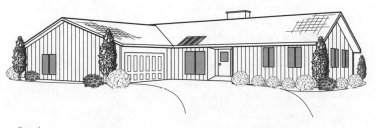

Ranch

Split-level

Town house

Victorian

Important Statistics

FIXED RATE MONTHLY P&I FACTORS

(Multiply mortgage amount × factor -1000)

INTEREST RATE	15 YEARS	20 YEARS	25 YEARS	30 YEARS
6.00	8.438568	7.164311	6.443014	5.995503
6.125	8.506250	7.236610	6.519640	6.076105
6.250	8.574229	7.309282	6.596694	6.157172
6.375	8.642504	7.382323	6.674172	6.238699
6.500	8.711074	7.455731	6.752072	6.320680
6.625	8.779938	7.529504	6.830387	6.403110
6.750	8.849095	7.603640	6.909115	6.485981
6.875	8.918543	7.678136	6.988252	6.569288
7.00	8.988283	7.752989	7.061792	6.653025
7.125	9.058312	7.828198	7.147732	6.737185
7.250	9.128629	7.903760	7.228069	6.821763
7.375	9.199233	7.979672	7.308797	6.906751
7.500	9.270124	8.055932	7.389912	6.992145
7.625	9.341299	8.132537	7.471410	7.077937
7.750	9.412758	8.209486	7.553288	7.164122
7.875	9.484499	8.286774	7.635540	7.250694
8.00	9.556521	8.364401	7.718162	7.337646
8.25	9.701404	8.520657	7.884501	7.512666
8.50	9.847396	8.678232	8.052271	7.689135
8.75	9.994481	8.837107	8.221436	7.867004
9.00	10.142666	8.997260	8.391964	8.046226
9.25	10.291923	9.158668	8.563818	8.226754
9.50	10.442247	9.321312	8.736967	8.408542
9.75	10.593627	9.485169	8.911274	8.591544
10.00	10.746051	9.650216	9.087007	8.775716
10.125	10.822652	9.733180	9.175273	8.868266
10.250	10.899509	9.816434	9.263833	8.961013
10.375	10.976622	9.899974	9.352682	9.054010
10.500	11.053989	9.983799	9.441817	9.147393
10.625	11.131609	10.067905	9.531233	9.240976
10.750	11.209480	10.152290	9.620927	9.334814
10.875	11.287600	10.236950	9.710894	9.428901
11.000	11.365969	10.321684	9.801131	9.523234
11.125	11.444585	10.407088	9.891632	9.617806
11.250	11.523446	10.492560	9.982395	9.712614
11.375	11.602551	10.578297	10.073416	9.807651
11.500	11.681898	10.664296	10.164690	9.902914
11.625	11.761486	10.750555	10.256213	9.998398
11.750	11.841314	10.837071	10.347982	10.094097
11.875	11.921379	10.923840	10.439993	10.190008
12.000	12.001681	11.010861	10.532241	10.286126
12.125	12.082217	11.098131	10.624724	10.382446

LOAN AMORTIZATION SCHEDULE A

Loan amount = $100,000
Interest rate = 7.00%
Loan years = 30
Payment amount = $665.31
Payments per year = 12

#	DATE	PAYMENT	PRINCIPAL	INTEREST	BALANCE
					100,000.00
1	JA/98	665.31	81.98	583.33	99,918.02
2	FE/98	665.31	82.45	582.86	99,835.57
3	MR/98	665.31	82.94	582.37	99,752.63
4	AP/98	665.31	83.42	581.89	99,669.21
5	MY/98	665.31	83.91	581.40	99,585.30
6	JN/98	665.31	84.40	580.91	99,500.90
7	JL/98	665.31	84.89	580.42	99,416.01
8	AU/98	665.31	85.38	579.93	99,330.63
9	SE/98	665.31	85.88	579.43	99,244.75
10	OC/98	665.31	86.38	578.93	99,158.37
11	NO/98	665.31	86.89	578.42	99,071.48
12	DE/98	665.31	87.39	577.92	98,984.09
YR 1 1998		7,983.72	1,015.91	6,967.81	98,984.09
TOTAL		7,983.72	1,015.91	6,967.81	
13	JA/99	665.31	87.90	577.41	98,896.19
14	FE/99	665.31	88.42	576.89	98,807.77
15	MR/99	665.31	88.93	576.38	98,718.84
16	AP/99	665.31	89.45	575.86	98,629.39
17	MY/99	665.31	89.97	575.34	98,539.42
18	JN/99	665.31	90.50	574.81	98,448.92
19	JL/99	665.31	91.02	574.29	98,357.90
20	AU/99	665.31	91.56	573.75	98,266.34
21	SE/99	665.31	92.09	573.22	98,174.25
22	OC/99	665.31	92.63	572.68	98,081.62
23	NO/99	665.31	93.17	572.14	97,988.45
24	DE/99	665.31	93.71	571.60	97,894.74
YR 2 1999		7,983.72	1,089.35	6,894.37	97,894.74
TOTAL		15,967.44	2,105.26	13,862.18	
25	JA/00	665.31	94.26	571.05	97,800.48
26	FE/00	665.31	94.81	570.50	97,705.67
27	MR/00	665.31	95.36	569.95	97,610.31
28	AP/00	665.31	95.92	569.39	97,514.39
29	MY/00	665.31	96.48	568.83	97,417.91
30	JN/00	665.31	97.04	568.27	97,320.87
31	JL/00	665.31	97.60	567.71	97,223.27
32	AU/00	665.31	98.17	567.14	97,125.10
33	SE/00	665.31	98.75	566.56	97,026.35
34	OC/00	665.31	99.32	565.99	96,927.03
35	NO/00	665.31	99.90	565.41	96,827.13
36	DE/00	665.31	100.49	564.82	96,726.64
YR 3 2000		7,983.72	1,168.10	6,815.62	96,726.64
TOTAL		23,951.16	3,273.36	20,677.80	

#	DATE	PAYMENT	PRINCIPAL	INTEREST	BALANCE
37	JA/01	665.31	101.07	564.24	96,625.57
38	FE/01	665.31	101.66	563.65	96,523.91
39	MR/01	665.31	102.25	563.06	96,421.66
40	AP/01	665.31	102.85	562.46	96,318.81
41	MY/01	665.31	103.45	561.86	96,215.36
42	JN/01	665.31	104.05	561.26	96,111.31
43	JL/01	665.31	104.66	560.65	96,006.65
44	AU/01	665.31	105.27	560.04	95,901.38
45	SE/01	665.31	105.89	559.42	95,795.49
46	OC/01	665.31	106.50	558.81	95,688.99
47	NO/01	665.31	107.12	558.19	95,581.87
48	DE/01	665.31	107.75	557.56	95,474.12
YR 4 2001		7,983.72	1,252.52	6,731.20	95,474.12
TOTAL		31,934.88	4,525.88	27,409.00	
49	JA/02	665.31	108.38	556.93	95,365.74
50	FE/02	665.31	109.01	556.30	95,256.73
51	MR/02	665.31	109.65	555.66	95,147.08
52	AP/02	665.31	110.29	555.02	95,036.79
53	MY/02	665.31	110.93	554.38	94,925.86
54	JN/02	665.31	111.58	553.73	94,814.28
55	JL/02	665.31	112.23	553.08	94,702.05
56	AU/02	665.31	112.88	552.43	94,589.17
57	SE/02	665.31	113.54	551.77	94,475.63
58	OC/02	665.31	114.20	551.11	94,361.43
59	NO/02	665.31	114.87	550.44	94,246.56
60	DE/02	665.31	115.54	549.77	94,131.02
YR 5 2002		7,983.72	1,343.10	6,640.62	94,131.02
TOTAL		39,918.60	5,868.98	34,049.62	
61	JA/03	665.31	116.21	549.10	94,014.81
62	FE/03	665.31	116.89	548.42	93,897.92
63	MR/03	665.31	117.57	547.74	93,780.35
64	AP/03	665.31	118.26	547.05	93,662.09
65	MY/03	665.31	118.95	546.36	93,543.14
66	JN/03	665.31	119.64	545.67	93,423.50
67	JL/03	665.31	120.34	544.97	93,303.16
68	AU/03	665.31	121.04	544.27	93,182.12
69	SE/03	665.31	121.75	543.56	93,060.37
70	OC/03	665.31	122.46	542.85	92,937.91
71	NO/03	665.31	123.17	542.14	92,814.74
72	DE/03	665.31	123.89	541.42	92,690.85
YR 6 2003		7,983.72	1,440.17	6,543.55	92,690.85
TOTAL		47,902.32	7,309.15	40,593.17	

#	DATE	PAYMENT	PRINCIPAL	INTEREST	BALANCE
73	JA/04	665.31	124.61	540.70	92,566.24
74	FE/04	665.31	125.34	539.97	92,440.90
75	MR/04	665.31	126.07	539.24	92,314.83
76	AP/04	665.31	126.81	538.50	92,188.02
77	MY/04	665.31	127.55	537.76	92,060.47
78	JN/04	665.31	128.29	537.02	91,932.18
79	JL/04	665.31	129.04	536.27	91,803.14
80	AU/04	665.31	129.79	535.52	91,673.35
81	SE/04	665.31	130.55	534.76	91,542.80
82	OC/04	665.31	131.31	534.00	91,411.49
83	NO/04	665.31	132.08	533.23	91,279.41
84	DE/04	665.31	132.85	532.46	91,146.56
YR 7 2004		7,983.72	1,544.29	6,439.43	91,146.56
TOTAL		55,886.04	8,853.44	47,032.60	
85	JA/05	665.31	133.62	531.69	91,012.94
86	FE/05	665.31	134.40	530.91	90,878.54
87	MR/05	665.31	135.19	530.12	90,743.35
88	AP/05	665.31	135.97	529.34	90,607.38
89	MY/05	665.31	136.77	528.54	90,470.61
90	JN/05	665.31	137.56	527.75	90,333.05
91	JL/05	665.31	138.37	526.94	90,194.68
92	AU/05	665.31	139.17	526.14	90,055.51
93	SE/05	665.31	139.99	525.32	89,915.52
94	OC/05	665.31	140.80	524.51	89,774.72
95	NO/05	665.31	141.62	523.69	89,633.10
96	DE/05	665.31	142.45	522.86	89,490.65
YR 8 2005		7,983.72	1,655.91	6,327.81	89,490.65
TOTAL		63,869.76	10,509.35	53,360.41	
97	JA/06	665.31	143.28	522.03	89,347.37
98	FE/06	665.31	144.12	521.19	89,203.25
99	MR/06	665.31	144.96	520.35	89,058.29
100	AP/06	665.31	145.80	519.51	88,912.49
101	MY/06	665.31	146.65	518.66	88,765.84
102	JN/06	665.31	147.51	517.80	88,618.33
103	JL/06	665.31	148.37	516.94	88,469.96
104	AU/06	665.31	149.24	516.07	88,320.72
105	SE/06	665.31	150.11	515.20	88,170.61
106	OC/06	665.31	150.98	514.33	88,019.63
107	NO/06	665.31	151.86	513.45	87,867.77
108	DE/06	665.31	152.75	512.56	87,715.02
YR 9 2006		7,983.72	1,775.63	6,208.09	87,715.02
TOTAL		71,853.48	12,284.98	59,568.50	

#	DATE	PAYMENT	PRINCIPAL	INTEREST	BALANCE
109	JA/07	665.31	153.64	511.67	87,561.38
110	FE/07	665.31	154.54	510.77	87,406.84
111	MR/07	665.31	155.44	509.87	87,251.40
112	AP/07	665.31	156.34	508.97	87,095.06
113	MY/07	665.31	157.26	508.05	86,937.80
114	JN/07	665.31	158.17	507.14	86,779.63
115	JL/07	665.31	159.10	506.21	86,620.53
116	AU/07	665.31	160.02	505.29	86,460.51
117	SE/07	665.31	160.96	504.35	86,299.55
118	OC/07	665.31	161.90	503.41	86,137.65
119	NO/07	665.31	162.84	502.47	85,974.81
120	DE/07	665.31	163.79	501.52	85,811.02
YR 10 2007		7,983.72	1,904.00	6,079.72	85,811.02
TOTAL		79,837.20	14,188.98	65,648.22	
121	JA/08	665.31	164.75	500.56	85,646.27
122	FE/08	665.31	165.71	499.60	85,480.56
123	MR/08	665.31	166.67	498.64	85,313.89
124	AP/08	665.31	167.65	497.66	85,146.24
125	MY/08	665.31	168.62	496.69	84,977.62
126	JN/08	665.31	169.61	495.70	84,808.01
127	JL/08	665.31	170.60	494.71	84,637.41
128	AU/08	665.31	171.59	493.72	84,465.82
129	SE/08	665.31	172.59	492.72	84,293.23
130	OC/08	665.31	173.60	491.71	84,119.63
131	NO/08	665.31	174.61	490.70	83,945.02
132	DE/08	665.31	175.63	489.68	83,769.39
YR 11 2008		7,983.72	2,041.63	5,942.09	83,769.39
TOTAL		87,820.92	16,230.61	71,590.31	
133	JA/09	665.31	176.66	488.65	83,592.73
134	FE/09	665.31	177.69	487.62	83,415.04
135	MR/09	665.31	178.72	486.59	83,236.32
136	AP/09	665.31	179.76	485.55	83,056.56
137	MY/09	665.31	180.81	484.50	82,875.75
138	JN/09	665.31	181.87	483.44	82,693.88
139	JL/09	665.31	182.93	482.38	82,510.95
140	AU/09	665.31	184.00	481.31	82,326.95
141	SE/09	665.31	185.07	480.24	82,141.88
142	OC/09	665.31	186.15	479.16	81,955.73
143	NO/09	665.31	187.23	478.08	81,768.50
144	DE/09	665.31	188.33	476.98	81,580.17
YR 12 2009		7,983.72	2,189.22	5,794.50	81,580.17
TOTAL		95,804.64	18,419.83	77,384.81	

#	DATE	PAYMENT	PRINCIPAL	INTEREST	BALANCE
145	JA/10	665.31	189.43	475.88	81,390.74
146	FE/10	665.31	190.53	474.78	81,200.21
147	MR/10	665.31	191.64	473.67	81,008.57
148	AP/10	665.31	192.76	472.55	80,815.81
149	MY/10	665.31	193.88	471.43	80,621.93
150	JN/10	665.31	195.02	470.29	80,426.91
151	JL/10	665.31	196.15	469.16	80,230.76
152	AU/10	665.31	197.30	468.01	80,033.46
153	SE/10	665.31	198.45	466.86	79,835.01
154	OC/10	665.31	199.61	465.70	79,635.40
155	NO/10	665.31	200.77	464.54	79,434.63
156	DE/10	665.31	201.94	463.37	79,232.69
YR 13 2010		7,983.72	2,347.48	5,636.24	79,232.69
TOTAL		103,788.36	20,767.31	83,021.05	
157	JA/11	665.31	203.12	462.19	79,029.57
158	FE/11	665.31	204.30	461.01	78,825.27
159	MR/11	665.31	205.50	459.81	78,619.77
160	AP/11	665.31	206.69	458.62	78,413.08
161	MY/11	665.31	207.90	457.41	78,205.18
162	JN/11	665.31	209.11	456.20	77,996.07
163	JL/11	665.31	210.33	454.98	77,785.74
164	AU/11	665.31	211.56	453.75	77,574.18
165	SE/11	665.31	212.79	452.52	77,361.39
166	OC/11	665.31	214.04	451.27	77,147.35
167	NO/11	665.31	215.28	450.03	76,932.07
168	DE/11	665.31	216.54	448.77	76,715.53
YR 14 2011		7,983.72	2,517.16	5,466.56	76,715.53
TOTAL		111,772.08	23,284.47	88,487.61	
169	JA/12	665.31	217.80	447.51	76,497.73
170	FE/12	665.31	219.07	446.24	76,278.66
171	MR/12	665.31	220.35	444.96	76,058.31
172	AP/12	665.31	221.64	443.67	75,836.67
173	MY/12	665.31	222.93	442.38	75,613.74
174	JN/12	665.31	224.23	441.08	75,389.51
175	JL/12	665.31	225.54	439.77	75,163.97
176	AU/12	665.31	226.85	438.46	74,937.12
177	SE/12	665.31	228.18	437.13	74,708.94
178	OC/12	665.31	229.51	435.80	74,479.43
179	NO/12	665.31	230.85	434.46	74,248.58
180	DE/12	665.31	232.19	433.12	74,016.39
YR 15 2012		7,983.72	2,699.14	5,284.58	74,016.39
TOTAL		119,755.80	25,983.61	93,772.19	

#	DATE	PAYMENT	PRINCIPAL	INTEREST	BALANCE
181	JA/13	665.31	233.55	431.76	73,782.84
182	FE/13	665.31	234.91	430.40	73,547.93
183	MR/13	665.31	236.28	429.03	73,311.65
184	AP/13	665.31	237.66	427.65	73,073.99
185	MY/13	665.31	239.05	426.26	72,834.94
186	JN/13	665.31	240.44	424.87	72,594.50
187	JL/13	665.31	241.84	423.47	72,352.66
188	AU/13	665.31	243.23	422.08	72,109.43
189	SE/13	665.31	244.67	420.64	71,864.76
190	OC/13	665.31	246.10	419.21	71,618.66
191	NO/13	665.31	247.53	417.78	71,371.13
192	DE/13	665.31	248.98	416.33	71,122.15
YR 16 2013		7,983.72	2,894.24	5,089.48	71,122.15
TOTAL		127,739.52	28,877.85	98,861.67	
193	JA/14	665.31	250.43	414.88	70,871.72
194	FE/14	665.31	251.89	413.42	70,619.83
195	MR/14	665.31	253.36	411.95	70,366.47
196	AP/14	665.31	254.84	410.47	70,111.63
197	MY/14	665.31	256.33	408.98	69,855.30
198	JN/14	665.31	257.82	407.49	69,597.48
199	JL/14	665.31	259.32	405.99	69,338.16
200	AU/14	665.31	260.84	404.47	69,077.32
201	SE/14	665.31	262.36	402.95	68,814.96
202	OC/14	665.31	263.89	401.42	68,551.07
203	NO/14	665.31	265.43	399.88	68,285.64
204	DE/14	665.31	266.98	398.33	68,018.66
YR 17 2014		7,983.72	3,103.49	4,880.23	68,018.66
TOTAL		135,723.24	31,981.34	103,741.90	
205	JA/15	665.31	268.53	396.78	67,750.13
206	FE/15	665.31	270.10	395.21	67,480.03
207	MR/15	665.31	271.68	393.63	67,208.35
208	AP/15	665.31	273.28	392.03	66,935.07
209	MY/15	665.31	274.86	390.45	66,660.21
210	JN/15	665.31	276.46	388.85	66,383.75
211	JL/15	665.31	278.07	387.24	66,105.68
212	AU/15	665.31	279.69	385.62	65,825.99
213	SE/15	665.31	281.33	383.98	65,544.66
214	OC/15	665.31	282.97	382.34	65,261.69
215	NO/15	665.31	284.62	380.69	64,977.07
216	DE/15	665.31	286.28	379.03	64,690.79
YR 18 2015		7,983.72	3,327.87	4,655.85	64,690.79
TOTAL		143,706.96	35,309.21	108,397.75	

#	DATE	PAYMENT	PRINCIPAL	INTEREST	BALANCE
217	JA/16	665.31	287.95	377.36	64,402.84
218	FE/16	665.31	289.63	375.68	64,113.21
219	MR/16	665.31	291.32	373.99	63,821.89
220	AP/16	665.31	293.02	372.29	63,528.87
221	MY/16	665.31	294.72	370.59	63,234.15
222	JN/16	665.31	296.44	368.87	62,937.71
223	JL/16	665.31	298.17	367.14	62,639.54
224	AU/16	665.31	299.91	365.40	62,339.63
225	SE/16	665.31	301.66	363.65	62,037.97
226	OC/16	665.31	303.42	361.89	61,734.55
227	NO/16	665.31	305.19	360.12	61,429.36
228	DE/16	665.31	306.97	358.34	61,122.39
YR 19 2016		7,983.72	3,568.40	4,415.32	61,122.39
TOTAL		151,690.68	38,877.61	112,813.07	
229	JA/17	665.31	308.76	356.55	60,813.63
230	FE/17	665.31	310.56	354.75	60,503.07
231	MR/17	665.31	312.38	352.93	60,190.69
232	AP/17	665.31	314.20	351.11	59,876.49
233	MY/17	665.31	316.03	349.28	59,560.46
234	JN/17	665.31	317.87	347.44	59,242.59
235	JL/17	665.31	319.73	345.58	58,922.86
236	AU/17	665.31	321.59	343.72	58,601.27
237	SE/17	665.31	323.47	341.84	58,277.80
238	OC/17	665.31	325.36	339.95	57,952.44
239	NO/17	665.31	327.25	338.06	57,625.19
240	DE/17	665.31	329.16	336.15	57,296.03
YR 20 2017		7,983.72	3,826.36	4,157.36	57,296.03
TOTAL		159,674.40	42,703.97	116,970.43	
241	JA/18	665.31	331.08	334.23	56,964.95
242	FE/18	665.31	333.01	332.30	56,631.94
243	MR/18	665.31	334.96	330.35	56,296.98
244	AP/18	665.31	336.91	328.40	55,960.07
245	MY/18	665.31	338.88	326.43	55,621.19
246	JN/18	665.31	340.85	324.46	55,280.34
247	JL/18	665.31	342.84	322.47	54,937.50
248	AU/18	665.31	344.84	320.47	54,592.66
249	SE/18	665.31	346.85	318.46	54,245.81
250	OC/18	665.31	348.88	316.43	53,896.93
251	NO/18	665.31	350.91	314.40	53,546.02
252	DE/18	665.31	352.96	312.35	53,193.06
YR 21 2018		7,983.72	4,102.97	3,880.75	53,193.06
TOTAL		167,658.12	46,806.94	120,851.18	

#	DATE	PAYMENT	PRINCIPAL	INTEREST	BALANCE
253	JA/19	665.31	355.02	310.29	52,838.04
254	FE/19	665.31	357.09	308.22	52,480.95
255	MR/19	665.31	359.17	306.14	52,121.78
256	AP/19	665.31	361.27	304.04	51,760.51
257	MY/19	665.31	363.37	301.94	51,397.14
258	JN/19	665.31	365.49	299.82	51,031.65
259	JL/19	665.31	367.63	297.68	50,664.02
260	AU/19	665.31	369.77	295.54	50,294.25
261	SE/19	665.31	371.93	293.38	49,922.32
262	OC/19	665.31	374.10	291.21	49,548.22
263	NO/19	665.31	376.28	289.03	49,171.94
264	DE/19	665.31	378.47	286.84	48,793.47
YR 22 2019		7,983.72	4,399.59	3,584.13	48,793.47
TOTAL		175,641.84	51,206.53	124,435.31	
265	JA/20	665.31	380.68	284.63	48,412.79
266	FE/20	665.31	382.90	282.41	48,029.89
267	MR/20	665.31	385.14	280.17	47,644.75
268	AP/20	665.31	387.38	277.93	47,257.37
269	MY/20	665.31	389.64	275.67	46,867.73
270	JN/20	665.31	391.91	273.40	46,475.82
271	JL/20	665.31	394.20	271.11	46,081.62
272	AU/20	665.31	396.50	268.81	45,685.12
273	SE/20	665.31	398.81	266.50	45,286.31
274	OC/20	665.31	401.14	264.17	44,885.17
275	NO/20	665.31	403.48	261.83	44,481.69
276	DE/20	665.31	405.83	259.48	44,075.86
YR 23 2020		7,983.72	4,717.61	3,266.11	44,075.86
TOTAL		183,625.56	55,924.14	127,701.42	
277	JA/21	665.31	408.20	257.11	43,667.66
278	FE/21	665.31	410.58	254.73	43,257.08
279	MR/21	665.31	412.98	252.33	42,844.10
280	AP/21	665.31	415.39	249.92	42,428.71
281	MY/21	665.31	417.81	247.50	42,010.90
282	JN/21	665.31	420.25	245.06	41,590.65
283	JL/21	665.31	422.70	242.61	41,167.95
284	AU/21	665.31	425.16	240.15	40,742.79
285	SE/21	665.31	427.64	237.67	40,315.15
286	OC/21	665.31	430.14	235.17	39,885.01
287	NO/21	665.31	432.65	232.66	39,452.36
288	DE/21	665.31	435.17	230.14	39,017.19
YR 24 2021		7,983.72	5,058.67	2,925.05	39,017.19
TOTAL		191,609.28	60,982.81	130,626.47	

#	DATE	PAYMENT	PRINCIPAL	INTEREST	BALANCE
289	JA/22	665.31	437.71	227.60	38,579.48
290	FE/22	665.31	440.26	225.05	38,139.22
291	MR/22	665.31	442.83	222.48	37,696.39
292	AP/22	665.31	445.41	219.90	37,250.98
293	MY/22	665.31	448.01	217.30	36,802.97
294	JN/22	665.31	450.63	214.68	36,352.34
295	JL/22	665.31	453.25	212.06	35,899.09
296	AU/22	665.31	455.90	209.41	35,443.19
297	SE/22	665.31	458.56	206.75	34,984.63
298	OC/22	665.31	461.23	204.08	34,523.40
299	NO/22	665.31	463.92	201.39	34,059.48
300	DE/22	665.31	466.63	198.68	33,592.85
YR 25 2022		7,983.72	5,424.34	2,559.38	33,592.85
TOTAL		199,593.00	66,407.15	133,185.85	
301	JA/23	665.31	469.35	195.96	33,123.50
302	FE/23	665.31	472.09	193.22	32,651.41
303	MR/23	665.31	474.84	190.47	32,176.57
304	AP/23	665.31	477.61	187.70	31,698.96
305	MY/23	665.31	480.40	184.91	31,218.56
306	JN/23	665.31	483.20	182.11	30,735.36
307	JL/23	665.31	486.02	179.29	30,249.34
308	AU/23	665.31	488.86	176.45	29,760.48
309	SE/23	665.31	491.71	173.60	29,268.77
310	OC/23	665.31	494.58	170.73	28,774.19
311	NO/23	665.31	497.46	167.85	28,276.73
312	DE/23	665.31	500.36	164.95	27,776.37
YR 26 2023		7,983.72	5,816.48	2,167.24	27,776.37
TOTAL		207,576.72	72,223.63	135,353.09	
313	JA/24	665.31	503.28	162.03	27,273.09
314	FE/24	665.31	506.22	159.09	26,766.87
315	MR/24	665.31	509.17	156.14	26,257.70
316	AP/24	665.31	512.14	153.17	25,745.56
317	MY/24	665.31	515.13	150.18	25,230.43
318	JN/24	665.31	518.13	147.18	24,712.30
319	JL/24	665.31	521.15	144.16	24,191.15
320	AU/24	665.31	524.19	141.12	23,666.96
321	SE/24	665.31	527.25	138.06	23,139.71
322	OC/24	665.31	530.33	134.98	22,609.38
323	NO/24	665.31	533.42	131.89	22,075.96
324	DE/24	665.31	536.53	128.78	21,539.43
YR 27 2024		7,983.72	6,236.94	1,746.78	21,539.43
TOTAL		215,560.44	78,460.57	137,099.87	

#	DATE	PAYMENT	PRINCIPAL	INTEREST	BALANCE
325	JA/25	665.31	539.66	125.65	20,999.77
326	FE/25	665.31	542.81	122.50	20,456.96
327	MR/25	665.31	545.98	119.33	19,910.98
328	AP/25	665.31	549.16	116.15	19,361.82
329	MY/25	665.31	552.37	112.94	18,809.45
330	JN/25	665.31	555.59	109.72	18,253.86
331	JL/25	665.31	558.83	106.48	17,695.03
332	AU/25	665.31	562.09	103.22	17,132.94
333	SE/25	665.31	565.37	99.94	16,567.57
334	OC/25	665.31	568.67	96.64	15,998.90
335	NO/25	665.31	571.98	93.33	15,426.92
336	DE/25	665.31	575.32	89.99	14,851.60
YR 28 2025		7,983.72	6,687.83	1,295.89	14,851.60
TOTAL		223,544.16	85,148.40	138,395.76	
337	JA/26	665.31	578.68	86.63	14,272.92
338	FE/26	665.31	582.05	83.26	13,690.87
339	MR/26	665.31	585.45	79.86	13,105.42
340	AP/26	665.31	588.86	76.45	12,516.56
341	MY/26	665.31	592.30	73.01	11,924.26
342	JN/26	665.31	595.75	69.56	11,328.51
343	JL/26	665.31	599.23	66.08	10,729.28
344	AU/26	665.31	602.72	62.59	10,126.56
345	SE/26	665.31	606.24	59.07	9,520.32
346	OC/26	665.31	609.77	55.54	8,910.55
347	NO/26	665.31	613.33	51.98	8,297.22
348	DE/26	665.31	616.91	48.40	7,680.31
YR 29 2026		7,983.72	7,171.29	812.43	7,680.31
TOTAL		231,527.88	92,319.69	139,208.19	
349	JA/27	665.31	620.51	44.80	7,059.80
350	FE/27	665.31	624.13	41.18	6,435.67
351	MR/27	665.31	627.77	37.54	5,807.90
352	AP/27	665.31	631.43	33.88	5,176.47
353	MY/27	665.31	635.11	30.20	4,541.36
354	JN/27	665.31	638.82	26.49	3,902.54
355	JL/27	665.31	642.55	22.76	3,259.99
356	AU/27	665.31	646.29	19.02	2,613.70
357	SE/27	665.31	650.06	15.25	1,963.64
358	OC/27	665.31	653.86	11.45	1,309.78
359	NO/27	665.31	657.67	7.64	652.11
360	DE/27	655.91	652.11	3.80	0.00
YR 30 2027		7,974.32	7,680.31	294.01	0.00
TOTAL		239,502.20	100,000.00	139,502.20	

LOAN AMORTIZATION SCHEDULE B

Loan amount = $100,000
Interest rate = 10.00%
Loan years = 30
Payment amount = $877.58
Payments per year = 12

#	DATE	PAYMENT	PRINCIPAL	INTEREST	BALANCE
					100,000.00
1	JA/98	877.58	44.25	833.33	99,955.75
2	FE/98	877.58	44.62	832.96	99,911.13
3	MR/98	877.58	44.99	832.59	99,866.14
4	AP/98	877.58	45.36	832.22	99,820.78
5	MY/98	877.58	45.74	831.84	99,775.04
6	JN/98	877.58	46.12	831.46	99,728.92
7	JL/98	877.58	46.51	831.07	99,682.41
8	AU/98	877.58	46.89	830.69	99,635.52
9	SE/98	877.58	47.28	830.30	99,588.24
10	OC/98	877.58	47.68	829.90	99,540.56
11	NO/98	877.58	48.08	829.50	99,492.48
12	DE/98	877.58	48.48	829.10	99,444.00
YR 1 1998		10,530.96	556.00	9,974.96	99,444.00
TOTAL		10,530.96	556.00	9,974.96	
13	JA/99	877.58	48.88	828.70	99,395.12
14	FE/99	877.58	49.29	828.29	99,345.83
15	MR/99	877.58	49.70	827.88	99,296.13
16	AP/99	877.58	50.11	827.47	99,246.02
17	MY/99	877.58	50.53	827.05	99,195.49
18	JN/99	877.58	50.95	826.63	99,144.54
19	JL/99	877.58	51.38	826.20	99,093.16
20	AU/99	877.58	51.80	825.78	99,041.36
21	SE/99	877.58	52.24	825.34	98,989.12
22	OC/99	877.58	52.67	824.91	98,936.45
23	NO/99	877.58	53.11	824.47	98,883.34
24	DE/99	877.58	53.55	824.03	98,829.79
YR 2 1999		10,530.96	614.21	9,916.75	98,829.79
TOTAL		21,061.92	1,170.21	19,891.71	
25	JA/00	877.58	54.00	823.58	98,775.79
26	FE/00	877.58	54.45	823.13	98,721.34
27	MR/00	877.58	54.90	822.68	98,666.44
28	AP/00	877.58	55.36	822.22	98,611.08
29	MY/00	877.58	55.82	821.76	98,555.26
30	JN/00	877.58	56.29	821.29	98,498.97
31	JL/00	877.58	56.76	820.82	98,442.21
32	AU/00	877.58	57.23	820.35	98,384.98
33	SE/00	877.58	57.71	819.87	98,327.27
34	OC/00	877.58	58.19	819.39	98,269.08
35	NO/00	877.58	58.67	818.91	98,210.41
36	DE/00	877.58	59.16	818.42	98,151.25
YR 3 2000		10,530.96	678.54	9,852.42	98,151.25
TOTAL		31,592.88	1,848.75	29,744.13	

#	DATE	PAYMENT	PRINCIPAL	INTEREST	BALANCE
37	JA/01	877.58	59.65	817.93	98,091.60
38	FE/01	877.58	60.15	817.43	98,031.45
39	MR/01	877.58	60.65	816.93	97,970.80
40	AP/01	877.58	61.16	816.42	97,909.64
41	MY/01	877.58	61.67	815.91	97,847.97
42	JN/01	877.58	62.18	815.40	97,785.79
43	JL/01	877.58	62.70	814.88	97,723.09
44	AU/01	877.58	63.22	814.36	97,659.87
45	SE/01	877.58	63.75	813.83	97,596.12
46	OC/01	877.58	64.28	813.30	97,531.84
47	NO/01	877.58	64.81	812.77	97,467.03
48	DE/01	877.58	65.35	812.23	97,401.68
YR 4 2001		10,530.96	749.57	9,781.39	97,401.68
TOTAL		42,123.84	2,598.32	39,525.52	
49	JA/02	877.58	65.90	811.68	97,335.78
50	FE/02	877.58	66.45	811.13	97,269.33
51	MR/02	877.58	67.00	810.58	97,202.33
52	AP/02	877.58	67.56	810.02	97,134.77
53	MY/02	877.58	68.12	809.46	97,066.65
54	JN/02	877.58	68.69	808.89	96,997.96
55	JL/02	877.58	69.26	808.32	96,928.70
56	AU/02	877.58	69.84	807.74	96,858.86
57	SE/02	877.58	70.42	807.16	96,788.44
58	OC/02	877.58	71.01	806.57	96,717.43
59	NO/02	877.58	71.60	805.98	96,645.83
60	DE/02	877.58	72.20	805.38	96,573.63
YR 5 2002		10,530.96	828.05	9,702.91	96,573.63
TOTAL		52,654.80	3,426.37	49,228.43	
61	JA/03	877.58	72.80	804.78	96,500.83
62	FE/03	877.58	73.41	804.17	96,427.42
63	MR/03	877.58	74.02	803.56	96,353.40
64	AP/03	877.58	74.63	802.95	96,278.77
65	MY/03	877.58	75.26	802.32	96,203.51
66	JN/03	877.58	75.88	801.70	96,127.63
67	JL/03	877.58	76.52	801.06	96,051.11
68	AU/03	877.58	77.15	800.43	95,973.96
69	SE/03	877.58	77.80	799.78	95,896.16
70	OC/03	877.58	78.45	799.13	95,817.71
71	NO/03	877.58	79.10	798.48	95,738.61
72	DE/03	877.58	79.76	797.82	95,658.85
YR 6 2003		10,530.96	914.78	9,616.18	95,658.85
TOTAL		63,185.76	4,341.15	58,844.61	

#	DATE	PAYMENT	PRINCIPAL	INTEREST	BALANCE
73	JA/04	877.58	80.42	797.16	95,578.43
74	FE/04	877.58	81.09	796.49	95,497.34
75	MR/04	877.58	81.77	795.81	95,415.57
76	AP/04	877.58	82.45	795.13	95,333.12
77	MY/04	877.58	83.14	794.44	95,249.98
78	JN/04	877.58	83.83	793.75	95,166.15
79	JL/04	877.58	84.53	793.05	95,081.62
80	AU/04	877.58	85.23	792.35	94,996.39
81	SE/04	877.58	85.94	791.64	94,910.45
82	OC/04	877.58	86.66	790.92	94,823.79
83	NO/04	877.58	87.38	790.20	94,736.41
84	DE/04	877.58	88.11	789.47	94,648.30
YR 7 2004		10,530.96	1,010.55	9,520.41	94,648.30
TOTAL		73,716.72	5,351.70	68,365.02	
85	JA/05	877.58	88.84	788.74	94,559.46
86	FE/05	877.58	89.58	788.00	94,469.88
87	MR/05	877.58	90.33	787.25	94,379.55
88	AP/05	877.58	91.08	786.50	94,288.47
89	MY/05	877.58	91.84	785.74	94,196.63
90	JN/05	877.58	92.61	784.97	94,104.02
91	JL/05	877.58	93.38	784.20	94,010.64
92	AU/05	877.58	94.16	783.42	93,916.48
93	SE/05	877.58	94.94	782.64	93,821.54
94	OC/05	877.58	95.73	781.85	93,725.81
95	NO/05	877.58	96.53	781.05	93,629.28
96	DE/05	877.58	97.34	780.24	93,531.94
YR 8 2005		10,530.96	1,116.36	9,414.60	93,531.94
TOTAL		84,247.68	6,468.06	77,779.62	
97	JA/06	877.58	98.15	779.43	93,433.79
98	FE/06	877.58	98.97	778.61	93,334.82
99	MR/06	877.58	99.79	777.79	93,235.03
100	AP/06	877.58	100.62	776.96	93,134.41
101	MY/06	877.58	101.46	776.12	93,032.95
102	JN/06	877.58	102.31	775.27	92,930.64
103	JL/06	877.58	103.16	774.42	92,827.48
104	AU/06	877.58	104.02	773.56	92,723.46
105	SE/06	877.58	104.88	772.70	92,618.58
106	OC/06	877.58	105.76	771.82	92,512.82
107	NO/06	877.58	106.64	770.94	92,406.18
108	DE/06	877.58	107.53	770.05	92,298.65
YR 9 2006		10,530.96	1,233.29	9,297.67	92,298.65
TOTAL		94,778.64	7,701.35	87,077.29	

#	DATE	PAYMENT	PRINCIPAL	INTEREST	BALANCE
109	JA/07	877.58	108.42	769.16	92,190.23
110	FE/07	877.58	109.33	768.25	92,080.90
111	MR/07	877.58	110.24	767.34	91,970.66
112	AP/07	877.58	111.16	766.42	91,859.50
113	MY/07	877.58	112.08	765.50	91,747.42
114	JN/07	877.58	113.02	764.56	91,634.40
115	JL/07	877.58	113.96	763.62	91,520.44
116	AU/07	877.58	114.91	762.67	91,405.53
117	SE/07	877.58	115.87	761.71	91,289.66
118	OC/07	877.58	116.83	760.75	91,172.83
119	NO/07	877.58	117.81	759.77	91,055.02
120	DE/07	877.58	118.79	758.79	90,936.23
YR 10 2007		10,530.96	1,362.42	9,168.54	90,936.23
TOTAL		105,309.60	9,063.77	96,245.83	
121	JA/08	877.58	119.78	757.80	90,816.45
122	FE/08	877.58	120.78	756.80	90,695.67
123	MR/08	877.58	121.78	755.80	90,573.89
124	AP/08	877.58	122.80	754.78	90,451.09
125	MY/08	877.58	123.82	753.76	90,327.27
126	JN/08	877.58	124.85	752.73	90,202.42
127	JL/08	877.58	125.89	751.69	90,076.53
128	AU/08	877.58	126.94	750.64	89,949.59
129	SE/08	877.58	128.00	749.58	89,821.59
130	OC/08	877.58	129.07	748.51	89,692.52
131	NO/08	877.58	130.14	747.44	89,562.38
132	DE/08	877.58	131.23	746.35	89,431.15
YR 11 2008		10,530.96	1,505.08	9,025.88	89,431.15
TOTAL		115,840.56	10,568.85	105,271.71	
133	JA/09	877.58	132.32	745.26	89,298.83
134	FE/09	877.58	133.42	744.16	89,165.41
135	MR/09	877.58	134.53	743.05	89,030.88
136	AP/09	877.58	135.66	741.92	88,895.22
137	MY/09	877.58	136.79	740.79	88,758.43
138	JN/09	877.58	137.93	739.65	88,620.50
139	JL/09	877.58	139.08	738.50	88,481.42
140	AU/09	877.58	140.23	737.35	88,341.19
141	SE/09	877.58	141.40	736.18	88,199.79
142	OC/09	877.58	142.58	735.00	88,057.21
143	NO/09	877.58	143.77	733.81	87,913.44
144	DE/09	877.58	144.97	732.61	87,768.47
YR 12 2009		10,530.96	1,662.68	8,868.28	87,768.47
TOTAL		126,371.52	12,231.53	114,139.99	

#	DATE	PAYMENT	PRINCIPAL	INTEREST	BALANCE
145	JA/10	877.58	146.18	731.40	87,622.29
146	FE/10	877.58	147.39	730.19	87,474.90
147	MR/10	877.58	148.62	728.96	87,326.28
148	AP/10	877.58	149.86	727.72	87,176.42
149	MY/10	877.58	151.11	726.47	87,025.31
150	JN/10	877.58	152.37	725.21	86,872.94
151	JL/10	877.58	153.64	723.94	86,719.30
152	AU/10	877.58	154.92	722.66	86,564.38
153	SE/10	877.58	156.21	721.37	86,408.17
154	OC/10	877.58	157.51	720.07	86,250.66
155	NO/10	877.58	158.82	718.76	86,091.84
156	DE/10	877.58	160.15	717.43	85,931.69
YR 13 2010		10,530.96	1,836.78	8,694.18	85,931.69
TOTAL		136,902.48	14,068.31	122,834.17	
157	JA/11	877.58	161.48	716.10	85,770.21
158	FE/11	877.58	162.83	714.75	85,607.38
159	MR/11	877.58	164.19	713.39	85,443.19
160	AP/11	877.58	165.55	712.03	85,277.64
161	MY/11	877.58	166.93	710.65	85,110.71
162	JN/11	877.58	168.32	709.26	84,942.39
163	JL/11	877.58	169.73	707.85	84,772.66
164	AU/11	877.58	171.14	706.44	84,601.52
165	SE/11	877.58	172.57	705.01	84,428.95
166	OC/11	877.58	174.01	703.57	84,254.94
167	NO/11	877.58	175.46	702.12	84,079.48
168	DE/11	877.58	176.92	700.66	83,902.56
YR 14 2011		10,530.96	2,029.13	8,501.83	83,902.56
TOTAL		147,433.44	16,097.44	131,336.00	
169	JA/12	877.58	178.39	699.19	83,724.17
170	FE/12	877.58	179.88	697.70	83,544.29
171	MR/12	877.58	181.38	696.20	83,362.91
172	AP/12	877.58	182.89	694.69	83,180.02
173	MY/12	877.58	184.41	693.17	82,995.61
174	JN/12	877.58	185.95	691.63	82,809.66
175	JL/12	877.58	187.50	690.08	82,622.16
176	AU/12	877.58	189.06	688.52	82,433.10
177	SE/12	877.58	190.64	686.94	82,242.46
178	OC/12	877.58	192.23	685.35	82,050.23
179	NO/12	877.58	193.83	683.75	81,856.40
180	DE/12	877.58	195.44	682.14	81,660.96
YR 15 2012		10,530.96	2,241.60	8,289.36	81,660.96
TOTAL		157,964.40	18,339.04	139,625.36	

#	DATE	PAYMENT	PRINCIPAL	INTEREST	BALANCE
181	JA/13	877.58	197.07	680.51	81,463.89
182	FE/13	877.58	198.71	678.87	81,265.18
183	MR/13	877.58	200.37	677.21	81,064.81
184	AP/13	877.58	202.04	675.54	80,862.77
185	MY/13	877.58	203.72	673.86	80,659.05
186	JN/13	877.58	205.42	672.16	80,453.63
187	JL/13	877.58	207.13	670.45	80,246.50
188	AU/13	877.58	208.86	668.72	80,037.64
189	SE/13	877.58	210.60	666.98	79,827.04
190	OC/13	877.58	212.35	665.23	79,614.69
191	NO/13	877.58	214.12	663.46	79,400.57
192	DE/13	877.58	215.91	661.67	79,184.66
YR 16 2013		10,530.96	2,476.30	8,054.66	79,184.66
TOTAL		168,495.36	20,815.34	147,680.02	
193	JA/14	877.58	217.71	659.87	78,966.95
194	FE/14	877.58	219.52	658.06	78,747.43
195	MR/14	877.58	221.35	656.23	78,526.08
196	AP/14	877.58	223.20	654.38	78,302.88
197	MY/14	877.58	225.06	652.52	78,077.82
198	JN/14	877.58	226.93	650.65	77,850.89
199	JL/14	877.58	228.82	648.76	77,622.07
200	AU/14	877.58	230.73	646.85	77,391.34
201	SE/14	877.58	232.65	644.93	77,158.69
202	OC/14	877.58	234.59	642.99	76,924.10
203	NO/14	877.58	236.55	641.03	76,687.55
204	DE/14	877.58	238.52	639.06	76,449.03
YR 17 2014		10,530.96	2,735.63	7,795.33	76,449.03
TOTAL		179,026.32	23,550.97	155,475.35	
205	JA/15	877.58	240.50	637.08	76,208.53
206	FE/15	877.58	242.51	635.07	75,966.02
207	MR/15	877.58	244.53	633.05	75,721.49
208	AP/15	877.58	246.57	631.01	75,474.92
209	MY/15	877.58	248.62	628.96	75,226.30
210	JN/15	877.58	250.69	626.89	74,975.61
211	JL/15	877.58	252.78	624.80	74,722.83
212	AU/15	877.58	254.89	622.69	74,467.94
213	SE/15	877.58	257.01	620.57	74,210.93
214	OC/15	877.58	259.16	618.42	73,951.77
215	NO/15	877.58	261.32	616.26	73,690.45
216	DE/15	877.58	263.49	614.09	73,426.96
YR 18 2015		10,530.96	3,022.07	7,508.89	73,426.96
TOTAL		189,557.28	26,573.04	162,984.24	

#	DATE	PAYMENT	PRINCIPAL	INTEREST	BALANCE
217	JA/16	877.58	265.69	611.89	73,161.27
218	FE/16	877.58	267.90	609.68	72,893.37
219	MR/16	877.58	270.14	607.44	72,623.23
220	AP/16	877.58	272.39	605.19	72,350.84
221	MY/16	877.58	274.66	602.92	72,076.18
222	JN/16	877.58	276.95	600.63	71,799.23
223	JL/16	877.58	279.25	598.33	71,519.98
224	AU/16	877.58	281.58	596.00	71,238.40
225	SE/16	877.58	283.93	593.65	70,954.47
226	OC/16	877.58	286.29	591.29	70,668.18
227	NO/16	877.58	288.68	588.90	70,379.50
228	DE/16	877.58	291.08	586.50	70,088.42
YR 19 2016		10,530.96	3,338.54	7,192.42	70,088.42
TOTAL		200,088.24	29,911.58	170,176.66	
229	JA/17	877.58	293.51	584.07	69,794.91
230	FE/17	877.58	295.96	581.62	69,498.95
231	MR/17	877.58	298.42	579.16	69,200.53
232	AP/17	877.58	300.91	576.67	68,899.62
233	MY/17	877.58	303.42	574.16	68,596.20
234	JN/17	877.58	305.94	571.64	68,290.26
235	JL/17	877.58	308.49	569.09	67,981.77
236	AU/17	877.58	311.07	566.51	67,670.70
237	SE/17	877.58	313.66	563.92	67,357.04
238	OC/17	877.58	316.27	561.31	67,040.77
239	NO/17	877.58	318.91	558.67	66,721.86
240	DE/17	877.58	321.56	556.02	66,400.30
YR 20 2017		10,530.96	3,688.12	6,842.84	66,400.30
TOTAL		210,619.20	33,599.70	177,019.50	
241	JA/18	877.58	324.24	553.34	66,076.06
242	FE/18	877.58	326.95	550.63	65,749.11
243	MR/18	877.58	329.67	547.91	65,419.44
244	AP/18	877.58	332.42	545.16	65,087.02
245	MY/18	877.58	335.19	542.39	64,751.83
246	JN/18	877.58	337.98	539.60	64,413.85
247	JL/18	877.58	340.80	536.78	64,073.05
248	AU/18	877.58	343.64	533.94	63,729.41
249	SE/18	877.58	346.50	531.08	63,382.91
250	OC/18	877.58	349.39	528.19	63,033.52
251	NO/18	877.58	352.30	525.28	62,681.22
252	DE/18	877.58	355.24	522.34	62,325.98
YR 21 2018		10,530.96	4,074.32	6,456.64	62,325.98
TOTAL		221,150.16	37,674.02	183,476.14	

#	DATE	PAYMENT	PRINCIPAL	INTEREST	BALANCE
253	JA/19	877.58	358.20	519.38	61,967.78
254	FE/19	877.58	361.18	516.40	61,606.60
255	MR/19	877.58	364.19	513.39	61,242.41
256	AP/19	877.58	367.23	510.35	60,875.18
257	MY/19	877.58	370.29	507.29	60,504.89
258	JN/19	877.58	373.37	504.21	60,131.52
259	JL/19	877.58	376.48	501.10	59,755.04
260	AU/19	877.58	379.62	497.96	59,375.42
261	SE/19	877.58	382.78	494.80	58,992.64
262	OC/19	877.58	385.97	491.61	58,606.67
263	NO/19	877.58	389.19	488.39	58,217.48
264	DE/19	877.58	392.43	485.15	57,825.05
YR 22 2019		10,530.96	4,500.93	6,030.03	57,825.05
TOTAL		231,681.12	42,174.95	189,506.17	
265	JA/20	877.58	395.70	481.88	57,429.35
266	FE/20	877.58	399.00	478.58	57,030.35
267	MR/20	877.58	402.33	475.25	56,628.02
268	AP/20	877.58	405.68	471.90	56,222.34
269	MY/20	877.58	409.06	468.52	55,813.28
270	JN/20	877.58	412.47	465.11	55,400.81
271	JL/20	877.58	415.91	461.67	54,984.90
272	AU/20	877.58	419.37	458.21	54,565.53
273	SE/20	877.58	422.87	454.71	54,142.66
274	OC/20	877.58	426.39	451.19	53,716.27
275	NO/20	877.58	429.94	447.64	53,286.33
276	DE/20	877.58	433.53	444.05	52,852.80
YR 23 2020		10,530.96	4,972.25	5,558.71	52,852.80
TOTAL		242,212.08	47,147.20	195,064.88	
277	JA/21	877.58	437.14	440.44	52,415.66
278	FE/21	877.58	440.78	436.80	51,974.88
279	MR/21	877.58	444.46	433.12	51,530.42
280	AP/21	877.58	448.16	429.42	51,082.26
281	MY/21	877.58	451.89	425.69	50,630.37
282	JN/21	877.58	455.66	421.92	50,174.71
283	JL/21	877.58	459.46	418.12	49,715.25
284	AU/21	877.58	463.29	414.29	49,251.96
285	SE/21	877.58	467.15	410.43	48,784.81
286	OC/21	877.58	471.04	406.54	48,313.77
287	NO/21	877.58	474.97	402.61	47,838.80
288	DE/21	877.58	478.92	398.66	47,359.88
YR 24 2021		10,530.96	5,492.92	5,038.04	47,359.88
TOTAL		252,743.04	52,640.12	200,102.92	

#	DATE	PAYMENT	PRINCIPAL	INTEREST	BALANCE
289	JA/22	877.58	482.91	394.67	46,876.97
290	FE/22	877.58	486.94	390.64	46,390.03
291	MR/22	877.58	491.00	386.58	45,899.03
292	AP/22	877.58	495.09	382.49	45,403.94
293	MY/22	877.58	499.21	378.37	44,904.73
294	JN/22	877.58	503.37	374.21	44,401.36
295	JL/22	877.58	507.57	370.01	43,893.79
296	AU/22	877.58	511.80	365.78	43,381.99
297	SE/22	877.58	516.06	361.52	42,865.93
298	OC/22	877.58	520.36	357.22	42,345.57
299	NO/22	877.58	524.70	352.88	41,820.87
300	DE/22	877.58	529.07	348.51	41,291.80
YR 25 2022		10,530.96	6,068.08	4,462.88	41,291.80
TOTAL		263,274.00	58,708.20	204,565.80	
301	JA/23	877.58	533.48	344.10	40,758.32
302	FE/23	877.58	537.93	339.65	40,220.39
303	MR/23	877.58	542.41	335.17	39,677.98
304	AP/23	877.58	546.93	330.65	39,131.05
305	MY/23	877.58	551.49	326.09	38,579.56
306	JN/23	877.58	556.08	321.50	38,023.48
307	JL/23	877.58	560.72	316.86	37,462.76
308	AU/23	877.58	565.39	312.19	36,897.37
309	SE/23	877.58	570.10	307.48	36,327.27
310	OC/23	877.58	574.85	302.73	35,752.42
311	NO/23	877.58	579.64	297.94	35,172.78
312	DE/23	877.58	584.47	293.11	34,588.31
YR 26 2023		10,530.96	6,703.49	3,827.47	34,588.31
TOTAL		273,804.96	65,411.69	208,393.27	
313	JA/24	877.58	589.34	288.24	33,998.97
314	FE/24	877.58	594.26	283.32	33,404.71
315	MR/24	877.58	599.21	278.37	32,805.50
316	AP/24	877.58	604.20	273.38	32,201.30
317	MY/24	877.58	609.24	268.34	31,592.06
318	JN/24	877.58	614.31	263.27	30,977.75
319	JL/24	877.58	619.43	258.15	30,358.32
320	AU/24	877.58	624.59	252.99	29,733.73
321	SE/24	877.58	629.80	247.78	29,103.93
322	OC/24	877.58	635.05	242.53	28,468.88
323	NO/24	877.58	640.34	237.24	27,828.54
324	DE/24	877.58	645.68	231.90	27,182.86
YR 27 2024		10,530.96	7,405.45	3,125.51	27,182.86
TOTAL		284,335.92	72,817.14	211,518.78	

#	DATE	PAYMENT	PRINCIPAL	INTEREST	BALANCE
325	JA/25	877.58	651.06	226.52	26,531.80
326	FE/25	877.58	656.48	221.10	25,875.32
327	MR/25	877.58	661.95	215.63	25,213.37
328	AP/25	877.58	667.47	210.11	24,545.90
329	MY/25	877.58	673.03	204.55	23,872.87
330	JN/25	877.58	678.64	198.94	23,194.23
331	JL/25	877.58	684.29	193.29	22,509.94
332	AU/25	877.58	690.00	187.58	21,819.94
333	SE/25	877.58	695.75	181.83	21,124.19
334	OC/25	877.58	701.55	176.03	20,422.64
335	NO/25	877.58	707.39	170.19	19,715.25
336	DE/25	877.58	713.29	164.29	19,001.96
YR 28 2025		10,530.96	8,180.90	2,350.06	19,001.96
TOTAL		294,866.88	80,998.04	213,868.84	
337	JA/26	877.58	719.23	158.35	18,282.73
338	FE/26	877.58	725.22	152.36	17,557.51
339	MR/26	877.58	731.27	146.31	16,826.24
340	AP/26	877.58	737.36	140.22	16,088.88
341	MY/26	877.58	743.51	134.07	15,345.37
342	JN/26	877.58	749.70	127.88	14,595.67
343	JL/26	877.58	755.95	121.63	13,839.72
344	AU/26	877.58	762.25	115.33	13,077.47
345	SE/26	877.58	768.60	108.98	12,308.87
346	OC/26	877.58	775.01	102.57	11,533.86
347	NO/26	877.58	781.46	96.12	10,752.40
348	DE/26	877.58	787.98	89.60	9,964.42
YR 29 2026		10,530.96	9,037.54	1,493.42	9,964.42
TOTAL		305,397.84	90,035.58	215,362.26	
349	JA/27	877.58	794.54	83.04	9,169.88
350	FE/27	877.58	801.16	76.42	8,368.72
351	MR/27	877.58	807.84	69.74	7,560.88
352	AP/27	877.58	814.57	63.01	6,746.31
353	MY/27	877.58	821.36	56.22	5,924.95
354	JN/27	877.58	828.21	49.37	5,096.74
355	JL/27	877.58	835.11	42.47	4,261.63
356	AU/27	877.58	842.07	35.51	3,419.56
357	SE/27	877.58	849.08	28.50	2,570.48
358	OC/27	877.58	856.16	21.42	1,714.32
359	NO/27	877.58	863.29	14.29	851.03
360	DE/27	858.12	851.03	7.09	0.00
YR 30 2027		10,511.50	9,964.42	547.08	0.00
TOTAL		315,909.34	100,000.00	215,909.34	

Important Documents

Real Estate Brokerage Services Disclosure

State law (laws vary by state) requires you, the consumer, to be informed about the types of services which real estate licensees may perform. The purpose of this disclosure is to give you a summary of these services.

A SINGLE AGENT is a licensee who represents only one party in a sale. That is, a single agent represents his/her client. The client may be either the seller or the buyer. A single agent must be completely loyal and faithful to the client.

A SUB-AGENT is another agent/licensee who also represents only one party in a sale. A sub-agent helps the agent represent the same client. The client may be either the seller or the buyer. A sub-agent must also be completely loyal and faithful to the client.

A LIMITED CONSENSUAL DUAL AGENT is a licensee for both the buyer and the seller. This may only be done with the written, informed consent of all parties. This type of agent must also be loyal and faithful to the client, except where the duties owed to the clients conflict with one another.

A CONTRACT BROKER assists one or more parties in a sale. A contract broker is not an agent and does not have the same obligations as an agent. The contract broker and licensees working with him/her perform the services set out in their contract.

State law imposes the following obligations on all real estate licensees to all parties, no matter their relationship:

1. To provide services honestly and in good faith;
2. To exercise reasonable care and skill;
3. To keep confidential any information gained in confidence, unless disclosure is required by law or duty to a client, the information becomes public knowledge, or disclosure is authorized in writing;
4. Present all written offers promptly to the seller;
5. Answer your questions completely and accurately.

Further, even if you are working with a licensee who is not your agent, there are many things that the licensee may do to assist you, the customer. Some examples are:

1. Provide information about properties
2. Show properties
3. Assist in making a written offer
4. Provide information on financing.

You should choose which type of service you want from a licensee and sign a brokerage service agreement. If you do not sign an agreement, by law the licensee working with you is a contract broker.

The licensee's broker is required by law to have on file an office policy describing the company's brokerage services. You should feel free to ask any questions you have.

The State Real Estate Law Commission requires the real estate licensee to sign, date, and provide you a copy of this form. Your signature is not required by law or rule, but would be appreciated.

Name of Licensee:_____

Signature: _____ Date: _____

Consumer Name: _____

Signature: _____ Date: _____

LIMITED NEW HOME WARRANTY

This Agreement made this _____day of _____ , 19_____ ,
by and between _____
(BUILDER) of _____ (BUILDER'S ADDRESS)
and _____ (PURCHASER)
of _____
(HOME/PROPERTY ADDRESS).
WHEREAS, Builder has caused to be built for sale to Purchaser or under contract
with Purchaser a Home situated on land located In the County of
_____ State of _____ , at the above property address;
and
WHEREAS, Builder does hereby agree to give a limited warranty on the Home
located at the above property for a period of one (1) year following closing or
occupancy by the Purchaser, whichever event shall first occur, upon the following
condition.

NOW, THEREFORE, In consideration of the payment of the purchase price of
this Home, and other good and valuable consideration, the receipt and sufficiency
of which is hereby acknowledged, and the premises and agreements hereinafter
set forth, the parties hereby agree as follows:

1. Not later than thirty (30) days after closing or occupancy, whichever event
shall first occur, the Purchaser shall deliver a written list of any minor omissions or
malfunctions not previously made known in writing to the Builder. To the extent
that such items are a normal Builder responsibility or not otherwise excluded
hereunder, corrections or adjustments will be made by the Builder.

2. Builder warrants the above Home to be free from latent defects for a period of
one (1) year following closing or occupancy, whichever event shall first occur.

A latent defect in construction is herein defined as a defect not apparent at time of
occupancy or closing but which becomes apparent within one (1) year from date
of closing or occupancy, whichever event shall first occur, and such defect has been
directly caused by Builder's failure to construct in accordance with the standards
of construction prevailing in the geographical area of the Home. It is stressed,
however, that normal characteristic behavior of building materials, wear and tear,
general maintenance, and like items, will not constitute a latent defect.

PROCEDURE: Should it appear that a possible latent defect (non-emergency nature)
has developed, Purchaser shall outline pertinent details in writing, and deliver same
to Builder. Following receipt of such notice, Builder will make an inspection. If a
latent defect exists the Builder will (at Builder's sole option) either (1) repair,
(2) replace or (3) pay to Purchaser the reasonable cost of such repair or replace due
to such latent defects(s); however, Builder shall not be obilgated to spend more
than the purchase price of the Home less the value of the land upon which the
Home is situated.

NOTWITHSTANDING, ANYTHING TO THE CONTRARY STATED HEREIN, THIS WARRANTY DOES NOT COVER ANY APPLIANCE, PIECE OF EQUIPMENT, OR ITEM WHICH IS A CONSUMER PRODUCT FOR PURPOSES OF THE MAGNUSON–MOSS WARRANTY ACT (15 U.S.C., §2301 THROUGH 2312). THIS WARRANTY IS GIVEN IN LIEU OF ANY AND ALL OTHER WARRANTIES, EITHER EXPRESSED OR IMPLIED, INCLUDING ANY IMPLIED WARRANTY OF MERCHANTABILITY, FITNESS FOR A PARTICULAR PURPOSE, HABITABILITY AND WORKMANSHIP, EXCEPT, IF APPLICABLE, SUCH WARRANTY AS SPECIFICALLY STATED IN ANY REQUIRED VA/FHA WARRANTY DELIVERED SIMULTANEOUSLY HEREWITH.

3. The Builder shall not be liable under this Agreement unless written notice of the latent defect shall have been given by Purchaser to Builder within the one (1) year warranty period. Steps taken by the Builder to correct any defect or defects shall not act to extend the warranty period described hereunder.

4. The purchaser shall have (90) ninety days, after expiration of the (1) one year warranty, to bring any legal action hereunder.

5. Builder hereby assigns to Purchaser all of Builder's rights, If any, under manufacturers' warranties on appliances and items of equipment included in the Home. Builder assumes no responsibility for such manufacturers' warranties and Purchaser should follow the procedures in these warranties if defects appear in such appliances and items of equipment.

6. Builder does not assume responsibillty for any of the following, all of which are expressly excluded from coverage under this Limited Warranty:

(a) Defects in appliances and pieces of equipment which are covered by manufacturer's warranties.

(b) Incidental, consequential, or secondary damages caused by a breech of this warranty.

(c) Defects which are the result of characteristics common to the materials used, such as (but not limited to) warping and deflection of wood; mildew and fading, chalking, and checking of paint due to sunlight; cracks due to drying and curing of concrete stucco, plaster, bricks and masonry; drying, shrinking and cracking of caulking and weatherstripping.

(d) Conditions resulting from condensation on, or expansion or contraction of, materials.

(e) Defective design or materials supplied by Purchaser or installed under his direction; or defects in, or caused by anything not built into, or installed in the Home pursuant to contract between Builder and Purchaser.

(f) Damages due to ordinary wear and tear, abusive use, or lack of proper maintenance of the Home.

Transfer of the Property or a Beneficial Interest in Borrower. If all or any part of the Property or any interest in it is sold or transferred (or if a beneficial interest in Borrower is sold or transferred and Borrower is not a natural person) without Lender's prior written consent, Lender may, at its option, require immediate payment in full of all sums secured by this Security Instrument. However, this option shall not be exercised by Lender if exercise is prohibited by federal law as of the date of this Security Instrument.

If Lender exercises this option, Lender shall give Borrower notice of acceleration. The notice shall provide a period of not less than 30 days from the date the notice is delivered or mailed within which Borrower must pay all sums secured by this Security Instrument. If Borrower fails to pay these sums prior to the expiration of this period, Lender may invoke any remedies permitted by this Security Instrument without further notice or demand on Borrower.

WITNESS THE HAND(S) and SEAL(S) OF THE UNDERSIGNED.

CAUTION: IT IS IMPORTANT THAT YOU THOROUGHLY READ THE CONTRACT BEFORE YOU SIGN IT.

_____ (Seal)
Borrower

_____ (Seal)
Borrower

_____ (Seal)
Borrower

NOTE

_____ , 20 _____   _____ _____
                                            (city)   (state)

_____
                      (Property Address)

1. BORROWER'S PROMISE TO PAY

In return for a loan that I have received, I promise to pay U.S. $ _____ (this amount is called "principal"), plus interest, to the order of the Lender. The Lender is
_____ . I understand that the Lender may transfer this Note. The Lender or anyone who takes this Note by transfer and who is entitled to receive payments under this Note is called the "Note Holder."

2. INTEREST

Interest will be charged on unpaid principal until the full amount of principal has been paid. I will pay interest at a yearly rate of _____ %.

The interest rate required by this Section 2 is the rate I will pay both before and after any default described in Section 6(B) of this Note.

3. PAYMENTS

A. Time and Place of Payments

I will pay interest and principal by making payments every month.

I will make my monthly payments on the _____ day of each month beginning on _____ . I will make these payments every month until I have paid all of the principal and interest and any other charges described below that I may owe under this Note. My monthly payments will be applied to interest before principal. If, on _____ , I still owe amounts under this Note, I will pay those amounts in full on that date, which is called the "maturity date."

I will make my monthly payments at _____ or at a different place if required by the Note Holder.

(B) Amount of Monthly Payments

My monthly payment will be in the amount of U.S. $ _____ .

4. BORROWER'S RIGHT TO PREPAY

I have the right to make payments of principal at any time before they are due. A payment of principal only is known as a "prepayment." When I make a prepayment, I will tell the Note Holder in writing that I am doing so.

I may make a full prepayment or partial prepayments without paying any prepayment charge. The Note Holder will use all of my prepayments to reduce the amount of principal that I owe under this Note. If I make a partial prepayment, there will be no charges in the due date or in the amount of my monthly payment unless the Note Holder agrees in writing to those changes.

5. LOAN CHARGES

If a law, which applies to this loan and which sets maximum loan charges, is finally interpreted so that the interest or other loan charges collected or to be collected in connection with this loan exceed the permitted limits, then: (I) any such loan charge shall be reduced by the amount necessary to reduce the charge to the permitted limit; (ii) any sums already collected from me which exceeded permitted limits will be refunded to me. The Note Holder may choose to make this refund by reducing the principal I owe under this Note or by making a direct payment to me. If a refund reduces principal, the reduction will be treated as a partial payment.

6. BORROWER'S FAILURE TO PAY AS REQUIRED

(A) Late Charge for Overdue Payments

If the Note Holder has not received the full amount of any monthly payment by the end of _____ calendar days after the date it is due, I will pay a late charge to the Note Holder. The amount of the charge will be _____ % of my overdue payment of principal and interest. I will pay this late charge promptly but only once on each late payment.

(B) Default

If I do not pay the full amount of each monthly payment on the date it is due, I will be in default.

(C) Notice of Default

If I am in default, the Note Holder may send me a written notice telling me that if I do not pay the overdue amount by a certain date, the Note Holder may require me to pay immediately the full amount of principal which has not been paid and all the interest that I owe on that amount. The date must be at least 30 days after the date on which the notice is delivered or mailed to me.

(D) No Waiver by Note Holder

Even if, at a time when I am in default, the Note Holder does not require me to pay immediately in full as described above, the Note Holder will still have the right to do so if I am in default at a later time.

(E) Payment of Note Holder's Costs and Expenses

If the Note Holder has required me to pay immediately in full as described above, the Note Holder will have the right to be paid back by me for all of its costs and expenses in enforcing this Note to the extent not prohibited by applicable law. Those expenses include, for example, reasonable attorneys' fees.

7. GIVING OF NOTICES

Unless applicable law requires a different method, any notice that must be given to me under this Note will be given by delivering it or by mailing it by first class mail to me at the Property Address above or at a different address if I give the Note Holder a notice of my different address.

Any notice that must be given to the Note Holder under this Note will be given by mailing it by first class mail to the Note Holder at the address stated in Section 3(A) above or at a different address if I am given a notice of that different address.

8. OBLIGATIONS OF PERSONS UNDER THIS NOTE

If more than one person signs this Note, each person is fully and personally obligated to keep all of the promises made in this Note, including the promise to pay the full amount owed. Any person who is a guarantor, surety or endorser of this Note, is also obligated to do these things. Any person who takes over these obligations, including the obligations of a guarantor, surety, or endorser of this Note, is also obligated to keep all of the promises made in this Note. The Note Holder may enforce its rights under this Note against each person individually or against all of us together. This means that any one of us may be required to pay all of the amounts owed under this Note.

9. WAIVERS

I and any other person who has obligations under this Note waive the rights of presentment and notice of dishonor. "Presentment" means the right to require the Note Holder to demand payment of amounts due. "Notice of dishonor" means the right to require the Note Holder to give notice to other persons that amounts due have not been paid.

10. UNIFORM SECURED NOTE

This Note is a uniform instrument with limited variations in some jurisdictions. In addition to the protections given to the Note Holder under this Note, a Mortgage, Deed of Trust or Security Deed (the "Security Instrument") dated the same date as this Note, protects the Note Holder from possible losses which might result if I do not keep the promises which I make in this Note. That Security Instrument describes how and under what conditions I may be required to make immediate payment in full of all amounts I owe under this Note. Some of those conditions are described as follows:

Transfer of the Property or a Beneficial Interest in Borrower. If all or any part of the Property or any interest in it is sold or transferred (or if a beneficial interest in Borrower is sold or transferred and Borrower is not a natural person) without Lender's prior written consent, Lender may, at its option, require immediate payment in full of all sums secured by this Security Instrument. However, this option shall not be exercised by Lender if exercise is prohibited by federal law as of the date of this Security Instrument.

If Lender exercises this option, Lender shall give Borrower notice of acceleration. The notice shall provide a period of not less than 30 days from the date the notice is delivered or mailed within which Borrower must pay all sums secured by this Security Instrument. If Borrower fails to pay these sums prior to the expiration of this period, Lender may invoke any remedies permitted by this Security Instrument without further notice or demand on Borrower.

WITNESS THE HAND(S) and SEAL(S) OF THE UNDERSIGNED.

CAUTION: IT IS IMPORTANT THAT YOU THOROUGHLY READ THE CONTRACT BEFORE YOU SIGN IT.

_____ (Seal)
                                                                Borrower

_____ (Seal)
                                                                 Borrower

_____ (Seal)
                                                                 Borrower

MORTGAGE

THIS MORTGAGE ("Security Instrument") is given on _____ 20 __ .
The guarantor is _____("Borrower"). This Security
Instrument is given to _____ , which is organized and existing under the
laws of _____, and whose address is
_____ ("Lender"). Borrower owes Lender the principal
sum of _____ Dollars (U.S.
$ _____ .) This debt is evidenced b Borrower's note dated the same date as this
Security Instrument ("Note") , which provides for monthly payments, with the full debt, if not paid
earlier, and payable on _____. This Security Instrument
secures to Lender: (a) the repayment of the debt evidenced by the Note, with interest, and all
renewals, extensions and modifications of the note; (b) the payment of all other sums, with interest,
advanced under paragraph 7 to protect the security of this Security Instrument; and (c) the
performance of Borrower's covenants and agreements under the Security Instrument and the Note.
For this purpose, Borrower does hereby mortgage, grant and convey to Lender and Lender's
successors and assigns, with power of sale, the following described property located in
_____ County, [name of state]:

Which has the address of _____ , _____
                                  (Street)   (City)
Alabama _____ ("Property Address");

　　　　TO HAVE AND TO HOLD this property unto Lender and Lender's successors and
assigns, forever, together with all the improvements now or hereafter erected on the property, and all
easements, appurtenances, and fixtures now or hereafter a part of the property. All replacements and
additions shall also be covered by the Security Instrument. All of the foregoing is referred to in this
Security Instrument as the "Property."

　　　　BORROWER COVENANTS that Borrower is lawfully seised of the estate hereby
conveyed and has the right to mortgage, grant and convey the Property and that the Property is
unencumbered, except for encumbrances of record. Borrower warrants and will defend generally the
title to the Property against all claims and demands, subject to any encumbrances of record.

　　　　THIS SECURITY INSTRUMENT combines uniform covenants for national use and
non-uniform covenants with limited variations to constitute a uniform security instrument covering
real property.

　　　　UNIFORM COVENANTS. Borrower and Lender covenant and agree as follows:

1. **Payment of Principal and Interest; Prepayment and Late Charges**. Borrower shall promptly
pay when due the principal of and interest on the debt evidenced by the Note and any prepayment
and late charges due under the Note.

2. **Funds for Taxes and Insurance.** Subject to applicable law or to a written waiver by Lender,
Borrower shall pay to Lender on the day monthly payments are due under the Note, until the Note is
paid in full, a sum ("Funds") of: (a) yearly taxes and assessments which may attain priority over this
Security Instrument as a lien on the Property; (b) yearly leasehold payments or ground rents on the
Property, if any; (c) yearly hazard or property insurance premiums; (d) yearly flood insurance
premiums, if any; (e) yearly mortgage insurance premiums, if any; and (f) any sums payable by
Borrower to Lender, in accordance with the provisions of paragraph 8, in lieu of the payment of
mortgage insurance premiums. These items are called "Escrow Items." Lender may, at any time,
collect and hold Funds in an amount not to exceed the maximum amount a lender for a federally
related mortgage loan may require for Borrower's escrow account under the federal Real Estate
Settlement Procedures Act of 1974 as amended from time to time, 12 U.S.C. 2601 et seq.
("RESPA"), unless another law that applies to the Funds sets a lesser amount. If so, Lender may, at
any time, collect and hold Funds in an amount not to exceed the lesser amount. Lender may estimate
the amount of Funds due on the basis of current data and reasonable estimates of expenditures of
future Escrow Items or otherwise in accordance with applicable law.

The Funds shall be held in an institution whose deposits are insured by a federal agency, instrumentality, or entity (including Lender if Lender is such an institution) or in any Federal Home Loan Bank. Lender shall apply the Funds to pay the escrow items. Lender may not charge Borrower for holding and applying the Funds, annually analyzing the escrow account, or verifying the Escrow Items, unless Lender pays Borrower interest on the Funds and applicable law permits Lender to make such a charge. However, Lender may require Borrower to pay a one-time charge for an independent real estate tax reporting service used by Lender in connection with this loan, unless applicable law provides otherwise. Unless an agreement is made or applicable law requires interest to be paid, Lender shall not be required to pay Borrower any interest or earnings on the Funds. Borrower and Lender may agree in writing, however, that interest shall be paid on the Funds. Lender shall give to Borrower, without charge, an annual accounting of the Funds, showing credits and debits to the Funds and the purpose for which each debit to the Funds was made. The Funds are pledged as additional security for the sums secured by this Security Instrument.

If the Funds held by Lender exceed the amount permitted to be held by applicable law, Lender shall account to Borrower for the excess Funds in accordance with the requirements of applicable law. If the amount of the Funds held by Lender at any time is not sufficient to pay the Escrow Items when due, Lender may so notify Borrower in writing, and, in such case Borrower shall pay to Lender the amount necessary to make up the deficiency. Borrower shall make up the deficiency in no more than twelve monthly payments, at Lender's sole discretion.

Upon payment in full of all sums secured by this Security Instrument, Lender shall promptly refund to Borrower any funds held by Lender. If, under paragraph 21, Lender shall acquire or sell the Property, Lender, prior to the acquisition or sale of the Property, shall apply any Funds held by Lender at the time of acquisition or sale as a credit against the sums secured by this Security Instrument.

3. **Application of Payments**. Unless applicable law provides otherwise, all payments received by Lender under paragraphs 1 and 2 shall be applied; first, to any prepayment charges due under the Note; second, to amounts payable under paragraph 2; third, to interest due; fourth, to principal due; and last, to any late charges due under the Note.

4. **Charges; Liens**. Borrower shall pay all taxes, assessments, charges, fines and impositions attributable to the Property which may attain priority over this Security Instrument, and leasehold payments or ground rents, if any. Borrower shall pay these obligations in the manner provided in paragraph 2, or if not paid in that manner, Borrower shall pay them on time directly to the person owed payment. Borrower shall promptly furnish to Lender all notices of amounts to be paid under this paragraph. If Borrower makes these payments directly, Borrower shall promptly furnish to Lender receipts evidencing the payments.

Borrower shall promptly discharge any lien which has priority over this Security Instrument unless Borrower: (a) agrees in writing to the payment of the obligation secured by the lien in a manner acceptable to Lender; (b) contests in good faith the lien by, or defends against enforcement of the lien in, legal proceedings which in the Lender's opinion operate to prevent the enforcement of the lien; or (c) secures from the holder of the lien an agreement satisfactory to Lender subordinating the lien to this Security Instrument. If Lender determines that any part of Property is subject to a lien which may attain priority over this Security Instrument, Lender may give Borrower a notice identifying the lien. Borrower shall satisfy the lien or take one or more of the actions set forth above within 10 days of the giving of notice.

5. **Hazard or Property Insurance**. Borrower shall keep the improvements now existing or hereafter erected on the Property insured against loss by fire, hazards included within the term "extended coverage" and any other hazards including floods or flooding, for which Lender requires insurance. This insurance shall be maintained in the amounts and for the periods that Lender requires. The insurance carrier providing the insurance shall be chosen by Borrower subject to Lender's approval which shall not be unreasonably withheld. If Borrower fails to maintain coverage described above, Lender may, at Lender's option, obtain coverage to protect Lender's rights in the Property in accordance with paragraph 7.

All insurance policies and renewals shall be acceptable to Lender and shall include a standard mortgage clause. Lender shall have the right to hold the policies and renewals. If Lender requires, Borrower shall promptly give to Lender all receipts of paid premiums and renewal notices. In the event of loss, Borrower shall give prompt notice to the insurance carrier and Lender. Lender may make proof of loss if not made promptly by Borrower.

Unless Lender and Borrower otherwise agree in writing, insurance proceeds shall be applied to restoration or repair of the Property damaged, if the restoration or repair is economically feasible and Lender's security is not lessened. If the restoration or repair is not economically feasible or Lender's security would be lessened, the insurance proceeds shall be applied to the sums secured by the Security Instrument, whether or not then due, with any excess paid to the Borrower. If Borrower abandons the property, or does not answer within 30 days a notice from Lender that the insurance carrier has offered to settle a claim, then Lender may collect the insurance proceeds. Lender may use the proceeds to repair or restore the Property or to pay sums secured by this Security Instrument, whether or not then due. The 30-day period begins when the notice is given.

Unless lender and Borrower otherwise agree in writing, any application of proceeds to principal not extend or postpone the due date of the monthly payments referred to in paragraphs 1 and 2 or shall change the amount of the payments. If under paragraph 21 the Property is acquired by Lender, Borrower's right to any insurance policies and proceeds resulting from damage to the Property prior to the acquisition shall pass to Lender to the extent of the sums secured by this Security Instrument immediately prior to the acquisition.

6. **Occupancy, Preservation, Maintenance and Protection of Property; Borrower's Loan Application; Leaseholds** . Borrower shall occupy, establish, and use the Property as Borrower's principal residence within sixty days after the execution of this Security Instrument and shall continue to occupy the Property as Borrower's principal residence for at least one year after the date of occupancy, unless Lender otherwise agrees in writing, which consent shall not be unreasonably withheld, or unless extenuating circumstances exist which are beyond Borrower's control. Borrower shall note destroy, damage or impair the Property, allow the Property to deteriorate, or commit waste on the Property. Borrower shall be in default if any forfeiture action or proceeding, whether civil or criminal, is begun that in Lender's good faith judgement could result in forfeiture of the Property or otherwise materially impair the lien created by this Security Instrument or Lender's security interest. Borrower may cure such a default and reinstate, as provided in paragraph 18, by causing the action or proceeding to be dismissed with a ruling that, in Lender's good faith determination, precludes forfeiture of the Borrower's interest in the Property or other material impairment of the lien created by this Security Instrument or Lender's security interest. Borrower shall also be in default if Borrower, during the loan application process, gave materially false or inaccurate information or statement to Lender (or failed to provide Lender with any material information) in connection with the loan evidenced by the Note, including, but not limited to, representations concerning Borrower's occupancy of the Property as a principal residence. If this Security Instrument is on a leasehold, Borrower shall comply with all the provisions of the lease. If Borrower acquires fee title to the Property, the leasehold and the fee title shall not merge unless Lender agrees to the merger in writing.

7. **Protection of Lender's Rights in the Property**. If Borrower fails to perform the covenants and agreements contained in this Security Instrument, or there is a legal proceeding that may significantly affect Lender's rights in the Property (such as a proceeding in bankruptcy, probate, for condemnation or forfeiture or to enforce laws or regulations), then Lender may do and pay for whatever is necessary to protect the value of the Property and Lender's rights in the property. Lender's actions may include paying any sums secured by a lien which has priority over this Security Agreement, appearing in court, paying reasonable attorneys' fees and entering on the Property to make repairs. Although Lender may take action under this paragraph 7, Lender does not have to do so.

Any amounts disbursed by Lender under this paragraph 7 shall become additional debt of Borrower secured by this Security Instrument. Unless Borrower and Lender agree to other terms of payment, these amounts shall bear interest from the date of disbursement at the Note rate and shall be payable, with interest, upon notice from Lender to Borrower requesting payment.

8. **Mortgage Insurance**. If Lender required mortgage insurance as a condition of making the loan secured by this Security Instrument, Borrower shall pay the premiums required to maintain the mortgage insurance in effect. If, for any reason, this mortgage insurance coverage required by Lender lapses or ceases to be in effect, Borrower shall pay the premiums required to obtain coverage substantially equivalent to the mortgage insurance previously in effect, at a cost substantially equivalent to the cost to Borrower of the mortgage insurance previously in effect, from an alternate mortgage insurer approved by Lender. If substantially equivalent mortgage insurance coverage is not available, Borrower shall pay to Lender each month a sum equal to one-twelfth of the yearly mortgage insurance premium being paid by Borrower when the insurance coverage lapsed or ceased to be in effect. Lender will accept, use and retain these payments as a loss reserve in lieu of mortgage insurance. Loss reserve payments may no longer be required, at the option of Lender, if mortgage insurance coverage (in the amount and for the period that Lender requires) provided by an insurer approved by Lender again becomes available and is obtained. Borrower shall pay the premiums required to maintain mortgage insurance in effect, or to provide a loss reserve, until the requirement for mortgage insurance ends in accordance with any written agreement between Borrower and Lender or applicable law.

9. **Inspection**. Lender or its agent may make reasonable entries upon and inspection of the Property. Lender shall give Borrower notice at the time of or prior to an inspection specifying reasonable cause for the inspection.

10. **Condemnation**. The proceeds of any award or claim for damages, direct or consequential, in connection with any condemnation or other taking of any part of the Property, or for conveyance in lieu of condemnation, are hereby assigned and shall be paid to Lender.

In the event of a total taking of the Property, the proceeds shall be applied to the sums secured by this Security Instrument, whether or not then due, with any excess paid to the Borrower. IN the event of a partial taking of the Property in which the fair market value of the Property immediately before the taking is equal to or greater than the amount of the sums secured by this Security Instrument shall be reduced by the amount of the proceeds multiplied by the following fraction: (a) the total amount of the sums secured immediately before the taking, divided by (b) the fair market value of the Property immediately before the taking. Any balance shall be paid to Borrower. In the event of a partial taking of the Property in which the fair market value of the Property immediately before the taking is less than the amount of the sums secured immediately before the taking, unless Borrower and Lender otherwise agree in writing or unless applicable law otherwise provides, the proceeds shall be applied to the sums secured by this Security Instrument whether or not the sums are due then.

If the Property is abandoned by the Borrower, or if, after notice by Lender to Borrower that the condemnor offers to make an award or settle a claim for damages, Borrower fails to respond to Lender within 30 days after the date the notice is given, Lender is authorized to collect and apply the proceeds, at its option, either to restoration or repair of the Property or to the sums secured by this Security Instrument, whether or not then due.

Unless Lender and Borrower otherwise agree in writing, any application of proceeds to principal shall not extend or postpone the due date of the monthly payments referred to in paragraphs 1 and 2 or change the amount of such payments.

11. **Borrower Not Released; Forbearance By Lender Not A Waiver**. Extension of the time for payment or modification of amortization of the sums secured by this Security Instrument granted by Lender to an successor in interest of Borrower shall not operate to release the liability of the original Borrower or Borrower's successors in interest. Lender shall not be required to commence proceedings against any successor in interest or refuse to extend time for payment or otherwise modify amortization of the sums secured by this Security Instrument by reason of any demand made by the original Borrower or Borrower's successors in interest. Any forbearance by Lender in exercising any right or remedy shall not be a waiver of or preclude the exercise of any right or remedy.

12. Successor and Assigns Bound; Joint and Several Liability; Co-signers. The covenants and agreements of this Security Instrument shall bind and benefit the successors and assigns of Lender and Borrower, subject to the provisions of paragraph 17. Borrower's covenants and agreements shall be joint and several. Any Borrower who co-signs this Security Instrument but does not execute the Note: (a) is co-signing this Security Instrument only to mortgage, grant and convey that Borrower's interest in the Property under the terms of this Security Instrument; (b) is not personally obligated to pay the sums secured by this Security Instrument; and (c) agrees that Lender and any other Borrower may agree to extend, modify, forbear or make any accommodations with regard to the terms of this Security Instrument or the Note without that Borrower's consent.

13. Loan Charges. If the loan secured by this Security Instrument is subject to a law which sets maximum loan charges, and that law is finally interpreted so that the interest or other loan charges collected or to be collected in connection with the loan exceed the permitted limits, then: (a) any such loan charge shall be reduced by the amount necessary to reduce the charge to the permitted limit; and (b) any sums already collected from Borrower which exceeded permitted limits will be refunded to Borrower. Lender may choose to make this refund by reducing the principal owed under the Note or by making a direct payment to the Borrower. If a refund reduces principal, the reduction will be treated as a partial prepayment without any prepayment charge under the Note.

14. Notices. Any notice to Borrower provided for in this Security Instrument shall be given by delivering it or by mailing it first class mail unless applicable law requires use of another method. The notice shall be directed to the Property Address or any other address Borrower designates by notice to Lender. Any notice to Lender shall be given by first class mail to Lender's address stated herein or any other address Lender designates by notice to Borrower. Any notice provided for in this Security Instrument shall be deemed to have been given to Borrower or Lender when given as provided in this paragraph.

15. Governing Law; Severability. This security Instrument shall be governed by federal law and the law of the jurisdiction in which the Property is located. In the event that any provision or clause of this Security Instrument or the Note conflicts with applicable law, such conflict shall not affect other provisions of this Security Instrument or the Note which can be given effect without the conflicting provision. To this end the provisions of this Security Instrument and the Note are declared to be severable.

16. Borrower's Copy. Borrower shall be given one conformed copy of the Note and of this Security Instrument.

17. Transfer of the Property or a Beneficial Interest in Borrower. If all or any part of the Property or any interest in it is sold or transferred (or if a beneficial interest in Borrower is sold or transferred and Borrower is not a natural person) without Lender's prior written consent, Lender may, at its option, require immediate payment in full of all sums secured by this Security Instrument. However, this option shall not be exercised by Lender if exercise is prohibited by federal law as of the date of this Security Instrument.

If Lender exercises this option, Lender shall give Borrower notice of acceleration. The notice shall provide a period of not less than 30 days from the date the notice is delivered or mailed within which Borrower must pay all sums secured by this Security Instrument. If Borrower fails to pay these sums prior to the expiration of this period, Lender may invoke any remedies permitted by this Security Instrument without further notice or demand on Borrower.

18. Borrower's Right to Reinstate. If Borrower meets certain conditions, Borrower shall have the right to have enforcement of this Security Instrument discontinued at any time prior to the earlier of: (a) 5 days (or such other period as applicable law may specify for reinstatement) before sale of the Property pursuant to any power of sale contained in this Security Instrument; or (b) entry of a judgment enforcing this Security Instrument. Those conditions are that Borrower: (a) pays Lender all sums which then would be due under this Security Instrument and the Note as if no acceleration had occurred; (b) cures any default of any other covenants or agreements; (c) pays all expenses incurred in enforcing this Security Instrument, including, but not limited to, reasonable attorneys' fees; and (d) takes such action as Lender may reasonably require to assure that the lien of this Security Instrument, Lender's rights in the Property and Borrower's obligation to pay the sums secured by this Security Instrument shall continue unchanged. Upon reinstatement by Borrower, Security Instrument and the obligations secured hereby shall remain fully effective as if no this acceleration had occurred. However, this right to reinstate shall not apply in the case of acceleration under paragraph 17.

19. **Sale of Note; Change of Loan Servicer.** The Note or a partial interest in the Note (together with this Security Instrument) may be sold one or more times without prior notice to the Borrower. A sale may result in a change in the entity (known as the "Loan Servicer") that collects monthly payments due under the Note and this Security Instrument. There also may be one or more changes of the Loan Servicer unrelated to a sale of the Note. If there is a change of the Loan Servicer, Borrower will be given written notice of the change in accordance with paragraph 14 above and applicable law. The notice will state the name and address of the new Loan Services and the address to which payments should be made. The notice will also contain any other information required by applicable law.

20. **Hazardous Substances.** Borrower shall not cause or permit the presence, use, disposal, storage, or release of any Hazardous Substances on or in the Property. Borrower shall not do, nor allow anyone else to do, anything affecting the Property that is in violation of any Environmental Law. The preceding two sentences shall not apply to the presence, use, or storage on the Property of small quantities of Hazardous Substances that are generally recognized to be appropriate to normal residential uses and to maintenance of the Property.

Borrower shall promptly give Lender written notice of any investigation, claim, demand, lawsuit or other action by any governmental or regulatory agency or private party involving the Property and any Hazardous Substances or Environmental Law of which Borrower has actual knowledge. If Borrower learns, or is notified by any governmental or regulatory authority, that any removal or other remediation of any Hazardous Substances affecting the Property is necessary, Borrower shall promptly take all necessary remedial actions in accordance with Environmental Law.

As used in paragraph 20, "Hazardous Substances" are those substances defined as toxic or hazardous substances by Environmental Law and the following substances: gasoline, kerosene, other flammable or petroleum products, toxic pesticides and herbicides, volatile solvents, materials containing asbestos or formaldehyde, and radioactive materials. As used in this paragraph 20, "Environmental Law" means federal laws and laws of the jurisdiction where the Property is located that relate to health, safety or environmental protection.

NON-UNIFORM COVENANTS. Borrower and Lender further covenant and agree as follows:

21. **Acceleration; Remedies. Lender shall give notice to Borrower prior to acceleration following Borrower's breach of any covenant or agreement in this Security Instrument (but not prior to acceleration under paragraph 17 unless applicable law provides otherwise). The notice shall specify: (a) the default; (b) the action required to cure the default; (c) a date, not less than 30 days from the date the notice is given to Borrower, by which the default must be cured; and (d) that failure to cure the default on or before the date specified in the notice may result in acceleration of the sums secured by this Security Instrument and sale of the Property. The notice shall further inform Borrower of the right to reinstate after acceleration and the right to bring a court action to assert the non-existence of a default or any other defense of Borrower to acceleration and sale. If the default is not cured on or before the date specified in the notice, Lender at its option may require immediate payment in full of all sums secured by this Security Instrument and the sale of the Property. The notice shall further inform Borrower of the right to reinstate after acceleration and the right to bring a court action to assert the non-existence of a default or any other defense of Borrower to acceleration and sale. If the default is not cured on or before the date specified in the notice, Lender at its option may require immediate payment in full of all sums secured by this Security Instrument without further demand and may invoke the power of sale and any other remedies permitted by applicable law, Lender shall be entitled to collect all expenses incurred in pursuing the remedies provided in this paragraph 21, including, but not limited to, reasonable attorneys' fees and costs of title evidence.**

If Lender invokes the power of sale, Lender shall give a copy of a notice to Borrower in the manner provided in paragraph 14. Lender shall publish the notice of sale once a week for three consecutive weeks in a newspaper published in _____ County, Alabama, and thereupon shall sell the Property to the highest bidder at public auction at the front door of the County Courthouse of this county. Lender shall deliver to the purchaser Lender's deed conveying the Property. Lender or its designee may purchase the Property at any sale. Borrower covenants and agrees that the proceeds of the sale shall be applied in the following order: (a) to all expenses of the sale, including, but not limited to, reasonable attorneys' fees; (b) to all sums secured by this Security Instrument; and (c) any excess to the person or persons legally entitled to it.

22. **Release**. Upon payment of all sums secured by this Security Instrument, Lender shall release this Security Instrument without charge to Borrower. Borrower shall pay any recordation costs.

23. **Waivers**. Borrower waives all rights of homestead exemption in the Property and relinquishes all rights of curtesy and dower in the Property.

24. **Riders to this Security instrument**. If one or more rider are executed by Borrower and recorded together with this Security Instrument, the covenants of each rider shall be incorporated into and shall amend and supplement the covenants and agreements of this Security Instrument as if the rider(s) were a part of this Security Instrument. [Check applicable box(es)]

☐ Adjustable Rate Rider ☐ Condominium Rider ☐ 1-4 Family Rider
☐ Graduated Payment Rider ☐ Planned Unit Development Rider ☐ Biweekly Payment Rider
☐ Balloon Rider ☐ Rate Improvement Rider ☐ Second Home Rider
☐ Other(s) [specify]

BY SIGNING BELOW, Borrower accepts and agrees to the terms and covenants contained in this Security Instrument and in any rider(s) executed by Borrower and recorded with it.

Witnesses:

_____   _____(Seal)
                                                              --Borrower
_____   _____(Seal)
                                                              --Borrower

GRIFFITH HOME ANALYSIS

PROPERTY   INSPECTION   REPORT

Property Address:

Prepared Expressly for:

Inspection Date:

Inspector Name:

GENERAL INFORMATION

Unit Occupied: **Yes**

Unit Type: **Single Family**

Space Below Grade: **Basement**

Client Present: **Yes**

Selling Realtor:

Report Delivery: **Realtor Office**

People Present: **Client, Clients Realtor**

Weather: **Cloudy**

Fee: # 275.00

FOR THE PURPOSES OF THIS REPORT WE HAVE DESIGNATED THE RIGHT-HAND(RH) SIDE OF THE HOME AS THE RIGHT-HAND SIDE WHEN ENTERING THE FRONT ENTRANCE.

REPORT LIMITATIONS

This report has been prepared for the sole and exclusive use of the client indicated above and is limited to and impartial opinion which is not a warranty that the items are defect-free. This report is limited to the foundation/ framing, mechanical, and electrical components of the property which were visible to the inspector on the date of the inspection and his opinion of their condition at the time of the inspection. The oral presentation given at the time of the inspection and this report are to be considered the complete inspection. Please read the attached contract which is a part of this report.

Page 1 Cover Page

| GRIFFITH HOME ANALYSIS | *SUMMARY* |

16 Office Park Circle; Suite 9b
Birmingham, AL 35223

Inspection # #####/11/15/

UNIFORM INSPECTION SUMMARY

The list of items below are taken from the inspection report accompanying this summary; and in the inspectors opinion, constitute items needing attention. A major concern is generally held to mean an item identified as either significantly affecting the residence and/or could be considered a potentially expensive repair or replacement. This summary should not be considered a complete list of deficiencies within the residence. Items needing further evaluation are also listed. Minor repairs and items needing less than $50.00 in repairs are not part of this report.

ITEM 1   Secure loose rear deck handrail and repair broken rear LH side deck handrail.

ITEM 2   Caulk the roof flashing at the rear HH plumbing vent pipes. Active leakage was noted in the attic area. No deterioration was present.

ITEM 3   Caulking is needed in the tub and/or shower areas of each of the bathrooms.

ITEM 4   Active leakage was noted in several areas of the finished basement. -LH side corner of the billiard room, front corner of the closet in the billiard room, front closet of basement hall bath. Moisture levels were measured and exceeded safe levels for wood. Consult a qualified foundation waterproofing contractor.

ITEM 5   A crack or hole was observed in the heat exchanger of the second level heater. An unsafe condition exist and immediate repair should be accomplished. A qualified HVAC technician should investigate and repair.

ITEM 6   The automatic reverse safety feature of the automatic garage door opener did not function properly.

ITEM 7   Caulking is needed at open joints and trim locations of the exterior millwork.

ITEM 8

ITEM 9

ITEM10

ITEM11

ITEM12

Property Address: Birmingham, AL
Report Prepared For:

SUMMARY

   PAGE 2

GRIFFITH HOME ANALYSIS

ATTIC

16 Office Park Circle; Suite 9b   Inspection # #####11/15/

General Information

Attic	Access	Inspection Method	Framing	Sheathing	Insulation	Thickness	
Main Stairs	Full	Entered	Wood Rafter	Plywood	Blown-in	8-10	+/-
					Roll-Batt	5-7	
				Wall Ins. –	Roll-Batt	3-5	

Component		Condition	
Access			The readily accessible areas of the attic were inspected. Some areas may not be easily accessible due to obstructions or insulation.
	Main	Satisfactory	
	Stairs	Satisfactory	
Framing			Framing showed no major defects or damage at the time of the inspection.
	Main	Satisfactory	
	Stairs		
Sheathing			Roof sheathing showed no major defects or damage.
	Main	Satisfactory	Moisture was detected when the stain in the attic area were tested. This indicates
	Stairs		active leakage–rear pipe vent
			No moisture was detected when the stain(s) in the attic were tested.–chimney area
Insulation			Attic insulation was sufficient for the homes in this area.
	Blown-In	Satisfactory	
	Roll-Batt	Satisfactory	
	Roll-Batt	Satisfactory	
Ventilation			Ventilation was normal.
	Main Attic	Satisfactory	
	Screens	Satisfactory	
	Exhaust Vent	Satisfactory	
	Exhaust vent	Satisfactory	
Exposed Wiring			
	General wiring	Satisfactory	
	Fixtures	Satisfactory	
Chimneys			No moisture was detected when the stain in the attic adjacent to the chimney was tested. Monitor for possible future leakage.
	Metal	Satisfactory	
Exhaust Vent			
	Whole house	Satisfactory	
	Kitchen	Not Applicable	
	Bathrooms	Satisfactory	

Property Address: Birmingham, AL
Report Prepared For:

Pre Move-In Inspection Form: Older Home

Date: _____

Address: _____

We, the Purchaser(s) of the above property, do hereby acknowledge and confirm that we have satisfied ourselves that the following items are satisfactory.

Kitchen:
    Stove:
        Oven   _____
        Broiler   _____
        Stove eyes   _____
        Self-cleaning oven   _____
    Range vent fan   _____
    Refrigerator
        Ice maker   _____
    Dishwasher   _____
    Garbage disposal   _____
    Trash compactor   _____
    Microwave   _____
Electrical: _____
Paddle Fans: _____
Attic Fans: _____
Security alarm system: _____
Bath #1:
    Toilet   _____
    Tub   _____
    Shower   _____
    Fan vents   _____
Bath #2:
    Toilet   _____
    Tub   _____
    Shower   _____
    Fan vents   _____
Bath #3:
    Toilet   _____
    Tub   _____
    Shower   _____
    Fan vents   _____
Fireplace:
    Gas starter   _____
Roof: _____
Plumbing: _____
Water Heater: _____
Garage door opener: _____
Heating: _____
Air conditioning: _____

Comments: _____

_____

_____

_____
Purchaser

_____
Purchaser

_____
Agent

Pre Move-In Inspection Form: New Home

Plumbing:

___ 1. Instructions on use of faucets emphasize cleaning of aerator and show water cutoffs.

___ 2. Instruction on use of shower and tub drain.

___ 3. Hot water heater:
         a. Popoff valve and line or pilot light
         b. If water not hot, check breaker first
         c. Always turn off breaker if draining tank completely
         d. Periodically flush tank

___ 4. If plumbing is stopped up and service man finds diapers, toys, etc. in line, homeowner will be billed for the call.

___ 5. Show main house water cutoff.

___ 6. Show location of tub inspection grilles and their purpose.

___ 7. One year warranty on plumbing fixtures.

Electrical:

___ 1. Show buyer which plugs are switch-controlled.

___ 2. Correct size light bulbs stamped on fixtures.

Heating and Air Conditioning:

___ 1. Full one year warranty—plus four years parts warranty on compressor.

___ 2. Location and operation of thermostat.

___ 3. If heat or A/C does not operate, check:
         a. Thermostat setting and heat/cool setting
         b. Breaker box to be sure breaker is in "on" position.

___ 4. Location of filters. Should be changed every 30 days year round. Possibly void warranty if not changed regularly.

___ 5. Name of air conditioning company to call for direct service.

Appliances:

___ 1. Instruction on use and care of range and vent-a hood (filters).

___ 2. Instruction on use and care of dishwasher.

___ 3. Instruction on use and care of disposal.
         a. Reset button on bottom.
         b. Unjam—call warranty department.

___ 4. Instructions on use and care of oven.

___ 5. If appliances do not operate, always check breaker box.

___ 6. Name of company to telephone for appliance service.

General Inside:

___ 1. Floor tile not warranted if damaged by neglect, such as casters not being used under furniture.

___ 2. Carpet has tendency to loosen in damp weather—but will stretch tight again in drier weather.

____ 3. Paint

        a. Not warranted—we do not touch up

        b. Kitchen and baths are enamel—may be washed

        c. Do not scrub latex painted interior walls

____ 4. Cracks in Sheetrock not warranted.

____ 5. Cracks in tile grout not warranted.

____ 6. Doors

        a. 1/4" to 1/2" warp is normal. Variation due to weather conditions.

        b. Clean weep holes in weather-stripping.

        c. Use paraffin or WD-40 to keep doors from sticking.

____ 7. Instruct in operation of fireplace, if applicable.

____ 8. Do not use strong cleaning products or abrasive material on marble vanity tops, lavatories, and kitchen counter tops.

____ 9. Bathroom door locks can be unlocked from the outside with small screwdriver or coat hanger.

General Outside:

____ 1. Explain functions and importance of weep holes and expansion joints.

____ 2. Show location and operation of breaker box and ground wire.

____ 3. Show location and explain secondary A/C drain.

____ 4. Show location and explain sink and sewer cleanouts (in case of emergency if sewer backs up, remove clean-out and allow sewer to overflow outside).

____ 5. Garage floors, porches, drives, walks, and patios will get hairline cracks not structurally significant, cannot be stopped and not warranted.

____ 6. Sunken utility lines and washed out yards not warranted.

____ 7. Dead grass not warranted. Grass is alive when planted but needs root growth fertilizer and plenty of water.

Please initial the following:

Vanities OK	_____
Tubs OK	_____
Kitchen Sink OK	_____
Appliances OK	_____
Carpet OK	_____
Kitchen Counter Tops OK	_____
Light Fixtures OK	_____
Mirrors OK	_____
Windows OK	_____
Floor Tile OK	_____

I have discussed each of the above items with a representative from _____ and understand them. I have been instructed in the use and care of the above listed items in my new home and find our home completed in a manner satisfactory and acceptable to us.

Date: _____

Customer Signature: _____

Address: _____

Sales Representative: _____

BUYER EXCLUSIVE AGENCY AGREEMENT (BEAA)

1. **Exclusive Agent**. The undersigned, _____ ("Buyer"), appoints "[name of realty co.]" ("Broker") as the exclusive agent of Buyer to assist Buyer in locating and acquiring real property acceptable to Buyer, and Broker accepts the Appointment. The desired property is generally described as follows:

Buyer agrees to work exclusively with Broker's licensee, _____ ("Licensee"), or another licensee of Broker acceptable to Buyer, in viewing properties, discussing properties with other brokers or prospective sellers and making offers on or conducting negotiations for the property. If Buyer is contacted directly by a seller or other real estate licensees, Buyer will refer them to Licensee or Broker.

2. **Term**. This Agreement shall be effective from the date signed by Broker and shall continue until the later of _____ _____ , or closing of the acquisition of the property.

3. **Broker's Services**. Broker, through Licensee or another licensee acceptable to Buyer, will provide to Buyer such of those brokerage services set forth on Attachment A hereto as Buyer may request from time to time. Buyer and Broker agree, however, that the services that Broker shall otherwise provide hereunder may or will be more limited if the circumstances described in paragraphs 4, 5, or 6 below apply.

4. **Limited Consensual Dual Agency for "in-House" Listings**. Buyer does _____ does not _____ desire to be shown Broker's "in-house" listings. (Buyer, please indicate preference by initials in appropriate space.) If Buyer desires to be shown Broker's "in-house" listings, the following paragraphs A and B shall apply:

A. Broker will act as the Limited Consensual Dual Agent of both Buyer and the seller of any such "in-house" listing, both with respect to showing the Property and in any subsequent negotiations or transaction between Buyer and the seller. Buyer has read the disclosure documents referred to in paragraph 11 below and understands the differences between the services that Broker can perform as a "single agent" and as a "limited consensual dual agent." Buyer specifically acknowledges that, as a limited consensual dual agent, Broker cannot negotiate price or other terms and conditions of any contract on any such in-house listings for Buyer or otherwise advocate the interests of either Buyer or the seller where those interests are in conflict.

B. If Buyer desires to make an offer on a Broker-listed property, Buyer agrees to execute Broker's Consensual Dual Agency Addendum form confirming Buyer's consent to limited consensual dual agency on a "property, seller and buyer specific" basis. Buyer shall not refuse such consent unless based on facts disclosed or a change of circumstances or events after the date of this Agreement. If either the seller or Buyer do not confirm such consent, Broker shall continue as agent of the seller with respect to that specific property but will, at the option of Buyer, provide non-agency brokerage services to Buyer with respect to that property as the agent of seller or refer Buyer to an attorney or another broker or show other properties to Buyer as the agent of Buyer. In any event, Broker shall not disclose to either Buyer or to the seller any confidential or privileged information regarding either party.

5. **Previous Agency with Seller**. Buyer may be shown a property where Broker or Licensee has previously represented the seller with respect to the property. The prior representation will not usually preclude Broker from now serving as Buyer's agent with respect to the property, but it would preclude Broker from disclosing to Buyer any confidential information about Seller that Broker learned as a result of the prior representation. If Licensee is aware of such prior representation, then Licensee shall inform Buyer of such prior representation and, if Buyer desires to make an offer on the property, may request both parties to execute Broker's Disclosure of Agency Status form.

6. **Other Potential Buyers**. Other potential buyers represented by Broker may be interested in the same or similar properties as Buyer. Buyer agrees that Broker may show to others at any time any property shown to Buyer, and may present and negotiate offers on such properties on behalf of others. Buyer and Broker agree that Broker shall not reveal to Buyer the terms of any other such offers and shall not reveal to other offers the terms of any offer by Buyer.

7. **Broker's Compensation**. Broker shall be compensated under this Agreement as follows:

A. If Buyer acquires an MLS-listed property with respect to which the listing broker pays Broker a selling commission at least equal to that normally paid by Broker to selling brokers for similar properties, Broker agrees to accept said commission as compensation under this Agreement, and Buyer authorizes Broker to accept the commission. Buyer hereby does _____ does not _____ instruct Broker to show to Buyer only those properties on which such commissions are offered by the listing broker.

B. If Buyer acquires a property on which Broker's commission is not paid as in A above, Buyer shall (or shall require Seller to) pay to Broker a fee of ____ % of the gross purchase price of the property. Any commission paid to Broker, as selling broker, by the seller shall be credited against the fee otherwise payable under this paragraph B by Buyer.

C. Broker shall be entitled to compensation if Buyer enters into an agreement during the term of this Agreement to acquire a property. Broker shall also be entitled to compensation if Broker showed or introduced the property to Buyer during the term of this Agreement and Buyer enters into an agreement within ____ days after expiration or termination of this Agreement to acquire the property. Broker's commission or fee shall be payable at closing if closing occurs. If a transaction fails to close because of Buyer's default, the commission or fee that would have been payable to Broker at closing shall be immediately due and payable by Buyer; if it fails to close through no fault of Buyer, the fee shall be waived by Broker.

8. Property Condition; Disclaimers.

A. Buyer understands that real estate brokers and licensees are not experts on matters of property condition or defects, hazardous substances, property boundaries, square footage or acreage, and other areas requiring specialty expertise. Salespeople may sometimes express opinions about the property, but such personal opinions are not meant to be, and cannot be relied upon, as representation of fact. Unless Buyer has personal expertise in such matters, Buyer is strongly encouraged to have the property inspected by professional inspectors satisfactory to Buyer. Buyer should also obtain a survey, title search (and title policy at closing) ant a termite inspection of property that Buyer desires to purchase. Any offer to purchase submitted by Buyer should normally be contingent upon Buyer's receipt and approval of all such matters prior to closing. Buyer may also want to consult a lawyer or an accountant for legal or tax advice.

B. The preprinted contract/offer forms customarily fused by Broker also contain provisions disclaiming any representations on the part of the real estate brokers/licensees involved in the transaction as to condition of the property, property lines, legal or tax consequences of the transaction, and various other matters. Buyer consents to the use of such standard forms, but reserves the right to object, prior to making any offer, to any such disclaimers that Buyer believes to be inaccurate.

C. Buyer also agrees to execute at closing, if requested by Broker, Broker's form reaffirming that neither Broker nor any of Broker's licensees have made any such representations.

9. **Attorney's Fees.** In the event that legal action is commenced to enforce this Agreement, the prevailing party shall be entitled to attorney's fees and court costs.

10. **Facsimile Signatures.** Buyer and Broker agree that this Agreement may be transmitted by facsimile for signature or to evidence signature by one or both parties, in which event a facsimile copy of the executed Agreement shall be effective.

11. **Related Documents and Disclosures.** Buyer acknowledges that Licensee has provided to Buyer the **"Real Estate Brokerage Services Disclosure"** prepared by the [name of state] Real Estate Commission, together with Broker's **Consumer Information Brochure**, copies of which documents are attached hereto, and has explained to Buyer the types of brokerage services generally available to consumers and those offered by Broker. Buyer has reviewed both documents carefully and understands the concepts addressed therein. In particular, but without limitation, Buyer understands the differences between Single Agency, Limited Consensual Agency and Contract Broker as expressed in these documents.

Buyer should consult an attorney if Buyer does not understand this Agreement or its legal effect. Buyer has read and approves this Agreement and hereby acknowledges receipt of a copy.

Buyer	Date	Licensee	Date

Buyer	Date	Broker	Date

CONSENSUAL DUAL AGENCY ADDENDUM
(Property, Seller and Buyer Specific)

THIS CONSENSUAL DUAL AGENCY ADDENDUM supplements the following existing agreements between [name of realty co] ("Broker") and the undersigned with respect to specific property located at _____ (the "Property"):

(i)**Buyer Exclusive Agency Agreement ("BEAA") between the undersigned Buyer(s) and Broker; and**

(ii)**Seller Exclusive Agency Agreement ("SEAA") between the undersigned Seller(s) and Broker.**

BACKGROUND

Under the SEAA, Seller has engaged Broker and _____ ("Listing Licensee") to sell the Property, as Seller's exclusive agent. Under the BEAA, Buyer has engaged Broker and _____ ("Selling Licensee") to assist Buyer in located and purchasing a property, as Buyer's exclusive agent. Buyer is interested in seeing Seller's property and possibly making an offer to acquire it, and Seller desires the Buyer to do so. Buyer and Seller have previously agreed that, under such circumstances, Broker and its licensees could represent both Buyer and Seller with respect to the Property as Limited Consensual Dual Agents. Buyer and Seller now wish to ratify and confirm such agreement.

AGREEMENT

1. Appointment as Limited Consensual Dual Agent. Accordingly, Seller, Buyer, and Broker hereby agree that Broker and its licensees shall represent both Buyer and Seller as Limited Consensual Dual Agents with respect to any transaction between Seller and Buyer regarding the Property. Seller and Buyer each waives any claims they may have regarding conflicts of interest or the appearance of conflicts of interest arising from this relationship.

2. Nature of Representation. As the Limited Consensual Dual Agents of Buyer and Seller, Broker and its licensees will show the Property to Buyer and work to facilitate communications and any subsequent transaction between the parties with respect to the Property. The salespeople will not negotiate price or nay terms or conditions of any offers or contracts, or otherwise advocate the position of one party against the other, with respect to the Property. Except for any specific disclosures required by law, neither Broker not its licensees shall disclose confidential information regarding one party to the other party which they believe could harm that party's bargaining position. Such information includes, but is not limited to, the maximum price that Buyer is willing to offer or the minimum price that Seller is willing to accept, negotiating strategies or other private matters. Unless specifically prohibited in writing by Buyer or Seller, respectively, Broker is authorized to disclose to Seller financial information regarding Buyer's ability to pay the purchase price or obtain financing and to provide to Buyer multiple listing service information regarding sales prices of properties comparable to the Property.

3. Related Documents and Disclosures. Seller and Buyer acknowledge that Broker has provided to Seller and Buyer the **"Real Estate Brokerage Services Disclosure"** prepared by the [name of state] Real Estate Commission, together with the Broker's **Consumer Information Brochure,** copies of which documents are attached hereto, and has explained to Seller and Buyer the types of brokerage services offered by Broker. Seller and Buyer have reviewed both documents carefully and understand the concepts expressed therein. In particular, but without limitation, Seller and Buyer understand the differences between Single Agency and Limited Consensual Dual Agency as expressed in these documents.

4. Facsimile Signatures. Buyer and Broker agree that this Agreement may be transmitted by facsimile for signature or to evidence signature by one or both parties, in which event a facsimile copy of the executed Agreement shall be effective.

Seller and Buyer should each consult an attorney before signing this Agreement if they do not understand this Agreement or its legal effect. Seller and Buyer have each read and approved this Agreement and hereby acknowledges receipt of a copy.

Buyer	Date	Seller	Date

Buyer	Date	Seller	Date

Selling Licensee	Date	Listing Licensee	Date

Acknowledged and Accepted:_____

                                Broker

FEDERAL TRUTH-IN-LENDING DISCLOSURE STATEMENT

Date: _____

File/Loan No.: _____

Borrowers: _____

_____

_____

Property

Location: _____

ANNUAL PERCENTAGE RATE The cost of your credit as a yearly rate.	FINANCE CHARGE The dollar amount the credit will cost you.	Amount Financed The amount of credit provided to you or on your behalf.	Total of Payments The amount you will have paid after you have made all payments as scheduled.
%	$	$	$

You have the right to receive at this time an itemization of the Amount Financed.

☐ I want an itemization.   ☐ I do not want an itemization.

Your payment schedule will be:

Number of Payments	Amount of Payments	When Payments are Due
	$	
	$	
	$	

INSURANCE: Credit life insurance and credit disability insurance are not required to obtain credit, and no such insurance will be applied for or provided unless you sign and agree to pay the additional cost.

Type	Premium	Term	Signature
Credit Life			I want to apply for credit life insurance. _____ Signature
Credit Disability			I want to apply for credit disability insurance. _____ Signature
Credit Life and Credit Disability			I want to apply for credit life and disability insurance. _____ Signature

You may obtain property insurance from anyone you want that is acceptable to creditor. If you get the

insurance from _____ you will pay $ _____ for a term of _____

SECURITY: You are giving a security interest in the property being purchased.

_____

_____

Filing fees $ _____   Non-filing insurance $ _____

LATE CHARGE: If payment is _____ late, you will be charged $ _____ / _____ % of the payment.

PREPAYMENT: If you pay off early, you

     ☐ May   ☐ will not   ☐ have to pay a penalty.

     ☐ May   ☐ will not   ☐ be entitled to a refund of part of the finance charge.

ASSUMPTION: Someone buying your home

     ☐ Cannot assume the remainder of the mortgage on the original terms.

     ☐ May, subject to conditions, be allowed to assume the remainder of the mortgage on the original terms.

See your contract documents for any additional information about nonpayment, default, any required repayment in full before the scheduled date, and prepayment refunds and penalties.

e means an estimate

I/We hereby acknowledge receipt of disclosures made in this notice.

_____ / _____

                                                DATE

_____ / _____

                                                DATE

_____ / _____

                                                DATE

ESTIMATED CASH REQUIRED TO PURCHASE

Purchaser _____   Type of Purchase _____

Address of Property _____

_____   Date _____

Purchase Price $_____
Down Payment (including earnest money) $_____
Mortgage Amount $_____

CLOSING COSTS:
Origination Fees $_____
Discount Points $_____
VA Funding Fee $_____
Attorney Fee $_____
Title Insurance Policy * $_____
Survey of Property (Av. 185) $_____
Credit Report ($55 - 65) $_____
Appraisal Fee (FHA $275, VA $300, conv. $350) $_____
Mtg. Recording Fee ($1.50/$1000 + $20) $_____
Deed Recording Fee ($1.00/$1000 + $10) $_____
Underwriting Fee ($150) $_____
Document Preparation Fee ($150 $_____
Tax Service Fee ($75) $_____
Lender Reinspection ($50) $_____
Express ($40) $_____
Flood Certification Fee ($19) $_____
Total Closing Costs $_____ b.

PREPAID ITEMS:
Hazard Insurance* $ _____ /year $_____ v(14 Months)
Ad Valorem Taxes $ _____ /year $_____ (2 months + Oct -
                                                        Mo of Closing)

Interest (Loan amount × % interest + 365 × number $_____
of days from closing to end of month)
Total of Prepaid Items   +$_____ c.

Total Cash Required to Purchase (approx)   =$_____ (a+b+c)
  Less Earnest Money   −$_____
Total Cash Required at Closing (approx) $_____
(This figure does not include prorated taxes & dues)

Mortgage in the Amount of $ _____ amortized over a period of _____ years
at an Annual Percentage Rate of _____ .

Monthly Deposit - Principal and Interest $_____
Monthly Deposit - Hazard Insurance $_____
Monthly Deposit - Ad Valorem Taxes $_____
Monthly Deposit - PMI * $_____

TOTAL MONTHLY PAYMENT (approx) $_____

The undersigned Purchasers acknowledge that this is an estimate. Lenders and Vendors will vary
their charges; therefore, these figures cannot be guaranteed by the Broker or his representative.

Purchaser _____   Purchaser _____

COMMITMENT FOR TITLE INSURANCE

LAWYERS TITLE INSURANCE CORPORATION, a Virginia corporation, herein called the Company, for valuable consideration, hereby commits to issue its policy or policies of title insurance, as identified in Schedule A, in favor of the proposed insured named in Schedule A, as owner or mortgagee of the estate or interest covered hereby in the land described or referred to in Schedule A, upon payment of the premiums and charges therefor; all subject to the provisions of Schedule a and B and to the Conditions and Stipulations hereof.

This Commitment shall be effective only when the identity of the proposed insured and the amount of the policy or policies committed for have been inserted in Schedule A hereof by the Company, either at the time of the issuance of this Commitment or by subsequent endorsement.

This Commitmen is preliminary to the issuance of such policy or policies of title insurance and all liability and obligations hereunder shall cease and terminate six (6) months after the effective date hereof or when the policy or policies committed for shall issue, whichever first occurs, provided that the failure to issue such policy or policies is not the fault of the Company. This Commitment shall not be valid or binding until countersigned by an authorized officer or agent.

IN WITNESS WHEREOF, the Company has caused this Commitment to be signed and sealed, to become valid when countersigned by an authorized officer or agent of the Company, all in accordance with its By-Laws. This Commitment is effective as of the date shown in Schedule A as Effective Date.

CONDITIONS AND STIPULATIONS

1. The term "mortgage," when used herein, shall include deed of trust, trust deed , or other security instrument.

2. If the proposed insured has or acquires actual knowledge of any defect, lien, encumbrance, adverse claim or other matter affecting the estate or interest or mortgage thereon covered by this Commitment other than those shown in Schedule B hereof, and shall fail to disclose such knowledge to the Company in writing, the Company shall be relieved from liability or any loss or damage resulting from any act of reliance hereon to the extent the Company is prejudiced by failure to so disclose such knowledge. If the proposed insured shall disclose such knowledge to the Company, or if the Company otherwise acquires actual knowledge of any such defect, lien, encumbrance, adverse claim or other matter, the Company at its option may amend Schedule B of this Commitment accordingly, but such amendment shall not relieve the Company from liability previously incurred pursuant to paragraph 3 of these Conditions and Stipulations.

3. Liability of the Company under this Commitment shall be only to the named proposed insured and such parties included under the definition of insured in the form of policy or policies committed for and only for actual loss incurred in reliance hereon in undertaking in good faith (a) to comply with the requirements hereof, or (b) to eliminate exceptions shown in Schedule B, or (c) to acquire or create the estate or interest or mortgage thereon covered by this Commitment, in no even shall such liability exceed the amount stated in Schedule A for the policy or policies committed for and such liability is subject to the insuring provisions and the Conditions and Stipulations and the Exclusions from Coverage of the form of policy or policies committed for in favor of the proposed insured which are hereby incorporated by reference and are made a part of this Commitment except as expressly modified herein.

4. Any action or actions or rights of action that the proposed insured may have or may bring against the Company arising out of the status of the title to the estate or interest or the status of the mortgage thereon covered by this Commitment must be based on and are subject to the provisions of this Commitment.

By:

(President)

Attest:

(Secretary)

SCHEDULE A   COMMITMENT FOR TITLE INSURANCE

1. Effective Date February 17, 1995 at 8:00 a.m.   CASE NO. 1

2. POLICY OR POLICIES TO BE ISSUED:

    (a) ALTA OWNER'S POLICY (10-17-92)   AMOUNT $200,000.00

    PROPOSED INSURED:
    John Doe

    (b) ALTA LOAN POLICY (10-17-92)   AMOUNT $180,000.00

    PROPOSED INSURED:
    White Water Lending, Inc.
    AND/OR ITS SUCCESSORS AND ASSIGNS AS THEIR INTERESTS MAY APPEAR.

    (c)NONE   AMOUNT $ NONE

    PROPOSED INSURED:
    NONE

3. TITLE TO THE FEE SIMPLE ESTATE OR INTEREST IN THE LAND DESCRIBED OR
    REFERRED TO INTHIS COMMITMENT IS AT THE EFFECTIVE DATE HEREOF INVESTED IN:

    George Washington and Martha Washington

4. THE LAND REFERRED TO IN THIS COMMITMENT IS DESCRIBED AS FOLLOWS:

    SEE ATTACHED SCHEDULE A - PARAGRAPH 4

COUNTERSIGNED AT Birmingham, Alabama   COMMITMENT NO. 1
                                                SCHEDULE A- PAGE 01
                                    fm/fm Rev. No.   /
_____   THIS COMMITMENT IS INVALID UNLESS THE INSURING
     Authorized Officer or Agent   PROVISIONS AND SCHEDULES A AND B ARE ATTACHED.

COMMITMENT FOR TITLE INSURANCE
SCHEDULE A — PARAGRAPH 4
CONTINUED

Lot 22, Lots 23 and 24, Map of 1600 Pennsylvania Avenue, as recorded in Map Book 26, Page 34, in the Office of the Judge of Probate of Jefferson County, Alabama.

Also, part of vacated Chestnut Road. All being situated in Section 19, Township 18 South, Range 2 West and being more particularly described as follows: Begin at the southeasterly corner of Lot 23, Map of Beacon Hill; thence run in a northeasterly direction along the northeasterly line of said Lot 23 and the northwesterly right of way line of U.S. No. 31 South (said course being situated on a curve to the left having a central angle of 12 degrees 54 minutes 57 seconds and a radius of 2216. 83 feet) for a distance of 499.73 feet to the end of said curve and the point of beginning of a spiral curve to the left; thence turn an angle from the tangent of last described course to the chord of said spiral of 0 degrees 17 minutes 12 seconds and run in a northeasterly direction along the spiral and along the northwesterly right of way of U.S... No. 31 South for a distance of 118.77 feet to the northeasterly corner of Lot 24, map of Beacon Hill; thence turn an angle of 98 degrees 27 minutes 46 seconds to the left from the chord of last described course and run in a southwesterly direction along the southeasterly right of way line of Shades Crest road for a distance of 154.76 feet to the northwesterly corner of Lot 24, map of Beacon Hill; thence turn an angle to the left of 82 degrees 36 minutes 42 seconds and run southeasterly for a distance of 20 feet; thence turn an angle to the right of 83 degrees 32 minutes 44 seconds to the tangent of the following described course, said course being situated on a curve to the left and having a central angle of 9 degrees 24 minutes 11 seconds and a radius of 678.70 feet; thence run along the arc of said curve and the southeasterly right of way of Shades Crest Road for a distance of 111.38 feet; thence turn an angle to the left from the tangent of last described course of 96 degrees 19 minutes 19 seconds and run in a southeasterly direction for a distance of 177.77 feet; thence turn an angle to the right of 101 degrees 52 minutes 06 seconds to the tangent of the following described course, said course being situated on a curve to the left, having a central angle of 17 degrees 03 minutes 35 seconds and a radius of 135.00 feet; thence run along the arc of said curve and thecenterline of vacated Chestnut Road in a southwesterly direction for a distance of 40.20 feet to the end of said curve and the point of beginning of a curve to the left, said curve having a central angle of 59 degrees 30 minutes and a radius of 230.00 feet; thence run along the arc of said curve and along the centerline of vacated chestnut Road in a southwesterly direction for a distance of 238.85 feet to the end of said curve; thence run along the tangent extended to said curve in a southerly direction for a distance of 69.84 feet; thence turn an angle to the left of 81 degrees 33 minutes 36 seconds to the tangent to the following described course, said course being situated on a curve to the right having a central angle of 32 degrees 19 minutes 36 seconds and a radius of 130 feet; thence run along the arc of said curve and the northerly right of way of line of Hickory Road for a distance of 73.35 feet to the end of said curve and the point of beginning of a curve to the left, said curve having a central angle of 12 degrees 50 minutes and a radius of 115 feet; thence run in a southeasterly direction along the arc of said curve and along the northerly right of way of Hickory Road for a distance of 25.76 feet to the end of said curve and the point of beginning of a curve to the left; said curve having a central angle of 17 degrees 29 minutes 29 seconds and a radius of 360 feet; thence run in a southeasterly direction along the arc of said curve and along the northerly right of way line of Hickory road for a distance of 109.90 feet tot he point of beginning.

COMMITMENT NO. 1
SCHEDULE A PARAGRAPH 4 CONT. Page 02
fm/fm Rev. No.   /

COMMITMENT FOR TITLE INSURANCE
SCHEDULE B—SECTION 1
REQUIREMENTS

THE FOLLOWING ARE THE REQUIREMENTS TO BE COMPLIED WITH:

ITEM (A)   Payment to or for the account of the grantors or mortgagors of the full consideration for the estate or interest to be insured

ITEM (B)   Proper instrument(s) creating the estate or interest to be insure must be executed and duly filled for record, to wit:

      1.   Warranty deed from the present owner(s) and spouse(s), if married, to the purchaser(s).

      2.   Mortgage from the purchaser(s) and spouse(s), if married, to the mortgagee(s).

ITEM (C)   We find of record numerous judgements, bankruptcies and/or tax liens against parties with names similar to the name(s) of George Washington, owner. We will require satisfactory affidavit proof that there are no outstanding judgments and/or tax liens against George Washington.

ITEM (D)   Proper satisfaction of the following judgment(s) or satisfactory proof that said judgment(s) is/are not against George Washington.

Recorded	:	Real Volume 2000, Page 999
Plaintiff	:	John Adams
Defendant	:	George Michael Washington
Date	:	April 15, 1994
Court	:	Civil Court
Case no.	:	SC400-200
Amount	:	$500.00
Attorney of record	:	Thomas Jefferson

ITEM (E) Proper satisfaction of mortgage by George Washington and wife, Martha Washington to United States Bank of America, dated July 4, 1991, and recorded Real Volume 1776, Page 42.

ITEM (F) Proper satisfaction of mortgage by George Washington and wife, Martha Washington to Colonist Credit Union, dated August 5, 1994, and recorded Real Volume 2100, Page 19.

(SEE ATTACHED CONTINUATION PAGE)

THIS COMMITMENT IS INVALID UNLESS
THE INSURING PROVISIONS AND
SCHEDULES A AND B ARE ATTACHED.

COMMITMENT NO. 1
SCHEDULE B- PAGE 01
fm/fm Rev. No.   /

COMMITMENT FOR TITLE INSURANCE
SCHEDULE B — SECTION 1
REQUIREMENTS

ITEM (G) A written statement from the Secretary of the Fire District that all assessments for fire dues have been paid, or written verification by the closing attorney that subject property does not lie within a constituted Fire District. Otherwise, exception will be made on Final Policy for any delinquent Fire District assessments.

NOTE 1: 1994 Taxes were paid under Unit No. 23-5641; Parcel No. 27-7-40-1-RR-01.

NOTE 2: If this lender requires a Short Form Residential Loan Policy, please notify this office as soon as possible and verify the requirements and/or documents needed to issue this policy.

NOTE 3: If this closing is based on an Equity Line Mortgage Pay-off Letter, you must determine that the account is frozen and no further advances will be made. You should have a release in hand or adequate assurances that the release is immediately forthcoming and provide the company with same.

NOTE 4: Upon receipt of an accurate survey, proof of possession and satisfactory evidence that all claims for labor, materials, taxes and special assessments have been paid items 3, 4, 5, 6, and 7 will be eliminated from Schedule B - Part 1 of the mortgage policy.

NOTE 5: The Company will require the attached Owner's Affidavit to be properly executed, acknowledged and returned to this office.

NOTE 6: In order to expedite the issuance of your Policy(ies) for Title Insurance, upon closing this transaction, forward a complete final title package to our policy department. You should include all necessary documentation completing requirements, issuing endorsements or giving affiliate coverage. Also, indicate (1) the date(s) that all required documents were recorded or sent for recording, (2) the type of policy(ies) requested, (3) the types of endorsements requested, (4) where the final policy(ies) is/are to be sent.

THIS COMMITMENT IS INVALID UNLESS
THE INSURING PROVISIONS AND
SCHEDULES A AND B ARE ATTACHED.

COMMITMENT NO. 1
SCHEDULE B- 1 CONT. PAGE 02
fm/fm Rev. No.   /

COMMITMENT FOR TITLE INSURANCE
SCHEDULE B—SECTION 2
EXCEPTIONS

The policy or policies to be issued will contain exceptions to the following unless the same are disposed of to the satisfaction of the Company.

1. Defects, liens, encumbrances, adverse claims or other matters, if nay, created, first appearing in the public records or attaching subsequent to the effective date hereof but prior to the date the proposed insured acquires for value of record the estate or interest or mortgage thereon covered by this Commitment.

2. Taxes due and payable October 1, 1995.

3. Rights of parties in possession.

4. Encroachments, overlaps, boundary line disputes, or other matters which would be disclosed by an accurate survey and inspection of the premises.

5. Any lien, or right to a lien, for services, labor, or materials heretofore or hereafter furnished, imposed by law and not shown by the public records.

6. Taxes or special assessments which are not shown as existing liens by the public record.

7. Easements, or claims of easements, not shown by the public records.

8. Title to all minerals within and underlying the premises, together with all mining rights and other rights, privileges and immunities relating thereto as recorded in Volume 48, Page 578 and Real 3357, Page 443.

9. Easement(s) as shown on recorded map.

10. Building restriction line(s) as shown on recorded map.

11. Deed and Right-of-Way Agreements recorded in Volume 2875, Page 361 and Deed 5153, Page 149 in said Probate Office.

12. Covenants, conditions, restrictions, easements, fees, and assessments of Vestlake Communities as recorded in Instrument #9406/9798.

13. Agreement and Easement in favor of Mountain Book Cablevision, Inc. recorded in Real Volume 4378, Page 503, in said Probate Office.

14. Conditions, reservations, restrictions, covenants, easements, fees and assessments set forth in Declaration of Watershed Protective Covenants recorded in Real Volume 4037, Page 122, in said Probate Office.

15. Terms, conditions, restrictions and release from damages contained in the deed to be insured herein.

16. Right-of-way granted South Central Bell Telephone Company recorded in Real Volume 4463, Page 959.

17. Easement and right-of-way granted the City of The Water Works and Sewer Board of the City of Birmingham recorded in Real 4527, Page 147 and Instrument #9403/1372.

NOTE: If policy to be issued in support of a mortgage loan, attention is directed to the fact that the Company can assume no liability under its policy, the closing instructions, or Insured Closing Service for compliance with the requirements of any consumer credit protection or truth in lending law in connection with said mortgage loan.

This commitment is invalid unless the Insuring Provisions and Schedules A and B are attached.

fm/fm   Rev. No.   /   SCHEDULE B— Section 2—Page 01   Commitment No. 1

Glossary of Terms

agent   A person authorized to work on another person's behalf in order to secure a contract to buy or sell a house.

amendatory clause   A clause in all FHA contracts stating that a home under contract must appraise for contract price or higher.

amortization   Schedule for making loan payments, usually on a monthly basis, wherein a certain amount of each payment is applied to the principal and a certain amount to interest.

appraisal   A qualified individual's estimate of the value of a property; required for obtaining a loan.

ARM   Adjustable Rate Mortgage. A loan that starts out at a lower interest rate than the current fixed rate and, after a period that ranges from one to seven years, adjusts upwards or downwards every year thereafter.

assessment   Any charges levied for municipal improvements or improvements or repairs of a condominium. Any known pending assessments must be disclosed in a real estate contract.

asset   Anything of monetary value a buyer owns that may help her creditworthiness.

assumption   A buyer's commitment to take on a seller's payments on a home in exchange for home ownership.

bad credit   Any late payments that appear on a person's credit report.

bad debt   Any revolving loan, mortgage, alimony and child support, or car payments that have never been made.

balloon loan   A loan that must be paid off in a shorter period of time than it is amortized for. Like the ARM, a balloon loan starts out at a lower interest rate than a fixed-rate loan; but unlike the ARM, it cannot be extended after the fixed-rate period ends. Instead, it "balloons," with the outstanding principal payable in full.

broker   A real estate licensee who has passed a local and state examination and is, therefore, qualified to run her own agency.

browser   A tool used at the top of a computer screen that displays Web documents and instructs you on other applications.

bullet   The date upon which a mortgage loan must be fully repaid. Especially common term among those who execute seller-held, or "purchase money" mortgages as the date by which purchaser will refinance and pay the remaining debt to the seller.

buyer-brokerage   A written agreement authorizing a real estate agent to work exclusively for a buyer in a real estate transaction. Sometimes called a "buyer agency agreement."

CMA   Competitive Market Analysis. A determination of a property's value by comparing it to other recently sold properties.

cap   The upper and lower interest rate thresholds in an ARM.

client   An individual who is represented by another individual in any professional context.

closing   The final step in transferring a deed from a seller to a purchaser.

closing costs   Fees paid to the lender for processing a mortgage loan.

commitment letter   A formal offer of a loan to a purchaser from a lender. The letter will spell out the terms and conditions of the loan.

Community Home Buyer Program A mortgage loan program specifically designed for homebuyers under a certain income level.

comparables Homes located in the vicinity of a home for sale that have recently sold and are comparable in size and list price of that home for sale. Used to determine the market value of a particular home.

conditions Specific terms in a contract that must be satisfied prior to a closing.

contingencies Certain provisions included in a contract that must be fully satisfied before that contract can close.

condominium A form of ownership in which the owner owns the interior walls and the airspace within as well as a percentage of the "common areas," which usually are maintained from owners' "maintenance fees."

conforming loan Any loan that follows Fannie Mae guidelines.

contract broker An agent who brings a buyer and a seller to the point of an executed contract, but who represents neither.

conveyance Any document transferring property from one person to another.

counteroffer Written response to an offer that changes one or more of the terms and conditions of that offer.

credit bureau An organization that collects credit information and organizes it into a credit report.

credit counseling Marginally ethical organizations that consolidate an individuals debt and receive payment for same while paying off a percentage of the individual's debt.

credit report An independent agency's compilation of an individual's debt information and debt payment history.

custom home A home built to an individual's or family's specifications as that individual's or family's personal residence.

deed A document of ownership transferred at closing from a seller to a purchaser.

default   Failure to make payments on a loan.

discount point   One percent, or a portion of a percent, of a loan charged to a purchaser by a lender as prepaid interest; in favorable economic times, discount points are used to "buy down" an interest rate.

download   To move a file from any remote computer or server onto your computer.

down payment   Money paid "up front" for the purchase of a home; all money except the loan amount and closing costs.

dual agent   A real estate agent who represents both the buyer and the seller in a transaction.

earnest money   Money to show good faith that accompanies an offer to purchase a piece of property. At a closing, the earnest money becomes part of the down payment.

easement   A right given by a landowner to let another person or a formal, recognized institution, such as an electric power company, use that landowner's property for a specific purpose.

EIFS   External Insulation Finishing System. The most common brand name is "dryvit," a form of artificial stucco usually sprayed over foam insulation covered by a metal mesh.

encroachment   The physical intrusion of an improvement on one piece of property onto another piece of property.

encumbrance   Any attachment to a title on a piece of property that is recorded as a debt, easement, or encroachment.

Equifax   A large national credit reporting bureau.

equity   Cash value of a property minus any and all debt on that property.

ergonomics   The study of the practical use of interior space. Also, the principals for how form should follow function.

escalation   Demand for total repayment of a debt. An escalation of payment can be demanded by a lender when an owner is deemed in default on his loan payments.

escrow Account established by a neutral party to hold monies in trust for a buyer or a seller (earnest money is put in such an account). Also, an account established by a lender to collect taxes and homeowner's insurance.

estate Any individual's personal, material holdings.

FHA mortgage Federal Housing Authority mortgage. FHA loans are guaranteed by the government and allow a buyer to put down less money than is required for all but a few conventional loans. Mortgage insurance is required on all FHA loans.

FNMA Commonly referred to as "Fannie Mae," a government organization overseeing standards for mortgage loans. Most mortgage loans are said to follow "Fannie Mae guidelines."

FSBO (pronounced "fisbo") For Sale By Owner. A home that is offered for sale without the use of a real estate agent.

Federal Flood Hazard Area As disclosed on a survey, an area in a community that has been identified by the federal government as flood-prone. People living in a Federal Flood Hazard Area are usually required to carry flood insurance.

Federal Truth-in-Lending Disclosure Form Form signed by a purchaser at the closing of a loan. Discloses the annual percentage rate, total principal of loan, interest that will be paid over the life of the loan, and the combined total of principal and interest over the life of the loan.

fee simple Refers to an inheritable ownership in a property.

FICA Tax taken out of an individual's income for Social Security.

fixed-rate mortgage Type of mortgage loan in which the interest rate remains unchanged throughout the life of that loan.

foreclosure The legal process of seizing a property from an owner because of default and then selling it.

freehold estate Any structure that a person owns, both outside walls and inside walls, and the space included therein.

full factual   A credit report that most mortgage lenders use to qualify applicants for loans. It combines information from two or more national credit reporting bureaus.

gift letter   A letter required in order for a buyer to furnish part of a down payment from a gift. The letter must state that its author has no intention of recouping his or her gift.

hold harmless   An executed agreement that an agency, organization, or individual is not responsible for damages caused by error or dispute regarding a piece of property.

homeowner's association   An organization usually formed in a subdivision or condominium, giving homeowners certain decision-making responsibilities for the welfare of the subdivision or condominium as a whole.

homeowner's insurance   Insurance coverage at least equal to the amount of the mortgage loan that protects a residential property against loss; required by all lenders.

home page   The first page your Web browser displays when you start it up.

homestead   One's recorded interest in a piece of property.

home warranty   A builder's guarantee to replace or repair any improperly functioning appliances or system components. Also, a service contract to protect appliances and systems in an older home.

HVAC   The heating and cooling delivery systems of any enclosed property. Stands for "heating, ventilating, and cooling."

hypertext   Any Web document that contains links to other documents. Selecting a link automatically displays the second document.

ISP   Internet Service Provider. An organization that supplies users with access to the Internet.

image   Any picture or graphic that appears on a Web page.

improvement   Anything added or modified on a property to give that property increased value.

inspection   An evaluation of the condition of a property by a professional.

interest rate   Percentage charged by a lender for issuing a loan. Fluctuates under the influence of a variety of economic factors.

Internet   The computer system that allows people using different computers to communicate with one another.

Internet server   A provider of computer lines that connect separate computer users.

joint tenancy   Refers to the equal, undivided ownership of a property by two or more individuals.

jumbo   A mortgage loan over a specified amount, outside of and above the amount of a conforming loan. Jumbo loans usually are offered at a slightly higher interest rate than conforming loans. Currently, the ceiling for conforming loans is $322,500.

leasehold estate   Property one lives in that is leased for a particular time. The individual's "leasehold" is determined by length of lease and monthly payment.

leveraging   Putting down the minimum down payment on a piece of property and financing the largest percentage possible.

lien   Any claim against a piece of property.

lien waiver   A disclosure showing that there are no liens on a piece of property. Usually signed by the seller at closing.

link   The text, graphic, or image you click on to make a hypertext jump to another Web page.

listing   Formal means of putting a piece of property on the market—if by a real estate agency, a written agreement with a termination date.

loan origination fee   Fee charged by a lender to process a loan. Usually one percent of the loan amount, although when interest rates are particularly favorable, the percentage can be reduced.

loss   As related to homeowner's insurance, any damage to a property covered under the insurance policy or any personal injury suffered on the premises.

lot   Any legally described piece of property, whether or not it has an improvement of any type situated on it.

lot yield   The number of lots a builder can expect to develop in a subdivision, based on an engineer's survey.

LTV   Loan-To-Value. Ratio used by lenders to determine the amount of down payment relative to the amount of financing. A down payment of 30 percent on a piece of property along with 70 percent financing is an LTV of 70 percent.

maintenance fee   Fee charged by a condominium or cooperative association for the upkeep of the overall property, including the grounds.

metes and bounds   A lengthy description of a plot of land, now, typically, given only for older homes built before subdivisions were divided into lot and block numbers.

minimum monthly payment   What mortgage lenders use to add up your total monthly credit indebtedness in determining your ratios.

mineral and mining rights   That part of a piece of property not conveyed as part of ownership.

MIP   Mortgage Insurance Premium. Insurance premium on FHA loans that indemnifies the lender against default.

MLS   Multiple Listing Service. A list of all homes for sale by real estate brokers in any given area, usually computerized. Agents use the MLS system to find houses in a specific area or price range to show their clients.

mortgage   The legal document that pledges a property as security for a loan.

Mortgagee Title Policy   A title policy that indemnifies a lender against a purchaser's default, or any liens and encroachments that compromise the lender's full rights to your property.

name affidavit   A statement generated from a title policy indicating that you are not the same person of a similar name to yours who has liens or judgments against her.

nonconforming loan   A loan that does not conform to standard Fannie Mae guidelines.

notary   A person authorized to stamp any document making it an official statement of record.

note   The specific terms of a mortgage, including payment amount and schedule of repayment.

on-site specialist   A real estate agent who works exculsively in one subdivision and represents one builder's or a group of builders' spec homes.

PA   Professional Association. A lending organization within a bank that offers nonconforming loans to a limited group of professionals, usually doctors or lawyers.

payoff   The final payment that closes a mortgage loan. Often, a lump sum repayment of an outstanding loan used to close the sale of a property.

PMI   Private Mortgage Insurance. Insurance premium on conventional loans of more than 80 percent LTV, charged to indemnify the lender against default.

point   One percent of a loan amount. Lenders charge points in exchange for lowering the interest rate.

possession   Date and time when a buyer takes over a property.

prequalification   A meeting with a lender and a buyer to determine the amount of money the buyer can borrow.

prequalification letter   A letter written by a loan officer, usually to accompany a contract for sale, indicating the purchaser's creditworthiness and how much of a mortgage the purchaser is eligible to obtain.

pre-paids   Homeowner's insurance, prorated taxes, and any loan interest payments to cover the period from the date of closing to the end of that month, paid in a lump sum to create an escrow account at closing.

principal   The amount of money borrowed and still owed on a loan.

promissory note　A security instrument pledging to repay a debt.

property tax　Annual state, county, and municipal assessments levied against a piece of property.

proration　The division of taxes and other fees that takes place at a closing. For example, if a seller has paid property taxes three months in advance, the amount of taxes for those three months would be returned to the seller at closing.

purchase money mortgage　A mortgage made by a purchaser directly to a seller. The seller becomes the lender.

ratios　The percentages of mortgage payment debt to gross monthly income and total debt to gross monthly income. For conventional loans, the standard ratios are 28 percent/ 36 percent.

recording　Entering a mortgage loan or a deed into courthouse records, thereby making them official documents.

relocation specialist　A real estate agent who deals exclusively with homebuyers moving from one community to another.

search directory　A Web site that indexes Web pages and enables you to search for the terms or categories you specify.

secondary market　The place where loans are bought and sold in large quantities.

septic tank　An enclosed underground structure on a property that sanitizes fouled water (sewage).

settlement agent　A person assigned to close the sale of a piece of property.

sewer　An underground system designed to carry fouled water from a piece of property.

single agency　An exclusive relationship between an agent and one other party, either a buyer or a seller, established to conduct a real estate transaction.

site　The location on any Web server.

spec house   A house built with a builder's money, usually on that builder's lot, with the expectation that the house will sell to an as yet unidentified purchaser.

subagent   An agent who helps the a purchaser buy a piece of property but who represents the seller.

survey   An engineer's drawing of the boundaries that separate one piece of property from another. If that property has improvements, also a drawing of the location of the improvements, done to scale.

TRW/Experian   A large national credit reporting bureau.

tenants in common   A divided ownership in a property held by two or more individuals.

termite bond   A statement pledging treatment of a home for termites. There are still some "repair" bonds pledging repairs of property damaged by termites during the time of treatment, but they are becoming increasingly rare.

terms   The duration, interest rate, and other specific features of a mortgage loan.

time is of the essence   A clause in a real estate offer demanding a response from a buyer or seller within a certain period of time in order to keep that offer alive and prioritize it above other offers.

title   The insured right of property ownership.

title insurance   Protection of buyers and lenders against losses incurred from disputes over title to a piece of property.

title plant   A microfiche or computer library that provides the complete title history of every piece of property in its regional domain.

town house   Attached dwelling in which owner owns exterior walls and all other exterior surfaces as well as interior ones.

Trans Union   A large national credit reporting bureau.

URL   Universal Resource Locator. The address that uniquely identifies a Web resource.

underwriting   The process of evaluating a loan to determine whether it is a good risk for the lender. Also determines whether loan documents are properly drawn up.

VA loan   A loan guaranteed by the Veterans Administration. New VA loans are available only to veterans, but existing VA loans may be assumed by nonveterans.

warranty deed   Any conveyance of property from one person or party to another person or property that in any way "warrants" that property's authenticity by legal description and legal history.

Web site or Web page   Anyone's location by "address" and accompanying data on the Internet.

will   A legal document drawn up by a competent individual bequeathing part or all of that individual's estate to others in the instance of that individual's death.

wood infestation report   A document showing whether or not a home is free of termites, other wood-decaying insects, or fungus. Now required of most mortgage lenders.

zoning   Municipal laws that establish how a property can be used.

Bibliography

Bierman, Todd and Masten, David. *The Fix Your Credit Workbook.* New York City: St. Martin's Press, 1998.

Bierman, Todd and Wice, Nathaniel. *The Guerrilla Guide to Credit Repair.* New York City: St. Martin's Press, 1994.

Dubois, Maurice. *Home Buyer's Confidential: The Insider's Guide to Buying Your Dream House, Condo, or Co-op.* New York City: Liberty Hall Press, 1991.

Eilers, Terry. *How to Buy the Home You Want for the Best Price in Any Market.* New York City: Hyperion, 1997.

Glink, Ilyce R. *10 Steps to Home Ownership: A Workbook for First-Time Buyers.* New York City: Times Books, 1996.

Irwin, Robert. *Tips & Traps When Negotiating Real Estate.* New York City: McGraw-Hill, Inc., 1995.

_____. *Tips & Traps When Buying a Home.* New York City: McGraw-Hill, Inc., 1997.

_____. *Tips & Traps When Mortgage Hunting.* New York City: McGraw-Hill, Inc., 1998.

_____. *How to Find Hidden Real Estate Bargains.* New York City: McGraw-Hill, Inc., 2002.

Irwin, Robert and Ganz, David L. *How to Get an Instant Mortgage.* New York City: John Wiley & Sons, Inc., 1997.

Resource Guide

The following is a list of companies and governmental agencies that provide information to help you with each stage of the home-buying process.

Information on Appraisals

American Society of Appraisers
555 Herndon Parkway, Suite 125
Herndon, VA 20170
(703) 478-2228; fax (703) 742-8471;
www.appraisers.org

This is a private organization to which almost all appraisers belong and pay dues. It publishes valuable information on the nature of the appraisal process.

Appraisal Foundation
1029 Vermont Avenue NW, Suite 900
Washington, DC 20005-3517
(202) 347-7722; fax (202) 347-7727;
www.appraisalfoundation.org

This private, nonprofit foundation is funded by several separate appraisal organizations. It establishes and publishes uniform standards for appraisals. Although these standards are routinely distributed to appraisers, they are also available to the general public.

Appraisal Institute
550 West Van Buren Street, Suite 1000
Chicago, IL 60607
(312) 335-4100; fax (312) 335-4400; www.appraisalinstitute.org

This institute issues educational designations for appraisers. Upon request, it also provides a list of members.

Credit Counseling

Consumer Credit Counseling Service
9009 West Loop So., Suite 700
Houston, TX 77096
(800) 873-2227; (713) 923-2227; www.cccsintl.org

Although CCCS is technically a nonprofit service with local representatives in every major U.S. city, be aware that national credit institutions fund it. Hence, although it might provide advice on improving your personal credit and keeping you out of bankruptcy, you should always consult an outside source, such as an accountant or tax adviser, before agreeing to any long-term debt workout schemes the CCCS recommends.

Credit Reporting Agencies

Equifax Information Service
Customer Correspondence
P.O. Box 105851
Atlanta, GA 30348; www.equifax.com
(800) 685-1111

Experian (formerly TRW)
12606 Greenville Avenue
P.O. Box 749-029
Dallas, TX 75374
(800) 831-5614

TransUnion
P.O. Box 8070
North Olmsted, OH 44070-8070
(800) 916-8800; www.transunion.com

These are the three major credit reporting agencies. Their addresses and phone numbers were current at the time of this book's publication; call the 800 information operator at (800) 555-1212 to confirm that the addresses and phone numbers have not changed. In their responses to your inquiries, the credit bureaus might direct future communications to local or regional offices. After you have regional phone numbers and addresses, direct all future communications to them.

If you have any complaints about how these credit reporting bureaus handle your inquiries, address them to:

Federal Trade Commission (FTC)
Attention: Credit Bureau Complaints
Pennsylvania Avenue and 6th Street NW
Washington, DC 20580
www.ftc.gov

Government and Government-Affiliated Agencies

Consumer Product Safety Division
Washington, DC 20207
(800) 638-2772; (301) 504-6816; fax (301) 504-0124

This is the toll-free number to call if you have a complaint or a concern about the safety of houses and buildings, including smoke alarms, electrical systems, indoor air quality, and insulation. The CPSD also publishes brochures on recall information and safety tips.

Fair Housing Information Clearing House
P.O. Box 6091
Rockville, MD 20850
(800) 343-3442

This agency provides numerous free brochures on almost every aspect of home buying, fair housing, and lending.

Federal Consumer Information Center
Pueblo, CO 81009
(719) 948-3334

FCIC publishes a free catalog of information regarding the thousands of consumer-oriented brochures published by the government.

Federal Housing Administration (FHA)
Washington, DC 20410
(202) 401-0388

FHA provides an extensive list of the many FHA loans available for home purchases and home improvements. It also publishes a worksheet that enables you to calculate down payment and closing costs associated with FHA loans.

Federal National Mortgage Association (Fannie Mae)
Consumer Information and Education
3900 Wisconsin Avenue NW
Washington, DC 20016
(202) 752-7000; www.fanniemay.com

Fannie Mae publishes free brochures on mortgage loans and most other aspects of the home-buying process.

Government National Mortgage Association (Ginnie Mae)
c/o HUD Consumer Information
451 Seventh Street SW
Washington, DC 20410
(202) 708-0926; www.hud.gov

Like Fannie Mae, Ginnie Mae publishes free brochures on mortgage loans and home buying.

U.S. Department of Housing and Urban Development (HUD)
451 Seventh Street SW
Room B100
Washington, DC 20410
(800) 767-7468

HUD provides free information on housing. Most importantly, HUD handles complaints regarding discrimination in the home-buying process. Through the national office, you can get a list of the local HUD offices.

U.S. Department of Veterans Affairs (VA)
810 Vermont Avenue NW
Washington, DC 20420
(202) 273-5400: www.va.gov

The VA publishes information on VA loans and all other services available to qualified veterans. Like FHA, the VA also publishes worksheets that include breakdowns of closing costs and other fees related to home buying.

Home Inspections

American Society of Home Inspectors (ASHI)
932 Lee Street, Suite 101
Des Plaines, IL 60016
(800) 743-2744; www.ashi.com

ASHI is the certifying agency for the largest number of qualified home inspectors. It also publishes brochures on the home inspection process and a list of ASHI-certified inspectors in the area where you're buying.

Index